A Century of Anecdote from 1760-1860

John Timbs

Contents

PREFACE. 7
A CENTURY OF ANECDOTE............................8

A CENTURY OF ANECDOTE
FROM 1760-1860

BY
John Timbs

PREFACE.

HORACE WALPOLE, in quoting from a volume of newly-published Memoirs, certain anecdotes of striking interest, characterizes them as "worthy of being inserted in the history of mankind, which, if well chosen and well written, would precede common histories, which are but repetitions of no uncommon events." This is a high standard of excellence, which few of the anecdote-books of modern times have attained: it has scarcely been reached by Walpole himself whose inexhaustible fund of anecdote, of gossip, of lively and fanciful conceits, of scandal, and of **bons-mots,** has won for him the character of "the best letter-writer in the English language." The habit of collecting anecdotes has afforded recreation to the learned as well as to the gay and sprightly, in all ages. In our time, the grave Lord Eldon left the world his Anecdote-Book, acknowledged to be one of the most entertaining works of its class.

The present work aims to be a collection of the best modern anecdote; but it has been particularly the object of the Editor to give the work a distinctive personal interest; and while it glances at striking events, the attractiveness of the **historiette** has been kept in view.

The classification of the work into sections—of Court and Fashionable Life, Political life, Men of Letters, Law and Lawyers, Eccentric Persons, &c.—may be found acceptable to various classes of readers. The collection commencing with the witty sayings of George Selwyn, and the elegant persiflage of Horace Walpole, concludes with the best anecdotes of Coleridge, Sydney Smith, and Rogers.

LONDON, *OCTOBER,* 1864

A CENTURY OF ANECDOTE.

COURT AND FASHIONABLE LIFE.

GEORGE SELWYN.

SELWYN, with brilliant wit and classic taste, combined qualities of a very contradictory nature. With good humour, kindness of heart, and great fondness for children, he united a morbid interest in the details of human suffering, and more especially a taste for witnessing criminal executions. Even frightful details of suicide and murder, the investigation of a disfigured corpse, or an acquaintance in his shroud, afforded him pleasure. When the first Lord Holland was on his death-bed, he was told that his friend Selwyn had called to inquire after his health. "The next time Mr. Selwyn calls," said Lord H., "show him up—if I am alive I shall be delighted to see him, and if I am dead he will be glad to see me."

Selwyn told a friend that Arthur More had had his coffin chained to that of his mistress. "How do you know?"—"Why, I saw them the other day in a vault in St. Giles's."

He was walking in Westminster Abbey with Lord Abergavenny, and met the man who showed the tombs. "Oh! your servant, Mr. Selwyn; I expected to have seen you here the other day, when the old Duke of Richmond's body was taken up."

Walpole having captured a housebreaker, sent to White's for Selwyn: the drawer, who had himself been lately robbed, received the message. He stalked up into the club-room, stopped short, and, in a hollow, trembling voice, said: "Mr. Selwyn, Mr. Walpole's compliments to you, and he has got a housebreaker for you."

Lord Pembroke met Selwyn, on the 1st of May, very much annoyed in the street with chimney-sweepers, who were clamorous, surrounded, daubed, and persecuted him; in short, they would not let him go till they had forced money from him. At length he made them a low bow, and cried, "Gentlemen, I have often heard of the *majesty* of the people; I presume your highnesses are in court mourning." This is Hannah More's version. Walpole gives Selwyn's words on meeting the chimney-sweepers wearing their crowns of gilt paper: "We have heard so much lately of the ***majesty of the people,*** that I suppose they are taken for the ***princes of the people,*** and that this is a Collar-day."

At the trials of Lords Kilmarnock and Balmerino, observing Mrs. Bethel, who had a hatchet-face, looking wistfully at the rebel lords, "What a shame it is," said Selwyn, "to turn her face to the prisoners till they are condemned."

Some ladies bantering him on his want of feeling, in attending to see Lord Lovat's head cut off, "Why," he said, "I made amends by going to the undertaker's, to see it sewn on again." At the undertaker's, after the head had been sewn on, and with the body, placed in the coffin, Selwyn, imitating the voice and manner of the Lord Chancellor at the trial, exclaimed, "My Lord Lovat, your lordship may rise."

Alluding to the practice of stage-criminals dropping a handkerchief on the scaffold, as a signal to the executioner to strike, "George," says Walpole, "never thinks but à la tête tranchée. He came to town t'other day to have a tooth drawn, and told the man that he would drop his handkerchief for the signal."

He went to Paris purposely to see Damien broken on the wheel, for attempting to assassinate Louis XV.: he got near the scaffold among the crowd, but was repulsed by one of the executioners, who, however, being told of Selwyn's object, caused the people to make way for him, exclaiming, "Faites place pour monsieur; c'est un

Anglais, et un *amateur*."

He delighted in a hoax. Dining with the Mayor and Corporation of Gloucester in 1758, when news arrived of our expedition having failed before Rochfort, the Mayor, turning to Selwyn, said: "You, sir, who are in the ministerial secrets, can, no doubt, inform us of the cause of this misfortune?"

Selwyn, though utterly ignorant upon the subject said, "I will tell you in confidence the reason, Mr. Mayor: the fact is, that the scaling-ladders, prepared for the occasion, were found, on trial, to be too short." The Mayor believed this solution, and told it to his friends; though Selwyn was aware that Rochfort lies on the river Charente, some leagues from the sea-shore, and that our troops had never even effected a landing on the French coast.

Walpole, speaking of the witty and notorious Lady Towns-hend, writes: "On Sunday, George Selwyn was strolling home to dinner. He saw my Lady Townshend's coach stop at Caraccioli's chapel. He watched it, saw her go in; her footman laughed; he followed. She went up to the altar, a woman brought her a cushion; she knelt, crossed herself and prayed. He stole up, and knelt by her. Conceive her face, if you can, when she turned, and found him close to her. In his demure voice, he said, 'Pray, madam, how long has your ladyship left the pale of our church?' She looked furies, and made no answer. Next day, he went to her, and she turned it off upon curiosity; but is anything more natural? No, she certainly means to go armed with every viaticum; the Church of England in one hand, Methodism in the other, and the Host in her mouth."

Selwyn's wit at the club is very amusing. One night, at White's, Sir L. Fawkener, the postmaster-general, was losing a large sum at piquet, when Selwyn, pointing to the successful player, said: "See, how he is robbing the mail." Observing Mr. Speaker Porisonby tossing about bank-bills, at a hazard-table, at Newmarket, "Look," said Selwyn, "how easily the Speaker passes the money-bills."

Walpole observing that there had existed the same indecision, irresolution, and want of system, in the politics of Queen Anne, that now distinguished those of the reign of George III., added, "But there is nothing new under the sun." "No," said Selwyn, "nor under the grandson."

A namesake of Charles Fox having been hung at Tyburn, the latter inquired of Selwyn whether he had attended the execution? "No," replied George, "I make a point of never frequenting rehearsals."

Selwyn was once wearied with the inquiries of a fellow-passenger in a stage-coach as to the state of his health. At length, to the repeated question of "How are you now, sir?"

Selwyn replied: "Very well, I thank you; and I mean to continue so for the rest of the journey."

A member of the Foley family having hurried off to the Continent, to avoid the importunities of his creditors,—"It is a **pass-over,**" remarked Selwyn, "that will not be much relished by the Jews."

Selwyn held several Government appointments, to which the wits of the day said, was added the post of "Receiver-General of Waif and Stray Jokes."

In Parliament, he often amused the House, during a long debate, by snoring in unison with the First Minister, Lord North. And when Burke was wearying his hearers by those long speeches which obtained for him the name of the "Dinner-bell," a nobleman entering the House just as Selwyn was quitting it, inquired, "Is the House up?" "No," replied George, "but Burke is."

Selwyn resided in Cleveland-row, St. James's, in the house rendered memorable by the quarrel which took place between Sir Robert Walpole and Lord Townsend, in the reign of George I., when the First Minister and Secretary of State seized each other by the throat; a scene which Gay burlesqued in the ***Beggar's Opera,*** under the characters of Peachum and Lockit.

When Lord Weymouth was about to be married, or, as he said, **turned off,** Selwyn told him he wondered that he had not been turned off before, for he still sat up drinking all night and gaming.

Selwyn, happening to be at Bath when it was nearly empty, was induced, for the mere purpose of killing time, to cultivate the acquaintance of an elderly gentleman he was in the habit of meeting in the rooms. In the height of the following season George encountered his old associate in St. James's-street. He endeavoured to pass unnoticed, but in vain. "What! don't you recollect me? "exclaimed the **cuttee.**—"I recollect you perfectly," replied Selwyn, "and when I next go to Bath I shall be most happy to become acquainted with you again."

Bruce was one day asked before Selwyn if the Abyssinians have any music? He replied, "They have one **Lyre.**" George whispered his neighbour, "They have one less since he left the country."

When a report was circulated that Sir Joshua Reynolds was to stand for the borough of Plympton on the next occasion of an election, the macaronies, clubmen and gentlemen generally laughed at the idea of an artist, or of a literary man, presuming to have a chance to get into the House of Commons. "He is not to be laughed at, however," said Selwyn; "he may very well succeed in being elected, for Sir Joshua is the ablest man I know, on a canvas."

In Walpole's time, an artist made a sketch as a companion to Copley's "Death of Lord Chatham." As the latter exhibits all the great men of Britain, the former was to record the Beauties. The subject chosen was the **Daughter of Pharaoh** saving Moses. The Princess-Royal was the Egyptian Infanta, accompanied by the Duchesses of Gloucester, Cumberland, Devonshire, Rutland, Lady Duncannon, &c. The sketch was to be seen **over against Brooks's:** George Selwyn said he could recommend a better companion for this piece, which should be **the Sons of Pharaoh** (faro) at the opposite house.

MASQUERADES.

During the food-riots in London, in 1772, when the condition of the middle and lower classes was one of extreme distress, they found little sympathy among persons of fashion. In the very midst of these distresses sprung up a rage for masquerades. At one of these licentious entertainments given at the Pantheon, in Oxford-street, it was calculated that not less than 10,000 guineas were expended by the revellers in dress and other luxuries. The trade of the metropolis would have profited by this, to a certain extent, had payment of liabilities been a recognised duty of the time. As a sample of the sort of persons, and their conduct at these orgies, may be cited from the various reports in different journals, the presence of groups of gentlemen from the universities, some of them attired as "Tom-fools, with cap and bells"; of clergymen, who gained applause for originality by trying to represent "old *sober* hackney-coachmen"; and of ladies, the Duchess of Ancaster at their head, in male attire. Dr. Goldsmith is named among those who masqueraded in "an old English dress"; and after lists of noble ladies, descriptions of their dresses, and praises of their wit and beauty, we find a sample of the easy virtue of the times in the presence of a group of "a lady abbess, and her nuns." The licence of speech, action, and allusion was astounding. At the Pantheon, the excited crew generally finished by breakfasting at daylight on the remains of the supper, and then going home "gloriously drunk." At Cornelys' masquerades in Soho-square, after a supper, marked by hard drinking and immodest singing, "which no lady need leave save those who are too immodest to stay," as the formula ran, the custom was to fling open the windows and pelt the eager, hungry, thirsty, and howling crowd below with half-empty bottles and the remains of the supper. The very Queen of Beauty at these orgies was young Gertrude Conway, niece of General Conway, daughter of Francis, first Marquis of Hertford, and only just married to George Villiers Earl of Grandison. She was the Queen of Fashion as well as of Beauty; and she excited the greatest admiration by giving frocks and tambour-waistcoats, as undress livery to her servants; and by the splendour of her chairmen, who never carried her abroad without feathers in their hats. This gay young wife died in 1782, in the thirty-second year of her age. In her masquerades lost their great patroness.

This species of entertainment was never encouraged by George III., at whose request Foote abstained from giving a masquerade at the Little Theatre in the Haymarket There were some curious scruples entertained even by people of pleasure at this time. The most fashionable of them appeared at the theatre in Lent attired in mourning; and at the same season masquerades were considered as out of place; but these scrupulous persons found a method of reconciling their sense of religion with their taste for dissipation:

"In Lent, if masquerades displease the town,
Call 'em ridottos and they still go down."

Madame Teresa Cornelys, a German by birth, and by profession a public singer, was one of the ***entrepreneurs*** of masquerades. Walpole describes her as a singular dame, and "the Heidegger of the age," She took Carlisle House, on the east side of Soho-square, enlarged it, and established here assemblies and balls by subscription. At first they scandalized, but soon drew in both righteous and ungodly. She went on building, and made her house a fairy palace for balls, concerts, and masquerades. Her opera, which she called "Harmonic Meetings," was splendid and charming. To avoid the Act, she pretended to take no money, and had the assurance to advertise that the subscription was to provide coats for the poor, for she vehemently courted the mob, and gained their favour. She then declared her masquerades were for the benefit of commerce. At last the bench of magistrates decided against her, and she was compelled to shut up the house. Her improvidence then reduced her to become a "vendor of asses' milk" at Knightsbridge; but she sank still lower, and died in 1797, in the Fleet Prison.

VAILS TO SERVANTS.

The giving of vails to servants was carried to great excess in the last century. Dr. King tells of a Lord Poor, a Roman Catholic peer of Ireland, who lived upon a small pension which Queen Anne had granted him. The Duke of Ormonde often invited him to dinner, and he as often excused himself. At last the duke kindly expostulated with him, and would know the reason why he so constantly refused to be one of his guests. My Lord Poor then honestly confessed that he could not afford it; "but," said he, "if your Grace will put a guinea into my hands as often as you are pleased to invite me to dine, I will not decline the honour of waiting on you." This was done, and Lord Poor was afterwards a frequent guest at the Duke's, in St. James's-square.

Lord Taaffe, of Ireland, a general officer in the Austrian service, who resided for a time in England, had another way of meeting this subject of vails. When his friends, who had dined with him, were going away, he always attended them to the door; and if they offered any money to the servant who opened it (for he never suffered but one servant to appear), he always prevented them, saying, in his manner of speaking *English,* "If you do give it, give it to me, for it was I that did buy the dinner."

It was at Newcastle House, at the north-west angle of Lincoln's Inn Fields, then the residence of the Duke of Newcastle, that the old and expensive custom of "vails-giving" received its death-blow. Sir Timothy Waldo, on his way from the Duke's dinner-table to his carriage, put a crown into the hand of the cook, who returned it, saying, "Sir, I do not take silver." "Don't you, indeed?" said Sir Timothy, putting the crown into his pocket; "then I do not give gold." Jonas Hanway's "Eight Letters to the Duke of—"had their origin in Sir Timothy's complaint.

AMENITIES OF SARAH, DUCHESS OF MARLBOUROUGH.

One of her Grace's principal charms was a prodigious abundance of fine hair; one day, at her toilet, in anger to her heroic lord, she cut off her commanding tresses, and flung them in his face.

Her eldest daughter and she were long at variance, and never reconciled. When the younger Duchess exposed herself by placing a monument and silly epitaph of her own composition and bad spelling, to Congreve, in Westminster Abbey, her mother, quoting the words, said, "I know not what **happiness** she might have in his company, but I am sure it was no **honour**" With her youngest daughter, the Duchess of Montagu, old Sarah agreed as ill. "I wonder," said the Duke of Marlborough to them, "that you cannot agree, you are so alike!" Of her grand-daughter, the Duchess of Man Chester, she affected to be fond. One day, she said to her, "Duchess of Manchester, you are a good creature, and I love you mightily—but you **have** a mother!" "And she has a mother!" "answered the Duchess of Manchester, who was all spirit, justice, and honour, and could not suppress sudden truth.

Sarah, who had risen to greatness and independent wealth by the weakness of a Queen, forgot, like the Duke d'Epernon, her own unmerited exaltation, and affected to brave successive courts, though sprung from the dregs of one. When the Prince of Orange came over, in 1734, to marry the Princess Royal Anne, a boarded gallery, with a penthouse roof, was erected for the procession from the windows of the great drawing-room at St. James's across the garden to the Lutheran Chapel in the Friary. The marriage was deferred for some weeks, and the boarded gallery remained, darkening the windows of Marlborough House. The Duchess cried, "I wonder when **my neighbour George** will take away his orange-chest!"—which the gallery did resemble.

Great was her fury when Henry Pox prevailed on the second Duke to go over to the court. With her warm, intemperate, humour, she said, "That was the Fox that had stolen her goose!" Repeated injuries at last drove the Duke to go to law with her, fearing that even no lawyer would come up to the Billingsgate with which she was animated herself. She appeared in the court of justice, and with some wit and infinite abuse, treated the laughing public with the spectacle of a woman who had held the reins of empire, metamorphosed into the widow Blackacre. Her grandson, in his suit, demanded a sword set with diamonds, given to his grandsire by the Emperor. "I retained it," said the beldam, "lest he should pick out the diamonds and pawn them."

Her insolent asperity once produced an admirable reply from the famous Lady

Mary Wortley Montagu. Lady Sundon had received a pair of diamond ear-rings as a bribe for procuring a considerable post in Queen Caroline's family for a certain peer; and decked with those jewels, paid a visit to the old Duchess; who, as soon as she was gone, said, "What an impudent creature to come hither with the bribe in her ear!" "Madam," replied Lady Mary Wortley, who was present, "how should people know where wine is sold, unless a bush is hung out."

Eventually, the Duke resigned everything to reinstate himself in the old Duchess' will, when she said, "It is very natural; he listed as soldiers do when they are drunk, and repented when he was sober."

Sarah, in a letter to Lord Stair, says, "I have made a settlement of a very great estate that is in my own power, upon my grandson, John Spencer, and his sons; but they are to forfeit it if any of them shall ever accept any employment military or civil, or any pension from any King or Queen of this realm, and the estate is to go to others in the entail. This, I think, ought to please everybody; for it will secure my heirs in being very considerable men. None of them can put on a fool's coat, and take posts from soldiers of experience and service, who never did anything but kill pheasants and partridges."

With this said will, her son-in-law, the Duke of Montagu, had bound up an old penny history-book, called "The Old Woman's Will of Ratcliffe Highway," only tearing away the title-page of the latter.

FINE COURTESY.

On one of George the First's journeys to Hanover, his coach broke. At a distance in view was a château of a considerable German nobleman. The King sent to borrow assistance. The possessor came, conveyed the King to his house, and begged the honour of his Majesty accepting a dinner while his carriage was repairing; and while the dinner was preparing, begged leave to amuse his Majesty with a collection of pictures, which he had formed in several tours to Italy. But what did the King see in one of the rooms but an unknown portrait of a person in the robes and with the regalia of the sovereigns of Great Britain! George asked whom it represented. The nobleman replied, with much diffident but decent respect, that in various journeys to Rome he had become acquainted with the Chevalier de St. George, who had done him honour of sending him that picture. "Upon my word," the King instantly, "it is very like to the family." It impossible to remove the embarrassment of the proprietor more good breeding.—*Walpole's Reminiscences.*

FLATTERING COMPARISON.

Then Prince William (afterwards Duke of Cumberland) was child, he was carried to his grandfather on his birthday, when the King asked him at what hour he rose. The Prince replied, "When the chimney-sweepers went about"—"Vat is de chimney-sweeper?" said the King. "Have you been so in England," said the boy, "and do you not know what a chimney-sweeper is? Why, they are like that man there;" pointing to Lord Finch, afterwards Earl of Winchelsea and Nottingham, of a family uncommonly dark and swarthy—the black funereal Finches."

THE HUSBAND'S ADVICE.

Sir John Germain, a short time before his decease, in 1718, having called his wife to his bedside, said: "Lady Betty, I have made you a very indifferent husband, and particularly of late years, when infirmities have rendered me a burden to myself; but I shall not be much. longer troublesome to you. I advise you never again to marry an old man; but I strenuously exhort you to marry when I am gone, and I will endeavor to put it in your power. You have fulfilled every obligation towards me in an exemplary manner, and I wish to demonstrate my sense of your merits. I have, therefore, by will, bequeathed you this estate, [Note *: Drayton, in Northamptonshire, "a most venerable heap of ugliness, 'with many curious bits.'"—*Walpole*]. which I received from my first wife; and which, as she gave it to me, so I leave it to you. I hope you will marry, and have children to inherit it" Lady Betty, though left young a widow, and though she survived Sir John fifty years, never married a second time."

KINGLY AFFECTION.

George II. and his son Frederick, Prince of Wales, several years previous to the decease of the latter, lived on terms of complete alienation, or rather hostility. The King, though he never visited his son during his last illness, sent constantly to make inquiries; and received accounts, every two hours, of his state and condition. He was so far from desiring the Prince's recovery, that, on the contrary, he considered it would be an object of the utmost regret. Nor did he conceal his sentiments on this point. He was one day engaged in conversation with the Countess of Yarmouth, when the page entered, announcing that the Prince was better: "There now," said his Majesty, "I told you that he would not die." On the evening of the Prince's decease, the King had his usual party at Lady Yarmouth's apartments, and had just sat down to cards, when a page brought, from Leicester House, the information that the Prince was no more. The King did not testify either emotion or surprise. Then, rising, he crossed the room to Lady Yarmouth's table, who was likewise playing at cards, and leaning over her chair, said to her in a low tone of voice, in German, "Freddy is dead." Having communicated it to her, the King instantly withdrew. She followed him, the company broke up, and the news became public. These particulars were communicated by one of the party to Sir N Wraxall.

UNLUCKY GARDENING.

The gardens of Lord Islay (afterwards Duke of Argyll) at Whitton, or rather upon **Hounslow Heath,** were very cultivated, and gave rise to the following epigram:—

"Old Islay, to show his fine delicate taste
In improving his gardens purloin'd from the waste,
Bade his gard'ner one day to open his views,
By cutting a couple of grand avenues:
No particular prospect his lordship intended,

But left it to chance how his walks should be ended.
With transport and joy he beheld his first view end
In a favourite prospect—a church that was ruin'd—

But alas! what a sight did the next cut exhibit!
At the end of the walk hung a rogue on a gibbet!
He beheld it and wept, for it caused him to muse on
Full many a Campbell that died with his shoes on.
All amazed and aghast at the ominous scene,
He order'd it quick to be clos'd up again
With a clump of Scotch firs, that served for a *screen*."
Walpole's Letters, vol. i. 173.

A DELICATE HINT.

When Mrs. Chevenix, the toy-woman of Bath, and her sister Bertrand, called upon Walpole, touching the property of Strawberry Hill, he showed them his cabinet of enamels instead of treating them with white wine. The Bertrand said, "Sir, I hope you don't trust all sorts of ladies with this cabinet." What an entertaining assumption of dignity!

GEORGE II. AT DETTINGEN.

Frederick the Great, in his *Histoire de mon Temps,* gives the following account of George II at Dettingen: "The King was on horseback, and rode forward to reconnoitre the enemy: his horse, frightened at the cannonading, ran away with his Majesty, and nearly carried him into the midst of the French lines: fortunately, one of his attendants succeeded in stopping him. General Cyrus Trapaud, then an ensign, by seizing the horse's bridle, enabled his Majesty to dismount in safety. 'Now that I am once on my legs' said he, 'I am sure I shall not run away' The King then abandoned his horse, and fought on foot at the head of his Hanoverian battalions With his sword drawn, and his body placed in the attitude of a fencing-master, who is about to make a lunge in carte, he continued to expose himself, without flinching, to the enemy's fire."

LADY SARAH LENNOX.

Lady Sarah, the youngest daughter of the second Duke of Richmond, was born in 1745; and it is said, that when sixteen, she refused an offer of marriage made her by George III., but that she ultimately accepted him. Kensington traditions describe Lady Sarah as making hay in the fields, then bordering the road, and exchanging a word or two with the young Prince as he rode by. But the royal lover deceived her, and she, instead of being bride at his wedding, was only a bridesmaid. Lady Sarah was speedily consoled; for the year after the union of George and Charlotte, she married, at the age of eighteen, the well-known baronet, Sir Thomas Charles Bunbury. Subsequently, a widow of the mature age of thirty-six, Lady Sarah married, in 1781, the Hon. George Napier, son of Francis, fifth Lord Napier. The first child of which she was the mother was the "Sir Charles Napier," the hero of Scinde, whose "very existence" is ludicrously described by his biographer and brother, Sir William, as "an offence to royal pride." The slowness of Sir Charles Napier's promotion is amusingly laid to this union. When Lady Sarah was seventy, this eldest son of a brave, honourable, but singularly arrogant family, wrote to Lady Sarah: "It is the greatest satisfaction to me that the Regent is fifty, and that I am only thirty-four;" and at an earlier period by fifteen years, he expresses his disgust against the Prince of Wales, "for taking the liberty of calling me Charles! 'Marry, come up, very dirty cousin.'" Lady Sarah Lennox died in 1826, being then in her eighty-first year.—**Dr. Doran: note to** Walpole's **Last Journals.**

REMARKABLE COINING STORY.

In the spring of 1746, an elderly woman gave information against her maid for coining, and the trial came on at the Old Bailey. The mistress deposed that having been left a widow several years ago, with four children, and no possibility of maintaining them, she had taken to coining: that she used to buy old pewter-pots, out of each of which she made as many shillings, &c, as she could pass for three pounds, and that by this practice she had bred up her children, bound them out apprentices, and set herself up in a little shop, by which she had got a comfortable livelihood; that she had now given over coining, and indicted her maid as accomplice. The maid in her defence said, "That when her mistress hired her, she told her that she did something up in a garret into which she must never inquire: that all she knew of the matter was, that her mistress had often given her moulds to clean, which she did, as it was her duty: that, indeed, she had sometimes seen pieces of pewter-pots cut, and did suspect her mistress of coining; but that she never had had, or put off, one single piece of bad money."

The judge asked the mistress if this was true; she answered, "Yes;" and that she believed her maid was as honest a creature as ever lived; but that, knowing herself in her power, she never could be at peace; that she knew, by informing, she should secure herself; and not doubting but the maid's real innocence would appear, she concluded the poor girl would come to no harm. The judge flew into the greatest rage; told her he wished he could stretch the law to hang her, and feared he could not bring off the maid for having concealed the crime; but, however, the jury did bring her in **not guilty.** Horace Walpole, who relates this story, adds: "I think I never heard a more particular instance of parts and villainy."

TOO GOOD FOR ANYTHING.

Walpole, in his Letters, 1749, presents us with an impersonation of this rare excellence in **le beau** Gibberne, whose position he thus cleverly describes, in a letter to Sir Horace Mann: "Gibberne has been with me again to-day, as his mother was a fortnight ago: she talked me to death, and three times, after telling me her whole history, she said, 'Well, then, sir, upon the whole,' and began it all again. **Upon the whole,** I think she has a mind to keep her son in England; and he has a mind to be kept, though in my opinion he is very unfit for living in England—he is too polished! For trade, she says, he is in a cold sweat if she mentions it; and so they propose, by the acquaintance, he says, his mother has among the quality, to get him that nothing called something. He seems a good creature; too good to make his way here."

FLORENTINE BLUNDERS.

The Chevalier Lorenzi, whom Walpole feasted with venison which he protested was "as good as beef," with all his thirst for English knowledge, vented as many absurdities as if he had a passion for Ireland too. He was transported with some Florentine works of art, of which he said, the Great Duke had the originals, and there never had been made any copies of them. He told a lady also that he had seen a sapphire of the size of her diamond ring, and worth more: she said that could not be. "Oh!" said he, "I mean, supposing your diamond were a sapphire."

A LOVERS OF POMP.

The Duchess of Buckingham, natural daughter of James II., in her journey to the Continent, always stopped at Paris, visited the church where lay the unburied body of James, and wept over it A poor Benedictine of the convent, observing her filial piety, took notice to her Grace that the velvet pall that covered the coffin was become threadbare—and so it remained.

Though the Duchess could not effect a coronation to her will, she indulged her pompous mind with such puppet-shows as were appropriate to her rank. She made a funeral for her husband as splendid as that of the great Marlborough; she renewed that pageant for her only son, a weak lad, who died under age; and for herself: and prepared and directed waxen dolls of him and of herself to be exhibited in glass-cases in Westminster Abbey. It was for the procession at her son's burial that she wrote to old Sarah of Marlborough to borrow the triumphal car that had transported the corpse of the Duke. "It carried my Lord Marlborough," replied the other, "and shall never be used for anybody else." "I have consulted the undertaker," replied the Buckingham, "and he tells me I may have a finer for twenty pounds."

One of her last acts was marrying her grandson to a daughter of Lord Hervey. The day which was appointed for his first interview with the Duchess was on the martyrdom of her grandfather: she received him in the great drawing-room of Buckingham House, seated in a chair of state, in deep mourning, attended by her women in like weeds, in memory of the royal martyr!

GOOD ADVICE.

Mrs. Leneve used often to advise Walpole never to begin being civil to people he did not care for: "for," said she, "you grow weary of them, and can't help showing it, and so make it ten times worse than if you had never attempted to please them."

COURT CHAPLAINS.

Odd stories are told of devotional exercises at Court While Caroline, Queen of George II., dressed, prayers used to be read in the outward room, where hung a nude Venus.

Mrs. Selwyn, bedchamber-woman in waiting, was one day ordered to bid the chaplain, Dr. Madox, afterwards Bishop of Worcester, begin the service. He said archly: "And a very proper altar-piece is here, madam!" Queen Anne had the same custom; and once, ordering the door to be shut while she shifted, the chaplain stopped. The Queen sent to ask why he did not proceed. He replied, "He would not whistle the Word of God through the keyhole."

A FRACAS AT COURT.

Walpole humorously describes the following romping scene: "There has been a great fracas at Kensington: one of the Mesdames [George IL's daughters] pulled the chair from under Countess Delorane at cards, who, being provoked that her monarch was diverted with her disgrace, with the malice of a hobby-horse, gave him just such another fall But alas! the monarch, like Louis XIV., is mortal in the part that touched the ground, and was so hurt and so angry, that the Countess is disgraced, and her German rival [Lady Yarmouth] remains in the sole and quiet possession of her royal master's favour."—***Letter to Sir Horace Mann,*** 1742.

DUBLIN SOCIETY.

Malone relates that Lord Chesterfield, when Lord-Lieutenant in Ireland, being asked one day whom he thought the greatest man of the time, said—"The last man who arrived from England, be he who he might." There is some truth in this. Dublin depends a great deal on London for topics of conversation, as every secondary metropolis must; and the last man who arrives from the great scene of action (if of any degree of consequence) is courted as being supposed to know many little particulars not communicated by letters or the public prints. Every person in a distant country-town in England experiences something of this on the arrival of a friend from the metropolis.

LORD CHESTERFIELD'S MISTAKE.

Lord Chesterfield, on being made Secretary of State to George the Second, found a fair young lad in the antechamber at St. James's, who, seeming much at home, the Earl, concluding it was one of the sons of Lady Yarmouth, the King's mistress, was profuse of attentions to the boy, and more prodigal still of his prodigious regard for his mamma. The shrewd lad received all his Lordship's vows with indulgence, and without betraying himself; at last, he said, "I suppose your Lordship takes me for Master Louis; but I am only Sir. William Russel, one of the pages."

"THOSE GODDESSES, THE GUNNINGS."

Maria and Elizabeth Gunning, who appeared at the Court. of George II.—one at the age of eighteen and the other nineteen—were two portionless girls, of surpassing loveliness. "They are declared," writes Walpole, "to be the handsomest women alive: they can't walk in the park, or go to Vauxhall, but such crowds follow them, that they are generally driven away." They made more noise than any of their beautiful predecessors since the days of Helen. One day, they went to see Hampton Court: as they were going into the Beauty Room, another company arrived; the housekeeper said, "This way, ladies; here are the beauties." The Gunnings flew into a passion, and asked her what she meant; they went to see the palace, not to be shown as a sight themselves.

The youngest of these fair sisters became the wife of James, Duke of Hamilton: he fell in love with her at a masquerade, and in a fortnight, met her at an assembly made to show Lord Chesterfield's new house, in May Fair. Duke Hamilton made violent love to her at one end of the room, while he was playing faro at the other end: that is, he saw neither the bank nor his own cards, which were of three hundred pounds each; he soon lost a thousand. Two nights after, "being left alone with her, while her mother and sister were at Bedford House, the Duke grew so impatient that he sent for a parson. Doctor Keith refused to perform the ceremony without licence or ring; the Duke swore he would send for the Archbishop; at last they were married with a ring of a bed-curtain, at half-an-hour after twelve at night, at May Fair Chapel. In less than three weeks, Maria Gunning followed her sister to the altar, her choice falling on Lord Coventry.

Nothing could exceed the curiosity excited by the beauty of the sisters, which interest was considerably increased by their splendid alliances. When the Duchess of Hamilton was presented, the crowd at the drawing-room was so great that even noble persons clambered upon chairs and tables to look at her. There were mobs at their doors to see them get into their chairs; and such crowds flocked to see the Duchess, when she went to her castle, that 700 persons sat up all night in and about an inn in Yorkshire, to see her get into her post-chaise next morning. Lady Coventry was equally run after: at Worcester, a shoemaker got two guineas and a half by showing at a penny a head a shoe that he was making for the Countess! She went to Paris, but her Lord, who was grave and ill-bred, would not allow her to wear either red or powder. The Duke of Luxemburg told him he had called up my Lady Coventry's coach; my lord replied, **Vous avez fort bien fait.** He was jealous, prudish, and scrupulous: once, at a large dinner-party, he coursed his wife round the table, and, suspecting she had stolen on a little red, seized her, and scrubbed her with a napkin. She was weak-minded, and had little or no tact; for her Ladyship it was who told George II. the only sight she was eager to see was a coronation. But the King was only diverted with the awkward blunder.

Lady Coventry died at twenty-seven: the quantity of paint she had laid on her face is said, by checking the perspiration, to have been the immediate cause of the disorder which occasioned her death. Her sister, the Duchess of Hamilton, survived her thirty years.

ROBBERY PANIC.

In 1750, when robberies were so frequent in London, that people were almost afraid of stirring out after dark, Miss Pelham left a pair of diamond earrings, which she had borrowed, in a hackney-chair; she had put them under the seat for fear of being attacked, and forgot them. The chairmen sunk them. The next morning, when they were missed, the damsel began to cry; her mother grew frightened, lest her infanta should vex herself sick, and summoned a jury of matrons to consult whether she should give her hartshorn or lavender drops. Mrs. Selwyn, who was on the panel, grew very peevish, and said, "Pho! give her **brilliant drops!**"

At the same period a lady at a card-party caused great consternation by calling out, at the top of her voice, *"Un voleur! un voleur!"*—meaning a **thief in the candle!**

REASONABLE EVASION.

One day it was proposed that the Duchess of Douglas should go to Court, and take advantage of the privilege of the *tabouret,* or right of sitting on a low stool in the Queen's private chamber, which it was alleged she possessed by virtue of her late husband's ancestors having enjoyed a French dukedom (Touraine), in the fifteenth century. The old lady made all sorts of excuses in her homely way; but when the Laird of Boysack started the theory, that the real objection lay in her Grace's fears as to the disproportioned size of the tabouret for the co-relative part of her figure, he was declared, amidst shouts of laughter, to have divined the true difficulty—her Grace enjoying the joke fully as much as any of them.

JESUIT FLOGGING.

Molinari, a Jesuit of the school at Kensington, had, for corrective purposes, a whip made of strong cord, with knots at regular intervals, with which he used to lash the hands of the scholars in such a way as to make the blood leap from them. It seemed to give him great pain to inflict this chastisement, but he felt ***the necessity of being severe.*** He had a very extraordinary method of reconciling the devouter student to this torture. He sentenced him first to nine lashes, and then ordered him to hold out his hand; "Offer it up to God and His saints," he would say, "as a sacrifice." He would then select nine saints. The first blow was to be suffered in honour of St. Ignatius,—"Allons, mon enfant, au nom du plus grand de tous les Saints—St. Ignace!" and down went the whip from a vigorous and muscular arm. "Oh! mon Dieu!" cried the little martyr, withdrawing his hand after the first operation. "Allons! mon enfant, au nom de St Francois Xavier!" and he then inflicted a second laceration upon the culprit. "Mais, mon Pére, ayez pitié—jamais, jamais, je ne ferai des solécismes—oh, mon Pére, jamais." The Jesuit was inexorable. "Allons, mon enfant, au nom de St. Louis de Gonzague;" and thus he proceeded till he had gone through his calendar of infliction.

ODD BELIEF.

The only thing talked of (writes Walpole in 1751) is a man who draws teeth with a sixpence, and puts them in again for a shilling. I believe it; not that it seems probable, but because I have long been persuaded that the most incredible discoveries will be made, and that, about the time, or a little after, I die, the secret will be found out how to live for ever,—and that secret, I believe, will not be discovered by a physician.

GEOGRAPHICAL LAPSUS.

"Walpole mentions that when the fanciful Whiston predicted that the world would be burnt in three years, the Duchess of Bolton packed up all her effects, and declared she was off to China, to get out of danger.

DEATH OF FREDERICK, PRINCE OF WALES.

Two men were heard lamenting the Prince's death in Leicester Fields: one said, "He has left a great many small children!"—"Ay," replied the other; "but what is worse, they belong to our parish!" But the most extraordinary reflections on his death were set forth in May Fair Chapel: "He had no great parts, but he had great virtues; indeed, they degenerated into vices: he was very generous, but I hear his generosity has ruined a great many people; and then, his condescension was such, that he kept very bad company."

ROYAL CRITICISM.

"Walpole, writing in 1751, says: A certain King (George II.) was last week at the play. The intriguing chambermaid in the farce says to the old gentleman: "You are villainously old; you are sixty-six; you can't have the impudence to think of living above two years." The old gentleman in the stage-box turned about in a passion, and said, "This is d—d stuff."

A MATCH FOR A QUEEN.

After Sir Paul Methuen had quitted Court, Queen Caroline, who thought she had the foolish talent of playing off people, frequently saw him when she dined abroad, during the King's absence at Hanover. Once that she dined with Lady Walpole at Chelsea, Sir Paul was there, as usual. People that play off others generally harp upon the same string. The Queen's constant topic for teazing Sir Paul was his passion for romances, and he was weary of it, and not in good humour with her. "Well, Sir Paul, what romance are you reading now?"—"None, Madam! I have gone through them all."—"Well! what are you reading then?"—"I am got into a very foolish study, Madam; the History of the Kings and Queens of England."—

AN OBLIVIOUS LADY.

Mrs. Vesey, a leader of fashion, a contemporary of the celebrated Mrs. Montague, was so forgetful that she sometimes hardly remembered her own name. It will scarcely be credited, that she could declaim against second marriages, to a lady of quality who had been twice, married, and though Mr. Vesey was her own second husband. When at last reminded of the circumstance, she only exclaimed, "Bless me, my dear, I had quite forgotten it" There was, indeed, some decay of mind in such want of recollection. Her sister-in-law, who lived in the same house with her, and who formed physically, as well as morally, a perfect contrast to Mrs. Vesey, superintended all domestic arrangements. From their opposite figures, qualities, and endowments, the one was called "Body," the other "Mind."

A TUNBRIDGE WELLS HOAX.

The Lilliputian Lady Newhaven arriving at Tunbridge, desired her friend, Mrs. Vesey, to explain to her and instruct her in the customs of the place. A man arrived ringing a bell—"for what?" said my lady: "Oh!" replied Mrs. Vesey, "to notify your arrival" At that instant, the man bawled out, "At one o'clock, at Mr. Pinchbeck's great room, will be shown the surprising tall woman."—**Walpole's Letters.**

ODDITIES OF FALSE HAIR.

I was struck the other day [writes Walpole to Sir Horace Mann] with a resemblance of mine host at Brandon to old Sarazin. You must know, the ladies of Norfolk universally wear perriwigs, and affirm that it is the fashion at London. "Lord, Mrs. White, have you been ill, that you have shaved your head?" Mrs. White, in all the days of my acquaintance with her, had a professed head of red hair: to-day she had no hair at all before, and at a distance above her ears, I discerned a smart brown bob, from beneath which had escaped some long strings of original scarlet—so like old Sarazin at two in the morning, when she has been losing at faro, and clawed her wig aside, and her old trunk is shaded with the venerable white wig of her own locks."

KITTY CANNON AND HER TWO HUSBANDS.

Lord Dalmeny, eldest son of the second Earl of Roseberry, some years before his death in 1755, casually encountered in London a lady who made a deep impression on him, and whom he induced to marry him, and accompany him on a tour of the continent. This union was without the knowledge of relations on either side, but the pair lived in great harmony and happiness till the lady was overtaken by a mortal illness. When assured that she was dying, she asked for pen and paper, and wrote the words: "lam the wife of the Rev. Mr. Gough, rector of Thorpe, in Essex; my maiden name was C. Cannon, and my last request is, to be buried at Thorpe." How she had happened to desert her husband does not appear; but Lord Dalmeny, while full of grief for her loss, protested that he was utterly ignorant of this previous marriage. In compliance with her last wishes, he embalmed her body, and brought it in a chest to England. Under the feigned name of Williams, he landed at Colchester, where the chest was opened by the custom-house officers under suspicion of its containing smuggled goods. The young nobleman manifested the greatest grief on the occasion, and seemed distracted under the further and darker suspicions which now arose. The body being placed uncovered in the church, he took his place beside it, absorbed in profound sorrow. At length, he gave full explanation of the circumstances, and Mr. Gough was sent for to come and identify his wife. The first meeting of the indignant husband with the sorrow-struck young man who had unwittingly injured him, was very moving to all who beheld it. Of the two, the latter appeared the most solicitous to do honour to the deceased. He had a splendid coffin made for her, and attended her corpse to Thorpe, where Mr. Gough met him, and the burial was performed with all due solemnity. Lord Dalmeny immediately after departed for London, apparently inconsolable for his loss. Kitty Cannon is, it is believed, the first woman in England that had two husbands to attend her to the grave together.

A DREAM VERIFIED.

"Walpole writes to Sir Horace Mann, Jan. 9, 1755: "I relate the following, only prefacing, that I do believe the dream happened, and happened right, among the millions of dreams that do not hit. Lord Bury was at, Windsor, when the express of his father's death arrived: he came to town time enough to find his mother and sisters at breakfast ' Lord! child,' said my Lady Albemarle, 'what brings you to town so early? He said he had been sent for. Says she, 'You are not well!' 'Yes,' replied Lord Bury, 'I am, but a little flustered with something. I have heard.' 'Let me feel your pulse,' said Lady Albemarle: 'Oh!' continued she, 'your father is dead! 'Lord! Madam,' said Lord Bury, 'how could that come into your head? I should rather have imagined that you would have thought it was my poor brother William, (who is just gone to Lisbon for his health.) 'No,' said my Lady Albemarle, 'I know it is your father; I dreamed last night that he was dead, and came to take leave of me!' and immediately swooned." Another account states that Lady Albemarle thought she saw her Lord dressed in white: "the same thing happened before the Duke of Richmond's death, and often has happened before the death of any of her family."

THE UNIVERSAL PANACEA.

Edward, Duke of York, was one day conversing at St. James's, with his brother George III., when the latter remarked that he seemed in unusually low spirits. "How can I be otherwise," said the Duke, "when I am subjected to so many calls from my creditors, without having a sixpence to pay them?" The King, it is said, immediately presented him with a thousand-pound note; every word of which he read aloud, in a tone of mock gravity; and then marched out of the room, singing the first verse of "God save the King."

QUEEN CHARLOTTE'S MARRIAGE.

When the Princess Charlotte of Mecklenburgh-Strelitz came over to be married to George III. she was ten days at sea, but gay the whole voyage, sung to her harpsichord, and left the cabin-door open. Walpole describes her as easy, civil, and not disconcerted. On the road they wanted to curl her toupet: she said she thought it looked as well as that of any of the ladies sent to fetch her; if the King bid her, she would wear a perriwig, otherwise she would remain as she was. When she caught the first glimpse of St. James's palace, she turned pale: the Duchess of Hamilton smiled. "My dear Duchess," said the Princess, "*you* may laugh; you have been married twice; but it is no joke to me."

After the marriage ceremony, as supper was not ready, the Queen sat down, sung and played on the harpsichord to the royal family, who all supped with her in private. They talked of the different German dialects: the King asked if the Hanoverian was not pure. "Oh, no, sir," said the Queen; "it is the worst of all."

She was not tall, nor a beauty; pale, and very thin, but looked sensible, and was genteel. A ridiculous circumstance happened during the presentations. Lord Westmoreland, not very young or clear-sighted, mistook Lady Sarah Lennox for the Queen, kneeled to her, and would have kissed her hand if she had not prevented him. With Lady Sarah the King was thought to be in love.

Queen Charlotte had always been, if not ugly, at least ordinary, but in her later years her want of personal charms became, of course, less observable, and it used to be said that she was grown better-looking. Mr. Croker one day said something to this effect to Colonel Disbrowe, her chamberlain. "Yes," replied he, "I do think that the *bloom* of her ugliness is going off."

A VILLAGE TALE.

At Teddington, there lived, in Walpole's time, a Captain Prescott, who was not only a tar but pitch and brimstone too. He beat his wife, a beautiful, sensible young woman, most unmercifully, so that a young footman, who lived with them five years, could not bear to witness such brutality, but left them, and went to live with Mrs. Clive. The Captain's wife then resolved to run away, and by the footman's assistance did, and got to London. Her father and friends came up, and she swore the peace against her husband. The cause was heard before Lord Mansfield. Mrs. Clive's servant was summoned as a witness. The Chief Justice asked him if he had not been aiding and abetting to his former mistress's escape. He said, Yes, he had. "You had I" said my Lord, "what, do you confess that you helped your master's wife to elope?" "Yes, my Lord," replied the lad, "and yet my master has never thanked me!" "Thanked you!" said Lord Mansfield, "thanked you! what, for being an accomplice with a wife against her husband?" "My Lord, said the lad, "if I had not, he would have murdered her, and then he would have been hanged." The Court laughed, and Lord Mansfield was charmed with the lad's coolness and wit.

DISTRESSED ORPHANS.

Shortly before the Coronation of George III., Walpole relates this incident. "I was extremely diverted t'other day with my mother's and my old milliner: she said she had a petition to present to me. 'What is it, Mrs. Burton?' 'It is in behalf of two poor orphans.' I began to feel for my purse. 'What can I do for them, Mrs. Burton?' 'Only if your honour would be so compassionate as to get them **tickets for the Coronation**' I could not keep my countenance, and these distressed **orphans** are two- and three-and-twenty! Did you ever hear a more melancholy case?

CORONATION OF GEORGE III.

The following are a few amusing eccentricities of the pageant.

My Lady Harrington, covered with all the diamonds she could borrow, hire, or seize, and with the air of a Roxana, was the finest figure at a distance: she complained to George Selwyn that she was to walk with Lady Portsmouth, who would have a wig and a stick. "Pho," said he, "you will only look as if you were taken up by the constable." She told this everywhere, thinking the reflection was on my Lady Portsmouth.

Walpole tells us that he dressed part of Lady Strafford's head, and made some of my Lord Hertford's dress; "for," adds he, "you know, no profession comes amiss to me, from a tribune of the people to a habit-maker. . . . Lord B—put rouge upon his wife and the Duchess of Bedford in the Painted Chamber; the Duchess of Queensbury told me of the latter, that she looked like an orange-peach, half red and half yellow."

Some of the peeresses were so fond of their robes, that they graciously exhibited themselves for a whole day before to all the company their servants could invite to see them. A maid from Richmond begged leave to stay in town, because the Duchess of Montrose was only to be seen from two to four.

The King complained that so few precedents were kept for their proceedings. Lord Effingham owned the Earl Marshal's office had been strangely neglected; but he had taken such care for the future, that the ***next coronation*** would be regulated in the most exact order imaginable. The King was so diverted with this flattering speech that he made the Earl repeat it several times.

Garrick exhibited the Coronation, and opening the end of the stage, discovered a real bonfire and real mob; the houses in Drury Lane let their windows at three-pence a-head. Rich promised a finer Coronation than the real one: for there was to be a dinner for the Knights of the Bath and the Barons of the Cinque Ports, which Lord Talbot refused them.

PLAIN SPEAKING AT COURT.

When old Mr. Richard Clive, through the elevation of his great son, Lord Clive, had been introduced into society for which his former habits had not well fitted him, he presented himself at the levée. The King asked him where Lord Clive was. "He will be in town very soon," said the old gentleman, loud enough to be heard by the whole circle, "and then your Majesty will have another vote".

ROCHESTER'S LETTERS.

Mr. Bentley used to tell of an old-devout Lady St. John, who burnt a whole trunkful of letters of the famous Lord Rochester, "for which," said Mr. Bentley, "her soul is now burning in heaven." The oddness, confusion, and wit of the idea are very striking.

A VISIT TO LADY MARY WORTLEY MAOTAGU.

Walpole, writing in 1762, describes his visit to this strange lady: "I found her in a little miserable bedchamber of a ready-furnished house, with two tallow-candles, and a bureau covered with pots and pans. On her head, in full of all accounts, she had an old black-laced hood, wrapped entirely round, so as to conceal all hair or want of hair. No handkerchief but up to her chin a kind of horseman's riding-coat, calling itself a ***pet-en-l'air,*** made of a dark green brocade, with coloured and silver flowers, and lined with furs; boddice laced, a foul dimity petticoat, sprig'd, velvet muffeteens on her arms, grey stockings and slippers. Her face less changed in twenty years than I could have imagined; I told her so, and she was not so tolerable twenty years ago that she need have taken it for flattery, but she did, and literally gave me a box on the ear. She is very lively, all her senses perfect, her language as imperfect as ever, her avarice greater. With nothing but an Italian, a French, and a

Russian, all men servants, and something she calls an *old* secretary, but whose age till he appears will be doubtful; she receives all the world, and crams them into this kennel. The Duchess of Hamilton, who came in just after me, was so astonished and diverted, that she could not speak to her for laughing."

SAVINGS A LIFE, AND AN EAR.

Lady Suffolk was early affected with deafness. Cheselden, the surgeon, then in favour at Court, persuaded her that he had hopes of being able to cure deafness by some operation on the drum of the ear, and offered to try the experiment on a condemned convict then in Newgate, who was deaf. If the man could be pardoned, he would try it; and if he succeeded, would practise the same cure on her ladyship. She obtained the man's pardon, who was cousin to Cheselden, who had feigned that prettied discovery to save his relation, and no more was heard of the experiment. The man saved his ear too—but Cheselden was disgraced at Court.

WALPOLE'S VISIT TO THE COCK-LANE GHOST.

The notorious Ghost in Cock-lane was set on foot in 1762 by a drunken parish-clerk; the Methodists adopted it, and the whole town thought of nothing else. "I went to hear it," says Walpole, "for it is not an *apparition,* but an *audition.* We set out from the Opera, changed our clothes at Northumberland-house, the Duke of York, Lady Northumberland, Lady Mary Coke, Lord Hertford, and I, all in one hackney-coach, and drove to the spot: it rained in torrents; yet the lane was full of mob, and the house so full we could not get in; at last they discovered it was the Duke of York, and the company squeezed themselves into one another's pockets to make room for us. The house, which is borrowed, and to which the ghost has adjourned, is wretchedly small and miserable; when we opened the chamber, in which were fifty people, with no light but one tallow-candle at the end, we rambled over the bed of the child to whom the ghost comes, and whom they are murdering by inches in such insufferable heat and stench. At the top of the room are ropes to dry clothes. I asked if we were to have rope-dancing between the acts? We heard nothing; they told us, as they would at a puppet-show, that it would not come that night till seven in the morning; that is, when there are only 'prentices and old women. We stayed, however, till half-an-hour after one. The Methodists have promised their contributions; provisions are sent in like forage, and all the taverns and ale-houses in the neighbourhood make fortunes. The most diverting part is to hear people wondering **when it will be found out,** as if there was anything to find out—as if the actors would make their noises when they can be discovered."

The girl—the clerk's daughter, twelve years old—it was said, was continually disturbed at night with the knocking and scratching of some invisible agent against the wainscot of whatever room she was in. These noises were made, it was said, by the departed spirit of a young gentlewoman of respectable family in Norfolk, buried in the vaults of the church of St John, Clerkenwell. She was said to have been poisoned by her husband with a drink of deleterious punch; and the girl she pursued was said to have slept with her in the absence of her husband. Investigation of the noises was courted, and the supposed spirit had publicly promised, by an affirmative knock, that she would attend any one of the gentlemen into the vault where her body was deposited, and give a token of her presence by a knock upon her coffin. An investigation took place on the night of February 1, 1762; Dr. Johnson was present, with other gentlemen, and printed an account of what they saw and heard. Knocks and scratches were heard, and the girl declared that she felt the spirit like a mouse upon her back. The spirit was then required to manifest itself; but no evidence of any preternatural power was exhibited. Nor was the promised "affirmative knock "in the vault given; nor could any confession be drawn from the girl. This solemn inquiry undeceived the world, and the contrivers of the imposture were punished for what they did. The father of the girl was set three times in the pillory, and imprisoned for one year in the King's Bench prison; but the mob, instead of pelting him in the pillory, collected a subscription for him. Oliver Goldsmith has described the whole of this strange affair in a pamphlet.

"IT IS VERY INCONVENIENT."

This was a cant phrase with Walpole, which had its rise in the following story:—The tutor of a young Lord Castlecomer, who lived at Twickenham with his mother, having broken his leg, and somebody pitying the poor man to the mother, Lady Castlecomer, she replied, "Yes, indeed, it is very inconvenient to my Lord Castlecomer."

As a companion to the above: A constable's journal kept during the Civil War, ended thus: "And there was never heard of such troublesome and distracted times as these five years have been, but *especially for constables.*"

YAWNING'S CATCHING.

One evening, at the commerce-table, at the Princess Amelia's, Horace Walpole was seen to gape—a great sin on any Palatine Hill. A few days after, the Princess, calling at Strawberry Hill, and spying the shield with Medusa's head on the staircase, she said to Walpole, "Oh! now I see where yon learnt to yawn."

LORD BATH AND HIS CREDITOR.

Lord Bath owed a tradesman eight hundred pounds, and would never pay him: the man determined to persecute him till he did; and one morning followed him to Lord Winchil-sea's, and sent up word that he wanted to speak with him. Lord Bath came down, and said, "Fellow, what do you want with me?"—"My money," said the man, as loud as ever he could bawl before all the servants. He bade him come the next morning, and then would not see him. The next Sunday the man followed him to church, and got into the next pew: he leaned over, and said, "My money; give me my money!" My lord went to the end of the pew; the man too: "Give me my money!" The sermon was on avarice, and the text, "Cursed are they that heap up riches." The man groaned out, "O Lord!" and pointed to my Lord Bath. In short, he persisted so much, and drew the eyes of all the congregation, that my Lord Bath went out and paid him directly.

LONG SIR THOMAS ROBINSON.

This eccentric person, who is now at rest in Westminster Abbey, was, when living, designated as "Long," to distinguish him from his namesake Sir Thomas Robinson, created Lord Grantham in 1761. Chesterfield being asked by the Baronet to write some verses upon him, immediately produced the epigram:

"Unlike my subject now shall be my song,
It shall be witty, and it shan't be long."

Long Sir Thomas, or "Long Tom," as he was familiarly called, filled the office of Commissioner of Excise and Governor of Barbadoes. He was a man of the world, or rather of the town, and a great pest to persons of high rank or in office. He was very troublesome to the Duke of Newcastle, the minister, and when on his visits to him he was told that his Grace was gone out, would desire to be admitted to look at the clock, or to play with the monkey that was kept in the hall, in hopes of being sent for in to the Duke. This he had so frequently done, that all in the house were tired of him. At length it was concocted among the servants that he should receive a summary answer to his usual questions; and, accordingly, at his next coming, the porter, as soon as he had opened the gate, and without waiting for what he had to say, dismissed him in these words: "Sir, his Grace has gone out, the clock stands, and the monkey is dead."

Long Sir Thomas distinguished himself also in this curious manner. When our King had not dropped the folly of calling himself also King "of France," and it was customary at the coronation of an English sovereign to have fictitious Dukes of Aquitaine and Normandy to represent the vassalage of France, Sir Thomas was selected to fill the second mock dignity at the coronation of George III, the last occasion on which the foolish phantoms appeared. Churchill alludes to the circumstance in his "Ghost;" hut he assigns a wrong dukedom to Sir Thomas:

"Could Satire not (though doubtful since

Whether the plumber is or prince)
Tell of a simple knight's advance,
To be a doughty peer of France?
Tell how he did a dukedom gain,
And Robinson was Aquitain."

We have said there were two Sir Thomas Robinsons—of whom one was tall and thin, the other short and fat: "I can't imagine," said Lady Townshend, "why the one should be preferred to the other; I see but little difference between them; the one is as ***broad*** as the other is ***long.***"

GROWING TOWARDS OLD.

Walpole, writing in 1767, says: "I have seen and remember so much that my life already appears very long; nay, the first part of it seems to have been a former life, so entirely are the persons worn out who were on the stage when I came into the world. You must consider, as my father was Minister then, that I almost came into the world at three years old. I was ten when I was presented to George the First, two nights before he left England for the last time. This makes me appear very old to myself, and Methuselah to young persons, if I happen to mention it before them. If I see another reign, which is but too probable, what shall I see then? I will tell you an odd circumstance. Nearly ten years ago, I had already seen six generations in one family, that of Waldegrave. I have often seen, and once been in a room with, Mrs. Godfrey, mistress of James II It is true she doted; then came her daughter the old Lady Waldegrave; her son the ambassador; his daughter, Lady Harriet, her daughter, the present Lady Powis; and she has children who may be married in five or six years; and yet I shall not be very old if I see two generations more! but if I do I shall be superannuated, for I think I talk already like an old nurse."

[Mr. P. Cunningham, upon this notes: "He (Walpole) had seen the Duchess of Tyrconnell, (Frances Jennings, of De Grammont,) in his father's house at Chelsea, as I gather from the MS. note in his own edition and copy of De Grammont, once in my possession.]

EXTRAVAGANCES OF FASHION.

What an amusing picture of the follies of the early years of the reign of George III. does the following anecdotic gossip by Walpole, writing from Strawberry Hill, May 6, 1770, afford: "What think you of a winter Ranelagh [the Pantheon] erecting in Oxford road, at the expense of 60,000*l.?* the new bank, including the value of the ground, and of the houses demolished to make room for it, will cost 300,000 *l.?*; and erected, as my Lady Townley says, **by sober citizens too!** I have touched before to you on the incredible profusion of our young men of fashion. I know a younger brother who literally gives a flower-woman half-a-guinea every morning for a bunch of roses for the nosegay in his button-hole. There has lately. been an auction of stuffed birds; and as natural history is in fashion, there are physicians and others who paid forty and fifty guineas for a single Chinese pheasant; you may buy a live one for five. After this, it is not extraordinary that pictures should be dear. We have at present three exhibitions. One West, who paints history in the taste of Poussin, gets 300)*l.* for a piece not too large to hang over a chimney. . . . Another rage is for prints of English portraits; I have been collecting them above thirty years, and, originally, never gave for a mezzotinto above one, or two shillings, the lowest are now a crown; most from half-a-guinea to a guinea. Lately, I assisted a clergyman [Granger] in compiling a catalogue of them; since the publication, scarce heads in books not worth threepence, will sell for five guineas. Then we have Etruscan vases, made of earthenware, in Staffordshire, [by Wedgwood] from two to five guineas; and ***ormoulu,*** never made here before, which succeeds so well, that a teakettle, which the inventor offered for one hundred guineas, sold by auction for one hundred and thirty. In short, we are at the height of extravagance and improvements, for we do improve rapidly in taste as well as in the former. I cannot say so much for our genius. Poetry is gone to bed, or into our prose; we are like the Romans in that too. If we have the arts of the Antonines,—we have the fustian also."

WAITING TO BE HANGED.

A Laird in the north of Scotland, who died some thirty or forty years ago, had as great a *penchant* for attending executions as the witty George Selwyn, and his local standing would appear to have made his presence at such exhibitions a sine quâ non. On one occasion' an unfortunate wretch was about to be "turned off;" the rope was adjusted, and every thing was ready. The hangman, however, stood waiting with apparent anxiety, evidently for an addition to the spectators. Being asked why he did not proceed with the business, he replied with a look of surprise at his questioner, "M—(naming the laird) is nae come yet." The hang-man's paramount desire to please the local dignitary (who we may suppose he looked upon in the light of a patron) under such circumstances, is fine.—***Notes and Queries,*** No. 106, Third Series.

A DIFFICULTY SOLVED.

Mrs. Rudd, who was tried at the Old Bailey in 1775, for felony, preparatory to her trial sent for some brocaded silks to a mercer; she pitched on a rich one, and ordered him to cut off the proper quantity; but the mercer reflecting that if she were hanged, as was probable, he should never be paid, pretended he had no scissars, but would carry home the piece, cut off what she wanted, and send it to Newgate. She saw his apprehension; pulled out her pocket-book; and, giving him a bank-note of twenty pounds, said, "There is *a pair of scissors.*"

WHAT HORACE WALPOLE SAW.

When Walpole was near his sixtieth year, he wrote: "As I was an infant when my father became Minister, I came into the world at five years old; knew half the remaining Courts of King William and Queen Anne, or heard then; talked of as fresh; being the youngest and; favourite child, was carried to almost the first operas, kissed the hand of George the First, and am now hearing the frolics of his great-great-grandson;—no, all this cannot have happened in one life! I have seen a mistress of James the Second, the Duke of Marlborough's burial, three or four wars; the whole career, victories, and death of Lord Chatham; the loss of America; the second conflagration of London by Lord George Gordon—and yet I am not so old as Methusalem by four or five centuries."

THE TWO PRINCES OF ANAMABOE.

In the London season of 1749, two black princes of Anamaboe were in fashion at all the assemblies. Their story is very much like that of Oroonoko, and is briefly this: A Moorish king, who had entertained, with great hospitality, a British captain trafficking on the coast of Africa, reposed such confidence in him as to intrust him with his son, about eighteen years of age, and another sprightly youth, to be brought to England and educated in the European manners. The captain received them, and basely sold them for slaves. He shortly after died; the ship coming to England, the officers related the whole affair; upon which the Government sent to pay their ransom, and they were brought to England, and put under the care of the Earl of Halifax, then at the head of the Board of Trade, who had them clothed and educated. They were afterwards received in the higher circles, and introduced to the King (George II.) on the 1st of February. In this year they appeared at Covent Garden Theatre, to see the tragedy of **Oroonoko,** where they were received with a loud clap of applause, which they returned with "a genteel bow." The tender interview between Imoinda and Oroonoko so affected the Prince, that he was obliged to retire at the end of the fourth act His companion remained, but wept all the time so bitterly, that it affected the audience more than the play.

NOT INFECTIOUS.

Old Lady Rosslyn was at home. Mrs.—was announced.
When the women were bundling off, "Sit still, sit still," said old Lady R., "it is na' catching."

DOMESTIC TROUBLE.

There is an odd mixture of complaint and remedy in the following passage from a letter of Walpole to the Countess of Ossory, written from Strawberry Hill: "I am in great distress, with a near relation dying in my house. You have heard me mention Mrs. Daye; they have let her come' here from Chichester in the last stage of an asthma and dropsy. I can neither leave her here with only servants, nor know how to convey her back; but I will not disturb your happiness with melancholy stories, Madam. For political mishaps, they are very durable. One loves one's country, but then one takes no more part than comes to the share of an individual; besides, where one has lived a good while, events strike one the less. I have seen my country's barometer up at Minden, and down at Derby. I have worn laurels and crackers, and sackcloth-and ashes. At last I am grown like sauntering Jack, and bear revolutions with much philosophy:

My billet at the fire is found,
Whoever is depos'd or crown'd;

but I go no further; one has grief enough of one's own, without fretting because cousin America has eloped with a Presbyterian parson."

CHALK STONE AND GOUT.

Walpole was a martyr to gout, with deposits of chalk in his fingers; yet, says Hannah More, "neither years nor sufferings can abate the entertaining powers of the pleasant Horace, which rather improve than decay; though he himself says, he is only fit to be a milkwoman, as the ***chalk-stones*** on his fingers'-ends quality him for nothing but ***scoring;*** but he declares he will not be a ***Bristol milkwoman***"—the Anne Yearsley, who so grossly imposed upon the good Hannah. What exquisite humour is there in his description of his sufferings: "A finger of each hand has been pouring out a hail of chalk-stones and liquid chalk; and the first finger, which

I hoped exhausted, last week opened again, and threw out a cascade of the latter, exactly with the effort of a pipe that bursts in the streets; the gout followed, and has swelled both hand and arm; and this codicil will cost me at least three weeks. I must persuade myself, if I can, that these explosions will give me some repose; but there are top many chalk-eggs in the other fingers not to be hatched in succession."

HOW TO ESCAPE AN OLD STORY.

Lord Cobham *would* tell stories, though he had few to tell, and those he told prosily. One day he was dining at Sir Richard Temple's. Bubb Dodington was present, and after dinner fell asleep, and had a pretty long nap. Temple rallied him, when Dodington tried to deny the fact, and offered to bet ten guineas that he would repeat all Cobham had been saying. His lordship accepted the wager, and dared Dodington to the proof. To his surprise, however, Bubb went through a story Cobham had been telling, nearly word for word. "Surely," said Temple, "you must possess the extraordinary faculty of sleeping with your eyes open." "Far from it," replied Dodington; "when I dozed off I knew that the period of the evening had arrived when Cobham would tell *that* story; so, I went to sleep accordingly."

THE ART OF BORROWING.

Bubb Dodington was one day walking down Bow-street, at the time it was well inhabited, and "resorted to by gentry for lodgings," when a borrowing acquaintance rushed from the opposite side of the way, and expressed great delight at meeting him; "for," said he, "I am wonderfully in want of a guinea." Dodington winced, and taking out his purse, showed that he had no more than half a guinea. "A thousand thanks," exclaimed the persecutor, half forcing the coin from between the owner's fingers, "that will do very well for the present;" and cleverly changed the subject to a good story. When they had parted, the brazen borrower returned to Dodington, saying: "By the bye, when will you pay me that half-guinea?"—"Pay you! what do you mean?" "Why, I *intended* to borrow a guinea of you, and have only got half; but I'm not in a hurry for t'other; name your own time—only pray keep it."

THE PALSIED GAMBLER.

Hannah More used to relate that a foreign ambassador, Count Adhemar, had a stroke of palsy, and that he was to have had a great assembly on the night of the day on which it happened. It was on a Sunday! The company went—some hundreds. The man lay deprived of sense and motion; his bedchamber joined the drawing-room, where was a faro-bank, held close to his bed's head. Somebody said, they thought they made too much noise. "Oh no," answered another, "it will do him good; the worst thing he can do is to sleep." A third said, "I did not think Adhemar had, been a fellow of such rare spirit; palsy and faro together is spirited indeed; this is keeping it up!"

The gentle Hannah related this to Walpole, who, in return, told her of a French gentleman at Paris, who, being in the article of death, had not signed his will, when the lawyer who drew it up was invited by his wife to stay supper. The table was laid in the dying man's apartment; the lawyer took a glass of wine, and addressing himself to the lady, drank "à la santé de notre aimable agonisant!" "I told Mr. Walpole," says Hannah, "he invented the story to out-do me, but he protested it was literally true."

LOSING A FORTUNE.

Sir John Bland is said to have ***flirted*** away his whole fortune at hazard. In one night he exceeded what was lost by the Duke of Bedford, having at one period of the night (though he recovered the greatest part of it) lost two-and-thirty thousand pounds. The citizens are said to have "put on their double-channeled pumps, and trudged to St James's-street, in expectation of seeing judgments executed on White's—angels with flaming swords, and devils flying away with dice-boxes, like the prints in Sadeler's hermits." Sir John lost this immense sum to a Captain Scott, who had nothing but a few debts and his commission.

A REFORMED GAMESTER.

Colonel Thomas Panton was a celebrated gamester of the time of the Restoration, and who, in one night, it is said, won as many thousands as purchased him an estate of above 1,500*l.* a-year. "After this good fortune," says Lucas, "he had such an aversion against all manner of games, that he would never handle cards or dice again; but lived very handsomely on his winnings to his dying day, which was in the year 1681. Colonel Panton was the last proprietor of the gaming-house called Piccadilly Hall, and was in possession of land on the site of the streets and buildings which bear his name, as early as the year 1664. Yet we remember to have seen it stated that Panton street was named from a particular kind of horse-shoe called a *panton;* and from its contiguity to the Haymarket, this origin was long credited.

LOCAL FAME.

"I remember," says Walpole, "how, long ago, I estimated local renown at its just value by a little sort of adventure that I will tell you; and since that there is an admirable chapter somewhere in Voltaire, which shows that more extended fame is but local on a little larger scale: it is the chapter of the Chinese who goes into a European bookseller's shop, and is amazed at finding none of the works of his most celebrated countrymen; while the bookseller finds the stranger equally ignorant of western classics. Horace then tells us how he went once with Mr. Rigby to see a window of painted glass at Messling, in Essex, and dined at a better sort of alehouse. The landlady waited on them, and was notably loquacious, entertaining them with the *bonmots* and funny exploits of Mr. Charles. Mr. Charles said this, Mr. Charles played such a trick; oh! nothing was so pleasant as Mr. Charles. But, how astonished the poor soul was when they asked *who Mr. Charles was;* and how much more astonished when she found they had never heard of Mr. Charles Luchyn, who, it seems, was a relation of Lord Grimston, had lived in their village, and been the George Selwyn of half a dozen cottages.

"If I had," adds Walpole, "a grain of ambitious pride left, it is what, in other respects, has been the thread that has run through my life, that of being forgotten: so true, except the folly of being an author, has been what I said last year to the Prince of Wales [George IV.] when he asked me if I was a Freemason, I replied, No, sir; I never was anything."

Lady Charleville, Walpole's neighbour, told him, that having some company with her, one had been to see Strawberry. "Pray," said another, "who is that Mr. Walpole?" "Lord," cried a third, "don't you know the great epicure Mr. Walpole?" "Pho," said the fourth, "great epicure! you mean the antiquarian."

When Horace bought a large parcel of bugles at a little shop in the city, and bade the proprietor send them to Sir Robert Walpole's, the shopkeeper coolly asked "Who is Sir Robert Walpole?"

COURT AND CITY.

The contempt of the City for the Court, and the characteristic follies of public men, were humorously satirised in the following anonymous lines, which were in circulation in 1773:

"Yon I love, my dearest life,
More than Georgey loves his wife;
More than Ministers to rule,
More than North to play the fool,
More than Camden to grimace,
More than Barrington his place,
More than Clive his black jagueer,
More than Bute the royal ear;
More than patriots love their price,
More than Fox loves cards and dice,
More than Cits the Court to spite,
More than Townshend not to fight,

More than Colebrook heaps of pelf,
More than Elliot loves himself,
More than Alderman his gut,
More than Hillsborough to strut;
More than cullies love a jilt,
More than Grosv'nor horns well gilt;
More than Dartmouth loves field preachers,
More than Huntingdon her teachers,
More than Carlisle those who cheat him,
More than Long Tom those who treat him,
More than Pomfret a lead-mine,
More than Weymouth play and wine,
More than fools at wits to nibble,
More than Walpole loves to scribble,
More than Lyttleton to write,
More than blackleg March to bite,
More than country squires their dogs,
More than Mawbey loves his hogs,
More than Tories love the Stuarts,
More than Whigs love all true hearts.
Thus, my fair, I love you more
Than ever man loved fair before."

WHAT IS ENNUI?

Walpole, in a letter to Mr. Chute, writes from Houghton the following ludicrous account of one of his visitors, who seems to sit as the centre figure of his picture of Ennui:

"I have an Aunt here, a family piece of goods, an old remnant of inquisitive hospitality and economy, who, to all intents and purposes, is as beefy as her neighbours. She wore me down so yesterday with interrogatories, that I dreamt all night, she was at my ear with 'whos,' and 'whys,' and 'whens,' till, at last, in my very sleep

I cried out, For God in heaven's sake, madam, ask no more questions.'

"Oh! my dear sir, don't you find that nine parts in ten of the world are of no use but to make you wish yourself with that tenth part? I am so far from growing used to mankind by living amongst them, that my natural ferocity and wildness does but every day grow worse. They tire me, they fatigue me; I don't know what to do with them; I fling open the windows, and fancy I want air; and when I get by myself, I undress myself, and seem to have a bad people in my pockets, in. my plaits, and on my shoulders! I indeed find this fatigue worse in country than in town, because one can avoid it there, and has more resources; but it is there too. I fear it is growing old; but I literally seem to have murdered a man whose name was Ennui, for his ghost is ever before me. They say there's no English word for *ennui;* I think you may translate it most literally by what is called entertaining people.' and 'doing the honours,' that is, you sit an hour with somebody you don't know and don't care for, talk about the wind and the weather, and ask a thousand foolish questions, which all begin with, 'I think you live a good deal in the country,' or 'I think you don't love this thing or that.' Oh! tis dreadful!"

DEATH OF LORD CHESTERFIELD.

Lord Chesterfield's declining years, though now and then brightened by flashes of wit and merriment, were clouded by sickness and despondency. His ruling passion was ruffled in his last moments, when his only expressed anxiety related to his friend, Dayrolles, being in the room without a chair to sit down upon. Chesterfield died March 24, 1773. He desired, by will, that his remains might be buried in the next burying-place to the place where he should die, and that the expense of his funeral might not exceed 100*l.* He died in Chesterfield House; and was accordingly interred in Grosvenor Chapel, South Audley-street, but his remains were afterwards removed to Shelford, in Nottinghamshire.

Lord Chesterfield is described by Lord ,Hervey as "very short, disproportioned, thick, and clumsily made; having a broad, rough-featured, ugly face, with black teeth, and a head big enough for a Polyphemus."

LORD CHESTERFIELD'S WILL.

Stanhope-street, May Fair, was built by Lord Chesterfield, on ground belonging to the Dean and Chapter of Westminster. The earl is said to have had a hard bargain of the ground; as appears from the following clause in his will:

"In case my said godson, Philip Stanhope, shall, at any time hereafter, keep, or be concerned in keeping of, any racehorses, or pack of hounds, or reside one night at New-market, that infamous seminary of iniquity and ill-manners, during the course of races there; or shall resort to the said races, or shall lose, in any one day, at any game or bet whatsoever, the sum of 500*l.;* then, in any of the cases aforesaid, it is my express will that he, my said godson, shall forfeit and pay out of my estate, the sum of 5,000*l.* for the use of the Dean and Chapter of Westminster."

Upon this Lord Mahon remarks, in his **History of England:** "The last sentence contains a lively touch of satire. The earl had found, or believed that he found, the Chapter of Westminster of that day exorbitant and grasping in their negotiation with him of land for the building of Chesterfield House [and the houses in Stanhope Street adjoining]; and he declared that he now inserted their names in his 'Will,' because he felt sure that if the penalty should be incurred, they would not be remiss in claiming it"

LATE HOURS.

Walpole, writing in 1777, gives a droll picture of the silly dissipation of the time. "The present folly," he says, "is late hours. Everybody tries to be particular by being too late; and as everybody tries it, nobody is so. It is the fashion now to go to Ranelagh two hours after it is over. You may not believe this, but it is literal The music ends at ten, the company go at twelve. Lord Derby's cook lately gave him warning. The man owned he liked his place, but said he should be killed by dressing suppers at three in the morning. The earl asked him coolly at how much he valued his life? that is, he would have paid him for killing him. You see, we have brought the spirit of calculation to perfection!"

Again: "About ten days ago, I wanted a housemaid, and one presented herself very well recommended. I said, 'But, young woman, why do you leave your present place?' She said she could not support the hours she kept; that her lady never went to bed till three or four in the morning. 'Bless me, child,' said I, why, you tell me you live with a bishop's wife; I never heard that Mrs. North (wife of the Bishop of Worcester) gamed or raked so late 'No, sir,' said she, 'but she is three hours undressing.' Upon my word, the edifice that takes three hours to demolish must at least be double the time in fabricating!"

Just at this ruinous time of frenzy, folly, and extravagance, a large party had returned from the opera; Lady Melbourne (the mother of the Prime Minister) was standing before the fire, and adjusting her feathers in the glass, says she, "Lord! they say the Stocks will blow up; that will be very comical All the ladies, Melbournes, and all the Bishops' wives that kill their servants by vigils are going about the town lamenting their poor orphans, and soliciting the peers to redress their grievances."

ROYAL FLATTERY.

When Admiral Keppel, the friend and legatee of Admiral Saunders, carried the latter's red ribbon to George III., his Majesty, as great a flatterer as any of his own flatterers, kept Keppel, though in opposition, long in the closet, yet said not a word of so meritorious an officer as Saunders, who had died in opposition. Keppel, provoked, said at last, "Your Majesty has lost a most brave and loyal subject" The King, with great quickness, answered, "I do not miss him while I have a Keppel."

MAY AND DECEMBER.

The Prince of Conti, the lover of Madame de Bouffleurs, was greatly attached to the sex, even when old. Perceiving that he did not succeed so well as he had formerly done, he one day said, "It is time for me to retire. Formerly, my civilities were taken for declarations of love, but now my declarations of love are taken only for civilities."

INSANITY AND REASON.

A poor man in Bedlam was ill-used by an apprentice because he would not tell him why he was confined there. The unhappy creature said at last, "Because God has deprived me of a blessing which you never enjoyed." There never was anything finer or more affecting.

SLEEPING AND WAKING.

Lady Beaulieu was complaining of being waked by a noise in the night: her Lord (an Irishman) replied: "Oh! for my part, there's no disturbing me; if they don't wake me before I go to sleep, there is no waking me afterwards."

THE HEALTH OF EUROPE.

Madame de Sevigné had a German friend, the Princess of Tarente, who was always in mourning for some sovereign prince or princess. One day, Madame de Sevigné happening to meet her in colours, made a low curtsey, and said, "Madame, je me réjouis de la santé de l'Europe."

A FEU-DE-JOIE.

During foggy weather, with a gleam of sunshine, on the cannon firing for George III. going to the House, somebody asked what it was for? M. de Choiseul replied, "Apparement, c'est qu'on voit le soleil."

KINGLY RETORT.

The Due de Lauragais was a very singular and eccentric person. He was a great **Anglomane,** and was the first introducer into France of horse-races à, l Anglaise; it was to him that Louis XV.—not pleased at his insolent **Anglomanie**—made so excellent a retort The King had asked him, after one of his journeys, what he had learned in England? Lauragais answered, with a kind of republican dignity, "A panser" (penser)—"Les chevaux? inquired the King.

STORY OF A PARROT AND MONKEY.

A young Madame de Choiseul longed for a parrot, that should be a miracle of eloquence; and, as every shop in Paris then sold macaws, parrots, cockatoos, &c, a parrot was soon found for the nymph; but she had another passion, and was enamoured of GeneralJackoo, a celebrated monkey, at Astley's: ingots of gold were offered for this monkey, but Astley demanded a **terre** for life; but fortunately, another miracle of a monkey was heard of, who was not in so exalted a sphere of life, being only in a kitchen, where he had learned to pluck fowls with inimitable dexterity. This dear animal was not invaluable, was bought, and presented to Madame de Choiseul, who immediately made him the secretaire de ses commandemens. The first time she went out, the two animals were locked up in her bedchamber. When the lady returned, Jackoo the second received her with all the empressement possible—but where was Poll?—found at last under the bed, shivering and cowering—and without a feather, as stark as any Christian. Now, the two animals had been presented by two rival lovers of Madame; and Walpole humorously tells us "Poll's presenter concluded that his rival had given the monkey with that very view, challenged him, they fought, and both were wounded; and an heroic adventure it was!"

BRED IN THE BONE.

A well-known Jack Brag, who had contrived to secure a limited reception in society, being one day in a party, where those present were speculating on what they would do in given contingencies, committed himself by exclaiming, "Now, if I was a gentleman," which, naturally enough, led ill-natured people to suppose that there had been a time when he was not. Still, everybody was at fault as to his original vocation, until, in an unlucky hour, he accompanied some of his new associates to a billiard-table. Immediately on entering the room, he took up a cue, and placed himself before the marking-board, so naturally that every doubt was dissipated, and the marker stood confessed.

It has been told of Mr. Arthur Moore, and was naturally true of Secretary Craggs, who began life as a footman, that, in the days of his opulence, he once handed some ladies into a carriage, and then, from the mere force of habit, got up behind it himself.

A VEAL DINNER.

At the table of Lord Polkemmet, when the covers were removed, the dinner was seen to consist of veal broth, a roast fillet of veal, veal cutlets, a florentine (an excellent Scotch dish, composed of veal), a calf's head, calf's-foot jelly. The worthy judge observing an expression of surprise among his guests, broke out in explanation: "Ou, ay, it's a cauf; when we kill a beast we just eat up one side, and down the tither."

The expressions he used to describe his own *judicial* preparations for the bench, were very characteristic: "Ye see I first read a' the pleadings, and then, after letting them wamble in my wame wi' the toddy twa or three days, I gie my ain interlocutor."

THE BEAUTIFUL DUCHESS OF DEVONSHIRE.

The personal exertions made by the Duchess of Devonshire in favour of Charles Fox, during the contested election for Westminster, in 1784, are well known. Accompanied by her sister, Lady Duncannon, she visited the abodes of the humblest amongst the electors; she dazzled and enslaved them by the fascination of her manners, the power of her beauty, and the influence of her high rank; and is known, on more than one occasion, to have carried with her the meanest one drunk to the hustings in her carriage. 'The fact of her having purchased the vote of a stubborn butcher by a kiss is, we believe, undoubted. It was during these scenes that the Irish mechanic paid Her Grace the well-known compliment: gazing with admiration at her beautiful countenance,' he said, "I could light my pipe at her eyes."

This beautiful woman died in 1786, at the age of forty-nine. Sir N. Wraxall relates: "During the month of July, 1811, I visited the vault in the principal church of Derby, where repose the remains of the Cavendish family. As I stood contemplating the coffin which contained the ashes of that admired female [the beautiful Duchess of Devonshire] the woman who accompanied me pointed out the relics of a **bouquet,** which lay upon the lid, nearly collapsed into dust. 'That nosegay,' said she, 'was brought here by the Countess of Bessborough, who had designed to place it with her own hands on her sister's coffin; but overcome by her emotions on approaching the spot, she found herself unable to descend the steps conducting to the vault. In an agony of grief she knelt down on the stones, as nearly over the place occupied by the corpse as I could direct, and there deposited the flowers, enjoining me the performance of an office to which she was unequal. I fulfilled her wishes.'"

PROFITABLE SUPERSTITIONS.

Hannah More writes thus of her own time: "In vain do we boast of the eighteenth century, and conceitedly talk as if human reason had not a manacle left about her, but that philosophy had broken down all the strongholds of prejudice, ignorance, and superstition; and yet at this very time Mesmer has got a hundred thousand pounds by animal magnetism in Paris, and Mainanduc is getting as much in London. There is a fortune-teller in Westminster who is making little less. Lavater's physiognomy books sell at fifteen guineas a set. The divining-rod is still considered oracular in many places. Devils are cast out by seven ministers; and to complete the disgraceful catalogue, slavery is vindicated in print, and defended in the House of Peers."

"POOR AS JOB."

Lady Margaret Compton said she was *as poor as Job.* "I wonder," said Lady Barrymore, "why people *say as poor as Job,* and never as rich, for in one part of his life he had great riches." "Yes," said Walpole, "Madam, but then they pronounce his name differently, and call him *Jobb*"

A LONG DINNER.

Of Mr. Hay, afterwards Lord Newton, one of the judges of the Court of Session, equally remarkable as a gourmand and a lawyer, it is told that a client calling on him one day at four o'clock, and being surprised to find him at dinner, and saying to the servant that he understood five to be Mr. Hay's dinner hour, "Oh, but, sir," said the man, "it is his yesterday's dinner."

A TIRESOME CRITIC.

Walpole one day met Mr. Villiers, at Lord Granville's, where, on the subject of Thomson's new play, he began to give the earl an account of Coriolanus, with reflections on his history. Lord Granville at last grew impatient, and said, "Well! well! it is an old story; it may not be true," and so got rid of the bore.

WILBERFORCE'S EARLY LIFE.

"When I left the University," writes Mr. Wilberforce, "so little did I know of general society, that I came up to London stored with arguments to prove the authenticity of Rowley's Poems; and now I was at once immersed in politics and fashion. The very first time I went to Boodle's, I won twenty-five guineas of the Duke of Norfolk. I belonged at this time to five clubs—Miles and Evans's, Brookes's, Boodle's, White's, Goostree's. The first time I was at Brookes's, scarcely knowing any one, I joined, in mere shyness, in play at the faro-table, where George Selwyn kept bank. A friend, who knew my inexperience, and regarded me as a victim decked out for sacrifice, called to me, 'What, Wilberforce, is that you? Selwyn quite resented the interference; and, turning to him, said, in his most expressive tone, 'O, sir, don't interrupt Mr. Wilberforce; he could not be better employed I' Nothing could be more luxurious than the style of these clubs. Fox, Sheridan, Fitzpatrick, and all your leading men frequented them, and associated upon the easiest terms; you chatted, played at cards, or gambled, as you pleased. I was one of those who met to spend an evening in memory of Shakspeare, at the Boar's-head, Eastcheap. Many professed wits were present, but Pitt was the most amusing of the party. We played a good deal at Goostree's; and I well remember the intense earnestness which he displayed when joining in those games of chance. He perceived their increasing fascination, and soon after suddenly abandoned them for ever."

INTRODUCTION OF TOOTHPICKS.

Lord Clermont, at a dinner-party, told the company that in the course of his reading he had found that Scipio first introduced the use of toothpicks from Spain. "I did not know so much," said Walpole, in a letter next day; "nor that his lordship ever did read, or knew that Scipio was anybody hut a racehorse. His classic author, probably, is 'Marsh upon the Gums.'"

A VAIN OLD COUNTESS.

When the Countess of Pomfret gave her lord's collection of statues to the University of Oxford, she went there at the public cost, to receive adoration. "A box," says Walpole, "was built for her near the Vice-Chancellor, where she sat three days together for four hours at a time to hear verses and speeches, to hear herself called Minerva; nay,' the public orator had prepared an encomium on her beauty, but being struck with her appearance, had enough presence of mind to whisk his-compliments to the beauties of her mind. It is amazing that she did not mash a few words of Latin, as she used to fricasee French and Italian! or that she did not torture some learned simile, like her comparing the tour of Sicily, the surrounding the triangle, to squaring the circle; or as when she said it was as difficult to get into an Italian coach, as for Cæsar to take Attica, which she meant for Utica."

A REPRIEVE.

After the execution of eighteen malefactors, in 1787, a woman was hawking an account of them, but called them *nineteen.* A gentleman said to her, "Why do you say *nineteen?* there were but *eighteen* hanged." She replied, "Sir, I did not know *you* had been reprieved"

CHIRMAN'S IMPUDENCE.

Mrs. Herbert, the bedchamber-woman in the household of Queen Charlotte, going in a hackney-chair, the chairmen were excessively drunk, and after tossing her and jolting her about for some minutes, set the chair down; and the foreman, lifting up the top, said, "Madam, you are so drunk, that if you do not sit still, it will be impossible to carry you."

KING AND PRINCES.

The following dialogue is related of Mr. Pope and the Prince of Wales:—"Mr. Pope, you don't love princes." "Sir, I beg your pardon." "Well, you don't love kings, then!" "Sir, I own I love the lion best before his claws are grown." Was it possible to make a better answer to such simple questions?

A DRAM-DRINKER'S MOTTO.

Mr. Chute, a friend of Walpole's, passing by the door of Mrs. Edwards, who died of drams, he saw the motto which the undertakers had placed to her escutcheon, Morsjanua vitæ: **he said it ought to have been** Mors aqua vitæ.

A STUCK UP HOST.

Lord John Townshend was at a grand dinner, where the smallness of the establishment obliged the entertainer, a coarse upstart, to transform the gardener, the stable-boy, and even the coachman, into waiters. Several awkward mishaps were the consequence. Among others, the coachman upset the butter-boat over Townshend's clothes. Determined to expose his pretentious host, his Lordship exclaimed aloud, as he wiped off the butter, "John, take my advice, and in future never grease anything but your wheels."

PURE DICTION.

The poet, Malherbe, the founder of the purity of the French language, was very sensitive on the score of diction. When, during his last moments, his confessor, by way of encouraging him, began to enlarge on the joys of Paradise, "Stop," cried Malherbe, "your ungrammatical style is giving me a distaste for them."

ENGLISH CREDULITY.

Pasquier, an old French author, says that in the time of Francis I. the French used to call their creditors "Des Anglois," from the facility with which the English gave credit to them in all treaties, though they had broken so many.

THE DISCOVERIES OF POSTERITY.

When Walpole began to plant the grounds at Strawberry , Hill, he used to talk very learnedly with the nurseryman, except that now and then a lettuce run to seed overturned all his botany, as he more than once took it for a curious West Indian flowering shrub. "Then," he says, "the deliberation with which trees grow is extremely inconvenient to my natural impatience. I lament living in so barbarous an age when we are come to see so little perfection in gardening. I am persuaded a hundred and fifty years hence it will be as common to remove oaks a hundred and fifty years old, as it is now to transplant tulip-roots. I have even begun a treatise or panegyric on the great discoveries made by posterity in all arts and sciences, wherein I shall particularly descant on the great and cheap convenience of making trout-rivers. I shall talk of a secret of roasting a wild boar and a whole pack of hounds alive, without hurting them, so that the whole chase may be brought up to table. Then the delightfulness of having whole groves of humming-birds, tame tigers taught to fetch and carry, pocket spying-glasses to see all that is doing in China, with a thousand other toys, which we now look upon as impracticable; and which pert posterity would laugh in one's face for staring at, while they are offering rewards for perfecting discoveries, of the principles of which we have not the least conception! If ever this book should come forth, I must expect to have all the learned in arms against me, who measure all knowledge backward: some of them have discovered symptoms of 'all arts in Homer; and Pineda (the Spanish Jesuit) had so much faith in the accomplishments of his ancestors, that he believed Adam understood all sciences but politics. But as these great champions for our forefathers are dead, and Boileau not alive to pitch me into a verse with Herrault, I am determined to admire the learning of posterity, especially being convinced that half our present knowledge sprung from discovering the errors of what had formerly been called so. I don't think I shall ever make any great discoveries myself, and therefore shall be content to propose them to my descendants, like my Lord Bacon, who, as Dr. Shaw says very prettily, in his Preface to Boyle, 'had the art of inventing arts; or rather, like a Marquis of Worcester, of whom I have seen a little book which he calls 'A Century of Inventions,' where he has set down a hundred machines to do impossibilities with, and not a single direction how to make the machines themselves."

PRIDE OF HERALDRY.

Walpole, writing to Sir Horace Mann, tells him that Mr. Chute, who was always thinking of blazoning his pedigree in the noblest colours, had just tapped a new and very great family for him: "in short," says Walpole to Sir Horace, "by your mother it is very clear that you are descended from Hubert de Burgh, Grand Justiciary to Richard II.; indeed, I think he was hanged; but that is a misfortune that will attend very illustrious genealogies; it is as common to them as to the pedigrees of

Paddington and Blackheath I have had at least a dozen great-grandfathers that came to untimely ends. All your virtuosos in heraldry are content to know that they had ancestors who lived five hundred years ago. A match with a low woman corrupts a stream of blood as long as the Danube—tyranny, villainy, and executions are mere flea-bites, and leave no stain."

Lord Chesterfield placed among the portraits of his ancestors two old heads, inscribed *Adam de Stanhope* and *Eve de Stanhope:* the ridicule is admirable.

Old Peter Le Neve, the herald, who thought ridicule consisted in not being of an old family, made this epitaph, and it was a good one, for young Craggs, whose father had been a footman: "Here lies the last who died before the first of his family!" This old Craggs, who was angry with Arthur Moore, who had worn a livery too, and who was getting into a coach with him, turned about and said: "Why, Arthur, I am always going to get up behind; are not you?"

TRUE DIGNITY.

We have (says Walpole) in our family an instance of real dignity of mind, and I set it down as the most honourable alliance in the pedigree. The Dowager Lady Walpole, you know, was a French staymaker's daughter. When Ambassadress in France, the Queen expressed surprise at her speaking so good French. Lady Walpole said she was a French woman. "Franchise?" replied the Queen." "Vous Francaise, Madame! et de quelle famille?" "D'aucune, Madame," answered my aunt "Don't you think that *aucune* sounded greater than Montmorency would have done? One must have a great soul to be of the *aucune* family, which is not necessary to be a Howard."

PRECEDENCE.

Two ladies contended for precedence in the court of Charles V. They appealed to the monarch, who, like Solomon, awarded: "Let the elder go first." Such a dispute was never known afterwards.

When King William landed, he said to Sir Edward Seymour, the Speaker, "Sir Edward, I think you are of the Duke of Somerset's family." "No, Sir; he is of mine," was the Speaker's reply.

"Precedence of rank," says Furetière, "has its charms, certainly; though I cannot go so far as a lady of my acquaintance, who wished to die before her husband. I inquired of her the reason of wishing so extraordinary a thing. 'Because,' said her ladyship, 'if my husband dies before me, I cannot put his arms on his tomb, because he is not a man of family; though, should I die first, he can claim a right of placing my arms on my tomb, because I am a woman of quality by birth.'"

SMALL PRECEDENT.

An amusing illustration of this weak point is told. "When Lord Baltimore would not come into the Admiralty, because in the new commission they had given Lord Vere Beauclerc the precedence, a gentleman at Tom's Coffee-house said, "It put him in mind of Penkethman's petition in *The Spectator*, where he complains that formerly he used to act second chair in Diocletian, but now was reduced to dance fifth flowerpot."

SPANISH GRANDEES.

In Spain, it is the ambition of grandees to unite in themselves as many grandee-ships as possible by the marriage of heiresses, whose names and titles are assumed by their husbands; whence the old story of a benighted grandee, who knocked at a lonely inn, and when asked, as usual, "Quienès?" ("Who is there?") replied, "Don Diego de Mendoza Silva Ribero Guzman Pimental Osario Ponce de Leon Gumaga, Accrora Tellez y Giron, Sandoval y Boxas, Velasco Man—" "In that case," interrupted the landlord, shutting his window, "go with God There is not room for half of you."

MARY QUEEN OF SCOTS.

What a drawback on *beaux sentiments* and romantic ideas is presented in Pasquier's account of the execution of the Queen of Scots: he says, "The night before, knowing her body must be stripped for her shroud, she would have her feet washed, because she used ointment to one of them which was sore." In a very old trial of her, which Walpole bought from Lord Oxford's collection, it is said that she was a large lame woman. Take sentiments out of their pantoufles and reduce them to the infirmities of mortality, what a falling off is there!

THE HOUSE OF HUDDLESTONE AND HOWARD.

Mr. Huddlestone believed himself to be lineally descended from Athelstane, of which his name was allowed to be an undeniable corruption; and amongst others by the Duke of Norfolk. These two worthies often met over a bottle to discuss the respective pretensions of their pedigrees; and on one of these occasions, when Mr. Huddlestone was dining with the Duke, the discussion was prolonged till the descendant of the Saxon Kings fairly rolled from his chair upon the floor. One of the younger members of the family hastened, by the Duke's desire, to re-establish him, but he sternly repelled the proffered hand of the cadet. "Never," he hiccuped out, "shall it be said that the head of the house of Huddlestone was lifted from the ground by a younger branch of the house of Howard." "Well, then, my good old friend," said the good-natured Duke, "I must try what I can do for you myself. The head of the house of Howard is too drunk to pick up the head of the house of Huddlestone, but he will lie down beside him with all the pleasure in the world;" so saying, the Duke also took his place upon the floor. The concluding part of this anecdote has been plagiarised, and applied to other people, but the authenticity of this version may be relied on.—*Quarterly Review.*

EPITAPH ON A BELLE.

Lord Conway's sister, Miss Jenny, a belle of Walpole's time, died suddenly with drinking too freely of lemonade at a subscription masquerade. Horace, in his sneering way, says, "It is not quite unlucky for her: she had outlived the Prince's love and her own face, and nothing remained but her love and her person," which was exceedingly bad. Her exit was commemorated in three doggrel lines:

Poor Jenny Conway,
She drank lemonade
At a masquerade:
So now she's dead and gone away.

WOMANLY CONSOLATION.

One night, at a large rout, great panic was expressed about the French; when Lady Rochford, looking down on her fan, said with great softness: "I don't know: I don't think the French are a sort of people that women need be afraid of."

ODD PAYMENT.

Caroline Vernon lost one night two hundred pounds at faro, and bade Martindale mark it up. He said he would rather have a draft on her banker. "Oh! willingly;" and she gave him one. Next morning he hurried to Drummond's, lest all her money should be drawn out "Sir," said the clerk, "would you receive the contents immediately?" "Assuredly." "Why, Sir, have you read the note?" Martindale took it; it was, "Pay to the bearer two hundred blows, well applied."

PUBLIC SPEAKING.

The Duchess of Gordon, "one of the Empresses of Fashion,' coming out of an assembly, said to Dundas, "Mr. Dundas, you are used to speak in public; will you call my servant?" This Duchess had more wit than any of Walpole's old sayers of good things; but she was also coarser than they ventured to be.

GARDENING AND PUNCTUATION.

Hannah More tells us that Capability Brown illustrated everything he said about gardening by some literary or grammatical allusion; and he compared his art to literary composition. "Now, *there,*" said he, pointing with his finger, "I make a comma; and there," pointing to another spot, "where a more decided turn is proper, I make a colon; at another part, where an interruption is desirable to break the view,—a parenthesis—now a full stop; and then I begin another subject"

CIVIC SAPIENCE.

Two stories are related of an absurd Lord Mayor, one about the copy of a letter taken after the original was lost—and the other—hearing of a gentleman who had the small-pox twice and died of it, he asked if he died the first time or the second.

LIFE OF A SPENDTHRIFT.

Among the celebrities of the latter half of the last century was General Sir John Irwin, who, besides a regiment and government conferred on him by the Crown, held, for several years, the post of Commander-in-Chief in Ireland. But no income, however large, could suffice for his expenses. At one of the entertainments which he gave to the Lord Lieutenant, in Dublin, he displayed as the centre piece of the dessert a representation of the fortress of Gibraltar invested by the Spanish force, executed in confectionery, a model of the celebrated rock, with the works, batteries, and artillery of the besiegers throwing sugar-plums against the walls. This piece of folly cost nearly 1,500*l.!*

Irwin was a great favourite of George III., who once observed to him, "They tell me, Sir John, that you love a glass of wine." "Those," replied Irwin, "who so informed your Majesty have done me great injustice; they should have said a bottle." Irwin's extravagant mode of living involved him in endless pecuniary difficulties; and while the General was abroad, in great distress, George III. twice sent him a present of 500*l.* His debts became so numerous, and his creditors so importunate, that he privately quitted his elegant house in Piccadilly, opposite the Green Park, and retired to the Continent. There he hired a chateau in Normandy; but his pecuniary difficulties continuing, he removed over the Alps, into Italy; he is said to have died at Padua, in May, 1788, in obscurity, but not in distress.

DISTINCTION WITHOUT DIFFERENCE.

In 1792, the Duchess of York gave a great entertainment at Oatlands on her Duke's birthday. A company of strollers came to Weybridge to act in a barn; she was solicited to go to it, and did out of charity, and carried all her servants. Next day a Methodist came to preach a charity sermon in the same theatre, and she consented to hear it on the same motive; but her servants desired to be excused on not understanding English "Oh!" said the Duchess, "but you went to the comedy, which you understood less, and you shall go to the sermon;" to which she gave handsomely, and for them.

CIVIC ENJOYMENT.

In 1800, on November 8, the usual festivities were kept up with great spirit at the Mansion House, it being the day of the Lord Mayor (Combe) retiring from office, and the assumption of its duties by his successor, Sir William Staines. The honest knight loved his pipe, and was accordingly indulged with one. In yielding up his place and honours to him, the late chief magistrate, Combe, had the good nature to share in the humour of his successor; and they were observed, after dinner, lighting their pipes at one candle, like the Duke of Buckingham's two Kings of Brentford, smelling at one nosegay.

Alderman Boydell, when he lived at the corner of Ironmonger-lane, in Cheapside, had a strange mode of refreshing himself on the morning after a civic feast: leaving his shop, he would go to the pump in Ironmonger-lane, and there taking off his wig, place his bare head beneath the cooling stream.

A CRUEL CASE.

Lady Cathcart, who died in 1798,'had four husbands, of whom Lord Cathcart was the third; the fourth was a Captain Macguire, an Irish officer, who, not much pleased with the posy on her wedding-ring—

If I survive,
I'll have five,

took her to Ireland, and kept her there, in solitary durance, for twenty years, when he died, and her Ladyship returned to dance at the Welwyn Assembly.

MR. PITT'S IDEAS OF WOMEN.

Mr. Pitt is stated, by Lady Hester Stanhope, to have ardently loved the daughter of Lord A—, and that he almost broke his heart when he gave her up. But he considered that she was not a woman to be left at her will when business might require it, and he sacrificed his feelings to his sense of public duty. "Yet (adds Lady Hester) Mr. Pitt was a man just made for domestic life, who would have enjoyed his own retirement, digging his own garden, and doing it cleverly too."

"There were other reasons," Mr. Pitt would say, against this match; "there is her mother, such a chatterer! and then the family intrigues. I can't keep them out of my house, and for my King's and country's sake, I must remain a single man." He used to say, he considered "no man ought to marry who could not give a proper share of his time to his wife; for how would it be if he was always at the House, or in business, and she always at the Opera, or whirling about in her carriage?"

"People," says Lady Hester, "thought Mr. Pitt did not care about women, and knew nothing about them; but they were very much mistaken. Mrs. B—, of Devonshire, when she was Miss W—, was so pretty, that Mr. Pitt drank out of her shoe. Nobody understood shape, and beauty, and dress, better than he did; with a flame of his eye he saw it all at once. But the world was ignorant of much respecting him. Whoever thought that there was not a better judge of women in London than he? and not only of women as they present themselves to the eye, but that his knowledge was so critical as to analyse their features and persons in a most masterly way? Not a defect, not a blemish, escaped him: he would detect a shoulder too high, a limp in the gait, where nobody else would have seen it; and his beauties were real, natural, beauties. In dress, too, his taste was equally refined I shall never forget when I had arranged the folds and drapery of a beautiful dress which I wore one evening, how he said to me, 'Really, Hester, you are bent on conquest to-night; but would it be too bold in me, if I were to suggest that that particular fold'—and he pointed to a triangular fall which I had given to one part—'were looped up so?'—and it was exactly what was wanting to complete the classical form of my dress.

"He had so much urbanity, too! I recollect returning late from a ball, when he had gone to bed fatigued; there were others beside myself, and we made a great deal of noise. I said to him next morning, 'I am afraid we disturbed you last night' 'Not at all,' he replied; 'I was dreaming of the Masque of Comus, Hester, and when I heard you all so gay, it seemed a pleasant reality.'"

Lady Hester then relates how Mr. Pitt's excellent heart was full of sympathy for persons whom others spurned; and on being told that a lady of this ill-treated class was expected to accompany a guest at Walmer Castle, "My dear Hester," said Mr. Pitt, "for God's sake, don't distress the poor woman, if she is coming—now, pray don't." He then gave orders that she should have the bedroom in the house, while others, who were expected, were to be sent to the village.

MR. PITT'S LOVE OF PORT WINE.

Mr. Rogers has left these reminiscences of the statesman's port-drinking: "During his boyhood, Pitt was very weakly; and his physician, Addington (Lord Sidmouth's father), ordered him to take port wine in large quantities; the consequence was, that when he grew up he could not do without it. Lord Grenville has seen him swallow a bottle of port in tumblerfuls before going to the House. This, together with his habit of eating late suppers (indigestible cold veal pies, &c.), helped, undoubtedly, to shorten his life. Huskisson, speaking to me of Pitt, said that his hands shook so much that, when he helped himself to salt, he was obliged to support the right hand with the left. Stothard, the painter, happened to be one evening at an inn on the Kent Road, when Pitt and Dundas put up there on their way from Walmer. Next morning, as they were stepping into their carriage, the waiter said to Stothard, "Sir, do you observe these two gentlemen? "Yes," he replied, "and I know them to be Mr. Pitt and Mr. Dundas." "Well, sir, how much wine do you suppose they drank last night?" Stothard could not guess, "Seven bottles, sir?"

LORD PRMBROKE'S PORT WINE.

Lord Palmerston one day related the following anecdote to a deputation of gentlemen, who waited upon him to urge the reduction of the wine duties. Referring to the question of adulterations, "I remember," said his lordship, "my grandfather, Lord Pembroke, when he placed wine before his guests, said: 'There, gentlemen, is my champagne, my claret, &c I am no great judge, and I give you this on the authority of my wine-merchant; but I can answer for my port, for I made it myself!' I have still his receipt, which I look on as a curiosity; but I confess *I have never ventured to try it.*" The following is the veritable receipt which Lord Pembroke adopted:— Eight gallons of genuine port wine, forty gallons of cider, brandy to fill the hogshead. Elder-tops will give it the proper roughness, and cochineal whatever strength of colouring you please. The quantity made should not be less than a hogshead. It should be kept fully two years in cask, and as long in bottle before it is used.

PORT WINE AND PARALYSIS.

Mr. Savory, of Bond-street, used to relate that a friend of his, a baronet, well known in the gay world, on his return home from a convivial party, was seized with paralysis, and suddenly deprived of speech and power of moving one side of his body. Either from feelings of desperation, or an impulse of mental aberration, the gentleman had a bottle of port wine brought to his bed-side, and having finished it, he turned with great composure on his side and went to sleep. That gentleman lived long after, his intellect wholly unimpaired, his speech restored, and his general health as good as it ever was; and he long discussed his bottle or two of port wine with apparent impunity.

A JUDGE OF WINE.

In Bow-street, Covent-garden, there was formerly a coffeehouse kept by Mat Williams, which was much frequented by actors. Incledon, who was one day president at a large dinner-party here, found great fault with the wine, and though, by his order, it was more than once changed for better, he was still dissatisfied, at the same time boasting what very fine wine he had in his cellar, "bin No. 2," brandishing in his hand his nectar-key, as he called it. Munden, who sat next to Incledon, when he put the key into his coat-pocket, whilst he was singing, adroitly took it out, and leaving the room, sent the key to Mrs. Incledon, by a person whom he could trust, with a message to deliver to the bearer six bottles of the old port wine, bin No. 2. When the man returned, Mat Williams, who was in the secret, brought up one of the bottles himself, and said he hoped the company would find it better; he had only six bottles of *that* wine in the house. Incledon still persisted that it was worse than any of the others. The joke continued till the last bottle made its appearance, when a bumper was drank to the president, as donor of the last six bottles, not a little to his astonishment, as may be imagined.

THE STRAWBERRY.

It is related of the convivial Mr. Alderman Faulkner, that one night, when he expected his guests to sit late, and try the strength of his claret and his head, he took the precaution to place in his wine-glass a strawberry, which his doctor, he said, had recommended to him on account of its cooling qualities. On the faith of this specific, he drank even more deeply, and, as might be expected, was carried away earlier than usual. When some of his friends condoled with him next day, and attributed his misfortune to six bottles of claret which he had drunk, the Alderman was extremely indignant. "The claret," he said, "was sound, and never could do anybody any harm; any discomfiture was altogether caused by that d—d single strawberry which I kept all night at the bottom of my glass."

A FAMOUS PIPE OF MADEIRA.

The bidding for the pipe of Madeira, at the sale of the effects of the late Duchess de Raguse, in 1858, caused a great commotion in Paris. This famous wine, known to *convives* as the "1814 pipe," was fished up near Antwerp in 1814, where it had lain in the carcase of a ship wrecked at the mouth of the Scheld in 1778, and which had rested there ever since. As soon as the valuable discovery was made known, Louis XVIII. despatched an agent to secure the precious relic. A share of the glorious beverage was presented to the French Consul, who had assisted at its discovery, and thus it came into the cellars of the Duke de Raguse. Only four-and-forty bottles were remaining, and these were literally sold for their weight in gold to Rothschild, who was opposed by Véron and Milland. Véron was angry, because he declared that he had made the reputation of the wine, by mentioning it in his Memoirs, on the occasion of the dinner given to Taglioni by the Duchess de Raguse, whereat the famous "1814" was produced, as the greatest honour to be paid to the great artist.

SAVING A BOTTLE OF WINE.

Dr. King relates an odd story of saving a bottle of port wine at the expense of a life, at Colby House, Kensington, opposite the road leading to the Palace. Here lived Sir Thomas Colby, who was his own butler, and inadvertently had left the key of the wine-cellar on his parlour-table; when, fearing his servants might seize the key, and steal a bottle of wine, Sir Thomas rose from his bed in the middle of the night, when he was in a very profuse perspiration, the effect of medicine he had taken: he walked downstairs and secured the key, but took cold, and died in a few days, intestate, leaving more than 200,000*l.* in the funds, which was shared among five or six day-labourers, his nearest relations.

THE CHANCELLOR'S "CONSTANTIA."

Sheridan was dining with Lord Thurlow, when his Lordship produced some fine Constantia, which had been sent him from the Cape of Good Hope. The wine tickled the palate of Sheridan, who saw the bottle emptied with uncommon regret, and set his wits to work to get another. The old Chancellor was not to be so easily induced to produce his curious Cape in such profusion, and foiled all the attempts to get another glass. Sheridan being piqued, and seeing the inutility of persecuting the immovable pillar of the law, turned towards a gentleman seated further down, and said "Sir, pass me up that decanter; for I must return to Madeira, since I cannot double the Cape."

RELIGIONS AND SAUCES.

When Ude, the celebrated French cook, first came to this country, two peculiarities struck him: the number of churches and chapels in London, and the frequency with which melted butter appeared at our tables. "What an extraordinary nation!" he exclaimed; "they have twenty religions, and only one sauce."

A PUN OF A DISH.

It was suggested to a distinguished **gourmet** what a capital thing a dish all fins (turbot's fins) might be made. "Capital," said he; "dine on it with me to-morrow," "Accepted."

"Would you believe it? when the cover was removed, the sacrilegious dog of an Amphytrion had put into the dish, "Cicero, **Definibus.**" "There is a work all fins," said he.

EATING OLIVES.

There is etiquette in eating olives. Cardinal Richelieu is said to have detected an adventurer, who was passing himself off as a nobleman, by his helping himself to olives with a fork; it being **comme il faut** to use the fingers for that purpose.

A DISTINCTION,

A gentleman discharged his coachman for overturning him in his carriage, on his road home from a dinner-party. The man, the next morning, craved pardon, by acknowledging his fault: "I had certainly drunk too much, sir," said he; "hut I was not *very* drunk, ***and gentlemen, you know, sometimes get drunk.*** " "Why," replied the master (the Hon. B. G, renowned for the smartness of his answers), "I don't say you were very drunk for a ***gentleman,*** but you were d—d drunk for a ***coachman.*** So get about your business."

COSTLY EPICURISM.

One day an epicure, entering the Bedford Coffee-house, in Covent-garden, inquired, "What have you for dinner, John?" "Anything you please, sir," replied the waiter. "Oh, hut what vegetables?" The ***legumes*** in season were named; when the customer, having ordered two lamb-chops, said, "John, have you cucumbers?" "No, sir, we have none yet, 'tis so very early in the season; but, if you please, I will step into the market and inquire if there are any." The waiter did so, and returned: "Why, sir, there are a few, but they are half-a-guinea apiece." "Half-a-guinea apiece! are they small or large? "Why, sir, they are rather small." "Then buy two." This anecdote has been related of various epicures; it occurred to Charles, Duke of Norfolk, who died in 1815.

On an early summer's-day, a ***gourmet*** entered the shop of a fruiterer in New Bond-street, and desired to be handed one of two very small baskets of strawberries from out the window; he ate the fruit, and then coolly desired to have the other basket; and having eaten this also, inquired what he had to pay: "Six-and-thirty shillings," was the reply, and the demand was quickly paid.

WEARING ROUGE.

There was a certain Bishop of Amiens, who was a saint, and yet had a good deal of wit. A lady went to consult him whether she might wear **rouge:** she had been with several **directeurs,** but some were so severe, and some so relaxed, that she could not satisfy her conscience, and therefore was come to Monseigneur to decide for her, and would rest by his sentence. "I see, Madam," said the good prelate, "what the case is: some of your casuists forbid **rouge** totally; others will permit you to wear as much as you please. Now, for my part, I love a medium in all things, and therefore I permit you to wear **rouge** on one cheek only."

A HARMLESS CASE.

Once, when Lord Onslow was absent from home for a fortnight, Lady Onslow invited an officer to keep her company, to the great scandal of a prudish lady her neighbour, and of whom she asked leave to carry him into her pew at church, which the other, though with marks of indignation and surprise, could not help permitting. Sunday came, and my Lady and the Major—yet, though the minister had begun the service, the prude could not help whispering Lady O., "You did not tell me the Major had grey hair."

GRACE MAL-A-PROPOS.

A milliner's apprentice, about to wait upon a duchess, was fearful of committing some error in her deportment. She therefore consulted a friend as to the manner in which she should consult this great personage, and was told that, on going before the duchess, she must say her Grace, and so on. Accordingly, away went the girl, and, on being introduced, after a very low curtsy, she said: "For what I am going to receive, the Lord make me truly thankful." To which the duchess answered: "Amen!"

THE DUKE OF QUEENSBURY.

This long-lived voluptuary pursued pleasure with as much ardour at fourscore as he had done at twenty. Known to be immensely rich, destitute of issue, and unmarried, he formed a mark at which every necessitous man or woman throughout the metropolis directed their aim. When he lay dying in his house in Piccadilly, opposite the Green Park, in December, 1810, his bed was covered with billets and letters to the number of at least seventy, mostly, indeed, addressed to him by females of every description and of every rank, from duchesses down to ladies of the easiest virtue. Unable, from his weak state, to open or peruse these letters, he ordered them, as they arrived, to be laid on his bed, where they remained, the seals unbroken, till he expired.

Sir Nathaniel Wraxall denies the truth of stories which were circulated and believed of the Duke; as among others, that he wore a glass eye, that he used **milk bath,** [Note *: There are many persons still living who remember the almost universal prejudice against drinking milk which prevailed in the metropolis, in consequence of its being supposed that this common necessary of life might have been retailed from the daily lavations of the Duke of Queensbury.—J. H. JESSE, 1843.] and other idle tales. It is, however, a fact that the Duke performed, in his own drawing-room, the scene of "Paris and the Goddesses." Three of the most beautiful women to be found in London presented themselves before him, precisely as the divinities of Homer are supposed to have appeared to Paris on Mount Ida; while **he,** habited like the Dardan Shepherd, holding a gilded apple in his hand, conferred the prize on her whom he deemed the fairest

Mr. Wilberforce records having, when a young man, dined with the Duke at his Richmond villa: Pitt, Lord and Lady Chatham, the Duchess of Gordon, and George Selwyn: [the latter continued in society till he really looked like the wax work figure of a corpse.] The dinner was early, that some of the party might be ready to attend the opera. The views from the villa were enchanting, and the Thames in all its glory; but the Duke looked on with indifference. "What is there," he said, "to make so much of in the Thames?—I am quite tired of it,—there it goes, flow, flow, flow, always the same."

Latterly, the Duke confined himself almost entirely to his mansion in Piccadilly, where, in fine sunny weather, he would sit

"Sunning himself in Huncamunca's eyes."

A parasol was held over his head, as he watched every attractive form, and ogled every pretty face that met his eye in the street. He retained in his household a French physician; and the Duke is known to have promised a large salary to his medical attendant, the late Mr. Fuller, on condition that the latter should keep him alive. [For his services, during seven years, sleeping in his Grace's house 1,215 nights, and during that time making 9,340 visits, of two hours each, Mr. Fuller recovered from the Duke's executors, by an action-at-law, 7,500*l.*] The Duke died at the age of eighty-six; and it was said he would have lived longer but for his imprudent indulgence in eating fruit.

RESOLUTE SCOTTISH LADIES.

Some amusing stories are told [Note *: By Dean Ramsay, in his entertaining **Reminiscences.**] of the "resolute" class of old ladies whom no misfortune or bereavement could daunt. Mrs. Baird, of Newbyth, the mother of General Sir David Baird, had always been spoken of as a grand specimen of this class. When the news arrived from India of the gallant but unfortunate action of '84 against Hyder Ali, in which her son, then Captain Baird, was engaged, it was stated that he and other officers had been taken prisoners, and chained together two and two. The friends were careful in breaking such sad intelligence to the mother, who was, however, too Spartan in her nature to require such considerate treatment. When she was made fully to understand the position of her son and his gallant companions, disdaining all weak and useless expressions of her own grief, and knowing well the restless and athletic habits of her boy, all she said was, "Lord pity the chiel that's chained to our Davy."

Another story illustrates the liberal view which a Scottish maiden could take of her own privileges, or of those of her accepted admirer. On her marriage day the youth to whom she was about to be united said to her in a triumphant tone, "Weel, Jenny, haven't I been unco ceevil?" alluding to the circumstance that during their whole courtship he had never even given her a kiss. Her quiet reply was, "Oo, ay, man—senselessly ceevil."

When one of these dames was dying, and her friends were round her bed, she overheard one of them saying to another, "Her face has lost its colour; it grows like a sheet of paper." "Then I'm sure it maun be **brown** paper" was the cool comment of the dying woman.

A notion of the stiff manner in which these old ladies could vindicate their principles or their personal dignity is afforded by the various stories told of Mrs. Helen Carnegy, of Craigo. On one occasion, as she sat in an easy chair, having assumed the habits and privileges of age, Mr. Mollison, the minister of the Established Kirk, called on her to solicit for some charity. She did not like being asked for money, and, from her Jacobite principles, she certainly did not respect the Presbyterian Kirk. When he came in, she made only an inclination of the head, and when he said deprecatingly, "Don't get up, madam," she at once replied, "Get up? I wadna rise out of my chair for King George himsel, let abee a Whig Minister." The same lady had a graduated scale for her courtesies, and which was adapted to different individuals in the town according as she placed them in the scale of her consideration. As she liked a party at quadrille, she sent out her servant every morning to invite the ladies required to make up the game in these terms:—"Nelly, you'll gang to Lady Carnegy's, and mak my compliments, and ask the **honour** of her Ladyship's company and that of the Miss Carnegies, to tea this evening; and if they canna come, gang to the Miss Mudies, and ask the **pleasure** of their company; and if they canna come, you may gang to Miss Hunter and ask the **favour** of her company; and if she canna come, gang to Lucy Spark and **bid her come.**"

An old Montrose lady walking in the street one frosty day, fairly fell down. A young officer, with much politeness, came forward, and picked her up, earnestly saying, "I hope, ma'am, you are no worse," to which she replied, looking at him very steadily, "Indeed, sir, I'm just as little the better."

Two Glasgow ladies, sisters, attended a sale by auction at a country-house. A dozen of silver spoons were handed round to the company; when returned to the auctioneer, he only found eleven. He ordered the door to be shut, that every one should be searched. One of the sisters, in consternation, whispered to the other, "Esther, ye hae nae gotten the spune?" to which the other replied, "Na; but I hae gotten Mrs. Siddons in my pocket" She had been attracted by a miniature of the great actress, and had pocketed it. The cautious reply of the sister was, "Then just drop her, Esther."

Another Montrose lady hated paying taxes, and always pretended to misunderstand their nature. One day, receiving a notice of such payment signed by the provost (Thorn), she broke out, "I dinna understand thae taxes; but I just think when Mrs. Thorn wants a new gown, the provost sends me a tax-paper."

A very strong-minded lady had been asking from a lady the character of a cook she was about to hire. The lady naturally entered a little upon her moral qualifications, and described her as a very decent woman; the reply to which was, "Oh, d—n her decency; can she make good collops?"

A late well-known-member of the Scottish bar, when a youth, was going to pay a visit in the country, and was making a great fuss about packing up his clothes. His old aunt was much annoyed at the bustle, and stopped him by the somewhat contemptuous question: "Wherever's this you're goin, Robby, that ye mak sic a grand wark about your claes?" The young man lost temper and pettishly replied, "I'm going to the devil." "'Deed, Robby, then," was the quiet answer, "ye need nae be sae nice; he'll just tak ye as ye are."

It is told of old Miss Johnstone, of Hawk Hill, that, when dying, a tremendous storm of rain and thunder came on, so as to shake the house. In a quaint, eccentric spirit, and with no thought of profane or light allusions, she looked up, and, listening to the storm, quietly remarked, in reference to her departure, "Ech, sirs! what a nicht for me to be fleeing thro' the air!"

Some people, not very scrupulous, put bad coppers into the plate at a chapel-door on Sundays, with which a good old lady paid her losses at cards during the week, and so, in the end, it came to be known through whose veins the *ill bawbees circulated.*

An old lady hearing that her farm-servant had become a *local* preacher among the Methodists, she attacked him: "Well, John, hast thee become preacher? Thee'lt never sound the trumpet in Zion. Thee'lt never be anything but a *ram's-horn preacher*" However, John's answer was not "bad—"Weel, Missus, I may be a ram's-horn preacher, but it was the rams'-horns that brought down the walls of Jericho."

Old Mrs. Robinson had invited a gentleman to dinner—he had accepted, with the reservation, "If I am spared."—"Weel, weel," said Mrs. Robinson, "if ye're dead, I'll no expect you."

How pithy and how wise, and also how Scotch, says Dean Ramsay, is the following: "A young lady, pressed by friends to marry a decent, but poor man, on the plea, 'Marry for love, and work for siller,' replied 'It's a' vera true, but a kiss and a tinniefu' (porringer) of cauld water make a gey wersh (insipid) breakfast.'"

CHARITY ON CREDIT.

A certain rich laird in Fife, whose weekly contribution to the church collection never exceeded one penny, one day, by mistake, dropped into the plate at the door a five-shilling piece; but discovering his error, before he was seated in his pew, hurried back, and was about to replace the dollar by his customary penny, when the elder in attendance cried out, "Stop, laird, ye may put *in* what ye like, but ye maun take naething *out!*" The laird, finding his explanations went for nothing, at last said, "A weel, I suppose I'll get credit for it in heaven." "Na, na, laird," said the elder, "ye'll only get credit for the *penny.*"

ENGLISH AND SCOTCH.

Some amusing tilts between English and Scottish conceit are related by Dean Ramsay. A lowland cattle-dealer expressed his surprise that Nelson should have issued his signal at Trafalgar in the terms, *"England expects,"* &c. He was met with the answer (which seemed highly satisfactory to the rest), "Ay, Nelson only said 'expects' of the English; he said naething of Scotland, for he **kent the Scotch** would do theirs."

A splenetic Englishman said to a Scotchman, something of a wag, that no man of taste would think of remaining any time in such a country as Scotland. To which the canny Scot replied, "Tastes differ; I'se tak' ye to a place, no far frae Stirling, whaur thretty thousand of your countrymen ha' been for five hundred years, an' they've nae thocht o' leavin' yet."

MECHANICAL WONDERS.

Sir Alexander Ramsay had been constructing, upon his estate in Scotland, a piece of machinery, which was driven by a stream of water running through the home farmyard. There were a thrashing-machine, a winnowing machine, a circular saw for splitting trees, and other contrivances. Observing an old man, who had long been about the place, looking very attentively at all that was going on, Sir Alexander said, "Wonderful things people can do now, Robby?" "Ay," said Robby, "indeed, Sir Alexander, I'm thinking if Solomon was alive now, he'd be thought naething o'!"—***Dean Ramsay.***

A SHORT HISTOR.

The shortest chronicle of the Reformation by Knox, and of the Wars of Claverhouse (Claver'se) in Scotland, which we know of, is that of an old lady who, in speaking of those troublous times, remarked, "Scotland had a sair time o't. First, we had Knox deavin' us we' his clavers, and syne we had Claver'se deavin' us wi' his knocks."

A LONG HORSE.

A curious correspondence once arose between Mr. Pitt and Mr. Dundas. When the latter applied to Pitt for the loan of a horse "the length of Highgate," Pitt wrote back to say that he was afraid he had not a horse in his possession quite so long as Mr. Dundas had mentioned, but he had sent the longest he had.

AN ELECTION BALL.

An old Scotch laird, at one of these entertainments, had attired himself in splendour for the occasion. The grandee, who was going round, of course showing civilities, said, "I didna ken ye, B—, you're so braw." "Nae," said the old squire; "and I dare say, ye'll no ken me for another seven year!"

SCOTTISH FEELING.

No example of the attachment of Scotchmen to old Scottish ways, and remembrances of their early days, has ever, says Dean Ramsay, struck me more than the story told of old Lord Lovat, which is amongst the many touching anecdotes which are traditionary of his unfortunate period. On his return from the trial at Westminster Hall, where he had been condemned to death for his adherence to the Stuart cause, he saw out of his coach-window a woman selling the sweet yellow gooseberries, which recalled the associations of youth in his native country. "Stop a minute," cried the old scoffer, who knew his days on earth were numbered; "stop a minute, and gie me a ha'porth of **honey-blobs,**" as if he had gone back in fond recollection to his schoolboy-days, in the High-street of Edinburgh, when honey-blobs had been among the pet luxuries of his young life.

[Doubtless, the sight of the honey-blobs reproved "the offending Adam" in the peer, and reminded him of what innocence had outlived.]

ONE BETTER THAN TWO.

Lord Mulgrave, who made the Expedition of discovery towards the North Pole, was formed on rather a heavy, colossal scale; and to distinguish him from his younger brother, the Honourable Charles Phipps, who had likewise a seat in Parliament, the former was denominated "Ursa Major." He was also called "Alphesibœus," it is supposed from some fancied anology between him and the awkward imitator of the Dancing Satyrs, in the fifth eclogue of Virgil's Bucolics.

Lord Mulgrave was distinguished by a singularity of physical conformation, having **two distinct voices:** the one, strong and hoarse; the other, weak and querulous; of both of which he occasionally availed himself. So extraordinary a circumstance, probably, gave rise to a story of his having fallen into a ditch in a dark night, and calling for aid in his shrill voice. A countryman coming up, was about to assist him; but Lord Mulgrave addressing him in a hoarse tone, the peasant immediately exclaimed, "Oh, if there are two of you in the ditch, you may help each other out of it."

THE DUKE OF SUSSEX'S ANNULLED MARRIAGE.

While travelling in Italy, in 1792, the late Duke of Sussex formed an attachment to Lady Augusta Murray, daughter of the Earl of Dunmore. The earl was not in Italy at the time; but Lady Dunmore consented to a private marriage of her daughter with the Duke, who was then about twenty years of age. The Duke could not have been ignorant of the Royal Marriage Act, which forbad the marriage of English princes with English subjects; and rendered the consent of the reigning sovereign necessary, even when the alliance was with persons of royal blood. Nor is it likely that such a statute could have been unknown to Lady Dunmore. The young couple, after a residence at Rome of several months, came to England. At the desire of the Duke and her friends, the lady consented to a second marriage ceremony, more public and regular than the first. The couple took lodgings in South Molton-street, at the house of a coal-merchant; merely that they might, by residence of one month in the parish of St George's, Hanover-square, be entitled to have their banns asked in the church of that parish. They were regularly married on the 5th of December, 1793, under the names of Augustus Frederick and Augusta Murray. It was an anxious time for the lady, seeing that she was about to become a mother, and had every motive for wishing to be recognised as a true wife. The King, however, never forgave the Duke for this marriage, and even instituted a suit against his own son in the Court of Arches, for annulling the marriage. The fact of the ceremony at St George's Church had to be rendered manifest by the testimony of the mother and sister of Lady Augusta, the clergyman who had performed the ceremony, the coal-merchant and his wife, and another witness who was present. So far as the Church was concerned, the marriage was, in all respects, a valid one; but the terms of the Royal Marriage Act were clear and decided; and after many months of anxious doubt the Duke and Lady Augusta were informed, by the irrevocable judgment of the court, that the marriage was no marriage at all in the eyes of the English law, and that their infant son was illegitimate. Lady Augusta, in a letter to a friend, written in 1811, said: "Lord Thurlow told me my marriage was good in law; religion taught me it was good at home; and not one divine of my powerful enemies could make me believe otherwise, or ever will." When the pair separated, the Duke settled on Lady Augusta an income out of the allowance he received from Parliament; but the King took care, through the whole remainder of his life, not to give the Duke a single office or post that would augment his resources.

FLIGHT OF THE PRINCESS CHARLOTTE.

In a fine evening (July 16th, 1814), about the hour of seven, when the streets are deserted by all persons of condition, the young Princess Charlotte rushed out of her residence in Warwick House, unattended; hastily crossed Cockspur-street; flung herself into the first hackney-coach she could find, and drove to her mother's house in Connaught-place. The Princess of Wales having gone to pass the day at her Blackheath villa, a messenger was despatched for her, another for her law adviser, Mr. Brougham, and a third for Miss Mercer Elphinstone, the young Princess's bosom friend. Brougham arrived before the Princess of Wales had returned; and Miss Elphinstone had only obeyed the summons. Soon after the Royal mother came, accompanied by Lady Charlotte Lindsay, her lady in waiting. It was found that the Princess Charlotte's fixed resolution was to leave her father's house, and that which he had appointed for her residence, and to live thenceforth with her mother. But Mr. Brougham is understood to have felt himself under the painful necessity of explaining to her that, by the law, as all the twelve Judges but one had laid it down in George L's reign, and as it was now admitted to be settled, the King or the Regent had the absolute power to dispose of the persons of all the Royal Family while under age. The Duke of Sussex, who had always taken her part, was sent for, and attended the invitation to join in these consultations. It was an untoward incident in this remarkable affair, that he had never seen the Princess of Wales since the investigation of 1806, which had begun upon a false charge brought by the wife of one of his equerries, and that he had, without any kind of warrant from the fact, been supposed by the Princess to have set on, or at least supported the accuser. He, however, warmly joined in the whole of the deliberations of that singular night.

As soon as the flight of the young lady was ascertained, and the place of her retreat discovered, the Regent's officers of state and other functionaries were despatched after her. The Lord Chancellor Eldon first arrived, but not in any particular imposing state, "regard being had "to his eminent station; for, indeed, he came in a hackney-coach. Whether it was that the example of the Princess Charlotte herself had for the day brought this simple and economical mode of conveyance into fashion, or that concealment was much studied, or that despatch was deemed more essential than ceremony and pomp—certain it is, that all who came, including the Duke of York, arrived in similar vehicles, and that some remained inclosed in them, without entering the Royal mansion. At length, after much pains and many entreaties, used by the Duke of Sussex and the Princess of Wales herself, as well as Miss Elphinstone and Lady C. Lindsay (whom she always honoured with a just regard), to enforce the advice given by Mr. Brougham, that she should return without delay to her own residence, and submit to the Regent, the young Princess, accompanied by the Duke of York and her governess, who had now been sent for and arrived in a Royal carriage, returned to Warwick House, between four and five o'clock in the morning. There was then a Westminster election in progress, in consequence of Lord Cochrane's expulsion; and it is said that on her complaining to Mr. Brougham that he, too, was deserting her, and leaving her in her father's power, when the people would have stood by her—he took her to the window, when the morning had just dawned, and, pointing to the Park, and the spacious streets which lay before her, said that he had only to show her a few hours later on the spot where she now stood, and all the people of this vast metropolis would be gathered together on that plain, with one common feeling in her behalf—but that the triumph of one hour would be dearly purchased by the consequences which must assuredly follow in the next, when the troops poured in, and quelled all resistance to the clear and undoubted law of the land, with the certain effusion of blood—nay, that through the rest of her life she never would escape the odium which, in this country, always attends those who, by breaking the law, occasion such calamities. This consideration, much more than any quailing of her dauntless spirit, or faltering of her filial affection, is believed to have weighed upon her mind, and induced her to return home.

This admirably written narrative of a very remarkable incident is attributed to Lord Brougham. The late Sir Frankland Lewis was accustomed to say that it was somewhat highly coloured throughout; it first appeared in the **Edinburgh Review.**

The Salon des Etrangers in Paris was, after the Restoration, a rendezvous for confirmed gamblers. It was conducted by the Marquis de Livry; he presented an extraordinary like ness to the Prince Regent of England, "who," says Captain Gronow, "actually sent Lord Fife over to Paris to ascertain this momentous fact." The play in these saloons was frequently of the most reckless character. The Captain tells us that "The Hon. George T—, who used to arrive from Lon don with a very considerable letter of credit expressly to try his luck at the Salon des Etrangers, at length contrived to lose his last shilling at *rouge et noir.* When he had lost every thing he possessed in the world, he got up and exclaimed, in an excited manner, 'If I had Canova's Venus and Adonis from Alton Towers, my uncle's country-seat, it should be placed on the *rouge,* for black has won fourteen times running.'"

But, perhaps, the most incurable gamester amongst the English was Lord Thanet, whose income was not less than 50,000*l.* a-year, every farthing of which he lost at play. When the gambling-tables were closed, he invited those who remained to play at chicken-hazard and ecarté; the consequence was that, one night, he left off a loser of 120,000*l.* When told of his folly and the probability of his having been cheated, he exclaimed, "Then I consider myself lucky in not having lost twice that sum."

Fox, the secretary of the Embassy, came nightly to the Salon; and if he possessed a Napoleon, it was sure to be thrown away at hazard, or ***rouge et noir.*** The late Henry Baring, however, one night recommended him to take to the dice-box. Fox replied, "I will do so for the last time, for all my money is thrown away upon this infernal table." Fox staked all he had in his pockets; he threw in ***eleven*** times, breaking the bank, and taking home for his share, 60,000 francs.

Marshal Blucher was another daily visitor, and played the highest stakes at ***rouge et noir:*** it is said that the Bank of France was called upon to furnish him with several thousand pounds, to reimburse him for the money lost at play.

London is the only place in all Europe where a man can find a secure retreat, or remain, if he pleases, many years unknown. If he pays constantly for his lodging, for his provisions, and for whatsoever else he wants, nobody will ask a question concerning him, or inquire whence he comes, whither he goes, &c. Dr. King relates the following evidence of this fact, in his pleasant volume of ***Anecdotes of his Own Time,*** published in 1819:

"About the year 1706 (says the Doctor), I knew one Mr. Howe, a sensible, well-natured man, possessed of an estate of 700*l.* or 800 *l.* per annum: he married a young lady of good family in the west of England, her maiden name was Mallet; she was agreeable in her person and manners, and proved a very good wife. Seven or eight years after they had been married, he rose one morning early, and told his wife he was obliged to go to the Tower to transact some particular business: the same day, at noon, his wife received a note from him, in which he informed her that he was under a necessity of going to Holland, and should probably be about three weeks or a month. He was absent from her ***seventeen years,*** during which time she neither heard from him, nor of him. The evening before he returned, whilst she was at supper, and with some of her friends and relations, particularly one Dr. Rose, a physician, who had married her sister, a billet, without any name subscribed, was delivered to her, in which the writer requested the favour of her to give him a meeting the next evening, in the Birdcage-walk, in St. James's park. When she had read her billet, she tossed it to Dr. Rose, and laughing, 'You see, brother,' said she, 'old as I am, I have got a gallant.' Rose, who perused the note with more attention, declared it to be Mr. Howe's handwriting; this surprised all the company, and so much affected Mrs. Howe, that she fainted away; however, she soon recovered, when it was agreed that Dr. Rose and his wife, with the other gentlemen and ladies who were then at supper, should attend Mrs. Howe the next evening to the Birdcage-walk. They had not been there more than five or six minutes, when Mr. Howe came to them, and after saluting his friends, and embracing his wife, walked home with her, and they lived together in great harmony from that time to the day of his death.

"But the most curious part of my tale remains to be related. When Howe left his wife, they lived in a house in Jermyn-street, near St. James's Church; he went no further than to a little street in Westminster, where he took a room, for which he paid five or six shillings a week, and changing his name, and disguising himself by wearing a black wig (for he was a fair man), he remained in this habitation during the whole time of his absence. He had had two children by his wife when he departed from her; but they both died young in a few years after. However, during their lives, the second or third year after their father disappeared, Mrs. Howe was Obliged to apply for an Act of Parliament to procure a proper settlement of her husband's estate, and a provision for herself out of it during his absence, as it was uncertain whether he was alive or dead: this Act he suffered to be solicited and passed, and enjoyed the pleasure of reading the progress of it in the votes, in a little coffee-house near his lodging, which he frequented. Upon his quitting his house and family in the manner I have mentioned, Mrs. Howe at first imagined, as she could not conceive any other cause for such an abrupt elopement, that he had contracted a large debt unknown to her, and by that means involved himself in difficulties, which he could not easily surmount; and for some days she lived in continual apprehensions of demands from creditors, of seizures, executions, &c. But nothing of this kind happened.

"Mrs. Howe, after the death of her children, thought proper to lessen her family of servants, and the expenses of her housekeeping; and, therefore, removed from her house in Jermyn-street to a little house in Brewer-street, near Golden-square. Just over against her lived one Salt, a corn-chandler. About ten years after Howe's abdication, he contrived to make an acquaintance with Salt, and was at length in such a degree of intimacy with him, that he usually dined with Salt once or twice a week. From the room in which they eat, it was not difficult to look into Mrs. Howe's dining-room, where she generally sate and received company; and Salt, who believed Howe to be a bachelor, frequently recommended his own wife to him as a suitable match. During the last seven years of this gentleman's absence, he went every Sunday to St. James's Church, and used to sit in Mr. Salt's seat, where he had a view of his wife, but could not easily be seen by her. After he returned home, he never would confess, even to his most intimate friends, what was the real cause of such singular conduct; apparently there was none: but whatever it was, he was certainly ashamed to own it. Dr. Rose has often said to me, that he believed his brother Howe would never have returned to his wife, if the money which he took with him, which was supposed to have been 1,000*l.* or 2,000*l.*, had not been all spent; and he must have been a good economist, and frugal in his manner of living, otherwise his money would scarce have held out; for I imagine he had his whole fortune by him, I mean what he carried away with him in money or bank-bills, and daily took out of his bag, like the Spaniard in Gil Bias, what was sufficient for his expenses."

Dr. King received this remarkable story from Dr. Rose and Mr. Salt, whom he often met at King's coffee-house, near Golden-square.

SCOTTISH HUMOUR.

Sydney Smith very unfairly said it required a surgical operation to get a joke into a Scotch understanding. "The only idea of wit," he said, "which prevails occasionally in the North, and which, under the name of 'wut,' is so infinitely distressing to people of good taste, is laughing immoderately at stated intervals." He might have drawn a distinction between English wit and Scotch humour in no way discreditable to the latter. Charles Lamb is a second witness in the same cause to prove a *alibi* as regards wit proper. Dean Ramsay, however, controverts this with, some show of success, though most of the peculiar zest which he ascribes to Scottish humour resolves itself into "the vehicle in which the humour is conveyed."

There is something distinctive in the following, but it is neither wit nor humour, but a shower of Scotch vocables. When an Aberdonian went up to visit his son, then the manager of the Opera-house, his answer on his return as to the nature of his son's business was this, "He just keeps a curn of wirricows and weanies, and gars them fizzle and loup and mak murgeons to the great foulk." Though this may not sustain the pretensions to peculiar humour, it will go far to sustain the claim to a distinctive language.

A Scotch nobleman, of no bright parts, was asked by the Duchess of Devonshire how it happened that the Scots in general made a much better figure from home than in Scotland. "Oh!" said he, "nothing is so easily accounted for. For the honor of the nation persons are stationed at every egress, to see that none leave the country but men of abilities." "Then," answered the Duchess, "I suspect your lordship was smuggled."

A poor laird of Macnab was in the habit of riding a most wretched horse to the Musselburgh races, where a young wit asked him, in a contemptuous tone, "Is that the same horse you had last year, laird?" "Na," said the laird, brandishing his whip in the interrogator's face, so emphatically as to preclude further questioning, "Na; but it's the same *whip*".

A miserly Scottish lord had picked up a small copper coin, and was observed to put it into his pocket by a beggar, who exclaimed, "O, gie't to me, my lord;" to which the quiet answer was, "Na, na; fin' a fardin for yersell, puir body."

The late Lord Airlie remarking to one of his tenants that it was a very wet season, "Indeed, my lord," replied the man, "I think the spiggot's out a' thegither."

PALMER'S CLARET.

Captain Gronow relates [Note *: In his lively volume of **Reminiscences,** &c.] that General Palmer having received from Parliament 100,000*l.* for his father's introduction of the mail-coach system, was induced to invest a large portion of his fortune in the purchase of a fine estate for the production of claret, in the neighborhood of Bordeaux. The management of the property he confided to a very plausible agent, under whose auspices Palmer's Claret began to be talked of in the clubs, and to be highly prized. The patronage of the Regent was solicited, and the Prince, from a kindly feeling for Palmer, who had before been introduced at Carlton House, gave a dinner, when his claret was to be tried. Sir Benjamin Bloomfield, Sir William Knighton, and Sir Thomas Tyrrwhitt were of the party, with Lord Yarmouth, known as "Red-herrings," from his rubicund whiskers, hair, and face, and from the town of Yarmouth largely importing that fish from Holland. The wine was produced, and was found excellent The Prince was delighted, told some of his best stories, quoted Shakespeare, and felicitously declared the bouquet of the wine as suited "to the holy Palmer's kiss." Lord Yarmouth alone sat in moody silence; on being asked the cause, he said that he had drunk claret which he much preferred at His Royal Highness table. The Prince ordered a bottle of this wine to be served with anchovy sandwiches; and His Royal Highness declared his own wine superior to Palmer's, adding that he should try to obtain a better wine from his estate. Palmer came from Carlton House much mortified; on Sir Thomas Tyrrwhitt attempting to console him, saying that it was the anchovies that had spoiled the taste of the connoisseurs, the General said, loudly enough to be heard by Lord Yarmouth, "No; it was the confounded red-herrings." Palmer took the advice of the Prince, rooted out his old vines, and planted new ones, at an immense cost, but with little or no result. He and his agent got into difficulties, mortgaged the property, and were eventually ruined; the General sold his commission, passed through the Insolvent Court, and was at last seen begging in the streets of London, so strongly had the tide of misfortune set in against him.

"TIPPING THE COLD SHOULDER."

Mr. Lockhart, in his admirable *Life* of his father-in-law, relates that many years ago, when the wealthy Mrs. Coutts visited Sir Walter Scott at Abbotsford, it so happened that there were already in the house several ladies, Scotch and English, of high birth and rank, who felt by no means disposed to assist their host and hostess in making Mrs. Coutts's visit agreeable to her. On the first day of her stay, Sir Walter Scott, during dinner, did everything in his power to counteract this influence of **the evil eye,** and something to overawe it; but the spirit of mischief had been fairly stirred, and it was easy to see that Mrs. Coutts followed these noble dames to the drawing-room in by no means that complacent mood which was customarily sustained, doubtless, by every blandishment of obsequious flattery in this mistress of millions. He cut the gentlemen's sederunt short, and soon after joining the ladies, managed to withdraw the youngest and gayest, and cleverest, who was also the highest in rank (a lovely Marchioness), into his armorial-hall adjoining. He said to her, "I want to speak a word with you about Mrs. Coutts. We have known each other a good while, and I know you won't take anything I can say in ill part. It is, I hear, not uncommon among the fine ladies in London to be very well pleased to accept invitations, and even sometimes to hunt after them, to Mrs. Coutts's grand balls and fêtes, *and then, if they meet her in any private circle, to practise on her the delicate* manœuvre *called* tipping the cold shoulder. *This you agree with me is shabby; but it is nothing new either to you or to me, that fine people will do shabbinesses for which beggars might blush, if they once stoop so low as to poke for tickets. I am sure you would not for the world do such a thing; but you must permit me to take the great liberty of saying, that I think the style you have all received my guest, Mrs. Coutts, in, this evening, is, to a certain extent, a sin of the same order. You were all told, a couple of days ago, that I had accepted her visit, and that she would arrive to-day to stay three nights. Now, if any of you had not been disposed to be of my party at the same time with her, there was plenty of time for you to have gone away before she came; and as none of you moved, and it was impossible to fancy that any of you would remain out of mere curiosity, I thought I had a perfect right to calculate on your having made up your minds to help me out with her." The beautiful Peeress answered, "I thank you, Sir Walter; you have done me the great honor to speak as if I had been your daughter, and depend upon it you shall be obeyed with heart and good-will." One by one, the other exclusives were seen engaged in a little* tête-à-tête *with her Ladyship. Sir Walter was soon satisfied that things had been put into a right train; the Marchioness was requested to sing a particular song,* because he thought it would please Mrs. Coutts. "Nothing could gratify her more than to please Mrs. Coutts." Mrs. Coutts's brow smoothed, and in the course of half an hour she was as happy and easy as ever she was in her life, rattling away at comic anecdotes of her early theatrical years, and joining in the chorus of Sir Adam's "Laird of Cockpen." She stayed out her three days—saw, accompanied by all the circle, Melrose, Dryburgh, and Yarrow—and left Abbotsford delighted with her host, and, to all appearance, with his other guests.

LORD PETERSHAM.

This eccentric nobleman, who was the eldest son of Charles, third Earl of Harrington, was a leader of fashion some thirty years since: he was tall and handsome: according to Captain Gronow, Lord Petersham very much resembled the pictures of Henry ?V. of France, and frequently wore a dress not unlike that of the celebrated monarch. He was a great patron of tailors, and a particular kind of great-coat was called after him a "Petersham." When young, he used to cut out his own clothes; he made his own blacking, which, he said, would eventually supersede every other. He was also a connoisseur in snuff, and one of his rooms was fitted up with shelves and beautiful jars for various kinds of snuff, with the names in gold. Here were also implements for moistening and mixing snuffs, and "Lord Petersham's mixture" is to this day a popular snuff. He possessed a fine collection of snuff-boxes, and it was said, a box for every day in the year. Captain Gronow saw him using a beautiful Sèvres box, which, on being admired, he said, was "a nice summer box, but would not do for winter wear." He was equally choice of his teas, and in the same room with the snuffs, upon shelves, were placed tea-canisters, containing Congou, Pekoe, Souchong, Gunpowder, Russian, and other fine kinds. Indeed, his father's mansion, Harrington House, was long famous for its tea-drinking: and the Earl and Countess, and family, received their visitors upon these occasions in the long gallery, and here the family of George the Third enjoyed many a cup of tea. It is told that when General Lincoln Stanhope returned from India after several years' absence, his father welcomed him with "Hallo, Linky, my dear boy! delighted to see you. **Have a cup of tea!**"

Lord Petersham's equipages were unique: the carriages and horses were brown; the harness had furniture of antique design; and the servants wore long brown coats, reaching to their heels, and glazed hats with large cockades. His Lordship was a liberal patron of the opera and the theatres; and two years after he had succeeded his father in the earldom (of Harrington), he married the beautiful Maria Foote, of Covent-garden Theatre.

SALLY LUNN CAKES.

Captain Gronow, in the second series of his piquant **Reminiscences,** tells us that Lady Harrington related to him a curious anecdote of these tea-cakes. She said, her friend Madame de Narbonne, during the emigration, determined not to live upon the bounty of foreigners, found means to amass money enough to open a shop at Chelsea, not far from the then fashionable Ranelagh. It had been the custom in France, before the Revolution, for young ladies in some noble families to learn the art of making preserves and pastry; accordingly, Madame de Narbonne commenced her operations under the auspices of some of her acquaintances; and those who went to Ranelagh made a point of stopping and buying some of her cakes. Her fame spread throughout the West-end of the town, and orders were given to have them sent for breakfast and tea in many large houses in St. James's. Madame de Narbonne employed a Scotch maid-servant to execute her orders; the name of this woman was *Sally Lunn;* and ever since a particular kind of tea-cake has gone by the name of *Sally Lunn.*

Hone, however, states Sally Lunn to have lived at Bath at the close of the last century; and that a baker and musician, of Bath, noticed her, bought her business, and set to music a song in praise of Sally Lunn and her fashionable cakes.

A BACCHANALIAN DUELLIST.

"A good old Irish gentleman," in the times of conviviality and dueling, was Mr. Bagenal, of Dunleckny, in the county Carlow—**King** Bagenal, as he was called through his extensive territories; and within their bounds no monarch was more absolute. Of high Norman lineage, polished manners, princely income, and boundless hospitality, Mr. Bagenal was popular with every class. A terrestrial paradise was Dunleckny for all lovers of good wine, good horses, good dogs, and good society. His stud was magnificent, and he had a large number of capital hunters for his visitors. He derived great delight from encouraging the young men who frequented his house to hunt and drink, and solve points of honor at twelve paces. His politics were popular: he was the mover of the grant of 50,000*l.* to Grattan in 1782; he was at that time member for the county of Carlow.

Enthroned at Dunleckny, he gathered around him a host of congenial spirits. He had a tender affection for pistols: a brace of "saw-handles," loaded, was often laid before him on the dinner-table. After dinner, the claret was produced in an unbroached cask. Bagenal's practice was to tap the cask with a bullet from one of his pistols, whilst he kept the other, **in terrorem,** for any of the guests who should fail in doing simple justice to the wine. He gave his junior guests the results of his own experience, for the regulation of their conduct "I am not a quarrelsome person," he would say; "I never was—I hate your mere duellist—but experience of the world tells me that there are knotty points in life in which the only solution is the ***saw-handle.*** Occasions will arise in which the use of them is absolutely indispensable to character. A man must show his proofs—in this world courage will never be taken upon trust."

His practice accorded with his precepts. Some pigs, the property of a gentleman who had recently settled near Dunleckny, strayed into an in closure of King Bagenal's, and rooted up a flower-knot. The incensed monarch ordered that the porcine trespassers should be shorn of their ears and tails; and he transmitted the severed appendages to the owner of the swine, with an intimation, that ***he,*** too, deserved to have his ears docked; and that only he had not got a tail, or he (King Bagenal) would sever the caudal member from his dorsal extremity. "Now," quoth Bagenal, "if he's a gentleman, he ***must*** burn powder after such a message as that." Nor was he disappointed. A challenge was given by the owner of the pigs; Bagenal accepted it with alacrity; only stipulating that, as he was old and feeble, being then in his 79th year, he should fight sitting in his arm-chair; and that as his infirmities prevented early rising, the meeting should take place in the afternoon. "Time was," said the old man, with a sigh, "that I would have risen before daybreak to fight at sunrise—but we can't do these things at seventy-eight Well, Heaven's will be done!"

They fought at twelve paces. Bagenal wounded his antagonist severely; the arm of the chair in which he sat was shattered, but he escaped unhurt; and he ended the day with a glorious carouse, tapping the claret, as usual, by firing a pistol at the cask.

The traditions of Dunleckny allege, that when Bagenal, in the course of his tour through Europe, visited the petty court of Mecklenburgh-Strelitz, the Grand Duke, charmed with his magnificence and the reputation of his wealth, made him an offer of the hand of the fair Charlotte—who, being politely rejected by King Bagenal, was afterwards accepted by King George the Third!—**Abridged from Daunt's Ireland and her Agitators.**

THE PRINCE OF WALES AND MRS. ROBINSON.

This lady was distinguished as a writer in verse and prose, as well as by her exquisite beauty and personal misfortunes. She was the daughter of a merchant at Bristol, of the name of Darby, who failing in business, and dying soon after, his widow took her lovely daughter to London, where, at sixteen, she was induced to marry a young attorney, of specious appearance, named Robinson. Her husband soon after falling into difficulties, Garrick encouraged her to try the stage for subsistence; and at nineteen she performed several parts with success: [Note *: Walpole, however, speaks of her as an indifferent actress in Lady Craven's comedy of the *Miniature Picture,* performed at Drury Lane, in May, 1780. His words are: "Mrs. Robinson (who is supposed to be the favourite of the Prince of Wales) thought on nothing out her own charms or him."—***Letter to Mason.***] she first appeared as Juliet, in 1776. Her beauty had already become known to the Prince of Wales; and one night, after she had played the part of Perdita, in the *Winter's Tale,* she received from the hands of Lord Maiden a lock of His Royal Highness' hair, enclosed in a billet, with these words—"To the ever adorable Perdita—Florizel, to be redeemed,"—in the Prince's handwriting. The vanity of a young woman in her situation rendered her an easy prey, and she soon after became the mistress of the Prince, and lived in a style of great splendour. The connexion, either from the incautiousness of His Royal Highness, the officiousness of false friends, or from some other causes, never well explained, produced much uneasiness to the royal family. The King thus wrote to Lord North:

20th August, 1781.

"My eldest son got last year into an improper connexion with an actress of indifferent character, through the friendly assistance of Lord Malden. He sent her letters and very foolish promises, which undoubtedly by her conduct she has cancelled. Col. Hotham has settled to pay the enormous sum of 5,000*l.* for the letters, &c. being returned. You will, therefore, settle with him."

Then followed the open shame and scandal of the Prince's breaking up this intrigue; of which, however, the following record, an abstract from the parish register of St. Mary-le-bone, may be added: "Georgiana Augusta Frederica Elliott, daughter of H. R. H. George Prince of Wales and Grace Elliott: born 30 March, and baptized 30 July, 1782."

At this date we find Walpole writing: "Charles Fox is languishing at the feet of Mrs. Robinson." George Selwyn says: "Who should the man of the people live with, but with the woman of the people?" This scandal was, doubtless, heightened for the sake of the joke. However, the habits of luxury which Mrs. Robinson had acquired during her royal connexion could not be shaken off. Her attachments were of a romantic cast: on the return of the celebrated trooper, Colonel Tarleton, from his guerilla warfare in the backwoods of America, she fell desperately in love with him; in a journey by night to render him a personal service, she caught cold, followed by a severe fever, and lost the sinews of her knees, being then only twenty-two. This affliction she never overcame, and was unable to stand upright or walk during the remainder of her life. She now devoted herself to literature, and many of her poetical pieces are of deep feeling and highly-wrought sentiment. She maintained her personal fascinations, and she might be considered as one of the loveliest women in England till her 42d year, when her sedentary life brought on dropsy of the chest, of which she died, in 1800, neglected and poor, at Englefield-green: she was interred at Old Windsor, where a plain tomb, placed over her grave, bears the following lines:

"Of Beauty's isle, her daughters must declare,
She who sleeps here was fairest of the fair;
But ah! while Nature on her favorite smiled,
And Genius claimed his share in Beauty's child,
Even as they wove a garland for her brow,
Sorrow prepared a willowy wreath of woe,
Mixed lurid nightshade with the buds of May,
And twined her darkest cypress with the bay,
In mildew tears steeped every opening flower,
Preyed on the sweets, and gave the canker power.
Yet O may Pity's angel from the grave,
The early victim of misfortune save,
And, as she springs to everlasting morn,
May Glory's fadeless crown her soul adorn."

After the death of Mrs. Robinson, her papers, with the hair and billet of the Prince of Wales, were purchased by Sir Richard Phillips, by whom her memoirs, as far as she had written them, were published. Her portrait was more than once painted; her favorite attitude being with her head resting upon her upraised arm, which was very beautiful.

THE PRINCE OF WALES AN ODD-FELLOW.

Near to the south end of Grosvenor-row, Chelsea, was a small public-house, "The Feathers," to which a curious anecdote is attached. A Lodge of Odd-Fellows, or some similar society, held its meetings here; and on one occasion, when a new member was being initiated into the mysteries of the fellowship, in rushed two persons, whose abrupt intrusion threw the whole assemblage into uproar. Summary punishment was proposed by an expeditious kick into the street; but just as it was about to be bestowed, the Secretary recognized one of the intruders as George, Prince of Wales. Circumstances instantly changed: it was, indeed, the Prince, out on a nocturnal ramble: accordingly, it was proposed that His Royal Highness and his companion should be admitted members. The Prince assented, and was chairman the remainder of the evening; and the chair in which he sat, ornamented, in consequence, with the triple plume, is still preserved in the parlour of the modern tavern in Grosvenor-street, West; and over it hangs a coarsely-painted portrait of the Prince, in the robes of the order. The old "Feathers" was removed in 1851, and on clearing the ground, coins, old horse-shoes, war-implements, and some human remains, were found.

At the intersection of the cross-roads, at the end of Grosvenor-place, suicides were subjected to the revolting burial then awarded by the law. The last person thus interred was named Griffiths, the son of a colonel, who had first murdered his father and then destroyed himself: this took place in 1823.—***Memorials of Knightsbridge.***

THE PRINCE OF WALES AND COLONEL HANGER.

This eccentric person was the youngest son of Gabriel, first Lord Coleraine, and was, by turns, a successful gamester; a prisoner in the King's Bench; a gallant soldier in King George's army, fighting against the Americans; and ultimately a flattered guest at the table of the Prince of Wales.

Hanger's extravagance in dress has been recorded by him-self. For one winter's dress-clothes only it cost him 900*l.:* on every birth-day, he had two suite: morning-dress cost 80*l.;* and ball-dress above 180*l.;* the latter including a satin coat, which thenceforth became the fashion. He was passionately fond of the turf: he once stood 3,000 guineas on one race—Shark against Leviathan—and won it. He was a considerable gainer by the turf; but he was subjected to strange reverses. Once, when he was dining with the Prince of Wales, at Carlton House, after the wine had for some time circulated, his good-humored volubility suddenly ceased, and he seemed for a time lost in thought. The Prince inquired the cause. "I have been reflecting, sir," replied the Colonel, "on the lofty independence of my present situation. I have compromised with my creditors, paid my washerwoman, and have three shillings and sixpence left for the pleasures and necessities of life," exhibiting at the same moment the amount in current coin, upon the royal board at which he sat.

After he had obtained his colonelcy, one day, the Prince condescendingly said, that "now he was rich, he would so far impose upon his hospitality as to dine with him;" at the same time insisting on the repast being anything but extravagant. "I shall give your Royal Highness a leg of mutton, and nothing more, by G—," warmly replied the Colonel. The day was named; and the Colonel had sufficient time to recur to his budget, and bring his ways and means into action. Long destitute of credit and resources, he counted upon the forestalment of the profits of his appointment, to entertain "the first gentleman in England;" but agents had flinty hearts and long memories, and would not advance: the day approached, and Hanger could boast little more than the once-vaunted half-crown and a shilling. The day arrived, and etiquette demanded that the proper officer should examine and report upon the nature of the expected entertainment, when the Colonel was found, with a dirty scullion for his aide-de-camp, in active preparation for his royal visitor; his shirt-sleeves tucked up, while he ardently basted the roasting leg of mutton, which shed its savoury exhalations upon a panfull of potatoes; and there were tankards of foaming ale, and bread à discretion. Although the Colonel's culinary skill was undoubted, and the Prince had enjoyed a steak-dinner at Alderman Combe's brewery, yet Hanger's feast was dispensed with, and due acknowledgment made for the evidences of his hospitality.

After many sufferings and vicissitudes, a coronet became Hanger's, by the death of his brother, Lord Coleraine; and it came opportunely, for he knew, by experience, its value, and he resolved to enjoy it. He had had enough of fashion, and had proved all its allurements. So he took a small house at Somers Town, near which stood a public-house he was fond of visiting; and there, as the price of his sanction, and in acknowledgment of his rank, a large chair by the fireside was exclusively appropriated to the peer. His Lordship died, unmarried, March 31, 1824, aged seventy-three, and with him the family honours became extinct.

THE EARLDOM OF BRIDGEWATER.

On the death of the Duke of Bridgewater, his relative, then General Egerton, claimed the earldom, but found a difficulty in complying with the established rule of the House of Lords—that before a nobleman can take his seat, he must produce his patent, or prove his descent from a former peer,—inasmuch as he could not find the registers of the marriage of his grandfather or father. The former, when Bishop of Hereford, had run away with Lady Harriet Bentinck, a daughter of Lord Portland, which occasioned the difficulty in that case. This was got over; but not so readily the other impediment; for though Lord Bridgewater knew that his father, when Bishop of Durham, had married Lady Sophia de Grey, a daughter of the Duke of Kent, and that the ceremony was performed at the Chapel Royal, George the Second attending to give away the bride; though all these were circumstances of public notoriety, still he could not find the marriage recorded in the St. James's register. For almost a twelvemonth he was thus prevented from taking his seat; when, having offered by advertisement a considerable reward to any one who should give him such information as should enable him to obtain the required document, his agent, Mr. Clarke, was waited upon one morning by a very old man, who stated that he could prove the marriage of Egerton, Bishop of Durham, with Lady Sophia de Grey, having himself acted as clerk on that occasion. He related that in consequence of the lameness of His Majesty, the ceremony was performed in the pew in which the King sat, instead of at the altar; and that pew being in St. Martin's, and not in St James's, the marriage was registered in the former parish. Search was immediately made at St. Martin's Church, and the entry found forthwith.—***From Sir Bernard Burke's Anecdotes of the Aristocracy, Second Series.***

GEORGE III. AND HANNAH LIGHTFOOT.

Although George the Third condemned, with great severity, the first amour of his eldest son—with Mrs. Robinson, the youth of the King was not spotless; but he fell into a like dereliction himself. [Note *: Dr. Doran, in his Notes to the *Last Journals of Horace Walpole,* has printed the following illustration of the royal household life from a note in the handwriting of Mrs. Piozzi, "The character of George III. was uniformly moral, and uniformly discreet. He was what we call 'a steady boy' in early youth. A confidential friend, and natural son, indeed, of one of my uncles, was about the court when Prince Frederic of Wales died. He told my mother the following story:—The Princess was sitting one day of her early widowhood, pensive, and melancholy; her two eldest sons were playing about the room, 'Brother,' said the second boy (Edward, Duke of York), 'when you and I are men grown, you shall be married, and *I* will keep a mistress.' 'Be quiet, Eddy,' replied the present king (George III.), 'we shall have anger presently for your nonsense: there must be no mistresses at all.' 'What you say?' cried old Augusta; 'you more need learn your pronouns, as the preceptor bid you do. Can you tell what is a pronoun?' 'Yes, very well,' replied Prince Edward; 'a pronoun is to a noun what a mistress is to a wife, a substitute and a representative.' "]. The story is variously told; but the following version, written by Sir Richard Phillips, who knew some of the parties, and took great pains to elicit the truth in the *Monthly Magazine,* may be relied on.

About the year 1756, there lived at the corner of Market-street, St. James's-market, a linen-draper named Wheeler, a Quaker, who had a beautiful niece, named Hannah Lightfoot, blown as "the fair Quakeress," from serving in her uncle's shop. The lady caught the eye of Prince George, in his walks and rides from Leicester House to St James's Palace, and she soon returned the attentions of such a lover. [Note*: In Exeter-street, Knightsbridge, resided a family named Perrin, one of whom, it has been said, was employed by the Duchess of Kingston to furnish a meeting between Prince George and Hannah Lightfoot.—*Memorials of Knightsbridge.*] She is said to have been privately married to the Prince, in 1759, in Kew Chapel: another story states that the marriage was celebrated at Curzon-street Chapel, by the Rev. Alexander Keith, with the Prince's brother, the Duke of York, as a witness: and it is stated that children were born of the marriage, of whom, a son, was sent, when a child, to the Cape of Good Hope, with the name of George Rex. This portion of the story, by Dr. Doran, receives some corroboration, from there being, in 1830, at the Cape, a Mr. George Rex, at the Knysna: a Correspondent of *Notes and Queries,* second series, vol xi understood from Rex that he had then (1830) been about thirty-four years a resident in the colony, was about sixty-eight years of age, of strong, robust appearance, and the exact resemblance in features to George III. This would bring him to about the time of the Prince's marriage to Hannah, as stated by Dr. Doran. On Mr. Rex's first arrival in the colony, he occupied a high situation in the Colonial Government, and received an extensive grant of land at the Knysna.

We now return to Sir Richard Phillips's version. The acquaintance alarming the Royal Family, it was contrived to marry the Quaker to a young grocer and former admirer, of the name of Axford, of Ludgate-hill The Prince, however, was inconsolable; and a few weeks after, as Axford was one evening from home, a royal carriage came to the door, and the lady was hurried into it by the attendants, and carried off at full speed. Where she was taken to, or what became of her, was never known. Some reported that she survived her lover: others that she died in 1765, after having had three sons, since general officers. Her death disturbed the royal mind. Axford, broken-hearted, retired to Warminster, set up a grocer's shop, married again, and had a family: he died in old age, about 1810, but not without having sought clamorously for information about his wife, at Weymouth and other places. [We remember a grocer of the above name and family at Ludgate-hill, and on the north side of Fleet-street, between 1822 and 1826.]

ATTEMPTS TO ASSASSINATE GEORGE THE THIRD.

Twice had his Majesty nearly fallen a victim to the fury of a maniac. On the morning of August 2, 1786, as the King was stepping out of his post-chariot, at the garden-entrance to St James's Palace, a woman, who was waiting there, pushed forward, and presented a paper, which his Majesty received with great condescension.

At that instant, she struck a concealed knife at the King's breast, which his Majesty happily avoided by bowing, as he received the paper. As she was making a second thrust, one of the yeomen caught her arm, and at the same instant, one of the King's footmen wrenched the knife out of her hand. The King, with great temper and fortitude, exclaimed: "I have received no injury: do not hurt the woman, the poor creature appears insane." His Majesty was perfectly correct in his humane supposition. She proved to be Margaret Nicholson; and after a long examination before the Privy Council, they were "clearly and unanimously of opinion, that she was, and is, insane." The knife struck against his Majesty's waistcoat, and made a slight cut, the breadth of the point, through the cloth; had not the King shrunk in his side, the blow must have been fatal. Several addresses of congratulation were presented to his Majesty, and knighthoods conferred, and the recipients became popularly known as "Peg Nicholson's Knights." She was committed to Bethlehem Hospital, in Moorfields, and thence removed to the new hospital, in St. George's Fields; she died here in 1828, in her 99th year, after a confinement of forty-two years.

Another attempt on his Majesty's life was made on the night of the 15th of May, 1800, when the King and Queen and the Court were present at Drury-lane Theatre. A maniac named Hadfield fired a pistol at the King from the pit of the theatre, when the arm of the assassin was arrested by a gentleman named Holroyd. Hadfield had been a gallant dragoon, and his face was seamed with scars which he had received in battle; he was adjudged to be insane, and committed to Bethlehem Hospital, where he employed himself with writing verses on the death of his birds and cats, his only companions in his long imprisonment, from 1802 until his death, in 1841.

"JACK ROBINSON" AND GEORGE III.

John Robinson, of Appleby, rose, under the patronage of Sir James Lowther, from being footboy in his service, to sit in Parliament for Westmoreland and Harwich, and Secretary of the Treasury, under Lord North's Administration, when he was caricatured as *the political ratcatcher.* He was made by Pitt Surveyor-General of His Majesty's Woods and Forests; when he died, there were found in his writing-desk upwards of 300 letters written to him by George III.

Mr. Serjeant Atkinson relates of Robinson: The King was once obliged in the chase to cross Wyke Farm (Robinson lived at Wyke House, near Brentford), when on riding up to one of the gates, he found it locked. He hailed a man close by, but the fellow seemed lazy or unwilling to do as he was bid. "Come, come," said the King, "open the gate." "Nay, **ye mun gang aboot,**" was the answer. "Gang aboot!" replied the King;—"open the gate, man—I'm the King!" "Why, may be," said the chap, "but ye mun gang aboot, if ye ert king;" and sure enough, the King was force to "gang aboot," which in plain English means that he was obliged to go round nearly the whole inclosure of Osterley Park. Robinson came home in the afternoon, and hearing of the King's disappointment, instantly ordered horses to his carriage, and drove post haste to Kew. He was admitted, as usual, without ceremony, and his Majesty, laughing, greeted him thus: "Ah, Robinson, I see you are in distress—be of good cheer! I wish I had such fine fellows in my pay as **auld gang aboot.** Tell him from me that I shall always be glad to see him." Robinson was at ease; and **auld gang aboot** very soon and very often found a more direct path than around the palings of Osterley Park to Kew Palace, where he always met with kindness. The King never saw Robinson afterwards without inquiring affectionately after "auld gang aboot."

SIR JOHN DINELY, BART.

This eccentric baronet, of the family of the Dinelys, of Charlton, descended, by the female line, from the Royal House of Plantagenet, having dissipated the wreck of the family estates, obtained the pension and situation of a poor knight of Windsor. His chief occupation consisted in advertising for a wife, and nearly thirty years were passed in assignations to meet the fair respondents to his advertisements. His figure was truly grotesque: in wet weather, he was mounted on a high pair of pattens; he wore the coat of the Windsor uniform, with a velvet embroidered waistcoat, satin breeches, silk stockings, and a full-bottomed wig. In this finery he might be seen strolling one day; and next out marketing, carrying a penny loaf, a morsel of butter, a quartern of sugar and a farthing candle. Twice or thrice a year he came to London, and visited Vauxhall Gardens and the theatres. His fortune, if he could recover it, he estimated at 300,000*l.* He invited the widow, as well as the blooming maiden of sixteen, and addressed them in printed documents, bearing his signature, in which he specified the sum the ladies must possess; he expected less property with youth than age or widowhood; adding that few ladies would be eligible that did not possess at least 10,000*l.* a-year, which, however, was nothing compared to the honour his high birth and noble descent would confer; the incredulous he referred to Nash's **Worcestershire.** He addressed his advertisements to "the angelic fair" from his house, in Windsor Castle (one of the poor knights' houses). He cherished to the last the expectation of forming a connubial connexion with some lady of property, but, alas! he died a bachelor in 1808.

THAT YOU MUST LOVE ME AND LOVE MY DOG.

An excellent story to this moral is told of Merry, of Della Cruscan memory. In tender youth, he loved and courted a modest appanage to the opera, in truth a dancer, who had won him by the artless contrast between her manners and situation. She seemed to him a native violet, that had been transplanted by some rude accident into that exotic and artificial hot-bed. Nor, in truth, was she less genuine and sincere than she appeared to him. He wooed and won this flower. Only for appearance' sake, and for due honour to the bride's relations, she craved that she might have the attendance of her friends and kindred at the approaching solemnity. The request was too amiable not to be conceded; and in this solicitude for conciliating the good-will of mere relations, he found a presage of her superior attentions to himself, when the golden shaft should have "killed the flock of all attentions else." The morning came; and at the Star and Garter, Richmond—the place appointed for the breakfasting—accompanied by one English friend, he impatiently awaited what reinforcements the bride should bring to grace the ceremony. A rich muster she had made. They came in six coaches—the whole ***corps de ballet***—French and Italian, men and women. Monsieur de B., the famous ***pirouetter*** of the day, led his fair spouse, but scraggy, from the banks of the Seine. The prima donna had sent her excuse. But the first and second buffa were there; and Signor Sc—, and Signora Ch—, and Madame V—, with a countless cavalcade besides of chorusers and figurantes, at the sight of whom Merry afterwards declared, that "then for the first time it struck him seriously that he was about to marry—a dancer." But there was no help for it. Besides, it was her day; these were, in fact, her friends and kinsfolk. The assemblage, though whimsical, was all very natural. But when the bride—handing out of the last coach a still more extraordinary figure than the rest—presented to him as the *father*—the gentleman that was to *give her away*—no less a person than Signor Delpini himself—with a sort of pride, as much as to say, "See what I have brought to do us honour!"—the thought of so extraordinary a paternity quite overcame him; and, slipping away under some pretence from the bride and her motley adherents, poor Merry took horse from the back-yard to the nearest sea-coast, from which, shipping himself to America, he shortly after consoled himself with a more congenial match in the person of Miss Brunton; relieved from his intended clown father, and a bevy of painted buffas for bridemaids.—**Charles Lamb.**

KISSING HANDS.

Dr. Leifchild has left the following amusing account of the reception of a deputation to George the Fourth, with its attendant ceremonies:—

"Not only had my father the honour of conversing with a royal duke, but while at Kensington he was introduced to royalty itself. He must be allowed to narrate the event in his own words:—'I was one of the ministers of the three denominations, Presbyterian, Baptist, and Independent, who proceeded to Carlton Palace, Pall Mall, with an Address of Congratulation to the Prince Regent upon his accession to the throne as George the Fourth. We were a motley group, of various dimensions, dresses, and appearance. We advanced in a somewhat confused manner through a long room, with noblemen in waiting on each side, like statues, to the King, who was seated on a low throne at the further end. He was lusty, pappy, and pale, in a kind of uniform, and with a cocked hat, which on our approach he took off with inimitable gracefulness. Dr. Rees, our senior, a Presbyterian, and a fine-looking man, read the address. The King's air of supine-ness had given way to a mirthful smile, as he saw the satisfaction on our countenances when we were admitted to the royal presence. At the close of the address he read a brief reply, and then unexpectedly addressed us *impromptu* in these words:—"The manner in which you have spoken of my late revered father must touch every heart, and none more than my own (laying his hand upon his breast). You may assure yourselves, gentlemen, of a continuance, while I sway the sceptre, of all the privileges you enjoyed under his auspicious reign." To this we had almost audibly said, "hear, hear." When the King was informed that we waived the usual privilege of *all* kissing hands on account of the fatigue it would occasion him, and that as twelve only of the clergy had been permitted to do so, six only of our number would be selected for the honour, he smilingly observed, "O you may *all* kiss hands." Upon this we all fell in a most humiliating posture on our knees to kiss his extended hand. Some of those who were large and aged men, especially Doctors Rees and Waugh, had great difficulty in rising, and retired backwards in some confusion, not being accustomed to such a movement. As we retired, the King said to us, "You may stay in the adjoining room till I return.' While waiting there, we saw a small deputation of Quakers advancing with an address, which one of their number held before him in a frame. One of the pages coming towards them to take off their hats, Dr. Waugh, who loved a joke, said to the foremost Quaker in an audible whisper, "Persecution, brother"; to which the brother significantly replied, while pointing upwards, "Not so bad to take off the hat as the head." We saw the King again as he returned in procession, and departed well pleased. I believe we were all remarkably loyal in our prayers the next Sunday.'"

ECCENTRIC MR. BLACKBURN.

This gentleman, one of the oldest members of the House of Commons, was very absent: once, Captain Gronow gave him a letter to frank, which he deliberately opened, and read in the Captain's presence; and on being asked if it amused him, he replied that he did not understand what it meant.

Mr. Blackburn was intimate with the Duke of Gloucester: one day, he accompanied His Royal Highness to shoot pheasants; when, suddenly, Mr. B. observing that the Duke's gun was cocked, asked His Royal Highness whether he always carried his gun cocked. "Yes, Blackburn, always," was the reply. "Well then, good morning, your Royal Highness; I will no longer accompany you."

At dinner, he would never surrender his place at table, even to royalty; so the Duke was obliged to sit near him. Whenever the royal servant filled the Duke's glass with wine-and-water, Mr. B. invariably drank it off; until, at length, the Duke having secured a glass, drank it off and said, "Well, Blackburn, I have done you at last." After dinner, in the drawing-room, the servant in royal livery was holding a tray with a cup of tea for the Duke. Mr. Blackburn, seeing nobody took the cup of tea, determined on drinking it; the servant retired a little, but Blackburn followed, and persisted; upon which the servant said, "Sir, it is for His Royal Highness." "D—n his Royal Highness, I will have this tea" The Duke exclaimed "That's right, Blackburn," and ordered the servant to hand it to him.—***Captain Gronow's Reminiscences.***

IRISH WIFE-HUNTING.

An old Catholic family chanced to be in pecuniary difficulties, and a rich wife was the prescribed remedy. A priest, a friend of the family, who, as matrimony is one of the seven sacraments, thinks himself in duty bound to promote so salubrious a rite, was consulted. He gave a couple of taps to his gold snuff-box, protested that there are risks in celibacy, that it is needful to husband the constitution and the estate, and observing that the young squire, though a little pale, was a pretty fellow, put his finger to his nose, and hinted at a young damsel in Newrow (a penitent of his reverence, and a mighty good kind of young woman, not long come from the Cork convent), with ruddy cheeks, and vigorous arms, a robust waist and antigallican toes. The parties were brought together. The young gentleman stuttered a compliment, the heart of the young lady and her wooden fan were in a flutter; the question was popped. The old people put their heads together. Consideration of the marriage, high blood, and equity of redemption upon one side; and rude health and twenty thousand pounds on the other. The bargain was struck; and to ensure the hymeneal negotiation, nothing remained but that Counsellor Bellew should look over the settlements.

Accordingly, a Galway attorney prepared the draft marriage settlement, with a skin for every thousand, and waited on Mr. Bellew. Laying thirty guineas on the table, and thinking that upon the credit of such a fee he might presume to offer his opinion, he commenced with an ejaculation on the fall of the good old families, until Mr. Bellew, after counting the money, cast a Caius Marius look upon him, and awed him into respect He unrolled the volume of parchment, and the eye of the illustrious conveyancer glistened at the sight of the ancient and venerable name that stood at the head of the indenture. But as he advanced through the labyrinth of limitations, he grew alarmed and disturbed, and on arriving at the words "on the body of the said Judy Mac Gilligan to be begotten," he dropped his pen, and put the settlement-away, with something of the look of a Frenchman, when he intimates his perception of an unusually bad smell. It was only after an interval of reflection, and when he had recalled the fiscal philosophy of Vespasian, that he was persuaded to resume his labours, but did not completely recover his tranquillity of mind, until turning the back of his brief, he marked that most harmonious of all monosyllables "paid," at the foot of the consolatory stipend.—***Savage's Irish Sketches.***

LONG STORIES.

Capt. George Robert Fitzgerald was one day rattling on in an ordinary, in a small town in Mayo county, when Mr. Garret Dillon, an old story-teller, shouted out: "Captain Fitzgerald, let me ask you this little question; do you intend to pay every man's club present?" "No, sir," replied Fitzgerald, "this is an ordinary, and not my private house." "Well, then, sir, as you have now for two long hours engrossed the whole talk to yourself, I lay down my watch on the table, and if you attempt to say a word for one hour, I will make it a personal matter with you." George Robert, to the surprise of the company, quietly submitted to the injunction; the hour passed on; Dillon told, as under restraint, some stories in his worst manner; and it was a relief to the company, when Fitzgerald, at the expiration of the injunction, with perfect good humour, commenced to talk as if he had never been interrupted.

SMALL SERVICE.

An English lady, who lived in the country, and was about to have a large dinner party, was ambitious of making as great a display as her husband's establishment, a tolerably large one, could furnish. So that there might seem to be no lack of servants, a great lad, who had been employed only in farm work, was trimmed and dressed for the occasion, and ordered to take his stand at the back of his mistress' chair, with strict injunctions not to stir from the place, nor do anything, unless she directed him; the lady well knowing, that, although no footman could make a better appearance as a piece of still life, some awkwardness would be inevitable, if he were put in motion. Accordingly, Thomas having thus been duly drilled and repeatedly enjoined, took his post at the head of the table, behind his mistress, and for awhile he found sufficient amusement in looking at the grand set-out, and staring at the guests: when he was weary of this, and of an inaction to which he was so little used, his eyes began to pry about nearer objects. It was at a time when our ladies followed the French fashion of having the back and shoulders under the name of the neck, uncovered much lower than accords either with the English climate, or with old English notions; a time when, as Landor expresses it, the usurped dominion of **neck** had extended from the ear downwards almost to where mermaids become fish. This lady was in the height, or lowness of that fashion; and between her shoulder-blades, in the hollow of the back, not far from the confines where nakedness and clothing met, Thomas espied what Pasquier had seen upon the neck of Mademoiselle des Roches.

The guests were too much engaged with the business and the courtesies of the table to see what must have been worth seeing, the transfiguration produced in Thomas's countenance by delight, when he saw so fine an opportunity of showing himself attentive, and making himself useful. The lady was too much occupied with her company to feel the flea; but, to her horror, she felt the great finger and thumb of Thomas upon her back, and, to her greater horror, heard him exclaim in exultation, to the still greater amusement of the party, "A vlea, a vlea! my lady, ecod I've caught 'en!"—*The Doctor.* [This reminds one of a story in Miss Hawkins's **Countess and Gertrude.**

A POSER.

At Plymouth there is, or was, a small green opposite the Government House, over which no one was permitted to pass. Not a creature was allowed to approach, save the General's cow; and the sentries had particular orders to turn away any one who ventured to cross the forbidden turf. One day old Lady D——, having called at the General's in order to make a short cut, bent her steps across the lawn, when she was arrested by the sentry calling out, and desiring her to return, and go the other road. She remonstrated; the man said he could not disobey his orders, which were to prevent any one crossing that piece of ground. "But," said Lady D——, with a stately air, "do you know who I am?" "I don't know who you be, ma'am," replied the immovable sentry, "but I knows who you b'aint—you b'aint the General's cow." So Lady D——wisely gave up the argument, and went the other way.

BEAU BRUMMEL.

Of all the beaux that ever flourished, exemplary of waistcoat and neckcloth, and having authoritative boots from which there was no appeal, Brummel appears to have been the chief He was born in 1778, and his father, having grown wealthy by speculating in the funds, sent young George Bryan Brummel, at the proper age, to Eton. There he was a general favourite, but was more distinguished for his love of fun and frolic than for study. Even at this early period he affected a peculiar elegance, and obtained from his schoolfellows the *sobriquet* of "Buck Brummel," the term **dandy** not being then in parlance.

Contests between the Etonians and the bargemen were frequent. Upon one of these occasions an unlucky bargee fell into the hands of the schoolboys, who, in resentment of their having been roughly handled by him in some previous quarrel, were about to fling him over the bridge into the river, when Brummel saved the poor fellow by exclaiming: "My good fellows, don't send him into the river! the man is evidently in a high state of perspiration, and it amounts almost to a certainty that he will catch cold!"

From Eton Brummel went to Oriel College, Oxford, where he did not remain long, for he was not much more than sixteen years old, when his father died, and in three months he was gazetted to a cornetcy in the 10th Hussars, then commanded by the Prince of Wales. Brummel had, when an Eton boy, been presented to the Prince on the terrace at Windsor Castle, and was soon received into high favour.

Brummel's assurance, at this early date, was sublime. A great law-lord gave a ball, at which a Miss J., one of the beauties of the day, was present; she declined all offers to dance until the young hussar made his appearance, and he, having proffered to lead her out, she acquiesced quietly, to the mortification of the disappointed candidates. In one of the pauses of the dance he found himself next an acquaintance, when he exclaimed, "Ha! you here? Do, my good fellow, tell me who that ugly man is leaning against the chimney-piece?" "Why, surely you must know him," replied the other; "'tis the master of the house." "No, indeed," said the cornet, coolly; "how should I? I never was invited."

Brummel soon grew weary of a soldier's life. His regiment, being at Brighton, was unexpectedly ordered to Manchester. The news arrived in the evening, and early next day Brummel made his appearance before the Prince of Wales, to whom he apologetically explained: "Why, the fact is, your Royal Highness, I have heard that we are ordered to Manchester. Now, you must be aware how disagreeable this is to *me!* I really could not go: think, your Royal Highness—*Manchester!* Besides, *you* would not be there. I have, therefore, determined, with your Royal Highness' permission, to sell out." The flattery was well-timed, and secured the Prince's acquiescence.

A year afterwards Brummel came into possession of his fortune, which had accumulated, during his minority, to thirty thousand pounds. He then took a house in May Fair, 4, Chesterfield-street, in which street George Selwyn resided some forty years previously. Brummel soon became famed for the excellence of his dinners, and the Prince was more than once his guest. Brummel subsequently removed to 22, South-street. He was not a mere coxcomb, but already a man of great shrewdness and observation, and strong satirical spirit. Madame de Stael is said to have stood in awe of him, and considered her having failed to please him as her greatest misfortune; while she placed the Prince of Wales having neglected to call upon her, only as a secondary cause of lamentation. However, Brummel is best known by his excess of affectation, which often resembled humour.

An acquaintance, in a morning call, having recently been travelling in the north of England, persisted in cross-questioning Brummel about the Lakes—which did he like best? Tired at length of affected raptures, Brummel turned to his valet, who chanced to be in the room—"Robinson?" "Sir?" "Which of the Lakes do I admire?" "Windermere, sir," replied the valet, who understood his master's humour. "Ah! yes, Windermere," repeated Brummel; "so it is,—Windermere."

The intimacy between Brummel and the Prince lasted some years; the quarrel which led to the estrangement is variously related: some said it was owing to Brummel desiring the Prince to ring the bell, an assertion which the Beau stoutly denied. Moore sings:

"Neither have I resentments, nor wish there should come ill
To mortal, except, now I think on't, to Beau Brummel;
Who threatened last year, in a superfine passion,
To cut me, and bring the old King into fashion."

Others said the offence arose from the friend's ridicule of the favourite mistress Fitzherbert. Brummel protested that it was he who had cut the Prince, in public, in the following manner:—Riding one day with a friend, who happened to be otherwise regarded, and encountering the Prince, who spoke to the friend, without noticing Brummel, he affected the air of one who waits aloof while a stranger is present; and then, when the great man was moving off, said to his companion, loud enough for the other to hear, "Eh! who is our fat friend?"

Although the loss of his royal friend estranged many from Brummel, they generally suffered for their timeserving. A notable instance of this occurred to a lady of fashion, named Thompson, residing near Grosvenor-square, and who had a formidable rival in a Mrs. Johnson of Finsbury-square. The West-end lady gave a ball, at which the Prince had consented to be present, Brummel of course not being invited. Great, then, was the lady's surprise when, at the moment she expected the Prince's arrival, in walked the unasked and obnoxious Beau Brummel The lady indignantly walked forth from the circle of her friends, and informed Brummel that he had not been invited. "Not invited, madam, not invited?" said the unwelcome visitor, in his blandest tones; "surely there must be some mistake;" and, leisurely feeling in all his pockets to spin out the time, and give a better chance for the Prince's arrival, while the hostess was in agony, he at length drew forth a card, which he presented to her. At a glance she saw it was that of her East-end rival, and, returning it hastily, she exclaimed, "That card, sir, is a Mrs. Johnson's; my name is Thompson." "Is it, indeed?" replied Brummel, affecting much surprise "Dear me, how unfortunate! really, Mrs. John—Thompson, I mean, I am very sorry for this mistake; but, you know, Johnson and Thompson, Thompson and Johnson, are so much the same kind of thing. Mrs. Thompson, I wish you a very good evening." And, making one of his most elaborate bows, he retired, slowly and mincingly, amidst the ill-suppressed laughter of all present, except the hostess herself, who was bursting with indignation, and totally at a loss to reply to such matchless effrontery. Here are a few more of Brummel's affectations, first collected in the **Literary Pocket-book.**

Having taken it into his head, at one time, to eat no vegetables, and being asked by a lady if he had never eaten any in his life, he said, "Yes, madam, I once ate a pea."

Being met limping in Bond-street, and asked what was the matter, he said he had hurt his leg, and "the worst of it was, it was his favourite leg."

Somebody inquiring where he was going to dine the next day, was told that he really did not know: "they put me in my coach, and take me somewhere."

He pronounced of a fashionable tailor that he made a good coat, an exceedingly good coat—all but the collar; nobody could achieve a good collar but his tailor.

Having borrowed some money of a City beau, whom he patronized in return, he was one day asked to repay it; upon which he thus complained to a friend, "Do you know what has happened?" "No." "Why, do you know, there's that fellow Tomkins, who lent me five hundred pounds; he has had the face to ask me for it; and yet I had called the dog Tom, and let myself dine with him."

"You have a cold, Mr. Brummel," observed one of a sympathising group. "Why, do you know," said he, "that on the Brighton-road, the other day, my infidel valet put me into a room with a damp stranger."

Being asked if he liked port, he said, with an air of difficult recollection, "Port? port?—oh, ***port!***—oh, ay; what, the hot intoxicating liquor so much drunk by the lower orders?"

A beggar petitioned him for charity, "even if it was only a farthing." "Fellow," said Brummel, softening the disdain of the appellation in the gentleness of his tone, "I don't know the coin."

Having thought himself invited to somebody's country-seat, and being given to understand, after one night's lodging, that he was in error, he told an unconscious friend in town, who asked him what sort of a place it was, "that it was an exceedingly good place for stopping one night in."

Speaking lightly of a man, and wishing to convey his maximum of contemptuous feeling, he said, "He is a fellow, now, that would send his plate up twice for soup."

It was his opinion, that port, not porter, should be taken with cheese. "A gentleman," said he, "never ***malts*** with his cheese; he always ***ports.***" Yet this is counter to his estimate of port.

It being supposed that he once failed in a matrimonial speculation, somebody condoled with him; upon which he smiled, with an air of better knowledge on that point, and said, with a sort of indifferent feel of his neckcloth, "Why, sir, the truth is, I had great reluctance in cutting the connexion, but what could I do? (Here he looked deploring and conclusive). Sir, I discovered that the wretch positively ate cabbage."

When he went visiting, he is reported to have taken with him costly and elaborate dressing apparatus, including a silver basin; "for," said he, "it is impossible to spit in clay."

On reference being made to him as to what sum would be sufficient to meet the annual expenditure for clothes, he said that, "with a moderate degree of prudence and economy, he thought it might be managed for eight hundred a year."

He told a friend that he was reforming his way of life. "For instance," said he, "I sup early, I take a—a—little lobster, an apricot-puff, or so, and some burnt champagne, about twelve; and my man gets me to bed by three."

Brummel maintained his supremacy in the fashionable world several years after he had been cast off by the Prince. But, in the end the Beau was ruined by gaming, and he was compelled to quit England, and take up his abode at Calais. It has been said, ludicrously enough, that Brummel and Bonaparte fell together. The Moscow of the former, according to his own account, was a crooked sixpence, to the possession of which his good fortune was attached, but which he unfortunately lost. Nevertheless, Brummel had not lost his friends: he subsisted long at Calais chiefly upon their bounty. He obtained the appointment of English Consul at Caen, where, however, he soon became deeply involved in debt: in the hope of getting a more lucrative situation, he addressed his former friend, Lord Palmerston, then in office, stating the consulate at Caen to be useless: his lordship thanked him for the information, but forgot to provide him with any other situation. He was again thrown upon the charity of his friends; but paralysis more than once attacked him; he was flung into prison at Caen by his French creditors, and confined there upwards of two months. On his release, he fell into idiotcy; he was placed by friends in the hospital of the *Bon Sauveur,* in a room that had once been occupied by the celebrated Bourrienne. Here he died, March, 30, 1840—a deplorable instance of wasted fortune and reckless folly, reminding us, that beaux, like princes, find but few real friends.

HOBY, THE BOOTMAKER.

Hoby, of St. James's-street, was not only the greatest and most fashionable bootmaker, but a Methodist preacher at Islington. He was said to employ three hundred workmen; and was privileged to say all sorts of things to his customers, whom he sometimes annoyed with his humour. Horace Churchill, an ensign in the Guards, one day entered Hoby's shop in a great passion, saying that his boots were so ill-made that he should never employ Hoby for the future. Hoby gravely called to his shopman, "John, close the shutters. It is all over with us. I must shut up shop. Ensign Churchill withdraws his custom from me."

Hoby was bootmaker to the Duke of Kent. Calling on his Royal Highness to try on some boots, the news arrived of Lord Wellington's great victory over the French army at Vittoria. The Duke was kind enough to mention the glorious news to Hoby, who coolly said: "If Lord Wellington had had any other bootmaker than myself, he would never have had his great and constant successes; for my boots and prayers bring his Lordship out of all his difficulties." He was bootmaker to the Duke of Wellington from his boyhood, and received innumerable orders in the Duke's handwriting, both from the Peninsula and France, which he always religiously preserved.

On one occasion the late Sir John Shelley came into Hoby's shop, to complain that his top-boots had split in several places. Hoby quietly said—"How did that happen, Sir John?" "Why, in walking to my stables." "Walking to your stables?" said Hoby, with a sneer; "I made the boots for riding, not walking."—***Captain Gronow's Reminiscences.***

AN ULTIMATUM.

A luckless undergraduate of Cambridge being examined for his degree, and failing in every subject upon which he was tried, complained that he had not been questioned upon the things which he knew. Upon which the examining master tore off about an inch of paper, and pushing it towards him, desired him to write upon that all he knew.—*The Doctor.*

SCOTTISH CONVIVIALITY

"It is hardly possible," says Lord Cockburn, "to realize the scenes which took place in society fifty years back. In many houses, when a party dined, the ladies going away was the signal for the commencement of a system of compulsory conviviality. No one was allowed to shirk. 'No daylight, no heeltaps,' was the wretched jargon in which were expressed the propriety and the duty of seeing that the glass, when filled, must be emptied and drained. The supper which came after the early Scotch dinner had a peculiar tendency to foster these toping customs. The master of the feast said, 'Let there be tumblers,' and there were tumblers in more senses than one, the guests at these symposia frequently disappearing beneath the table. It was not a custom merely, but involved a different moral view, and theory of social life. The duty of hospitality was so misinterpreted that, in one case which he mentions, a London merchant, of formal manners and temperate habits, was pursued from the table of his host to his bedroom, and bottles and glasses were brought to his bedside, when, losing all patience, the wretched victim gasped out in his indignation, 'Sir, your hospitality borders upon brutality.'"

Of this deep-rooted character, Dean Ramsay relates the following illustration, communicated to him as coming from Mr. Mackenzie, the well-known author of the *Man of Feeling.* Mackenzie had been involved in a regular drinking-party, and was keeping as free from the usual excesses as he was able, when, as he marked companions around him falling victims to the power of drink, his attention was called to a small pair of hands that were working at his throat. On asking what it was, a voice replied, "Sir, I'm the lad that's to louse the neckcloths." To such an extent were the guests liable to become helpless, and such was the risk of apoplexy or suffocation, from their inability to untie their cravats, that it was the appointed duty of one of the household in this instance to perform this office for the protection of their jugulars.

There had been a carousing party at Colonel Grant's, the late Lord Seafield; and, as the evening advanced towards morning, two Highlanders were in attendance to carry the guests upstairs, it being understood that none could by any other means arrive at their sleeping apartments. One or two of the guests, however, whether from their abstinence or their superior strength of head, were walking upstairs, and declined the proffered assistance. The attendants were utterly astonished, and indignantly exclaimed, "Aigh, it's sare cheenged times at Castle Grant, when gentlemens can gang to bed on their ain feet."

Formerly in Scotland a funeral was a feast, and sometimes a fortune was well-nigh consumed in celebrating the great event. In the account of the funeral expenses of Sir Hugh Campbell, of Calder or Cawdor, there were charges for an enormous quantity of food and drink consumed. At the funeral of Mrs. Forbes, of Culloden, the mourners all got drunk. The festivities were conducted by her son Duncan, well known as the Lord President Forbes. The company sat so long and drank so freely, that when the word was given for the procession to form, and for the mourners to march to the burial-ground, the coffin was forgotten. The whole troop of jolly mourners found themselves at the grave with nothing to put in it. Special messengers were sent back for the poor dead lady, whose remains were "then deposited in the grave with all the decorum which could be mustered in such anti-funereal circumstances."

Nor were such death-scenes peculiar to the Highlands. There is a singular story told of Lord Forglen, on the authority of Auchinleck, James Boswell's father. On the day of Lord Forglen's death, his physician called on him as usual. "How does my lord do?" inquired the doctor, as he entered the house. "I houp he's weel," answered the manservant, with a solemnity which told what he meant. The doctor was then shown into a room where two dozen of wine were laid out under a table. Other persons presently came in, and the manservant, making them all sit down, began to describe to them his master's last moments, and, at the same time, to push the bottle about briskly. After a glass or two, the company rose to depart; but they were detained by the man. "No, no, gentlemen; not so," he said, "it was the express will o' the dead that I should fill ye a' fou, and I maun fulfil the will o' the dead." "And, indeed," said the doctor, who afterwards told the story, "he did fulfil the will o' the dead; for, before the end o't, there was na ane o' us able to bite his ain thoomb."

Of the reckless Scotchman, Dr. Archibald Pitcairn was a good example. He was an Edinburgh physician of high repute, a man of great wit and pleasantry, a hater of Calvinism, a supposed atheist, and a dreadful Bacchanalian. He would sometimes be drunk twice a-day. It was the habit of professional men in those days to meet their clients in some tavern; and it is told of him that he ordered his servants, whenever he should be detained at the tavern overnight, to provide him with a clean shirt next morning. They obeyed his orders on one occasion, day after day, till the number of clean shirts amounted to six, all of which he duly put on; but when he made his way home, it was discovered that the whole six were upon him, one over the other.

At Glasgow, forty years ago, when the time had come for the ***bowl*** to be introduced, some jovial and thirsty member of the company proposed as a toast, "The trade of Glasgow, and ***the outward bound***" The hint was taken, and silks and satins moved off to the drawing-room.

LADY BLESSINGTON AT GORE HOUSE.

Wilberforce, the philanthropist, resided in Gore House, just one mile from the turnpike at Hyde Park Corner, from 1808 until 1821: with its three acres of pleasure-ground, and fine old trees, it was then a delightful retreat. After the philanthropist, a few unknown persons held the place ere the next celebrity, one of a totally opposite character, reigned: this was Lady Blessington, who came to reside here in 1836; and the opposition of ideas called forth by these tenants seems to have suggested to James Smith this ***impromptu:***

"Mild Wilberforce, by all beloved,
Once owned this hallowed spot,
Whose zealous eloquence improved
The fettered Negro's lot;
Yet here still slavery attacks
When Blessington invites:
The chains from which he freed the blacks,
She rivets on the whites."

To Gore House came novelists and dramatists and poets, actors, statesmen, and refugees. "Here Louis Napoleon, just escaped from captivity at Ham, first came for the shelter of an English roof; and afterwards—deep lesson, too—a few years later, she went forth as privately, perhaps, as her guest had entered, from the palace of which she had been queen, to seek in the capital of him whom she had harboured that support she had so freely bestowed on him; the late refugee then having an empire rapidly falling into his hands. Her object was not gained, and on this occasion 'hope left a wretched one that sought her.' Lady Blessington finally quitted Gore House, April 14, 1849."

During a continental tour, Lady Blessington was introduced to the Count D'Orsay. "He was a great favourite of Lord Blessington, whose daughter by his first wife was, when quite a young girl, fetched from school to marry him; and a promise also is said to have been given from the Count to his Lordship, and from the Count's mother to Lady Blessington, that they (the Count and her Ladyship) would never leave each other. Be that as it may, they lived together for above a quarter of a century, and increase of years seemed still stronger to consolidate the engagement. D'Orsay led a gay and extravagant life in London, considerably beyond his means, in great measure appearing to consider his patronage sufficient payment. He undoubtedly possessed great abilities, was an excellent artist, and a humourist of the first water. But his conduct to his wife was cruel in the extreme: she was spurned by him entirely, he still pocketing an income from her father's estates! For a long time he could only make his exit from Gore House on Sundays, for fear of arrest; and his extravagances vastly accelerated the day of retribution. He and Lady Blessington retired to Paris, and Gore House was stripped of its contents by public sale. There, whatever was the cause, they met not with the reception anticipated. Lady Blessington died soon after, on June 4, 1849. D'Orsay designed her monument, and in little more than three years after, his career was ended. He died July 1, 1852."—*Davis's Memorials of Knightsbridge.*

The Count D'Orsay painted an interesting memorial of Gore House, and its celebrities: a view in the pleasure-grounds in the rear of the mansion, with portraits of the Duke of Wellington, Lady Blessington, the painter (D'Orsay), and other celebrities.

DISTINCTIONS OF DRESS.

The meeting of two gentlemen in a theatre lobby is a happy illustration of the confusion a similarity of dress occasions. Coming from different points, each in a great hurry, one addressed the other with, "Pray, are you the box-keeper?" "No," replied the other; "are you?"

Girard, the famous French painter, when very young, was the bearer of a letter of introduction to Lanjuinais, then of the Council of Napoleon. The young painter was shabbily attired, and his reception was extremely cold; but Lanjuinais discovered in him such striking proofs of talent, good sense, and amiability, that, on Girard's rising to take leave, he rose too, and accompanied his visitor to the antechamber. The change was so striking, that Girard could not avoid an expression of surprise. "My young friend," said Lanjuinais, anticipating the inquiry, "we receive an unknown person according to his dress—we take leave of him according to his merit."

PRUDENTIAL CONSIDERATION.

The lady of a distinguished officer died in one of our colonies, just previous to which she expressed a wish to be buried in England, and was, accordingly, deposited in a cask of rum, for the purpose of transport home, but remained in the cellar after the officer's second marriage; the detention being occasioned by his expectation that the duty on the spirit imported into England, in which the dear departed was preserved, would, in a few years, be either lowered or taken off altogether! Strange as this may seem, it is true.—*Theodore Hook.*

PLEASURES OF A CROWD.

"Pray, sir," said a person who had previously been the backmost of a crowd, to another who had just joined it; "pray, sir, have the kindness not to press upon me; it is unnecessary, since there is no one behind to press upon you!" "But there may be presently," said the other; "besides, sir, where's the good of being in a crowd, if one mayn't shove?"—*Poole.*

BORE-CIDE.

A certain well-known provincial bore, having left a tavern party, of which Burns was one, he, the bard, immediately demanded a bumper, and addressing himself to the chairman, said: "I give you the health, gentlemen all, of the waiter that called my Lord out of the room."—*Lockhart.*

"THERE'S A LANGUAGE THAT'S MUTE."

A gentleman, one Sunday morning, was attracted to watch a young country girl on the high road from the village to the church, by observing that she looked hither and thither, this way and that upon the road, as if she had lost her thimble. The bells were **settling** for prayers, and there was no one visible on the road except the girl and the gentleman, who recognised in her the errand-maid of a neighbouring farmer. "What are you looking for, my girl?" asked the gentleman, as the damsel continued to pore along the dusty road. She answered, gravely: "Sir, I'm looking to see if my master be gone to church." Now, her master had *a wooden leg.*

PERSONAL RETALIATION.

Tom Raikes, who was very much marked with the smallpox, having one day written an anonymous letter to Count D'Orsay, containing some piece of impertinence, had closed it with a wafer, and stamped it with something resembling the top of a thimble. The Count soon discovered who was the writer, and in a roomful of company, thus addressed him: "Ha! ha! my good Raikes, the next time you write an anonymous letter, you must not seal it with your nose."

LORD ALVANLEY.

Among the witticisms attributed to Lord Alvanley is a **bon mot,** which gave rise to the belief that Solomon, the Jew money-lender, caused the downfall and disappearance of Brummel; for, on some friends of his observing that if he bad remained in London, something might have been done for him by his old associates, Alvanley replied, "He has done quite right to be off; it was Solomon's judgment."

When Sir Lumley Skeffington's spectacle of the *Sleeping Beauty,* produced at a great expense on the stage, reappeared after some years' seclusion, Alvanley, on being asked who that smart-looking individual was, answered, "It is a second edition of the *Sleeping Beauty,* bound in calf, richly gilt, and illustrated by many cuts."

A gay man named Judge, imprisoned in the King's Bench, was said to be the first instance of a judge reaching the *bench* without being previously called to the bar; to which Alvanley replied, "Many a bad judge has been taken from the bench and placed at the bar."

"SWEERING AT LAIRGE."

A late Duke of Atholl had invited a well-known personage, a writer of Perth, to come up and meet him at Dunkeld for the transaction of some business. The Duke mentioned the day and hour when he should receive the man of law, who accordingly came punctually at the appointed time and place. But the Duke had forgotten the appointment, and gone to the hill, from which he would not return for some hours. A Highlander present described the Perth writer's indignation, and his mode of showing it, by a most elaborate course of swearing. "But whom did he swear at? was the inquiry made of the narrator, who replied, "Ou, he didna sweer at onything parteecular, but juist stude in ta middle of ta road and swoor at lairge." "Sweering at lairge," however, even in former days, was more the tendency of the upper classes than of the Scottish peasantry, one of whom thus rebuked the late Lord Rutherford on his exclaiming gruffly at the Scottish climate, "What a d—mist!" The shepherd, a tall, grim figure, turned sharp round upon him. "What ails you at the mist, sir? It wats the grass and slockens the ewes;" adding, with much solemnity, "It's God's wull," and there upon he turned from his Lordship with lofty indignation.

MATTER-OF-FACT-MEN.

"You must beware," says Charles Lamb, "of indirect expressions before a Caledonian. Clap an extinguisher on your irony, if you are unhappily blest with a vein of it. Remember, you are upon your oath. I have a print, a graceful female, after Leonardo da Vinci, which I was showing off to Mr.—. After he had examined it minutely, I asked him how he liked "my beauty" (a foolish name it goes by among my friends), when he very gravely assured me that he 'had very considerable respect for my character and talents'—so he was pleased to say—'but had not given himself much thought for the degree of my personal pretensions.'"

Lamb was present at a party of North Britons, where a son of Burns was expected, and happened to drop a silly expression in his South British way, that he wished it were the father instead of the son, when four of them started up at once, that it was impossible, because he (the father) was dead.

MARVELLOUS OYSTER-EATING.

"While I was at Versailles," narrates the author of the ***Physiologie de Gout,*** "I came frequently in contact with M. Laperte, who was voraciously fond of oysters, of which he complained he could never get his bellyful. This pleasure I resolved to give him, and for that purpose invited him to dine with me. He came. I kept company with him to the third dozen of oysters, and then allowed him to go on alone. He swallowed on steadily' to the ***thirty-second dozen***—that is to say, during more than an hour—when I stopped my guest just as he remarked, that he was ***beginning*** to enjoy his treat. "Alas!" I exclaimed, "it is quite clear that you are not to have your bellyful of oysters to-day. Let us begin dinner." We dined, and Laperte acquitted himself with the vigour and appetite of a man who had been suffering from a long fast."

THE LATE MARQUIS OF HERTFORD.

One day, when the noble marquis was going alone from Aldborough to Sudborne, on the road he met a cart with one horse, deeply laden with coals, which, from the badness of the road, and the deepness of the ruts, was in great danger of being overturned; the marquis endeavoured to pass it, when the carter, not knowing who the stranger was, said to his lordship, "Come, ya' a might tie your horse to a tree and come and help me." At this request the marquis instantly stopped and dismounted, asking the carter what he should do to help him? "Why, lay hold here and shove hard," was the ready reply, which, being complied with, they together soon got the cart out of the difficulty: the marquis then asked if there was anything more to do. "Why, no," said the carter, feeling his pocket; "if I had sixpence I would give it thee, but if you ***wool*** go down to the Crown with me, you shall take part of a pot of beer." The marquis declined the offer and mounted; the countryman, however, observed, "Why, you ride a very good horse; perhaps we shall see one another again." "That may be," was the reply; "but it is not very likely, and here is a half-crown for you to drink the Marquis of Hertford's health," and then rode on, leaving the poor fellow in fear and astonishment, at the event that had passed.

It will be recollected by some readers that the former church of St Dunstan-in-the-West, Fleet-street, within memory possessed one of London's wonders: it had a large gilt dial overhanging the street, and above it two figures of savages, life-size, carved in wood, and standing beneath a pediment, each having in his right hand a club, with which he struck the quarters upon a suspended bell, moving his head at the same time. To see the men strike was considered very attractive; and opposite St. Dunstan's was a famous field for pickpockets, who took advantage of the gaping crowd. Among those who were struck by the oddity of the figures was the Marquis of Hertford, who, when a child, and a good child, was taken by his nurse to see the giants of St. Dunstan's as a reward; and he used to say, when he grew to be a man he would buy those giants. Many a child of rich parents may have said the same; but, in the present case, the Marquis kept his word. When the old church of St. Dunstan was taken down, in 1830, Lord Hertford attended the second sale of the materials, and purchased the clock, bells, and figures for 200*l.*; and he had them placed at the entrance to the grounds of his villa in the Regent's-park, thence called "St Dunstan's Villa;" and here the figures do duty to the present day.

"ARMS FOUND."

Mrs. Butler, in her entertaining *Journal,* relates this droll story:—A gentleman of New York sent a die of his crest to a manufacturer, to have it put upon his gig-harness. The man sent home the harness when it was finished, but without the die: after sending for it several times, the owner called, when the reply was, "Oh, why, I didn't know you wanted it" "I tell you I wish to have it back." "Oh, pooh, pooh! you can't want it much now, do you?" "I tell you, sir, I desire to have the die back immediately." Ah, well, come now, what'll you take for it?" "D'ye think I mean to sell my crest? Why, you might as well ask me to sell my name." "Why, you see, a good many folks have seen it, and want to have it on their harness, as it's a pretty looking concern enough."

MATHEMATICS AT FAULT.

An English nobleman in Paris proposed to run his horse against time, at a rate which appeared to be impossible. He found plenty of persons to take bets, and he staked an immense sum on the event. Some friendly *savans* tried in vain to dissuade him from abiding the event: for they assured him that besides losing his fortune he would kill his horse. Nay, they proved it mathematically. They reckoned the volume of air the horse would displace at each bound, multiplied the weight of this by the necessary velocity, ascertained the strength of the horse by a dynamometer; and putting W for the weight, V for the velocity, and P for the power, proved, without running far into the calculus, that the achievement was impossible. The sporting man thanked his scientific friends, testified to the wonders of mathematics, ran his horse—and won!

Again, while the **Great Western** steam-ship was on the stocks at Bristol, one of the philosophers at the meeting of the British Association, which was held at the time in that city, calculated away the possibility of the steamer ever crossing the Atlantic. He computed that, for each horse-power of steam, one ton of coals would be required for every 1,425 miles. "Taking this as a basis of the calculation," he said, "and allowing one-fourth of a ton of coals per horse-power as spare fuel, the tonnage necessary for the fuel and machinery, on a voyage from England to New York, would be 370 tons per horse-power, which, for a vessel with engines of 400 horse-power, would be 1,480 tons." Now, as the tonnage of the **Great Western** was only 1,340 tons, with engines of 450 horse-power, for her to cross the Atlantic was, according to the theorist, utterly impossible. The "impossibility" was, however, performed, some twelve times per year, from the launch of the ship in 1838.

COMMERCIAL PEERAGES.

Among recent creations it may be mentioned that the title of Lord Belper, in 1856, was chosen by Mr. Strutt, on account of his family connexion with that place, to the manufacturing prosperity of which his uncle, the late Mr. Jedediah Strutt, contributed so largely. In the retiring address which he issued to his constituents on accepting the Chiltern Hundreds, prior to his elevation to the peerage, Lord Belper alluded to his own position as being still a manufacturer, thus identifying himself still with the order from which he is sprung. "The name, style, and title" which his Lordship chose, is almost better known upon the Continent than in this country, for there is scarcely a woman who plies her knitting-needle in the towns and villages of Germany but makes use of materials on the wrapper of which the name of Belper is printed in large characters. It may be of interest to remark here that Lord Belper is by no means the first person of commercial antecedents and connexions who has been raised to the peerage. Though George III. was very averse to the elevation of any one except members of the old county families, he created the London banker, Mr. Robert Smith, Lord Carrington, and conferred the Rendlesham peerage on the Thellussons. William IV. revived the barony of Ashburton in the person of Mr. Alexander Baring, who was many years head of the great commercial house which bears his name; and since the accession of her Majesty, Mr. Poulett-Thompson, of Manchester, and Mr. Jones Loyd, of Lothbury, have been respectively gazetted as Lord Sydenham and Lord Overstone. The case of Lord Belper, however, differs in one respect from that of the above noblemen, inasmuch as it is understood that his elevation to the peerage does not imply that he has withdrawn from his manufacturing engagements.

A RICHMOND HOAX.

One of the best practical jokes in Theodore Hook's clever **Gilbert Gurney** is Daly's hoax upon the lady who had never been at Richmond before, or, at least, knew none of the peculiarities of the place. Daly desired the waiter, after dinner, to bring some "maids of honour"—those cheesecakes for which the place has time out of mind been celebrated. The lady stared, then laughed, and asked, "What do you mean by 'maids of honour'?" "Dear me!" said Daly, "don't you know that this is so courtly a place, and so completely under the influence of state etiquette, that everything in Richmond is called after the functionaries of the palace? What are called cheesecakes elsewhere, are here called maids of honour; a capon is called a lord chamberlain; a goose is a lord steward; a roast pig is a master of the horse; a pair of ducks, grooms of the bedchamber; a gooseberry tart, a gentleman usher of the black rod; and so on." The unsophisticated lady was taken in, when she actually saw the maids of honour make their appearance in the shape of cheesecakes; she convulsed the whole party by turning to the waiter, and desiring him, in a sweet, but decided tone, to bring her a gentleman usher of the black rod, if they had one in the house quite cold!

SCOTTISH SERVANTS.

Dean Ramsay, in his very characteristic **Reminiscences,** illustrating the habits of old Scottish domestic servants, relates several amusing traits of their eccentricity, telling of simpler times than the present.

An instance of *fixedness* is afforded by an old coachman long in the service of a noble lady, and who gave all the trouble and annoyance which he conceived were the privileges of his position in the family. At last, the lady fairly gave him notice to quit, and told him he must go. The only satisfaction she got was the quiet answer, "Na, na, my lady; I druve ye to your marriage, and I shall stay to drive ye to your burial."

A gentlewoman's praise of English mutton was a great annoyance to the Scottish prejudices of Sandy, who had been fifty years domesticated in the family. One day, however, he had a real triumph upon the subject. The smell of the joint roasting had become very offensive through the house. The lady called out to Sandy to have the doors closed, adding, "That must be some horrid Scotch mutton you have got." To his delight, this was a leg of English mutton his mistress had expressly chosen. She significantly told a friend, "Sandy never let that down upon me."

Boaty, who long acted as Charon of the Dee at Banchory, was a first-rate salmon-fisher, and was much sought for by amateurs. One day he was in attendance with his boat on a sportsman, who caught salmon after salmon, and between each fish-catching took a pull at his flask, without offering Boaty any participation in the refreshment. Boaty got annoyed, and seeing no prospect of amendment, deliberately pulled the boat to shore, shouldered the oars, rods, landing-nets, and fishing apparatus, which he had provided, and set off homeward. His companion, keen for more sport, was amazed, and peremptorily ordered him to come back. But all the answer made by the offended Boaty was, "No, no; them 'at drink by themsells may just fish by themsells."

At a large dinner-party, one of the family noticed that a guest—Mrs. Murray—was looking for the proper spoon to help herself with salt The old servant, Thomas, was appealed to; he took no notice, and was appealed to more peremptorily, "Thomas, Mrs. Murray has not a salt-spoon," to which he replied most emphatically, "Last time Mrs. Murray dined here, we *lost* a salt-spoon."

An old servant, who took a similar charge of everything that went on in the family, having observed that his master thought he had drank wine with every lady at the table, but had overlooked one, jogged his memory with the question, "What ails ye at her wi' the green gown?"

An old servant was standing at a sideboard, and attending to the wants of a pretty large dinner-party; when the calls grew so numerous and frequent, that the attendant got bewildered, lost his temper, and at length, he gave vent to his indignation in this remonstrance, addressed to the whole company, "Cry a' thegither, that's the way to be served."

An aged Forfarshire lady, knowing the habits of her old and spoilt servant, when she wished a note to be taken without loss of time, held it open, and read it over to him, saying, "There, noo, Andrew, ye ken a' that's in't; noo dinna stop to open it, but jast send it aff."

A nursery-maid was leading a little child up and down a garden. "Is't a laddie or a lassie?" asked the gardener. "A laddie," said the maid. "Weel," said he, "I'm glad o' that, for there's ower many women in the world." "Heck, man," said Jess, "did ye no ken there's aye maist sawn o' the best crap?"

POWER OF THE EYE.

When Thomas Grenville was a young man he one day dined with Lord Spencer at Wimbledon. Among the company was George Pitt (afterwards Lord Rivers), who declared that he could tame the most furious animal by looking at it steadily. Lord Spencer said, "Well, there is a mastiff in the courtyard here which is the terror of the neighbourhood, will you try your powers on him?" Pitt agreed to do so; and the company descended into the courtyard. A servant held the mastiff by a chain. Pitt knelt down at a short distance from the animal, and stared him sternly in the face. They all shuddered. At a signal given, the mastiff was let loose, and rushed furiously towards Pitt—then suddenly checked his pace, seemed confounded, and, leaping over Pitt's head, ran away, and was not seen for many hours afterwards.

Mr. Rogers, who relates this story, tells us also how he profited by Pitt's experience, as follows:—"During one of my visits to Italy, while I was walking a little before my carriage, on the road, not far from Vicenza, I perceived two huge dogs nearly as tall as myself, bounding towards me from out a gateway, though there was no house in sight. I recollected what Pitt had done; and, trembling from head to foot, I yet had resolution enough to stand quite still and eye them with a fixed look. They gradually relaxed their speed from a gallop to a trot, came up to me, stopped for a moment, and then went back again."

RUINOUS EPICURISM.

A gentleman of Gloucestershire had one son, whom he sent abroad, to make the grand tour of the Continent, where he paid more attention to the cookery of nations and luxurious living, than anything else. Before his return, his father died, and left him a large fortune. He now looked over his notebook to discover where the most exquisite dishes were to be had, and the best cooks obtained. Every servant in his house was a cook; his butler, footman, housekeeper, coachman, and grooms—all were cooks. He had also three Italian cooks—one from Florence, another from Sienna, and a third from Viterbo—for dressing one Florentine dish! He had a messenger constantly on the road between Brittany and London, to bring the eggs of a certain sort of plover found in the former country. He was known to eat a single dinner at the expense of 50*l.*, though there were but two dishes. In nine years he found himself getting poor, and this made him melancholy. When totally ruined, having spent 150,000*l.*, a friend one day gave him a guinea to keep him from starving; and he was found in a garret next day **broiling an ortolan,** for which he had paid a portion of the guinea!

POLITICAL LIFE.

INTEGRITY OF EARL STANHOPE.

THIS eminent soldier, who carried arms under King William III. in Flanders, and under the Duke of Schomberg and Earl of Peterborough, at the close of his military career, became an active Whig leader in Parliament, took office under Sunderland, and was soon after raised to the peerage. His death was very sudden. He was of a constitutionally warm and sensitive temper. In the course of the discussion of the South Sea Company's affairs, which so unhappily involved some of the leading members of the Government, the Duke of Wharton (Feb. 4, 1721) made some severe remarks in the House of Lords, comparing the conduct of ministers to that of Sejanus, who had made the reign of Tiberius hateful to the old Romans. Stanhope, in rising to reply, spoke with such vehemence in vindication of himself and his colleagues, that he burst a blood-vessel, and died the next day. "May it be eternally remembered," says the **British Merchant,** "to the honour of Earl Stanhope, that he died poorer in the King's service than when he came into it Walsingham, the great Walsingham, died poor; but the great Stanhope lived in the time of the South Sea temptations!"

PHILIP, EARL OF CHESTERFIELD.

When the independent Philip, 2d Earl of Chesterfield, made one of his occasional visits to the House of Lords (from Geneva), a new doorkeeper, seeing him about to press into the House in a dress of extreme simplicity, impeded his entrance with this remark, "Now then, honest man, go back! you can have no business in such a place as this, honest man!"

EXECUTION OF LORDS KILMARNOCK AND BALMERINO.

Walpole relates many eccentric traits of these Rebel Lords, on their trial and execution. When they were to be brought from the Tower in separate coaches, there was some dispute in which the axe must go—old Balmerino cried, "Come, come, put it with me." At the bar, he played with his fingers upon the axe, while he talked to the gentleman-gaoler; and one day, somebody coming up to listen, he took the blade, and held it like a fan between their faces. During the trial, a little boy was near him, but not tall enough to see; he made room for the child, and placed him near himself. He said that one of his reasons for pleading **not guilty** was, that so many ladies might not be disappointed of their show.

At the trial, Lord Leicester went up -to the Duke of Newcastle, and said, "Never heard so great an orator as Lord Kilmarnock! if I was your Grace, I would pardon him, and make him **paymaster;**" alluding to Mr. Pitt, who had lately been preferred to that post, from the fear the ministry had of his abusive eloquence.

George Selwyn begged Sir William Saunderson to get him the High Steward's wand, after it was broke, as a curiosity; but that he behaved so like an attorney the first day, and so like a pettifogger the second, that he would not take it to light his fire with.

Lady Cromartie, who is said to have drawn her husband into the Rebellion, went to Leicester House, with four of her children, to bespeak the interest of the Princess of Wales for her lord. The Princess saw her, and made no other answer than by bringing in her own children, and placing them by her; "which," says Gray, "if true, is one of the prettiest things I ever heard." Lord Cromartie was reprieved.

Balmerino kept up his spirits to the same pitch of gaiety. In the cell at Westminster, he showed Lord Kilmarnock how he must lay his head; bid him not wince, lest the stroke should cut his skull or his shoulders, and advised him to bite his lips. As they were to return, he begged they might have another bottle together, as they should never meet any more till—, then pointed to his neck. At getting into the coach, he said to the gaoler, "Take care, or you'll break my shins with this damned axe."

Lord Kilmarnock was extremely poor: he had been known to dine with a man who sold pamphlets at Storey's-gate, St James's-park; and the man at the tennis-court said, "he would often have been glad if I would have taken him home to dinner." He was certainly so poor, that in one of his wife's intercepted letters she tells him she has plagued her steward for a fortnight for money, and can get but three shillings. The Duke of Argyle telling him how sorry he was to see him engaged in such a cause, "My lord," says he, "for the two kings and their rights I cared not a farthing which prevailed; but I was starving, and, by God, if Mahomet had set up his standard in the Highlands, I had been a good Mussulman for bread, and stuck close to the party, for I must eat."

At the Tower they stopped up Balmerino's windows because he talked to the populace; then he had only one, which looked directly upon all the scaffolding. They brought in the death-warrant at his dinner. His wife fainted. He said, "Lieutenant, with your damned warrant you have spoilt my lady's stomach."

Walpole was not at the execution of the Rebel Lords, but had two persons come to him directly, who were at the next house to the scaffold; and he saw another person who was on it. Just before they came out of the Tower, Balmerino drank a bumper to King James's health. As the clock struck ten they came forth on foot, Lord Kilmarnock all in black, his hair unpowdered in a bag, supported by Forster, the great Presbyterian, and by Mr. Home, a young clergyman; his friend, Lord Balmerino, followed alone, in a blue coat, turned up with red (his rebellious regimentals), a flannel waistcoat, and his shroud beneath; their hearses following. They were conducted to a house near the scaffold. Here they parted. Balmerino embraced the other, and said, "My lord, I wish I could Buffer for both!"

Kilmarnock remained an hour and a half in the house. At last he came to the scaffold, certainly much terrified, but with a resolution that prevented his behaving in the least meanly or unlike a gentleman. "When he beheld the fatal scaffold covered with black cloth, the executioner with his axe and his assistants, the sawdust, which was soon to be drenched with his blood, the coffin prepared to receive the limbs which were yet warm with life—above all, the immense display of human countenances which surrounded the scaffold like a sea, all eyes bent on the sad object of the preparation—his natural feelings broke forth in a whisper to the friend on whose arm he leaned, 'Home, this is terrible!' No sign of indecent timidity, however, affected his behaviour." (Sir Walter Scott.) He took no notice of the crowd; only to desire that the baize might be lifted up from the rails that the mob might see the spectacle. He stood and prayed some time with Forster, who wept over him, exhorted and encouraged him. He delivered a long speech to the sheriff, and, with a noble manliness, stuck to the recantation he had made at his trial; declaring he wished that all who embarked in the same cause might meet the same fate. He then took off his bag, coat, and waistcoat, with great composure, and, after some trouble, put on a napkin-cap, and then several times tried the block; the executioner, who was in white, with a white apron, out of tenderness, concealing the axe behind himself At last, the earl knelt down, with a visible unwillingness to depart, and, after five minutes, dropped his handkerchief, the signal, and his head was cut off at once, only hanging by a bit of skin, and was received in a scarlet cloth by four of the undertaker's men, kneeling, who wrapped it up and put it into the coffin with the body; orders having been given not to expose the heads, as used to be the custom.

The scaffold was immediately new strewn with saw-dust, the block new covered, the executioner new dressed, and a new axe brought. Then came old Balmerino, treading with the air of a general. As he mounted the scaffold, he read the inscription on his coffin, as he did again afterwards: he then surveyed the spectators, who were in amazing numbers, even upon masts of ships in the river, and, pulling out his spectacles, read a speech, which is variously reported. . . . He said, if he had not taken the sacrament the day before, he would have knocked down Williamson, the Lieutenant of the Tower, for his ill usage of him. He took the axe and felt it, and asked the headsman how many blows he had given Lord Kilmarnock; and gave him three guineas. Two clergymen, who attended him, coming up, he said, "No, gentlemen, I believe you have already done me all the service you can." Then he went to the corner of the scaffold, and called very loud for the warder to give him his perriwig, which he took off; and put on a nightcap of Scotch plaid, and then pulled off his coat and waistcoat and lay down; but being told he was on the wrong side, vaulted round, and immediately gave the sign by tossing up his arm, as if he were giving the signal for battle. He received three blows, but the first certainly took away all sensation. He was not a quarter of an hour on the scaffold; Lord Kilmarnock above half a one. Balmerino certainly died with the intrepidity of a hero, but with the insensibility of one too. As he walked from his prison to execution, seeing every window and top of house filled with spectators, he cried out, "Look, look, how they are all piled up like rotten oranges."

EXECUTION OF SIMON LORD LOVAT.

Of this cunning old creature, whose character seems a mixture of tyranny and pride in his villainy, Walpole relates some strange extravagances. In his own Highland domain, he governed despotically, either burning or plundering the lands or houses of his open enemies, or taking off his secret ones by the assistance of his cook, who was his poisoner in chief. He had two servants who married each other without his consent; he said "You shall have enough of each other," and stowed them in a dungeon that had been a well, for three weeks. "When he came to the Tower, he told them, that if he were not so old and infirm, they would find it difficult to keep him there. They told him they had kept much younger. "Yes," said he, "but they were inexperienced: they had not broke so many gaols as I have." At his own house, he used to say, that for thirty years of his life he never saw a gallows but it made his neck ache. His last act was to shift his treason upon his eldest son, whom he forced into the rebellion. He told Williamson, the Lieutenant of the Tower, "We will hang my eldest son, and then my second shall marry your niece." One day, that Williamson complained that he could not sleep, he was so haunted with *rats*—he replied, "What do you say, that you are so haunted with ***Ratcliffes?***"

The first day, as he was brought to his trial, a woman looked into the coach and said, "You ugly old dog, don't you think you'll have that frightful head cut off?" he replied, "You ugly old—, I believe I shall!" The last two days he behaved ridiculously, joking, and making everybody laugh, even at the sentence. When he withdrew, he said "Adieu, my lords, we shall never meet again in the same place." He said he would be hanged; for that his neck was so short and bended, that he should be struck in the shoulders. "I did not think it possible," says Walpole, "to feel so little as I did at so melancholy a spectacle, but tyranny and villainy, wound up by buffoonry, took off all edge of concern. The foreigners were much struck: Nicolini seemed a great deal shocked, but he comforts himself with the knowledge he thinks he has gained of the English constitution."

In the next letter Walpole sends some account of Lovat's death: he was beheaded, and died extremely well, without passion, affectation, buffoonery, or timidity: his behaviour was natural and intrepid. He professed himself a Jansenist; made no speech, but sat down a little while in a chair on the scaffold, and talked to the people about him. He lay down quietly, gave the sign soon, and was despatched at a blow.

Lord Lovat was not only the last person beheaded on Tower-hill, but was the last person beheaded in this country, April 9, 1747. During the day, a scaffolding built near Barking-alley fell, with nearly 1,000 persons on it, and twelve were killed.

Hogarth painted Lovat's portrait: he met him at St. Alban's (Nichols says Barnet), on his road to London. Hogarth says: "I took this likeness when Simon Fraser was relating on his fingers the number of the rebel forces—such a chieftain had so many men, &c. He received me with much cordiality—embraced me when I entered, and kissed me, though he was under the hands of the barber. The muscles of his neck appeared of unusual strength—more so than I had ever seen."

Hogarth also etched Lovat's portrait: when the plate was finished, a printseller offered its weight in gold for it. The impressions could not be taken off fast enough to meet the demand, which produced about twelve pounds per day for several weeks.

SIR ROBERT WALPOLE'S BRIBERY.

During Sir Robert Walpole's administration, he wanted to carry a question in the House of Commons, to which he knew there would be great opposition, and which was disliked by some of his own dependents. As he was passing through the

Court of Requests, he met a member of the Opposition, whose avarice he imagined would not reject a large bribe. He took him aside, and said, "Such a question comes on this day; give me your vote, and here is a bank-hill of 2,000*l*.," which he put into his hands. The member made him this answer: "Sir Robert, you have lately served some of my particular friends; and when my wife was last at Court, the King was very gracious to her, which must have happened at your instance. I should, therefore, think myself very ungrateful (putting the bank-bill into his pocket) if I were to refuse the favour you are now pleased to ask me."

Sir Robert was called the Grand Corrupter in the libels of his time: he is said to have thought all mankind rogues, and to have remarked that every one had his price. Pope refers to this:

"Would he oblige me, let me only find
He does not think me what he thinks mankind."
Or as he at first printed it:
"He thinks one poet of no venal kind."

That Walpole said something very much like the saying attributed to him is what even his son does not deny; but there is reason to believe that he said it with a qualification—"all *those* men have their price," not "all men have their price."

The saying as recorded by Richardson, the painter, who had ample means of being well-informed, was in these words: "There was not one, how patriot soever he might seem, of whom he did not know the price." (***Richardsoniana,*** 8vo. 1776, p. 178.) Dr. King, whose means of information were as good as Richardson's, records a remark made during a debate in Parliament by Walpole to Mr. W. Leveson, the brother of the Jacobite Lord Gower. "You see," said Sir Robert, "with what zeal and vehemence these gentlemen oppose; and yet I know the price of every man in this house except three, and your brother is one of them." Dr. King adds that Sir Robert lived long enough to know that my Lord Gower had his price as well as the rest. (***King's Anecdotes,*** p. 44.) His son modifies the saying: "Some are corrupt," Sir Robert Walpole said; "but I will tell you of one who is not; Shippen is not" (***Walpo-***

liana, i. 38.) And Sir Robert said, that "it was fortunate so few men could be prime ministers, as it was best that few should thoroughly know the shocking wickedness of mankind. I never heard him say that all men had their prices; and I believe no such expression ever came from his mouth."

Lord Brougham, also, doubts whether the above words were ever used by Walpole; or, if used, whether they are properly interpreted. "His famous saying that 'all men have their price,'" said Lord Brougham, "can prove nothing unless 'price' be defined; and if a large and liberal sense is given to the word, the proposition more resembles a truism than a sneer, or an ebullition of official philanthropy. But it has been positively affirmed that the remark was never made; for it is said that an important word is omitted, which wholly changes the sense; and that Walpole only said, in reference to certain actions or profligate adversaries, and their adherents resembling themselves, "all ***these*** men have their price." (***Coxe's Life of Walpole,*** vol. i. p. 757.) His general tone of sarcasm, when speaking of patriotism and political gratitude, and others of the more fleeting virtues, is well-known. "Patriots," he said, "are easily raised; I have myself made many a one. 'Tis but to refuse an unreasonable demand, and up springs a patriot!" So the gratitude of political men he defined to be "a lively sense of favours to come."

"DOWNRIGHT SHIPPEN."

Some notion of the free use made in Shippen's days of the current coin as a political agent, may be gathered from the fact which Shippen himself related to the celebrated Dr. Middleton. The Prince of Wales, to justify his satisfaction with a speech which the sturdy old Jacobite had made, sent him 1,000***l.*** by General Churchill, Groom of his Bedchamber. Shippen refused it. That Sir Robert Walpole himself had known of similar attempts made on Shippen's virtue by the Hanoverian party, is pretty evident from his well-known saying respecting that honest man, quoted in the preceding page.

A VISIT FROM THE PRETENDER.

Dr. King, in his volume of *Political and Literary Anecdotes of his own Times,* relates some interesting particulars of the short visit of the Pretender to England, in 1750, when he only stayed in London five days. Dr. King had some long conversations with him here, and for some years after held a constant correspondence with him, not, indeed, by letters, but by messengers, not couriers, but "gentlemen of fortune, honour, and veracity." The Doctor describes the Pretender as tall and well-made, but stooping a little. "He has an handsome face and good eyes; I think his *busts,* which about this time were commonly sold in London, are more like him than any of his pictures which I have yet seen." Dr. King then relates, in a note, the following corroboration of the striking resemblance of the bust. "He (the Pretender) came one evening to my lodgings and drank tea with me: my servant, after he was gone, said to me, that he thought my new visitor very like Prince Charles. 'Why,' said I, 'have you ever seen Prince Charles?' 'No, sir,' replied the fellow, 'but this gentleman, whoever he may be, exactly resembles the busts which are sold in Red Lion-street, and are said to be the busts of Prince Charles.' The truth is, these busts were taken in plaster of Paris from his face."

Dr. King relates that as to Prince Charles's religion, "He is certainly free from all bigotry and superstition, and he would readily conform to the religion of the country. With the Catholics he is a Catholic; with the Protestants he is a Protestant; and to convince the latter of his sincerity he often carried an English Common Prayer-book in his pocket." He also once selected a nonjuring minister to christen one of his illegitimate children. The Prince was very avaricious: Dr. King knew him, with 2,000 louis d'ors in his strong box, pretend he was in great distress, and borrow money from a lady in Paris, who was not in affluent circumstances.

THE PRETENDER'S HEALTH.

When Lord Mansfield (then Mr. Murray) was examined before the Privy Council, about the year 1747, for drinking the Pretender's health on his knees (which he certainly did), it was urged against him, among other things, to show how strong a well-wisher he was to the cause of the exiled family, that, when he was employed as Solicitor-General against the **rebels** who were tried in 1746, he had never used that term, but always called them ***unfortunate gentlemen.*** When he came to his defence he said the fact was true; and he should only say that "he pitied that man's loyalty who thought that ***epithets*** could add to the guilt of treason!"—an admirable instance of a dexterous and subtle evasion.

CONFERRING THE GARTER.

Two of our sovereigns appear to have shown ill manners and temper in conferring the insignia and decorations of this noble order. George the Second, who strongly disliked Lord Temple, "Squire Gawkey," as he was nicknamed, was compelled by political arrangements, very repugnant to his feelings, to invest that nobleman with the Order of the Garter; when the king took so little pains to conceal his aversion both to the individual and to the act, that, instead of placing the riband decorously over the shoulder of the new knight, his Majesty, averting his head, and muttering indistinctly some expressions of dissatisfaction, threw the riband across him, and turned his back at the same instant in the rudest manner. George the Third exerted more restraint over his passions than did his grandfather, yet even he could be ill-tempered. When he invested the Marquis Camden with the Garter, he showed much ill-humour in his countenance and manner. However, as he knew the ceremony must be performed, Mr. Pitt having pertinaciously insisted upon it, the king took the riband in his hand, and turning to the Duke of Dorset, the assistant knight-companion, before the new knight approached, asked him if he knew Lord Camden's Christian name. The duke, after inquiring, informed him that it was John Jeffreys. "What, what!" said the king, "John Jeffreys! the first Knight of the Garter, I believe, that was ever called John Jeffreys;" the king not considering his descent sufficiently illustrious.

In 1782, at the time of Lord North's resignation, there were on the king's table four Garters unappropriated, which the new ministers naturally considered as lawful plunder. One only of the number fell to the share of the sovereign, which he was allowed, though not without some difficulty, to confer on his third son, Prince William Henry, afterwards King William IV. The Duke of Devonshire, as head of the Whig party, was invested with one blue riband, and the Duke of Richmond with another. Lord Shelburne took for himself, as was to be expected, the fourth Garter. At the investment never did three men receive the Order in so dissimilar and characteristic a manner. The Duke of Devonshire advanced up to the sovereign, with his phlegmatic, cold, and awkward air, like a clown. Lord Shelburne came forward, bowing on every side, smiling and fawning like a courtier. The Duke of Richmond presented himself, easy, unembarrassed, and with dignity, like a gentleman.

POLITICAL INFAMY.

There are several degrees of infamy, but none beyond that of one Digges, a political hack, who was so infamous a fellow, that Dr. Franklin said of him, "If Digges was not damned, the devil would be useless."

A TRIFLING MISTAKE.

In the House of Peers, during the examination of the magistrates of Edinburgh, touching the particulars of the Porteous Mob, in 1736, the Duke of Newcastle having asked the Provost with what kind of shot the town-guard, commanded by Porteous, had loaded their muskets, received the unexpected reply, "Ou, just sic as ane shoots dukes and fools wi'!" The answer was considered as a contempt of the House of Lords, and the poor Provost would have suffered from misconception of his patois, had not the Duke of Argyle (who must have been exceedingly amused) explained that the worthy chief magistrate's expression, when rendered into English, meant to describe the shot used for ***ducks and waterfowl.***

SCOTTISH CONCEIT.

In the time of the Rebellion of 1745, Duke Hamilton was extolling Scotland to William the Third, to such a length, that the King could no longer bear it. "My Lord," said his Majesty, "I only wish it was a hundred thousand miles off, and that you was king of it."

TIT FOR TAT.

At the stormy Westminster election, in 1750, a chairmaker, having voted for Lord Trentham, the Prince of Wales sent one of his servants to the man to say that the Prince would employ him no more. "I am going to bid another person make his Royal Highness a chair." "With all my heart," said the chairmaker; "I don't care what they make him, so they don't make him a throne."

STICKING TOGETHER.

How genially the Scotch stick together in spite of their religious differences in the last century is illustrated in the following incident: Stirling, of Keir, and some other gentlemen, were tried for high treason in Edinburgh in 1708. They were charged with drinking the health of the Pretender, plotting a French invasion, and encouraging insurrection. They escaped through the hard swearing of the witnesses brought against them, one of these being Stirling's own servant who without any direction from his master had managed to swear very neatly in his favour. Riding home from the trial, Stirling turned about in mere curiosity, and asked the servant whether he had really forgotten certain occurrences. "I ken very weel what you mean, laird," was the man's reply, "but my mind was clear to trust my saul to the mercy o' Heaven rather than your honour's body to the mercy o' the Whigs."

FRENCH AND ENGLISH.

Dean Ramsay relates that during the long French war, two old ladies in Stranraer were going to the kirk, when one said to the other, "was it no' a wonderful thing that the Breetish were aye victorious over the French in battle?" Not a bit," said the other old lady, "dinna ye ken the Breetish aye say their prayers before gaen into battle?" The other replied, "But canna the French say their prayers as weel?" The reply was most characteristic, "Hoot! jabbering bodies, who could *understan'* them?"

SCOTTISH INDEPENDENCE.

The Earl of Buchan (David Stuart Erskine), who died in his eighty-eighth year, in 1829, was, in his early years, taken by the hand by Mr. Pitt—but upon a subsequent occasion, when an election of Scotch Peers took place, his lordship having, like the other Peers, received a government circular letter, naming the individuals to be elected, he retired from public life, considering this letter an insult to the peerage of Scotland,—and upon that occasion wrote a letter to the minister, in which is this remarkable sentence: "If the privileges of Scotland are endeavoured to be violated, *I shall know how to make my porridge in my helmet, and stir it with my sword!*"

AN ARCHBISHOP ON DUELLING.

The hold on society which the practice of Duelling had once attained is illustrated by an anecdote told by Walpole, of the Archbishop of York, who, when a sermon he had recently preached was attacked in the House of Lords as too servile in its advocacy of divine right, said openly that, "though as a Christian and a bishop he ought to bear wrongs, there were injuries that would provoke any patience; and that he, if insulted, should know how to chastise any petulance." We must take the story as we find it told by Walpole; but if it were true as he gives it, it shows the curious change society has undergone since—and which it underwent, indeed, during—the time of George III. In 1820 it would have been thought as extraordinary as it would be thought now, if an archbishop, standing up publicly in ecclesiastical costume, were to declare that he could stand a good deal, but that he must shoot any one who criticised his sermons. Duelling also gives the text for another of Walpole's best stories. Hutchinson, Provost of Dublin, quarrelled with Tisdale, the Irish Attorney-General, and after having abused him in the grossest terms, sent him a challenge. Tisdale refused to fight him, urging that he himself was seventy-three, but laying very little stress on that. His principal objection was that they were not on an equality with reference to the pleasure to be derived from the contest "If I should kill Hutchinson," he said, "I should get nothing but the pleasure of killing him; whereas, if he kills me, he will get my place of Secretary of State, of which he has the reversion."

LET WELL ALONE.

Walpole was long of opinion that few persons know **when** to die: *i.e.* when to go out of the world. He thought that when any personage had shone as much as possible, he should be heard of no more. Thus, Voltaire ought to have pretended to die after Alzire, Mahomet, and Semiramis, and not have produced his wretched last pieces: Lord Chatham should have closed his political career with his immortal war: and how weak was Garrick, when he quitted the stage, to limp after the tatters of fame by writing and reading pitiful poems; and even by ***sitting*** to read plays which he had acted with such fire and energy! We have another example in Mr. Anstey; who, if he had a friend upon earth, would have been obliged to him for being knocked on the head, the moment he had published the first edition of the Bath Guide; for, even in the second, he had exhausted his whole stock of inspiration, and has never written anything tolerable since. When such unequal authors print their works together, one may apply in a new light the old hacked simile of Mezentius, who tied together the living and the dead.

THE PULTENEY GUINEA.

William Pulteney, afterwards Earl of Bath, was remarkable alike for his oratorical talents and his long and consistent opposition to the measures of Sir Robert Walpole, the great Whig Minister. On the 11th of February, 1741, a time when party feeling was at its height, Walpole received an intimation in the House of Commons that it was the intention of the Opposition to impeach him. To this menace he replied with his usual composure and self-complacence, merely requesting a fair and candid hearing, and winding up his speech with the quotation—

"Nil conscire sibi, nulli pallescere culpœ."

With his usual tact, Pulteney immediately rose, and observed, "that the right honourable gentleman's logic and Latin were alike inaccurate, and that Horace, whom he had just misquoted, had written 'nullâ pallescere culpâ.'" Walpole maintained that his quotation was correct, and a bet was offered. The matter was thereupon referred to Nicholas Hardinge, Clerk of the House, an excellent classical scholar, who decided against Walpole. The Minister accordingly took a guinea from his pocket, and flung it across the house to Pulteney. The latter caught it, and holding it up, exclaimed, "It's the only money I have received from the Treasury for many years, and it shall be the last." This guinea having been carefully preserved, finally came into the hands of Sir John Murray, by whom it was presented, in 1828, to the British Museum, The following memorandum, in the handwriting of Pulteney, is attached to it:—"This guinea I desire may be kept as an heirloom. It was won of Sir Robert Walpole in the House of Commons; he asserting the verse in Horace to be 'nulli pallescere culpæ,' whereas I laid the wager of a guinea that it was 'nullâ palescere culpâ.' He sent for the book, and, being convinced that he had lost, gave me this guinea. I told him I could take the money without any blush on my side, but believed it was the only money he ever gave in the House where the giver and the receiver ought not equally to blush. This guinea, I hope, will prove to my posterity the use of knowing Latin, and encourage them in their learning."

DIVIDED DANGER.

When Lord Bath was told of the first determination of turning Pitt out of the ministry, and letting Fox remain, he said, it put him in mind of a story of the Gunpowder Plot The Lord Chamberlain was sent to examine the vaults under the Parliament House, and, returning with his report, said he had found five-and-twenty barrels of gunpowder; that he had removed ten of them, and hoped the other fifteen would do no harm.

OPENING LETTERS.

We have heard much of this "State necessity" in our day, but little that redounds so much to the honour of an English statesman as the following:—One morning, when Pulteney (afterwards Earl of Bath) was in office, a man came to him offering his service, that he could open any letter folded in any form, could take a copy of the letter, and make it up again in such a manner, that the writer of the letter himself could not distinguish whether the seal had been touched, or how the letter had been opened. The man withdrew into another room, a short letter was written, was folded up in the most artful manner, was sealed with a finely cut coat of arms, and then sent to the man in the room adjoining. In a quarter of an hour the man returned with the letter and the copy of the letter, and neither Mr. Pulteney, nor a friend who had been sitting with him at the time, could discover the least traces of the letter's having been opened. The man therefore hoped that his honour would employ him, or recommend him to some other person. He replied, that he regretted that there existed such a dangerous enemy to society; so far from employing or recommending him, he would punish him if he had it in his power. 'Go your ways,' said he, 'and seek your reward elsewhere.' The man was soon after taken into the Secretary of State's office."—***Newton, Life and Anecdotes,*** prefixed to his Works.

"TOTTENHAM IN HIS BOOTS."

This ***sobriquet*** was acquired by Charles Tottenham, Esq. of Tottenham Green, Co. Wexford, and a Member of the Irish Parliament, under the following circumstances: The Members of the House of Commons formerly attended ***in full dress,*** an arrangement first broken through as follows. A very important constitutional question was debating between Government and the Opposition—namely, as to the application of a sum of 60,000*l.*, then lying unappropriated in the Irish treasury. The numbers seemed to be nearly poised; it had been 'supposed that the majority would be inclined to give it to the King, while the Opposition would recommend laying it out upon the country,—when the serjeant-at-arms reported that a Member wanted to force himself into the House ***undressed,*** in dirty boots, and splashed up to his shoulders. The Speaker could not oppose custom to privilege, and was necessitated to admit him. It proved to be Mr. Tottenham, covered with mud, and wearing a pair of huge jack-boots! Hearing that the question was likely to come on sooner than he had expected, he had (lest he should not be in time) mounted his horse at Tottenham-green, set off in the night, ridden nearly sixty miles up to the

Parliament House direct, and rushed in, without washing or changing himself, to vote for the country. He arrived just at the critical moment, and his **casting-vote** gave a majority of one to the country party!

This incident could not die while the Irish Parliament lived: and "Tottenham in his Boots" remained to a very late period a standing toast at certain patriotic Irish tables. It should be added that, by an order of the Parliament, all members were to appear in the House in full court dress, under a penalty of 500*l.,* which fine, Mr. Tottenham having incurred, had to pay; he was the last who did so, for his bold conduct put an end to its farther exaction.

Soon after the affair, a portrait of the hon. member was painted by Stephens, and engraved by A. Millar, in the attitude of ascending the steps of the Parliament House, in Dublin, in his travelling dress—*in his boots.* This picture is in the possession of the head of the house of Tottenham—the Marquess of Ely.

BOYLE ROCHE'S BULLS.

Sir Boyle Roche, the Irish member, excelled in bulls. "I wish," said he, one day, when opposing an anti-ministerial motion, "I wish, Mr. Speaker, this motion at the bottom of the bottomless pit" At another time, in relation to English connexion, he observed—"England, it must be allowed, is the mother-country, and, therefore, I advise them (England and Ireland) to live in filial affection together like sisters as they are and ought to be." A question of smuggling practices in the Shannon being under consideration,—"I would," said Sir Boyle, "have two frigates stationed on the opposite points of the mouth of the river, and there they should remain fixed, with strict orders not to stir; and so, by cruising and cruising about, they would be able to intercept everything that should attempt to pass between."

A DROVE OF BULLS.

In a debate on the Leather Tax, in 1795, in the Irish House of Commons, the Chancellor of the Exchequer, Sir John Plunkett, observed, with great emphasis, "That in the prosecution of the present war, every man ought to give his last guinea to protect the remainder." Mr. Vandeleur said, "however that might be, the tax on leather would be severely felt by the barefooted peasantry of Ireland." To which Sir Boyle Roche replied that "this could be easily remedied by making the under-leathers of wood."

A KING'S SPEECH.

When George the Second, in his Speech, told his Parliament his reason for dissolving it was its being so near dissolution, Lord Cornbury said it put him in mind of a gaoler in Oxfordshire who was remarkably humane to his prisoners: one day he said to one of them, "My good friend, you know you are to be hanged on Friday se'night; I want extremely to go to London; would you be so kind as to be hanged next Friday?"

A MINISTERIAL REPROOF.

On one of the many occasions when the implacable hatred of the House of Brunswick towards that of Brandenburg broke out, Sir Robert Walpole said to George the Second, "Will your Majesty engage in an enterprise which must prove both disgraceful and disadvantageous? Why, Hanover will be no more than a breakfast to the Prussian army."

TALKING POLITICS.

As politics spoil conversation, Walpole once proposed that everybody should forfeit half-a-crown who said anything tending to introduce the idea either of ministers or opposition. Upon this Hannah More, who was present, added that whoever mentioned *pit-coal,* or a *fox-skin,* muff should be considered as guilty; and it was accordingly voted.

INVASION PANIC.

When, in 1756, the Duke of Newcastle expected the French every hour, one night he was terribly alarmed: on his table he found a mysterious card with only these words: "Charles is very well, and is expected in England every day." It was plainly some secret friend that advertised him of the Pretender's approaching arrival. He called up all the servants, ransacked the whole house to know who had been in his dressing-room:—at last it came out to be an answer from the Duchess of Queensbury to the Duchess of Newcastle about Lord *Charles* Douglas.

NARROW ESCAPE.

When, in 1759, there was a successful debate in the House of Commons on the Bill for fixing the augmentation of the salaries of the judges, Charles Townshend said, the book of *Judges* was saved by the book of *Numbers.*

PERUQUIERS' PETITION.

On the 11th of February, 1765, a petition was presented to King George III., by the master peruke-makers of the metropolis, setting forth the distresses of themselves and an incredible number of others dependent on them, from the almost universal decline of their trade, in consequence of gentlemen so generally beginning to wear their own hair. What business remained to their profession was, they said, nearly altogether taken from them by French artists. They had a further ground of complaint in their being obliged to work on Sunday, which they would much rather have spent in their religious duties, "learning to fear God and honour the king [a bit of flattery]." Under these circumstances, the distressed peruke-makers prayed his Majesty for means of relief. The king—though he must have scarcely been able to maintain his gravity—returned a gracious answer. But the public, albeit but little converted from the old views regarding the need of protection to industry, had the sense to see the ludicrous side of the petition, and some one quickly regaled them by publishing a petition from the *Body Carpenters,* imploring his Majesty to wear a wooden leg, and to enjoin all his servants to appear in the royal presence with the same graceful decoration.

CARLTON HOUSE INTRIGUE.

Lord Bute is known to have enjoyed a higher place in the Princess Dowager of Wales's favour, if not in her affection, than seemed compatible with strict propriety. His visits to Carlton House were always performed in the evening, when he commonly made use of the chair and chairmen of Miss Vansittart, a lady of the Princess' household. The curtains of the chair were closely drawn, to conceal the arrival, though this may have been done from apprehension of insult from the populace, for Lord Bute was very unpopular. Miss Chudleigh, then maid-of-honour at Carlton House, made a smart repartee upon these visits: when reproached by her royal mistress, for the irregularities of her conduct, she replied: ***"Votre Altesse Royale sait, que chacun a son But."***

As George III was accustomed to repair frequently in the evening to Carlton House, and there pass a considerable time, the world supposed that the Sovereign, his mother, and the ex-minister met in order to concert and to compare their views; thus forming a sort of interior Cabinet, which controlled and directed the ostensible Administration.

LEVÉE HUMOURS.

Lord Bute's first levée was crowded. Bothmar, the Danish minister, said, "La chaleur est excessive!" George Selwyn replied, "Pour se mettre au froid, il faut aller cher Monsieur le Due de Newcastle!" There was another George nòt quite so tender. George Brudenel was passing by: somebody in the mob said, "What is the matter here?" Brudenel answered, "Why, there is a Scotchman got into the Treasury, and they can't get him out."

POLITICAL CONFIDENCE.

When the Ministry of 1766 sought the confidence of Lord Chatham, he replied, their characters were fair enough, and he was always glad to see such persons engaged in the public service; but, turning to them with a smile, very courteous, but not very respectful, he said—"Confide in you? oh, no—you must pardon me, gentlemen—*youth* is the season of credulity—confidence is a plant of slow growth in an aged bosom."

LITTLE CAUSE AND GREAT EFFECT.

When, in 1772, negotiations for peace between the Russians and the Turks were in progress, the Empress ordered Count Orloff, her negotiator, confident Minister, and paramount gallant, to accord all that she could with any reason concede, but not to mention the surrender of the Crimea till the last moment, in hopes that, rather than lose all she was willing to give up, they would yield that country. In the meantime she had fallen in love with a lieutenant of her guards, and preferred him rapidly. Orloff, getting intelligence of this new favourite, was so impatient to get rid of him, that, without opening on the other points, he abruptly made the demand of the Crimea; was refused; broke off the treaty, and getting into a postchaise, disguised like a courier, hurried back to St. Petersburg, announced the rupture of the negotiation, was disgraced, and saw his rival remain in possession. Thus, the Empress and her lover-minister's impetuosity prevented the conclusion of so destructive a war, and was a new instance of what little passions influence the fate of kingdoms.

LORD CHATHAM'S CHARLATANERIE.

Some of Lord Chatham's sallies are examples of an approach made to the ludicrous by the sublime, as in the following instance. It is related that in the House of Commons, (when Mr. Pitt,) he began a speech with the words "Sugar, Mr. Speaker,"—and then, observing a smile to pervade the audience, he paused, looked fiercely around, and with a loud voice, rising in its notes, and swelling into vehement anger, he is said to have pronounced the word "Sugar!" three times, and having thus quelled the house, and extinguished every appearance of levity or laughter, turned round and disdainfully asked, "Who will laugh now?" Lord Brougham has well referred to this incident as an instance of the extraordinary power of Chatham's manner, and the reach of his audacity in trusting to those powers.

Lord Chatham (when Mr. Pitt) on some occasion made a very long and able speech in the Privy Council, relative to some naval matter. Every one present was struck by the force of his eloquence. Lord Anson, who was no orator, being then at the head of the Admiralty, and differing entirely in opinion from Mr. Pitt, got up, and only said these words,—"My Lords, Mr. Secretary is very eloquent, and has stated his own opinion very plausibly. I am no orator, and all I shall say is, that he knows nothing at all of what he has been talking about." This short reply, together with the confidence the Council had in Lord Anson's professional skill, had such an effect on every one present, that they immediately determined against Mr. Pitt's proposition.

LORD CHATHAM'S WAR PREDICTION.

The probability, indeed certainty, of England being sooner or later engaged in a war with France, consequent on her unfortunate dissensions with her revolted colonies in America, had been insisted upon by Lord Chatham in the House of Lords, as early as in the month of May preceding. "The French Court," said he, "are too wise to lose the opportunity of separating America from Great Britain; it would, perhaps, be folly in France to declare it now, while the Americans are giving full employment to our arms, and pouring into her lap their wealth and produce, which France is enjoying in peace. War, however, with France is not the less certain because it had not been declared." War broke out with France in the month of May, 1778, exactly a year after the delivery of Lord Chatham's prophetic speech.

POLITICAL GRATITUDE.

When Lord Chatham died,—which Walpole thought of no great consequence, but to himself—the House of Commons chose to bury him and father his children. In this fit of gratitude, two men chose not to be involved, but voted against attending his funeral; one was the Archbishop of Canterbury (Cornwallis), who owed the tiara to him; the other, Lord Onslow, who formerly used to wait in the lobby to help him on with his great-coat.

The City wanted to bury Lord Chatham in St. Paul's; which, it was said, would literally be "robbing Peter (Westminster Abbey, St. Peter's) to pay Paul."

The Rev. Mr. Mason writes to Walpole: "Pray give me an account of the funeral, and, if you have time, order your gardener to pluck a bouquet of onions, and send it with my compliments to Lord John, that he may put them in his handkerchief to weep with greater facility."

BRIBING MEMBERS OF PARLIAMENT.

About the year 1767 one Roberts, who had been Secretary to the Treasury, and Mr. Pelham, divulged some strange details of the mode in which the House of Commons was managed in his time, when a number of members received from him at the end of every Session a stipend in bank notes, the sums varying from 500*l.* to 800*l.* per annum. Roberts, on the day of the Prorogation, took his stand in the Court of Requests, and as the gentlemen passed, in going to or returning from the House, Roberts conveyed the money in a squeeze of the hand. The names of the recipients were entered in a book, which was preserved with the deepest secrecy, it being never inspected by any one except the king and Mr. Pelham. On the decease of that minister, in 1754, his brother, the Duke of Newcastle, and others of the succeeding Cabinet, were anxious to obtain information of the private state of the House, and besought Roberts to give up the book containing the names of the bribed. This Roberts refused to do, except by the king's command, and to his Majesty in person. Of this refusal the ministers acquainted the king, who sent for Roberts to St. James's, where he was introduced into the closet, more than one of the ministers being present. George II ordered him to return him the book in question, which injunction was complied with. At the same time, taking the poker in his hand, the king put it into the fire, made it red hot, and thrust the book into the flames, where it was immediately burnt. He considered it too confidential a register to be transferred to the new ministers, and as having become extinct with the administration of Mr. Pelham.

Another official person, who had been private secretary to the Earl of Bute, and seventeen years Treasurer of the Ordnance, testified to the Peace of 1763 having been carried by money: he secured above 120 votes, with 80,000*l.* set apart for the purpose, forty members receiving 1,000*l.* and 500*l.* each.

THE RESULT OF THE AMERICAN WAR WITH GREAT BRITAIN FORETOLD.

"I prophesied," said Colonel Barré, "on passing the Stamp Act, in 1765, what would happen thereon; and I now, in March 1769, I now fear I can prophesy further troubles; that if the whole people are made desperate, finding no remedy from Parliament, the whole continent will be in arms immediately, and perhaps ***these provinces lost to England for ever.***" This was in March 1769, and certainly a very remarkable prediction.—Professor Smyth's ***Lectures on Modern History.***

About the time of the breaking out of the war in 1812, between Great Britain and the United States, a whale ascended the Delaware to Philadelphia, ninety miles from the ocean, and was caught. None had since been known to do so until the beginning of the rebellion of the Southern States in 1861, when another whale came up to Philadelphia, and was caught.

AMERICAN WAR.

When, in 1781, George III., in his speech, threatened the continuation of the American war, the livery of London voted a severe remonstrance to the king, beseeching him to remove both his public and ***private*** counsellors, and using, Walpole says, "these ***stunning*** and memorable words, 'Your armies are captured, the wonted superiority of your service is annihilated, your dominions are lost.' Words that could be used to no other king; nothing had ever lost so much without losing all. If James II. had lost his crown, yet the crown lost no dominions." The king was, of course, very indignant; and the day before the sheriffs went to know when he would receive the address, he said to a young man who was hunting with him, "I must go to town to-morrow to receive those ***fellows in furs;*** they will not be very glad to see me, nor I them."

GEORGE III. AND AMERICAN INDEPENDENCE.

In the ***Men and Times of the American Revolution,*** we find the following picture, by Ukanah Watson, of "How George the Third appeared when he declared the Independence of the United States:"

"After waiting nearly two hours, the approach of the king was announced by a tremendous roar of artillery. He entered by a small door on the left of the throne, and immediately seated himself upon the chair of state, in a graceful attitude, with his right foot resting upon a stool. He was clothed in royal robes. Apparently agitated, he drew from his pocket the scroll containing his speech. The Commons were summoned, and after the bustle of their entrance had subsided, he proceeded to read his speech. I was near the king, and watched with intense interest every tone of his voice, and every emotion of his countenance. It was to me a moment of thrilling and dignified exultation. After some general and usual remarks, he continued:—'I lost no time in giving the necessary orders to prohibit the further prosecution of offensive war upon the continent of North America. Adopting, as my inclination will always lead me to do, with decision and effect whatever I collect to be the sense of my Parliament and my people, I have pointed all my views and measures, in Europe, as in North America, to an entire and cordial reconciliation with the colonies. Finding it indispensable to the attainment of the object, I did not hesitate to go to the full length of the powers vested in me, and offer to declare them.'—Here he paused, and was in evident agitation; either embarrassed in reading his speech, by the darkness of the room, or affected by a very ***natural emotion.*** In a moment he resumed:—'and offer to declare them ***free and independent States,*** In thus admitting their separation from the Crown of these Kingdoms, I have sacrificed every consideration of my own to the wishes and opinions of my people. I make it my humble and ardent prayer to Almighty God that Great Britain may not feel the evils which might result from so great a dismemberment of the empire, and that America may be free from the calamities which have formerly proved, in the mother country, how essential monarchy is to the enjoyment of constitutional liberty. Religion, language, interests, and affections may, and I hope will, yet prove a bond of permanent union between the two countries.' It is remarked that George III. is celebrated for reading his speeches in a distinct, free, and impressive manner. On this occasion he was evidently embarrassed; he hesitated, choked, and executed the painful duties of the occasion with an ill grace that does not belong to him."

GEORGE WASHINGTON.

Washington was remarkably silent and serious, and when he banqueted his prisoner, Lord Cornwallis, spoke little, never smiled, but happening to ask if it was true that Lord Dunmore was returning to resume his government of Virginia, and being answered in the affirmative, the hero burst out into a fit of laughter. This was the Philosopher laughing at the Ass that has left mumbling ***thistles*** for clover that is out of his reach.—***Walpole's Letters,*** 1782.

A KNOWING OLD CRONE.

At the time of the renewal of war, after the peace of Amiens, a gentleman, who was fishing in a sequestered spot not far from London, was accosted by an old woman of the neighbourhood, who entered into conversation with him on various matters. After a little, he asked her if she were not alarmed about Bonaparte's landing on the island. "Oh dear no!" she answered; "I am up to all that. He was expected here when I was a young woman, and he nearly came. At that time they called him the Pretender, and now they call him Bonaparte."

POLITICAL WINDOW BREAKING.

Upon the rejoicings on the acquittal of Admiral Keppel, Feb. 11, 1779, it happened at three in the morning that Charles Fox, Lord Derby, and his brother Major Stanley, and two or three more young men of quality, having been drinking at Almack's till that late hour, suddenly thought of making the tour of the streets, and were joined by the Duke of Ancaster, who was very drunk, and which showed it was no premeditated scheme—the latter was a courtier, and had actually been breaking windows. Finding the mob before Sir Hugh Palliser's house in Pall Mall, some of the young Lords said, "Why don't you break Lord George Germaine's windows?" The populace had been so little tutored, that they asked who he was, and being encouraged, broke his windows. The mischief pleasing the juvenile leaders, they marched to the Admiralty, forced the gates, and demolished Palliser's and Lord Lilburne's windows. Lord Sandwich, exceedingly terrified, escaped through the garden, with his mistress, Miss Reay, to the Horse Guards, and there betrayed a most manifest panic.—***Walpole's Last Journals,*** vol. ii. p. 343.

THE RIOTS OF 1780.

For Lord George Gordon's share in the Riots of London, in 1780, he was brought to trial in the Court of King's Bench, but, principally through the powerful eloquence of Erskine, was acquitted.

Malone relates that Lord Mansfield told Mr. W. Gerard Hamilton, that what he most regretted to have lost by the burning of his house (at the time of the Riots, set on foot about three years before by that wicked canting hypocrite Lord George Gordon) was a speech that he had made on the question how far the privilege of Parliament extended; that it contained ***all the eloquence*** and ***all the law*** he was master of; that it was fairly written out; and that he had no other copy. Mr. Daines Barrington informed Malone that the book here alluded to contained ***eight*** speeches made in the House of Lords; all fairly written for the press, ***and now*** irreparably lost

A person begging alms of Lord George Gordon, said, "God bless you, my Lord! you and I have been in all the prisons in London." "What do you mean!" cried Lord George;

"I never was in any prison but the Tower." That is true, my Lord," said the other, "and I have been in all the rest."

Lord George, in 1781, arranged to become a candidate for London in Parliament; but, it was said that he dropped his pursuit on finding that *the City did not choose to be burnt once a year for his amusement.*

Lord George asked Mr. Selwyn if he would choose him again for Luggershall? He replied, "His constituents would not." "Oh, yes, if you would recommend me, they would choose me if I came from the coast of Africa!" "That is according to what part of the coast you came from; they would certainly if you came from the *Guinea* Coast."

When Walpole was told that the Abbé de Sieyes was busy in forming a new constitution for France, be replied: "We have one monster who is going to create as much anarchy, that he too, I suppose, may form a new constitution! There has been in the papers a pathetic lamentation that Lord George Gordon is still in durance! So are the tigers and hyæna in the Tower, and I hope his Lordship will not find bail before they do!"

In 1788, Lord George having been twice convicted of libel, he was compelled to seek safety in flight; but being arrested in Holland, and sent back to England, he was committed to Newgate. It is singular to reflect, that after involving London in all the horrors of insurrection, anarchy, and conflagration, he should have escaped any punishment for these proceedings, which cost the lives of so many individuals, and the destruction of so many edifices; while he expiated, by a rigorous imprisonment to the end of his days in Newgate, the publication of a libel on the Queen of France, who herself perished on the scaffold. Lord George Gordon died in Newgate, on November 1, 1793: he had been converted to Judaism; but his last moments are said to have been embittered by the consciousness that his body would not be allowed sepulture among the Jews.

A CLOSE QUESTION.

When, in 1782, it was settled that Lord George Germaine should retire from the Ministry, and Lord North notified that necessity to him, Lord G. said, with spirit and good sense, "You say I must go, my Lord;—very well—but pray, *why is your*

Lordship to stay ?

"USED TO IT."

In 1782, when we lost Minorca, Walpole said, "It made no more impression than if the King had lost his pocket-handkerchief. We are like the fish-woman, who, being reproached with the cruelty of skinning eels alive, replied, 'Ah, poor things, they be used to it!' She mistook her own habitude for theirs. We are at once so dissipated and so accustomed to misfortunes that, though flayed to the bone, we forget the amputation of a finger in a moment."

MINISTERIAL METAMORPHOSIS.

Upon the change of Ministry in 1782, great was the change in the aspect of the House of Commons. The Treasury Bench and places behind it were now occupied by the new Ministry, emerged from their obscure lodgings, or from Brookes's, having thrown off their blue and buff uniforms, and being now in court-dresses, decorated with swords, lace, and hair-powder. Some degree of ridicule attached to this extraordinary metamorphosis. It happened that just then Lord Nugent's house in Great George-street had been broken open, and robbed of a variety of articles; among others, of a number of pairs of laced ruffles. He caused the particulars of the stolen articles to be advertised in the newspapers, where they were minutely specified. Coming down to the House of Commons, a gentleman, who accidentally sat next to him, asked his Lordship if he had yet discovered any of the articles recently lost. "I can't say that I have," answered he, "but I shrewdly suspect that I have seen some of my lace ruffles on the hands of the gentlemen who now occupy the Treasury Bench." This reply, the effect of which was infinitely increased by the presence of Fox and Burke, occasioned much laughter.

"THE DINNER BELL."

There sat in the Parliament of 1783, David Hartley, member for Hull, the intolerable length and dulness of whose speeches rendered him a nuisance even to his own friends. His rising operated like a dinner bell. One day, when he had thus wearied out the patience of his audience, having reduced the House from 300 to about 80 persons, half asleep, just at a time when he was expected to close, he unexpectedly moved that the Riot Act should be read, as a document, to prove some assertion he had made. Burke, who sat close by him, and who had been for more than an hour and a half bursting with impatience to speak upon the question, finding himself so cruelly disappointed, bounced up, exclaiming, "The Riot Act, my dear friend, the Riot Act! to what purpose? don't you see that the mob is already quietly dispersed?" This sarcastic wit, increased in effect by the despairing tone of Burke, convulsed every person present except Hartley, who never changed countenance, and insisted on the Riot Act being read by one of the clerks.

Mr. Jenkinson, afterwards Earl of Liverpool, used to relate that Hartley, having risen to speak, at about five o'clock, in the Session of 1779, and it being summer, and generally understood that he would continue a long time on his legs, Mr. Jenkinson profited by the occasion to breathe some country air. He walked, therefore, from the House to his residence in Parliament-street; from whence, mounting his horse, he rode to a place that he rented some miles out of town. There he dined, strolled about, and returned to London. As it was then near nine, he sent his servant to the House, to inquire who had spoken in the course of the debate, and when a division might be expected. The footman brought back for answer, that Mr. Hartley continued still speaking, but was expected to close soon, and that no other person had yet risen. In fact, when Mr. Jenkinson entered the House, Hartley remained exactly in the same place and attitude as he was near five hours before, regardless of the general impatience, or of the profound repose into which the majority of his hearers were sunk. However incredible this story appears, Wraxall declares that he has related it without exaggeration.

TREASURY DEPREDATIONS.

When, in 1783, Mr. Pitt introduced his bill to regulate fees in public offices, he exposed some strange malversations. One of the charges specified a sum of 340*l.* paid to the Secretary of the Treasury for the article of **whipcord.** The annual expenditure of the First Minister for his individual stationery did not fall short of 1,300*l.* Lord North, when called on, made nevertheless not only a plausible, but a very satisfactory defence to most of the alleged items. Robinson undertook to give some sort of explanation of whipcord, which Lord North could not master; but it diverted more than satisfied its hearers. [Has it not something to do with the Treasury whipper-in?]

Wraxall tells us that he knew a lord of trade who had a borough, and a very large fortune, and was in Parliament; on his being sworn in at the Board of Trade, he issued an order to provide a great number of pewter inkstands for his own use, which he after transmuted into one composed of silver. He might be seen at the levée, dressed in a suit of green velvet, made out of the materials ordered in his public character for the ostensible purpose of making bags to contain office-papers. His friends and correspondents could recognise the stationery, of which he had made an ample provision, more than ten years after the Board of Trade itself; abolished by Burke's bill, had ceased to have any existence.

Few places of considerable emolument, in any department, were given wholly unfettered to the nominal occupant. Under Lord Rockingham's first administration, in 1765, we find Wilkes **quartered** on the whole of the Treasury and Admiralty Boards, to the annual amount of 1,040*l.;* the marquis paying him 500*l.*, the inferior lords of the Treasury 60*l.* each, and the members of the Board of Trade, each 40*l.* This curious fact is stated in Horne's letter to Junius, 31st July, 1771, and was not denied. Wraxall knew a lady of quality, who, being the daughter of a person high in office, was commonly said to have "rode" sixteen persons at one time, to whom her father had given places, under that express condition or reservation; she is said to have outlived them all. Governments, military appointments, offices in the Excise and Customs; in a word, places of every description, at home and abroad, were frequently loaded with ***riders.***

A WESTMINSTER ELECTION IN 1784.

Walpole, in a letter to Sir Horace Mann, April 11, 1784, writes:—"Mr. Fox is still struggling to be chosen for Westminster, and maintains so sturdy a fight, that Sir Cecil Wray, his antagonist, is not yet three hundred ahead of him, though the Court exerts itself against him in the most violent manner, by mandates, arts, &c.—nay, sent a body of two hundred and eighty of the Guards to give their votes as householders, which *is* legal, but which my father in the most quiet seasons would not have dared to do. At first the contest threatened to be bloody: Lord Hood (the Admiral) being the third candidate, and on the side of the Court, a mob of three hundred sailors undertook to drive away the opponents; but the Irish chairmen, being retained by Mr. Fox's party, drove them back to their element, and cured the tars of their ambition of a naval victory, In truth, Mr. Fox has all the popularity in Westminster; and, indeed, is so amiable and winning, that, could he have stood in person all over England, I question whether he could not have carried the Parliament The beldames hate him; but most of the pretty women in London are indefatigable in making interest for him, the Duchess of Devonshire in particular. I am ashamed to say how coarsely she has been received by some worse than tars! But nothing has shocked me so much as what I heard this morning: at Dover they roasted a poor *fox* alive by the most diabolic allegory! a savage meanness that an Iroquois would not have committed. Base, cowardly wretches! how much nobler to have hurried to London, and torn Mr. Fox himself piecemeal! I detest a country inhabited by such stupid barbarians. I will write no more to-night; I am in a passion!"

LORD SANDWICH IN OFFICE, AND IN LOVE.

Lord Sandwich, when First Lord of the Admiralty, used to give notice to the numerous candidates for professional advancement, that he paid no attention to any memorial that extended beyond a single page. "If any man," he said, "will draw up his case, and will put his name to the bottom of the first page, I will give him an immediate reply: where he compels me to turn over the page, he must await my leisure."

When Mr. Eden, afterwards Lord Auckland, deserted Fox for Pitt, he sent, in justification of his apostasy, a circular letter to his former political colleague. The reply of Lord Sandwich was:—"Your letter is before me, and will presently be behind. I remain, Sir, your most humble Servant."

Charles Butler has left this characteristic sketch of the Minister: "Lord Sandwich might serve as a model for a man of business. He rose early, and, till a late dinner, dedicated his whole time to business: he was very methodical; slow, but not wearisome; cautious, not suspicious; rather a man of sense than a man of talent; he had much real good nature; his promises might be relied on. His manners partook of the old Court; and he possessed, in a singular degree, the art of attaching persons of every rank to him. Few homes were more pleasant or instructive than his Lordship's: it was filled with rank, beauty, and talent, and every one was at ease. He professed to be fond of music, and musicians flocked to him: he was the soul of the Catch Club, and one of the Directors of the concerts of Ancient Music; but he had not the least ear for music, and was equally insensible of harmony and melody."

This, however, it must be admitted, is but the bright side of the character of Lord Sandwich: he led a gay life, and lived in open concubinage, notwithstanding his high official position; and his male associates were some of the most unblushing profligates of the lax London society of the last century. He was by no means a handsome man; when seen in the street, he had an awkward, careless gait. Two gentlemen observing him, one remarked, "I think it is Lord Sandwich coming;" which the other thought to be a mistake, "Nay," said the first gentleman, "I am sure it is Lord Sandwich, for if you observe, he is walking down both sides of the street at once." But Lord Sandwich used to tell a better story of himself: "When I was at Paris," he said, "I had a dancing-master; the man was very civil, and on my taking leave of him, I offered my service in London. 'Then,' said the man, bowing, 'I would take it as a particular favour, if your lordship would never tell any one of whom you learned to dance.'" There is a line in the Heroic Epistle:—

"See Jemmy Twitcher shambles Stop, stop thief—"

alluding to his Lordship's shambling gait. ***Jemmy Twitcher*** was the name given to him by the satirists of the period; and a very scarce volume contains his "life, adventures, and amours, exhibiting many striking proofs to what baseness the human heart is capable of descending."

In the days of his hot youth, Sandwich had for his companions Sir Francis Dashwood, afterwards Lord Despenser; Thomas Potter, M.P., son of the Archbishop; and John Wilkes, with other men of fashion and loose morals. This precious set kept their orgies at Medmenham Abbey, their amusements being obscenity and mockery of the rites of religion: they dressed themselves up like Franciscan monks, drank wine out of sacramental vessels in honour of Venus, &c.; and over the door of the Abbey, which had once been a Cistercian monastery, they inscribed from Rabelais, "Fays ce que voudras," (Do what you will). Churchill thus describes the place, in his Candidate:—

"Whilst womanhood in habit of a nun,
At Medmenham lies, by sluggard monks undone;
Whilst Paul the aged chalks behind the door
A nation's reckoning, like an alehouse score,
Compelled to hire a foe to cast it up;
[Sandwich] shall pour from a, communion-cup
Libations to the goddess without eyes,
And hob and nob in cyder and excise."

According to Walpole, Lord Sandwich had been expelled the Beef-steak Club for blasphemy; yet he it was who, in the House of Lords, described Wilkes's "Essay on Woman" as "an indecent and blasphemous publication," and got the thing voted a breach of privilege. Churchill has left a coarse portrait of Sandwich, commencing—

"From his youth upwards to the present day,
When vices more than years have mark'd him grey,
When riotous excess, with wasteful hand
Shakes life's frail glass, and hastes each ebbing sand,
Unmindful from what stock he drew his birth,
Untainted with one deed of real worth,

Lothario, holding honour at no price,
Folly to folly added, vice to vice,
Wrought sin with greediness, and sought for shame
With greater zeal than good men work for fame."

The Lothario refers to Lord Sandwich's amour with Miss Reay, whom he first saw behind the counter of a milliner's shop, No. 4, at the west-end corner of Tavistock-court, the south side of Covent-garden Market: he had Miss Reay removed from her situation, had her education completed, and made a proficient in music and singing—and then she became his Lordship's mistress. He took her to his country-seat, Hinchinbrooke, in Huntingdonshire, and there introduced her to his family circle, to the distress of Lady Sandwich. At this time, Captain Hackman, 68th Foot, was recruiting at Huntingdon: he appeared at a ball, was asked by Lord Sandwich to Hinchinbrooke, was introduced to Miss Reay, became violently enamoured of her, made proposals, and was sent into Ireland, where his regiment was. He sold out; came back on purpose to be near the object of his affection; took orders, but could not bend the inflexible fair, in a black coat more than in a red. He could not live without her. He now resolved to kill himself, and that in her presence; for this purpose he followed her to London, and went to Covent-garden Theatre, where, seeing her coquet with Macnamara, a young Irish Templar, Hackman determined suddenly to despatch her too. He rushed out of the theatre, and provided himself with a pair of pistols, with which he returned to the Piazza, and at the close of the performance, as Miss Reay was being handed into her carriage, Hackman shot her dead. He was secured, tried at the Old Bailey for the murder, and hanged at Tyburn, April 19, 1779. In a Grub-street ballad of the time, we are told

"A Sandwich favourite was this fair,
And her he dearly loved;
By whom six children had, we hear;
This story fatal proved.

A clergyman, O wicked one,
In Covent Garden shot her;

No time to cry upon her God,
It's hoped he's not forgot her."

After the death of Miss Reay, Lord Sandwich lived in complete retirement; he survived her twelve years. She had borne him nine children, five of whom were alive at the time of her death. One of these attained to distinction, namely, Mr. Basil Montagu, a lawyer of eminence, who died in 1851, in his 82nd year: he was an honest, liberal-minded, and benevolent man.

A curious book sprung out of the above assassination: it was published in 1780, entitled **Love and Madness,** and professed to comprise the correspondence between Hackman and Miss Reay. The author was Dr. Herbert Croft: the basis of the work is fact, and some of the letters may be genuine; but most of them are apocryphal, though cleverly fictitious.

LORD NORTH'S WIT AND HUMOUR.

Among his political adversaries, Lord North had not a single enemy. With an unwieldy figure and a dull eye, the quickness of his mind seemed intuition. Lord Sandwich once said: "I must have pen and ink, and write down, and ruminate: give Lord North a bundle of papers, and he'll turn them over,—perhaps while his hair is dressing; and he instantly knows their contents and bearings." His wit was never surpassed (says Charles Butler), and it was attended with this singular quality, that it never gave offence, and the object of it was sure to join with pleasure in the laugh. One night, the House of Commons was in ill-humour, and Lord North deprecated the too great readiness to take offence which then seemed to possess the House. "One member," he said, "who spoke of me, called me 'that thing of a minister;' to be sure," he said, patting his large form, "I am a thing; the member, therefore, when he called me a thing, said what was true, and I could not be angry with him; but, when he added, that thing called a minister, he called me that thing, which, of all things, he himself wished to be, and therefore," said Lord North, "I took it as a compliment." Such good-natured sallies dropped from him incessantly.

A few only of Lord North's sayings have reached us, and these, as might be expected, are rather things which he had chanced to coat over with some sarcasm or epigram that tended to preserve them; they consequently are far from giving an idea of his habitual pleasantry and the gaiety of thought which generally pervaded his speeches. Thus, when a vehement declaimer, calling aloud for his head, turned round and perceived his victim unconsciously indulging in a soft slumber, and, becoming still more exasperated, denounced the Minister as capable of sleeping while he ruined his country, the latter only complained how cruel it was to be denied a solace which other criminals so often enjoyed, that of having a night's rest before their fate. When surprised in a like indulgence during the performance of a very inferior artist, who, however, showed equal indignation at so ill-timed a recreation, he contented himself with observing how hard it was that he should be grudged so very natural a release from considerable suffering; but, as if recollecting himself added, that it was somewhat unjust in the gentleman to complain of him for taking the remedy which he had himself been considerate enough to administer. The same good humour and drollery quitted him not when in opposition. On Mr. Martin's proposal to have a starling placed near the chair, and taught to repeat the cry of "Infamous coalition!" Lord North coolly suggested, that, as long as the worthy member was preserved to them, it would be a needless Waste of the public money, since the starling might well perform his office by deputy.

Gibbon well described Lord North as "the Palinurus of the State," who might safely indulge in his slumbers, with his Attorney and Solicitor-General on either hand remaining at their posts to watch out the long debate.

Lord North's habits of somnolency led to many a *contretems.* It was constitutional somnolency, which attacked him alike on the Treasury-bench and in private society. One evening, he called on a lady of condition, and charming mind and person, whom he found in a violent altercation with her sister-in-law. Lord North attempted to interpose as a mediator; but they were not to be pacified without legal assistance. He consented, therefore, to wait until the lady of the house should return from her solicitor's chambers in Lincoln's Inn, Seating himself in an arm-chair before the fire, he soon fell into a profound sleep, from which he was not awakened by the entrance of one of the maid-servants; who, seeing a corpulent man, with a blue riband across his breast, asleep in her mistress's drawing-room, and being unacquainted with the First Minister's person, ran down into the kitchen to give the alarm.

One evening, in a full House of Commons, Lord North took off on the point of his sword, the *wig* of Mr. Welbore Ellis, and carried it a considerable way across the floor, without ever suspecting or perceiving it. It happened thus: Mr. Ellis, the Treasury of the Navy, always sat at the lowest corner of the Treasury Bench, a few feet removed from Lord North. The latter having occasion to go down the House, previously laid his hand upon his sword, holding the chafe of the scabbard forward, nearly in a horizontal direction! Mr. Ellis stooping at the same instant that Lord North rose, the point of the scabbard came in contact with the Treasurer's wig, which it completely took off, and bore away. The accident was wholly unseen by Lord North, who received the first intimation of it from the involuntary bursts of laughter that it occasioned in every quarter of the House. Mr. Ellis, however, without altering a muscle of his countenance, and preserving the most perfect gravity in the midst of the general convulsion, having received back his wig, readjusted it to his head, and waited patiently until the House had recovered from the effect of so droll an occurrence.

About this time Lord North was elected Knight of the Garter; and he practised the charity, enjoined by ,the rules of chivalry, by a distribution every Sunday morning, at the door of his residence in Downing-street, of broken victuals and five shillings and threepence to each of twenty poor persons there assembled by order.

When the Rioters, in 1780, had nearly filled the little square at the end of Downing-street, and Lord North and his friends in the Minister's residence Were debating how the noisy mob should be treated, Mr. St. John held a pistol in his hand, and was much excited; Lord North, who never lost an occasion of jesting, exclaimed: "I am not half so much afraid of the mob, as of Jack St. John's pistol."

When Lord North had resigned the premiership, somebody at White's, missing two of his principal confidants, asked where they were? "Sitting up with the corpse, I suppose," said Selwyn. This was quite in character for him, who loved to see executions and dead bodies.

After his going out of office, one night, in the House of Commons, Lord North sat opposite to the Treasury-bench; somebody said, "I see, my Lord, you have taken your place;" he replied, "Yes, a place for life." It was better what he said on the first gazette of the new Administration, "I was abused for lying gazettes, but there are more lies in this one than in all mine—yesterday his Majesty **was pleased** to appoint the Marquis of Rockingham, the Duke of Richmond, Mr. Charles Fox, &c. &c. &c." The new Administration was called the **Regency,** as they governed in the place of the King. Lord Effingham, from his strange figure and dress, and his two staffs, as Deputy Earl Marshal and Treasurer of the Household, was called *the Devil on two sticks.*

Lord North bore his political elevation with modesty, and showed equanimity in his fall. On the evening when he announced his resignation in the House of Commons, [March 20, 1782,] snow was falling, and the weather was bitterly cold. Lord North's carriage was waiting. As he was passing through the great-coat room of the House of Commons, many members (chiefly his opponents) crowded the passage. When his carriage was announced, he put one or two of his friends into it, and then making a bow to his opponents said, "Good night, gentlemen; it is the first time I have known the advantage of being in the secret."

Lady Charlotte Lindsay tells of her father, Lord North, that "His manners were those of a high-bred gentleman, particularly easy and natural; indeed, good breeding was so marked a part of his character that it would have been affectation in him to have been otherwise than well-bred. With such good taste and good breeding, his raillery could not fail to be of the best sort—always amusing and never wounding. He was the least fastidious of men, possessing the happy art of extracting any good that was to be extracted out of anybody. He never would let his children call people **bores;** and I remember the triumphant joy of his family, when, after a tedious visit from a very prosy and empty man, he exclaimed: 'Well, that man *is* an insufferable bore!' He used frequently to have large parties of foreigners and distinguished persons to dine with him at Bushy Park. He was himself the life and soul of these parties. To have seen him then you would have said that he was there in his true element. Yet, I think that he had really more enjoyment when he went into the country on a Saturday and a Sunday, with only his own family, or one or two intimate friends: he then entered into all the jokes and fun of his children, was the companion and intimate friend of his elder sons and daughters, and the merry, entertaining playfellow of his little girl, who was five years younger than any of the others. To his servants he was a most kind and indulgent master: if provoked by stupidity or impertinence, a few hasty, impatient words might escape him; but I never saw him *really out of humour.* He had a drunken, stupid groom, who used to provoke him; and who, from this circumstance, was called by the children, 'the man that puts papa in a passion;' and I think he continued all his life putting papa in a passion and being forgiven, for I believe he died in his service."

UNWELCOME WISH.

Mr. Elliot, a lord of trade, in Lord North's Administration, was descended from Sir John Elliot, who was imprisoned in the Tower by Charles I. A country gentleman, dining with Mr. Elliot, at his house in Cornwall, and intending to compliment him on his ancestry, said, "I hope soon to see you in the same situation."

A PLURALIST IN OFFICE.

Hutchinson's rapacity for office was insatiate. He was in possession of many posts, some sinecures, and all lucrative, when he applied to the Lord Lieutenant Townshend for more. Townshend laughed, and said he had nothing but a Majorship of Dragoons, which Hely is reported to have accepted, employing a deputy to fulfil the duty for a small emolument When Hutchinson first appeared at the English Court, George III asked Lord North who he was; a query to which his lordship gave a well-known reply. "He is the Secretary of State for Ireland; a man on whom if your Majesty was pleased to bestow the United Kingdom, he would ask for the Isle of Man as a potato-garden."

LORD CHANCELLOR THURLOW.

Thurlow was the son of a Norfolk clergyman, from whom he received the rudiments of his education. He was then sent to the grammar-school at Canterbury, at the suggestion of Dr. Donne (according to Sir Egerton Brydges) to gratify a malignant feeling towards the head-master, by placing under his care "a daring, refractory, clever boy, who would be sure to torment him." The motive ascribed to Donne seems improbable; and Thurlow remained at the Canterbury school several years, until he removed to Caius College, Cambridge, where he gained no academical honours, and was compelled to leave Cambridge abruptly, in consequence of turbulent and indecorous behaviour towards the dean of his college. Soon after he was entered a member of the Society of the Inner Temple.

To Nando's, a coffee-house in Fleet-street, at the east corner of Inner-Temple-lane, Thurlow used to resort at this early period of his life. It was here, when only a young man, that his skill in argument obtained for him, from a stranger, the appointment of a junior counsel in the great cause of Douglas *v* the Duke of Hamilton, which had the effect of bringing his talents, industry, and legal acquirements under the immediate notice of persons of power and influence, and of thus opening the way to subsequent elevation.

Yet, in 1782, when Lord North was removed from power, and the Rockingham Ministry was formed, Thurlow remained in possession of the great seal, by express command of the King; thus furnishing an instance without a parallel in the history of English party of a Lord Chancellor retaining office under an Administration to the leading features of whose policy he was resolutely opposed.

Lord Thurlow over-estimated his personal influence with the king, in treating Mr. Pitt with **hauteur,** and Lord North foretold that whenever Pitt said to the king, "Sire, the Great Seal must be in other hands," the king would take the seal from Lord Thurlow, and never think any more about him. It turned out exactly as Lord North had said: the king took the Great Seal from Lord Thurlow, and never concerned himself about him afterwards. This mortified Thurlow severely, and he is known to have said, "No man has a right to treat another in the way in which the king has treated me: we cannot meet again in the same room." He now became so incensed with Mr. Pitt and his Ministry, as to accuse them of having imposed upon the king in advising a measure for the encouragement of the growth of timber in the New Forest.

About the year 1790, when Thurlow was supposed to be on no very friendly terms with the Minister (Mr. Pitt), a friend asked the latter how Thurlow drew with them? "I don't know," said the Premier, "how he draws, but he has not refused his oats yet."

After the Cabinet to which he belonged was broken up, and he was made a baron, and laid on the shelf, in the hope of regaining his ascendancy, he took an uncomfortable villa, which had only the recommendation of being in the vicinity of Windsor Castle; and here, for three years, he was to be seen dancing attendance upon royalty, unnoticed and neglected by the king, who, when he heard of his late chancellor's death after an illness of a few hours, having cautiously inquired of the messenger if he were really dead, coldly observed, "Then he has not left a worse man behind him;" though the phrase which the king actually used was, says Lord Brougham, less decorous, and more unfeeling than the above.

LORD THURLOW'S THUNDER.

The celebrated reply of Lord Thurlow to the Duke of Grafton, who had reproached him with his plebeian extraction, and his recent elevation to the Peerage, is described as superlatively great He rose from the woolsack, and advanced slowly to the place from which the Chancellor generally addressed the House: then, fixing on the Duke the look of Jove when he grasps the thunder;—"I am amazed," he said, in a civil tone of voice, "at the attack which the noble Duke has made upon me. Yes, my lords," considerably raising his voice, "I am amazed at his Grace's speech. The noble Duke cannot look before him, behind him, or on either side of him, without seeing some noble peer, who owes his seat in this house to his successful exertions in the profession to which I belong. Does he not feel it is as honourable to owe it to these, as to being the accident of an accident?—To all these noble lords, the language of the noble Duke is as applicable and as insulting as it is to myself. But I don't fear to meet it single and alone. No one venerates the peerage more than I do,—but, my lords, I must say, that the peerage solicited me—not I the peerage. Nay more,—I can say and will say, that, as a peer of parliament,—as Speaker of this right honourable House,—as Keeper of the Great Seal,—as guardian of his Majesty's conscience,—as Lord High Chancellor of England,—nay, even in that character alone in which the noble Duke would think it an affront to be considered,—but which character none can deny *me;*—as A MAN, I am at this moment as respectable;—I beg leave to add,—I am at this time as much respected as the proudest peer I now look down upon." The effect of this speech, both within the walls of parliament, and out of them, was prodigious. It gave Lord Thurlow an ascendancy in the House, which no chancellor had ever possessed; it invested him in public opinion, with a character of independence and honour; and this, although he was ever on the unpopular side of politics, made him always popular with the people.—***Charles Butler.***

LORD THURLOW AND LORD LOUGHBOROUGH.

Lord Thurlow disliked and made light of Lord Loughborough, as attested in some good stories. Once, when the latter Lord was making a considerable impression in the House of Lords, on a subject which Lord Thurlow had not studied in detail, the latter was heard to mutter, "If I was not as lazy as a toad at the bottom of a well, I could kick that fellow Loughborough heels over head any day in the week." It was this ceaseless antagonism between Thurlow and Loughborough which led George III. to say, in a letter to Lord Eldon, just after he had been raised to the woolsack, "The King felt some pleasure at hearing that the Lord Chancellor sat the other day on the woolsack between Rosslyn (formerly Loughborough) and Thurlow, who ever used to require an intermediate power to keep them from quarrelling."

Lord Thurlow told George IV. (who repeated it to Lord Eldon) that "the fellow (Lord L.) had ***the gift of the gab*** in a marvellous degree, but that he was no lawyer"—adding, "In the House of Lords I get Kenyon, or somebody, to start some law doctrine, in such a manner that that fellow must get up to answer it, and then I leave the woolsack, and give him such a thump in his bread-basket, that he cannot recover himself." Dr. Johnson, in comparing the two, says: "I never heard anything from him (Loughborough) that was at all striking; and depend upon it, sir, it is when you come close to a man in conversation, that you discover what his real abilities are. To make a speech in a public assembly is a knack. Now, I honour Thurlow, sir; Thurlow is a fine fellow; he fairly puts his mind to yours."

The struggle between the two law lords was kept up throughout the arrangements for the Regency. Sheridan entered actively into a negotiation with Lord Thurlow, to secure his co-operation in consideration of his being allowed to retain the office of Chancellor; while Fox had promised to bestow the Great Seal, in the event of a change, upon Lord Loughborough, who, on the other hand, kept a watch upon the mysterious movements of Thurlow. Suddenly, he broke off his negotiation with the Prince's party, and declared for the King and Mr. Pitt; it is thought from his having speculated upon the King's recovery.

Thurlow's intrigues were masterpieces of slyness. On one occasion, during the Regency communications at Windsor, he let his colleagues go to Salt-hill, while he contrived to dine at the Castle. On another occasion, during these manœuvres of the Chancellor at Windsor, he betrayed, to the no small amusement of his colleagues, the secret of an interview which he had just had with the Prince, by coming to the Council with His Royal Highness' hat in his hand, instead of his own!

A manœuvre of another description is related of Lord Thurlow, during the debate on the Regency. Dr. Watson, Bishop of Llandaff, in a speech supporting the claims of the Prince of Wales, incidentally cited a passage from Grotius, with regard to the definition of the word ***right*** "The Chancellor, in his reply," says the Bishop, in his ***Memoirs,*** "boldly asserted that he perfectly well remembered the passage I had quoted from Grotius, and that it solely respected natural, but was inapplicable to civil, rights. Lord Loughborough, the first time I saw him after the debate, assured me that before he went to sleep that night, he looked into Grotius, and was astonished to find that the Chancellor, in contradicting me, had presumed on the ignorance of the House, and that my quotation was perfectly correct. What miserable shifts do great men submit to in supporting their parties! The Chancellor Thurlow," continues the Bishop, "was an able and upright judge, but as the Speaker of the House of Lords, he was domineering and insincere. It is said of him, that in the Cabinet he opposed everything, proposed nothing, and was ready to support anything. I remember Lord Camden saying to me one night, when the Chancellor, was speaking, contrary, as he thought, to his own conviction, 'There, now, I could not do that: he is supporting what he does not believe a word of.' "

LORD THURLOW AT WARREN HASTINGS' TRIAL.

On one occasion, during the progress of the trial of Warren Hastings, Mr. Fox, struck by the solemnity of Lord Thurlow's appearance, said to the Speaker, "I wonder whether any one ever was so wise as Thurlow looks." Lord Brougham describes Fox's remark with a difference: "it was more solemn and imposing than almost any other person's in public life; so much so, that it proved dishonest, since no man could *be* so wise as he *looked."* "Nor," says Lord Brougham, "did Thurlow neglect any of the external circumstances, how trifling soever, by which attention and deference could be secured on the part of his audience. Not only were his periods well rounded, and the connecting matter or continuing phrases well flung in, but the tongue was so hung as to make the sonorous voice peal through the hall, and appear to convey things which it would be awful to examine too near, and perilous to question. Nay, to the more trivial circumstances of his place, when addressing the House of Lords, he scrupulously attended. He rose slowly from his seat, he left the woolsack with deliberation; but he went not to the nearest place, like ordinary chancellors, the sons of mortal, men; he drew back by a pace or two, and, standing, as it were, askance, and partly behind the huge bale he had quitted for a season, he began to pour out, first in a growl, and then in a clearer and louder roll, the matter which he tad to deliver; and which, for the most part, consisted in some positive assertions, some personal vituperation, some sarcasms at classes, some sentences pronounced upon individuals, as if they were standing before him for judgment; some vague mysterious threats of things purposely not expressed, and abundant protestations of conscience and duty, in which they who keep the consciences of kings are apt to indulge."

Lord Campbell has described from recollection the appearance of the great Chancellor "bent with age, dressed in an old-fashioned grey coat, with breeches and gaiters of the same stuff, a brown scratch wig, tremendous white bushy eyebrows, eyes still sparkling with intelligence, dreadful crowsfeet round them, very deep lines in his countenance, and shrivelled complexion of a sallow hue."

They who had never seen Lord Thurlow might well imagine they heard him, if they had access to such excellent imitators as George the Fourth and Lord Holland.

JOHN WILKES-HIS PLACE-HUNTING, AND HIS WIT.

Wilkes was, at his entrance into public life, "a friend of the elder Pitt's;" and the ***Chatham Correspondence*** shows that he continued to profess to be so, and was a candidate for office under him. In 1761 he addressed to him a letter, a model of its class, avowing his pride "to have Mr. Pitt his patron and friend," and his desire for a scene of business. "I wish," he writes, "the Board of Trade might be thought a place in which I could be of any service;" adding, "among all the chances and changes of a political world, I will never have an obligation in a parliamentary way but to Mr. Pitt and his friends." Wilkes did not succeed; but, contriving to mix himself up with the constitutional questions of "general warrants" and "parliamentary privilege," such men as Mr. Pitt, though they disapproved of the violence and despised the calumnies of Wilkes, they used him as the tool of their ambition. Wilkes, encouraged by such support, grew so violent, that in 1763, Mr. Pitt denounced, in Parliament, the ***North Briton,*** and its author, as "the blasphemer of his God, and the libeller of his King," and repudiated all connexion with Wilkes.

Mr. Malone relates, in his ***Memoirs,*** that Wilkes, about the time when his ***North Briton*** began to be much noticed, dined one day with Mr. Rigby, and after dinner honestly confessed that he was a ruined man, not worth a shilling; that his principal object in writing was to procure himself some place, and that he should be particularly pleased with one that should remove him from the clamour and importunity of his creditors. He mentioned the office of Governor of Canada, and requested Mr. Rigby's good offices with the Duke of Bedford, so as to prevail on that nobleman to apply to Lord Bute for that place. Mr. Rigby said the Duke had not much intercourse with Lord Bute; neither could it be supposed that his lordship would purchase Mr. Wilkes's silence by giving him a good employment. Besides, he could have no security that the same hostile attacks would not be still made against him by Mr. Wilkes's coadjutors; Lloyd and Churohill, after he had left England. Wilkes solemnly assured him there need not be the least apprehension of that, for that he would make Churchill his chaplain, and Lloyd his secretary, and take them both with him to Canada. The Duke, at Rigby's request, made the application. Lord Bute would not listen to it, and even treated the affair with contempt When this was told to Mr. Wilkes, he observed to Mr. Rigby that Lord B. had acted very foolishly, and that he might five to lament that he and his colleagues had not quitted England, as much as King Charles did that Hampden and Cromwell had not gone to America, after the famous representation of the state of the nation in 1641; for now he should never cease his attacks till he had made him the most unpopular man in England. He kept his word. Malone relates this information from Mr. Rigby.

Wilkes well understood this cunning, which was the secret of his popularity: he was compelled to follow, that he might seem to lead, or, at least, to go two steps with his followers, that he might get them to go three with him.

Of Wilkes's convivial wit no doubt can remain. Gibbon, who passed an evening with him in 1762, when both were militia officers, says, "I scarcely ever met with a better companion: he has inexhaustible spirits, infinite wit and humour, and a great deal of knowledge." He adds, "A thorough profligate in principle as in practice; his life stained with every vice, and his conversation full of blasphemy and indecency. These morals he glories in, for shame is a weakness he has long since surmounted." This, no doubt, is greatly exaggerated, and the historian, believing him really to confess his political profligacy, is perhaps in error also: "he told us that in this time of public dissension he was resolved to make his. fortune." Possibly this was little more than a variety of his well-known saying to some one who was fawning on him with extreme doctrines, "I hope you don't take me for a Wilkite?" His examination, powerfully humorous certainly, on Lord Thurlow's solemn hypocrisy in the House of Lords, is well known., When, that consummate piece of cant; was performed with all the solemnity which the actor's incredible air, eyebrows, voice, could lend the imprecation, "If I forget my sovereign, may my God forget me!" Wilkes, seated on the steps of the throne, eyeing him askance with his inhuman squint and demoniac grin, muttered, "Forget you! He'll see you d—d first."

Wilkes's notoriety led to his head being often painted as a public-house sign, which, however, did not invariably raise the original in estimation. An old lady, in passing a public-house, distinguished as above, to which her companion had called her attention, "Ah!" replied she, "Wilkes swings everywhere but where he ought."

Wilkes's ugliness was proverbial: his squint has been immortalised by Hogarth. Yet, even this natural obliquity he turned to humorous account. When Wilkes challenged Lord Townshend, he said, "Your lordship is one of the handsomest men in the kingdom, and I am one of the ugliest. Yet, give but half an hour's start, and I will enter the lists against you with any woman you choose to name, because you will omit attentions on account of your fine exterior, which I shall double on account of my plain one." He used to add that it took him just half an hour to talk away his face. He was so exceedingly ugly that a lottery-office keeper is said to have offered him ten guineas not to pass his window whilst the tickets were drawing, for fear of his bringing ill-luck upon the house.

Wilkes, in an ironical speech on Lord George Germaine, said the noble lord might conquer America, but he believed it would not be in Germany. This rhodomontade of Lord Chatham had been so often applied, that it seemed difficult to allude to it with novelty any more. Lord George, whose insolence bore him up against all his disgraces, repeated this sarcasm himself in council, and commended it Complaining to the King of the neglects and dilatoriness of the Admiralty and Ministry, and of the badness of the transports, he said, "But I must say, sir, that the two heaviest and worst sailors are King George and the Lord North;" and he bragged of having said it.

The following epigram on Mr. Wilkes, in consequence of becoming a favourite at Court in April. 1784, and having once more come into Parliament for Middlesex, in conjunction with the **Court Candidate,** Mr. Mainwaring, appeared in a newspaper of the time:—

POLITICAL CONSISTENCY.

"What! Liberty-Wilkes, of oppression the hater,
Call'd a turncoat, a Judas, a rogue, and a traitor!
What has made all our patriots so angry and sore?
Has Wilkes done that now which he ne'er did before?

Consistent was John all the days of his life;
For he loved his best friends as he loved his own wife;
In his actions he always kept self in his view,
Though false to the world, to John Wilkes he was true.

Luttrell and Wilkes were standing on the Brentford hustings, when Wilkes asked his adversary, privately, whether he thought there were more fools or rogues among the multitude of Wilkites spread out before them. "I'll tell them what you say, and put an end to you," said the Colonel; but, perceiving the threat gave Wilkes no alarm, he added, "Surely you don't mean to say you could stand here one hour after I did so?" "Why (the answer was), you would not be alive one instant after." "How so?" "I should merely say it was a fabrication, and they would destroy you in the twinkling of an eye!"

Horne Tooke having challenged Wilkes, who was then **Sheriff** of London and Middlesex, received the following laconic reply:—"Sir, I do not think it my business to cut the throat of every desperado that may be tired of his life; but, as I am at present High Sheriff of the city of London, it may happen that I shall shortly have an opportunity of attending you in my official capacity, in which case I will answer for it that *you shall have no ground* to complain of my endeavours to serve you."

Walpole is more tender towards Wilkes than might have been expected. When the Lord of Strawberry was ill in Paris, in 1765, Wilkes called twice to see him. "He was very civil," says Walpole, "but I cannot say entertained me much. I saw no wit; his conversation shows how little he has lived in good company. He has certainly one merit, notwithstanding the bitterness of his pen, that is, he has no rancour."

Boswell, dining with the sheriffs and judges at the Old Bailey, complained that he had had his pocket picked of his handkerchief. "Poh, poh!" said Alderman Wilkes, "it is nothing but the ostentation of a Scotchman, to let the world know that he had possessed a pocket-handkerchief."

Wilkes's wit was so constantly at his command that wagers were laid, that, from the time he quitted his home near Storey's Gate till he reached Guildhall, no one would address him who would leave him without a smile or a hearty laugh. Notwithstanding their feuds, Lord Sandwich and Wilkes were partial to each other. Charles Butler once was not punctual in an appointment with Lord Sandwich, when it was mentioned to his lordship that the delinquent had dined with Mr. Wilkes. "Well, then," said Lord Sandwich, "Wilkes has so often made me break appointments with others, that it is but fair he should once make a person break his appointment with me."

Wilkes frequently noticed the multitude of peers created during Mr. Pitt's administration, as a circumstance likely to be attended with an important consequence not generally foreseen. "While the relation between the minister and the newly-made peers shall subsist, their subserviency," he used to say, "to his measures will continue; but, when this relation ceases, the probability is that, as the succeeding ministers will not have the means of attaching them, they will form a silent, sulky opposition—a dead weight on every administration. Will it not then be found that the descendants of Mr. Pitt's peers will be *mutes to strangle his successors?*"

Wilkes had written the history of his life, and earnestly requested Charles Butler to be his executor, under a condition of printing it entire and unaltered. Butler read the manuscript, but declined the charge: it is said that, on the death of Wilkes, the cover of the book of manuscript was found without any of the leaves.

Dr. Franklin has left this plain-spoken estimate of Wilkes and 45: "This really an extraordinary event, to see an outlaw and exile, of bad personal character, not worth a farthing, come over from France, set himself up as a candidate for the capital of the kingdom, miss his election only by being too late in his application, and immediately carrying it for the principal county. The mob, spirited up by numbers of different ballads, sung or roared in every street, requiring gentlemen and ladies of all ranks, as they passed in their carriages, to shout for 'Wilkes and liberty!' marking the same words on all their coaches with chalk, and No. 45 on every door; which extends a vast way along the roads into the country. I went last week to Winchester, and observed that for fifteen miles out of town there was scarce a door or window-shutter next the road unmarked; and this continued, here and there, quite to Winchester, which is sixty-four miles."

Wilkes, of course, in his constant tilts, did not escape retaliation. The following is attributed to Sheridan:—

"Johnny Wilkes, Johnny Wilkes,
Thou greatest of bilks,
How changed are the notes you now sing;
Your famed forty-five
Is Prerogative,
And your blasphemy, 'God save the King.' "

Mr. Rogers thus relates his first impression of Wilkes;—"One morning, when I was a lad, Wilkes came into our banking-house to solicit my father's vote. My father happened to be out, and I, as his representative, spoke to Wilkes. At parting, Wilkes shook hands with me; and I felt proud of it for a week after. He was quite as ugly, and squinted as much, as his portraits make him; but he was very gentlemanly in appearance and manners. I think I see him at this moment, walking through the crowded streets of the City, as Chamberlain, on his way to Guildhall, in a scarlet coat, military boots, and a bag-wig—the hackney-coachmen in vain calling out to him, 'A coach, your honour.' "

Wilkes resided occasionally at Hamilton Lodge, in Kensington Gore. Sometimes he had high visitors here: a memorandum of his refers to a dinner given here to Counts Woronzow and Nesselrode; and, if we are to set down Sir Philip Francis as "Junius," here Junius visited, as Mrs. Rough, Wilkes's daughter, said, frequently; and he once cut off a lock of her hair when a child. Wilkes, to the last, kept up a certain fashionable status: he died in No. 30, Grosvenor-square; and was buried in Grosvenor Chapel, South Audley-street, where is a tablet with this inscription from his own pen, "The remains of John Wilkes, a Friend to Liberty."

BURKE AT THE "ROBIN HOOD."

The debating club called "The Robin Hood Society" met in Essex-street, in the Strand, in the reign of George the Second. It became famous as the scene of Burke's earliest eloquence. To discipline themselves in public speaking at its meetings was then, the custom among law-students, and others intended for public life; and it is said that at the Robin Hood, Burke had commonly to encounter an opponent whom nobody else could overcome, or at least silence. This person was the president, who sat in a large gilt chair. Goldsmith, who was of the club, was so struck with his eloquence and imposing aspect, that he thought Nature had meant him for a Lord Chancellor. "No, no,"! whispered Derrick (another member), who knew him to be a wealthy baker from the City, "only for a Master of the Rolls."

A DAY WITH EDMUND BURKE.

Mr. Hardy, in his *Memoirs of Lord Charlemont,* relates: "One of the most satisfactory days, perhaps, that I ever passed in my life was going with him, tête-à-tête, from London to Beaconsfield. He stopped at Uxbridge whilst the horses were feeding, and happening to meet some gentlemen, of I know not what militia, who appeared to be perfect strangers to him, he entered into discourse with them at the gateway of the inn. His conversation at that moment completely exemplified what Johnson said of him: 'That you could not meet Burke for half an hour under a shed, without saying he was an extraordinary man.' He was on that day altogether uncommonly instructive and agreeable. Every object of the slightest notoriety, as we passed along, whether of natural or local history, furnished him with abundant materials for conversation. The house at Uxbridge, where the Treaty was held during Charles the First's time; the beautiful and undulating grounds of Bulstrode, formerly the residence of Chancellor Jeffries; and Waller's tomb, in Beaconsfield churchyard, which, before we went home, we visited, and whose character—as a gentleman, a poet, and an orator—he shortly delineated, but with exquisite felicity of genius, altogether gave an uncommon interest to his eloquence; and, although one-and-twenty years have now passed since that day, I entertain the most vivid and pleasing recollection of it."

BURKE'S TABLE-TALK.

In 1863 there were printed, for private circulation, some extracts from Mr. Burke's table-talk at Crewe Hall, written down by Mrs. Crewe. Here are a few specimens [Note *: From a paper in the *Saturday Review.*]:—

When Langton, with reference to a conversation in which Johnson, as usual, had taken the lead, remarked that he should have been glad to hear more from another person (meaning Burke), Burke exclaimed, "Oh, no; it is enough for me to have rung the bell to him."

Johnson one day said:—

"What I most envy Burke for is his being constantly the same. He is never what we call humdrum; never unwilling to begin to talk, nor in haste to leave off. . . . Burke, sir, is such a man, that if you met him for the first time in the street when you were stopped by a drove of oxen, and you and he stepped aside to take shelter but for five minutes, he'd talk to you in such a manner that, when you parted, you would say, 'This is an extraordinary man.' Now, you may be long enough with me without finding anything extraordinary."

At the same time he denied him wit:—

"No, sir; he never succeeds there. 'Tis low; 'tis conceit I used to say Burke never once made a good joke."

Boswell vehemently maintains the contrary; and Reynolds declared that he had often heard Burke say, in the course of an evening, ten good things which would have served a noted wit to live upon for a twelvemonth.

Burke's happiest flights of fancy are those by which he points arguments and illustrates reflections too grave and deep to suggest humorous associations. Thus, in defending the trappings of royalty—"The feather that adorns the royal bird supports his flight; strip him of his plumage, and you fix him to the earth;" or when he accused Pitt of contemplating a commercial treaty with France as an affair of two firms, and not of two great nations, as "a contention between the sign of the **Fleur de Lis** and the sign of the **Old Red Lion,** which should obtain most custom."

Mrs. Piozzi describes Burke as a reckless, haphazard talker, troubling himself little about the consequences of what he said. One evening, at Sir Joshua Reynolds's, he spoke so strongly in praise of some island in the West Indies, that Mrs. Horneck, a widow with two beautiful daughters, resolved to lose no time in purchasing land there. She did so, and lost a large part of her slender income. "Dear sir," said I (Mrs. Piozzi), when we met next, "how fatal has your eloquence proved to poor Mrs. Horneck." "How fatal her own folly!" replied he; "Ods! my life, must one swear to the truth of a song?"

When some one mentioned Fox's attachment to France and French manners, Burke answered, "Yes, his attachment has been great and long; for, like a cat, he has continued faithful to the house after the family has left it." On its being remarked that no persons held together for any long continuance who called themselves democrats, taking the fact at once for granted, he replied, "Birds of prey are not gregarious." He said that Mr. Windham "often reminded him of Eddystone Lighthouse, dashed at by waves, but continuing steadily to give light to surrounding objects."

Mr. Burke thought that lounging rides on horseback had been of late one of the great checks to economy in all families among the gentry. Very few younger brothers, said he, are able to keep two horses, and two horses must be kept when they are in the habit of riding every day; and if they are neat and elegant in their ideas (as all gentlemen ought to be), this expense incurs that of an additional servant, besides necessary accoutrements, such as saddles, bridles, boots, &c., which create endless bills, and will run a man very fast into debt. Few besides elder brothers, he said, ever thought of riding in the middle of the day, except on particular occasions, till within the last thirty years. Men, indeed, who possessed parks, farms, or other objects to look after out of doors, kept horses in their stalls also for pleasure; but men who could have no other object but that of sauntering made more use of their own limbs, and found fitter employment for both their time and money.

Mrs. Piozzi confirms Wraxall's remark, that Burke's Irish accent was as strong as if he had never quitted the banks of the Shannon.

Burke frequently introduced coarse and low expressions even in his most splendid passages. The "pigging together in a truckle-bed," and "the sow of imperial augury," will, probably, occur to the reader. The effect of such expressions was sometimes great, and then redeemed them; but they sometimes deformed and disgusted. "The Venus of Phidias," Wilkes used to say, "was so lovely, that the Athenians called her the Venus of roses: lovely, too, generally speaking, is the Venus of Burke; but she sometimes is the Venus of whisky."

BURKE AND BARRY AT A STEAK-DINNER.

Many a middle-aged reader may recollect the dilapidated house of James Barry, the painter, in Castle-street, Oxford Market: he was extremely negligent of his person and dress, and not less so of his house, in which he had resided nearly twenty years; and until the time of his death it remained almost proverbial for its dirty and ruinous state. Here Barry gave a dinner to Burke—the statesman watched the steak while the painter ran to a neighbouring public-house for a pot of porter. Allan Cunningham has thus pleasantly described the visit: "Sir," said Barry, "you know I live alone; but if you will come and help me to eat a steak, I shall have it tender and hot from the most classic market in London—that of Oxford." The day and the hour came, and Burke, arriving at No. 36, Castle-street, found Barry ready to receive him. The fire was burning brightly, the steak was put on to broil, and Barry, having spread a clean cloth on the table, put a pair of tongs in the hands of Burke, saying, "Be useful, my dear friend, and look to the steak till I fetch the porter." Burke did as he was desired; the painter soon returned with the porter in his hand, exclaiming, "What a misfortune! the wind carried away the fine foaming top as I crossed Titchfield-street." They sat down together; the steak was tender, and done to a moment. The artist was full of anecdote, and Burke often declared that he never spent a happier evening in his life.

BURKE AND CHATHAM REPUTED MAD.

Perhaps, if there is one man to whom a reader of English history would point as having seen more than what lay immediately under his nose, as being that rare animal in political life, one who entertained wide and philosophical views instead of having faith in the expediency-doctrine of the moment—that man is Edmund Burke. "He possessed," says Coleridge, "and had sedulously sharpened that eye which sees all things, actions, and events in relation to the laws which determine their existence and circumscribe their possibility. He referred habitually to principles; he was a scientific statesman."

When the far-seeing sagacity of Burke, in foretelling the unhappy results of the French Revolution, first struck into the minds of his party, from which he had been separated, it was reported that he was in a state of mind bordering on insanity; especially after he had, in the House of Commons, addressed to the chair, with much vehemence of manner, the words of St. Paul, "I am not mad, most noble Festus; but speak the words, of truth and soberness." Burke's niece ventured to name to him the above absurd rumour, when he very sensibly replied, "Some part of the world, my dear—I mean the Jacobins, or unwise part of it—think, or affect to think, that I am mad; but, believe me, the world, twenty years hence, will, and with reason too, think from their conduct that they must have been mad." These rumours, however, gained strength, particularly after the death of Burke's son: he was said to wander about his grounds kissing his cows and horses; but his affection for domestic animals had been remarkable from his early manhood, and Reinagle painted him patting a favourite cow. This picture brought from London to Beaconsfield an old friend, to ascertain the truth or falsehood of the story—when Burke, without knowing the object of his visit, unsuspiciously showed him portions of the **Letters on a Regicide Peace,** which he was then writing. The circumstance of his being seen to throw his arms round the neck of his son's favourite horse, to weep and sob convulsively, as he kissed the animal, had, moreover, a greater share in substantiating the rumour than had Reinagle's picture.

Lord Chatham, contemporary with Burke, was also alleged to have been insane. Horace Walpole fosters this scandal, and the fact of the earl placing himself under Dr. Addington, originally a "mad doctor," strengthened the rumour; but Addington had been the village doctor at Hayes, where Lord Chatham resided. His ill-managed expenditure and his freaks of extravagance backed the report, which, after all, was little better than an invention of political enemies.

MR. FOX'S GAMING.

Fox's love of play was desperate. A few evenings before he voted the repeal of the Marriage Act, in February, 1772, he had been to Brompton, on two errands: one to consult Justice Fielding on the penal laws; the other to borrow 10,000 *l.,* which he brought to town at the hazard of being robbed. Fox was a member of Almack's Club, in Pall Mall, where they played only for rouleaus of 50 *l.* each rouleau; and generally, there was 10,000 *l.* of specie on the table. The gamesters' dresses for play were remarkable: they began by pulling off their embroidered clothes, and put on frieze greatcoats, or turned their coats inside outward, for luck. They put on pieces of leather, (such as are worn by footmen, when they clean their knives,) to save their lace ruffles; and to guard their eyes from the light, and to prevent tumbling their hair, they wore high-crowned straw hats, with broad brims, adorned with flowers and ribbons; and masks to conceal their emotions when they played at quinze. Each gamester had a small neat stand by him, with a large rim, to hold his tea; and a wooden bowl, with an edge of ormoulu to hold rouleaus.

Fox played admirably at whist and at picquet: with such skill, indeed, that at Brookes's Club, it was calculated that he might have made 4,000 *l.* a-year, had he confined himself to those games. But his misfortune arose from playing games at chance, particularly at Faro, when he almost inevitably rose a loser. Once, indeed, and once only, he won about eight thousands pounds in the course of a single evening. Part of the money he paid away to his creditors, and the remainder he lost almost immediately. Before he attained his thirtieth year, he had completely dissipated everything that he could either command, or could procure by the most ruinous expedients, in order to raise money, after losing his last guinea at the Faro table. He was reduced for successive days to such distress, as to borrow money from the waiters of Brookes's Club. The very chairmen, whom he was unable to pay, used to dun him for their arrears. Great sums were borrowed of Jews at exorbitant premiums. Fox called his outward room, where the Jews waited till he rose, the *Jerusalem Chamber.* His brother Stephen was enormously fat; George Selwyn said he was in the right to deal with Shylocks, as he could give them pounds of flesh.

Walpole remarks that in the debate on the Thirty-nine Articles, Feb. 6, 1772, Fox did not shine, "nor could it be wondered at. He had sat up playing at hazard at Almack's, from Tuesday evening the 4th, till five in the afternoon of Wednesday the 5th. An hour before he had recovered 12,000 *l.* that he had lost, and by dinner, which was at five o'clock, he had ended losing 11,000 *l.* On the Thursday, he spoke in the above debate; went to dinner at past eleven at night; from thence to White's, where he drank till seven the next morning; thence to Almack's, where he won 6,000 *l.*; and between three and four in the afternoon he set out for Newmarket. His brother Stephen lost 11,000 *l.* two nights after, and Charles 10,000 *l.* more on the 13th; so that, in three nights, the two brothers, the eldest not twenty-five, lost 32,000 *l.*

Towards the close of this year, Fox was publicly spoken of as having been more successful at Newmarket than had been the lot of many adventurers there for years.

The newspapers calculated his winnings at 28,000 *l.* Fox was said to have the finest stud in the kingdom; he refused 3,000*l.* for his favourite horse Pantaloon.

It is, however, remarkable that amidst the wildest excesses of youth, even while the perpetual victim of his passion for play, Fox eagerly cultivated at intervals his taste for letters. One morning, after he had passed the whole night in company with Topham Beauclerc at the Faro-table, the two friends were about to separate. Fox had lost throughout the night, and was in a frame of mind approaching desperation. Beauclerc's anxiety for the consequences led him to be early at Fox's lodgings; and on arriving there he inquired, not without anxiety, whether he had risen. The servant replied that Mr. Fox was in the drawing-room, when Beauclerc walked upstairs, and cautiously opened the door, expecting to behold a frantic gamester stretched upon the floor, bewailing his losses, or plunged in moody despair; but he was astonished to find him reading a Greek Herodotus. "What would you have me do?" said Fox, "I have lost my last shilling."

MR. FOX AND THE "SENSIBLE WOMAN."

In the summer of 1773, a cunning woman who had been transported a few years before, advertised herself in. London as ***a sensible woman*** who gave advice on all emergencies for half-a-guinea. She pretended to be related to Ministers, and called herself the Hon. Mrs. Grieve. Among the dupes whom she caught in her snares was Charles Fox. According to Walpole, this woman undoubtedly had uncommon talents and a knowledge of the world. She persuaded Fox, desperate with his debts, that she could procure for him, as a wife, a Miss Phipps, with a fortune of 80,000 *l.,* who was just arrived from the West Indies. There was such a person coming over, but not with half the fortune, nor known to Mrs. Grieve. With this bait, she amused Mr. Fox for many months, appointed meetings, and once persuaded him that, as Miss Phipps liked a fair man, and as he was remarkably black, he must powder his eyebrows. Of that intended interview he was disappointed by the imaginary lady's falling ill of what was afterwards pretended to be the small-pox. After he had waited some time, Mrs. Grieve affected to go to see if Miss Phipps was a little better, and able to receive her swain; but on opening the door, a servant-maid, who had been posted to wait on the stairs, as coming down with the remains of a basin of broth, told Mrs. Grieve that Miss Phipps was not well enough to receive the visit. Had a novice been the prey of these artifices, it would not have been extraordinary, but Charles Fox had been in the world from his childhood, and been treated as a man long before the season. He must have known there could not have been an Hon. Mrs. Grieve, nor such a being as she pretended to be. In one respect she had singular *finesse:* instead of asking him for money, which would have detected her plot at once, she was so artful as to lend him 300 *l.,* or thereabouts; and she paid herself by his chariot Standing frequently at her door, which served to impose on her more vulgar dupes.

ME. FOX DISMISSED FROM THE. MINISTRY.

In 1774, Fox was dismissed from the ministry for his flippant behaviour to Lord North. Edmund Burke had great weight with him; and Burke, tired of a hopeless opposition, of desperate fortune, and apt to deal in monied projects, had, in concert with Garrick the actor, engaged Fox in soliciting Lord North for a grant of land in America. If it succeeded, Burke and Fox would have sold their shares; if it miscarried, Fox would be a great acquisition to the discontented. Lord North refused the grant—Fox attacked him, and was turned out. Upon this, George Selwyn said to Fox, "Charles, for the future, I will fast and eat salt fish on the day you were turned out. You shall be my Charles the Martyr now. I am tired of the old one, your great-grandfather: his head can never be sewed on again: but as yours can be, I'll stick to you." Fox was infinitely hurt at his disgrace, and had reasons enough. When Lord North complained of his flippancies to the King, his Majesty, who hated him, said, "Why don't you turn him out? you may if you will." Fox knew not where to turn: at first, he said he would study the law: his character was so decried that the scandalous mob believed he was turned out for robbing the treasury.

The immediate cause and manner of Fox's dismissal was his forcing Lord North to vote with him; he had previously given offence by his motion on the Royal Marriage Bill. On the 24th of February he was dismissed from the Board of Treasury, on which occasion Lord North wrote him the following laconic note: "His Majesty has thought proper to order a new Commission of Treasury to be made out, in which I do not see your name.—NORTH."

FOX IN DIFFICULTIES.

Walpole gives, in one of his letters, the following lamentable picture of Fox's fallen fortune. "As I came up St. James's-street, I saw a cart and porters at Charles's (Fox) door; coppers and old chests of drawers loading. In short, his success at faro has awakened a host of creditors; but unless his bank had swelled to the size of the Bank of England, it could not nave yielded a sop apiece for each. Epsom, too, had been un-propitious; and one creditor has actually seized and carried off his goods, which did not seem worth removing. As I returned full of this scene, whom should I find sauntering by my own door, but Charles? He came up and talked to me at the coach-window, on the Marriage Bill, with as much *sang froid* as if he knew nothing of what had happened. I have no admiration of insensibility to one's own faults, especially when committed out of vanity. Perhaps the whole philosophy consisted in the commission. If *you* could have been as much to blame, the last thing you would bear well would be your own reflections. The more marvellous Fox's parts are, the more one is provoked at his follies, which comfort so many rascals and blockheads, and make all that is admirable and amiable in him only matter of regret to those who like him as I do."

Fox was sitting one evening at Brookes's, in a deep reverie, with his knife in his hand. "There," said Fitzpatrick, "I might describe Charles meditating on the ruin of his country, ingeminating the words 'peace, peace!' and ready to plunge the knife in his own bosom," "Yes," rejoined Hare, in the same ironic, dolorous tone, "and he would have done so, but happening to look on the handle of the knife, he saw it was silver, and put it into his pocket."

FOX'S HUMOUR.

Charles Butler, when spending the day with Mr. Fox, at St. Ann's-hill, mentioned that he had "never read Adam Smith's celebrated work on the 'Wealth of

Nations.'" "To tell you the truth," said Mr. Fox, "nor I either. There is something in all these subjects which passes my comprehension—something so wide, that I could never embrace them myself, nor find any one who did."

The Stamp-duty on receipts was first introduced during the short reign of the Administration composed of "All the Talents." Fox was at the time in pecuniary difficulties, which led Sheridan to write,—

"'I would,' says Fox, 'a tax devise;
That should not fall on me.'
'Then tax receipts,' Lord North replies,
'For these you never see.'"

During the Westminster election of 1789, one of the mob called out to Mr. Fox, a candidate, "Well, Charley, are not you sick of your *coalition?*" "Poor gentleman!" cried an old woman in the crowd, "why should not he like a *collation?*"

FOX AND GIBBON.

Of the sale of Fox's library we find the following memorandum in Walpole's manuscript Notes, quoted in Earl Russell's *Life of Fox:*—

"1781, June 20. Sold by auction, the library of Charles Fox, which had been taken in execution. Amongst the books was Mr. Gibbon's first volume of 'Roman History,' which appeared, by the title-page, to have been given by the author to Mr. Fox, who had written in it the following anecdote:—'The author at Brookes's said there was no salvation for the country till six heads of the principal persons in the administration were laid on the table; eleven days later, the same gentleman accepted the place of Lord of Trade under those very ministers, and has acted with them ever since!' Such was the avidity of bidders for the smallest production of so wonderful a genius, that by the addition of this little record, the book sold for three guineas."

Gibbon said that "Charley's black collier would soon sink Billy's painted galley;" but Mr. Fox said more truly—"Pitt will do for us, if he should not do for himself."

MB. ROGERS'S RECOLLECTIONS OF MR. FOX

"It is quite true, as stated in several accounts of him, that Fox, when a very young man, was a prodigious dandy, wearing a little odd French hat, shoes with red heels, &c. He and Lord Carlisle once travelled from Paris to Lyons for the express purpose of buying waistcoats; and during the whole journey they talked about nothing else. Fox (in his earlier days, I mean), Sheridan, Fitzpatrick, &c. led **such** a life! Lord Tankerville assured me that he has played cards with Fitzpatrick at Brookes's from ten o'clock at night till near six o'clock the next afternoon, a waiter standing by to tell them 'whose deal it was,' they being too sleepy to know. After losing large sums at hazard, Fox would go home—not to destroy himself, as his friends sometimes feared, but—to sit down quietly, and read Greek. He once won about eight thousand pounds; and one of his bond-creditors, who soon heard of his good luck, presented himself and asked for payment. 'Impossible, Sir,' replied Fox; 'I must first discharge my debts of honour.' The bond-creditor remonstrated 'Well, Sir, give me your bond.' It was delivered to Fox, who tore it in pieces, and threw them into the fire. 'Now, Sir,' said Fox, 'my debt to you is a debt of honour;' and immediately paid him.

"I saw Lunardi make the first ascent in a balloon which had been witnessed in England. It was from the Artillery-ground. Fox was there with his brother, General F. The crowd was immense. Fox, happening to put his hand down to his watch, found another hand upon it, which he immediately seized. 'My friend,' said he to the owner of the strange hand, 'you have chosen an occupation which will be your ruin at last' 'O, Mr. Fox,' was the reply, 'forgive me, and let me go! I have been driven to this course by necessity alone; my wife and children are starving at home.' Fox, always tender-hearted, slipped a guinea into the hand, and then released it. On the conclusion of the show Fox was proceeding to look what o'clock it was. 'Good God,' cried he, 'my watch is gone!'—'Yes,' answered General F., 'I know it is; I saw your friend take it.' 'Saw him take it! and you made no attempt to stop him?' 'Really, you and he appeared to be on such good terms with each other that I did not choose to interfere.'

Very shortly before Fox died he complained of great uneasiness in his stomach; and Cline advised him to try the effect of a cup of coffee. It was accordingly ordered; but, not being brought so soon as was expected, Mrs. Fox expressed some impatience; upon which Fox said, with his usual sweet smile, 'Remember, my dear, that good coffee cannot be made in a moment.' Lady Holland announced the death of Fox in her own odd manner to those relatives and intimate friends of his who were sitting in a room near his bed-chamber, and waiting to hear that he had breathed his last;—she walked through the room with her apron thrown over her head. Trotter's ***Memoirs of Fox,*** though incorrect in some particulars, is a very pleasing book. Trotter died in Ireland: he was reduced to great straits; and Mrs. Fox sent him, at different times, as much as several hundred pounds, though she could ill spare the money. How fondly the surviving friends of Fox cherished his memory! Many years after his death I was at a fête given by the Duke of Devonshire at Chiswick House. Sir Robert Adair and I wandered about the apartments, up and down stairs. 'In which room did Fox expire?' asked Adair. I replied, 'In this very room.' Immediately Adair burst into tears with a vehemence of grief such as I hardly ever saw exhibited by a man."

WILLIAM PITT'S EARLY LIFE.

One morning, some law lord (thought to have been Lord Mansfield) paid a visit to Lord Chatham, at his country residence at Hayes. Whilst they were conversing, his son William came through the library. Lord——asked who is that youth? Lord Chatham said, "That is my second son—call him back and talk to him." They did so, and Lord——was struck by a forwardness of knowledge, a readiness of expression, and unyieldingness of opinion, which even then was remarkable in the future minister. When he had left them, Lord Chatham said: "That is the most extraordinary youth I ever knew. All my life I have been aiming at the possession of political power, and have found the greatest difficulty in getting or keeping it. It is not on the cards of fortune to prevent that young man's gaining it, and if ever he does so, he will be the ruin of his country."

Mr. Pitt, member for Sir James Lowther's close borough of Appleby, delivered his maiden speech in February, 1781, in support of Mr. Burke's motion for Reforming the Civil List. His speech, early in June, on the American War, elicited praise even from his opponents. "He promises to be the first speaker ever heard in the House," said a Member to Fox. "He is that already" was the chivalrous, or rather the manly, reply of Charles Fox.

The story told of Mr. Pitt's refusing to marry Mademoiselle Neckar, (afterwards Madame de Staël,) when the match was proposed by the father, rests upon a true foundation; not so, however, the form of the answer, that "he was already married to his country"—thought to have been a jest.

A CASTING VOTE.

Lord Malmesbury has given this sketch of the Prime Minister, Pitt, on the night when the vote first went against Dundas. "I sat wedged close to Pitt himself the night we were 216 to 216; and the Speaker, Abbot (after looking as white as a sheet, and pausing for ten minutes) gave the casting vote against us. Pitt immediately put on the little cocked hat that he was in the habit of wearing when dressed for the evening, and jammed it deeply over his forehead, and I distinctly saw the tears trickling down his cheeks. We had overheard one or two such as Colonel Wardle say they would see ' how Billy looked after it.' A few young ardent followers of Pitt, with myself locked their arms together, and formed a circle in which he moved, I believe unconsciously, out of the House; and neither the Colonel nor his friends could approach him."

A NARROW ESCAPE.

In the autumn of 1784, Mr. Pitt had nearly fallen a victim to the frolic of a festive meeting. Returning late at night, on horseback, from Wimbledon to Addiscombe, the seat of Mr. Huskisson, near Croydon, where the party had dined; Lord Thurlow, then Chancellor, Pitt, and Dundas, found the turnpike-gate between Tooting and Streatham, thrown open. Being in elevated spirits, and having no servant near them, they passed through the gate at a brisk pace, without stopping to pay the toll; regardless of the remonstrance or threats of the turnpike-man, who, running after them, and believing them to belong to some highwaymen, who had recently committed depredations on that road, discharged the contents of his blunderbuss at their backs. Happily, he did no injury. To this narrow escape of the Prime Minister, which furnished matter of pleasantry, though perhaps not of rejoicing, to the Opposition, allusion is made in the ***Rolliad;***

> "How as he wander'd darkling o'er the plain,
> His reason lost in Jenkinson's champagne,
> A peasant's hand, but that just Fate withstood,
> Had shed a Premier's, for a robber's blood."

AN OPPORTUNITY LOST.

During the co-operation of all parties against Mr. Addington's government, in the spring of 1804, Mr. Pitt and Mr. C. Long were one night passing the door of Brookes's Clubhouse, on their way from the House of Commons, when Mr. Pitt, who had not been there since the Coalition of 1784, said he had a great mind to go in and sup. His wary friend said, "I think you had better not," and turned aside the well-conceived intention. "When," says Lord Brougham, "we reflect on the high favour Mr. Pitt was then in with the Whigs, and consider the nature of Mr. Fox, as well as his own, we can have little doubt of the cordial friendship which such a night would have cemented, and that the union of the two parties would have been complete."

DEFENDERS OP THEIR COUNTRY.

In 1805, Pitt had a meeting of country gentlemen, chiefly militia colonels, to consider his "Additional Force Bill." One of the meeting objected to a clause for calling out the Force, which he insisted should not be done, "except in case of actual invasion." Pitt replied "That would be too late;" but the speaker still insisted on the case of actual invasion. By-and-by, they came to another clause, to render the Force more disposable; the same gentleman objected again, and insisted very warmly that he would never consent to its being sent out of England. "Except, I suppose," rejoined Pitt, "in case of actual invasion."

PITT'S LAST MOMENTS.

The news of Austerlitz was the last blow which killed Pitt. The gout, which had hitherto confined its attacks to his extremities, assailed some vital organ. He was not without hopes of getting better. Lord Wellesley found him in high spirits, though before the interview was over, Pitt fainted in his presence. His last moments are described by the Hon. James Stanhope, who was present in the room when he died; so that at length we seem to have authentic information of a scene which has hitherto been very imperfectly described. "I remained the whole of Wednesday night with Mr. Pitt," says Mr. Stanhope in a paper drawn up by him, and of which Earl Stanhope has availed himself in his *Life of Pitt.* "His mind seemed fixed on the affairs of the country, and he expressed his thoughts aloud, though sometimes incoherently. He spoke a good deal concerning a private letter from Lord Harrowby, and frequently inquired the direction of the wind; then said, answering himself 'East; ah! that will do; that will bring him quick.' At other times he seemed to be in conversation with a messenger, and sometimes cried out 'Hear, hear,' as if in the House of Commons. During the time he did not speak he moaned considerably, crying, 'Oh, dear! Oh, Lord!' Towards twelve the rattles came in his throat, and proclaimed approaching dissolution.... At about half-past two he ceased moaning.... I feared he was dying; but shortly afterwards, with a much clearer voice than he spoke in before, and in a tone I shall never forget, 'Oh, my country! how I leave my country!' [referring, as it was natural for him to do, to the disastrous state of the continental war produced by the battle of Austerlitz.] From that time he never spoke or moved, and at half-past four expired without a groan or struggle," 23d January, 1806. He received the Sacrament from the Bishop of Lincoln. Mr. Pitt gave his watch to his servant, who handed it over to Mr. Dundas, M.P., more than twenty years after

Mr. Pitt's death. That watch, a mourning-ring, and box containing the hair, were bequeathed to the Rt Hon. R. N. Hamilton; and the watch is now preserved in the Fitzwilliam Museum, at Cambridge.

"Pitt is the most forgiving and easy-tempered of men," says Lord Malmesbury. "He is the most upright political character I ever knew or heard of," says Wilberforce. "I never once saw him out of temper," says George Rose. One day, when the conversation turned upon the quality most needed in a Prime Minister, and one said "Eloquence," another "Knowledge," and a third "Toil," Pitt said, "No; Patience." It was an answer worthy of the great statesman, and recalls that of Newton, who said that he owed his splendid discoveries to the power of fixed attention. Pitt was wonderfully patient, and this, which is commonly regarded as a slow virtue, he combined with uncommon readiness and rapidity of thought. "What an extraordinary man Pitt is!" said Adam Smith; "he makes me understand my own ideas better than before."

PITT'S HABITS OF WORK.

His extraordinary and systematic exertions told seriously against Mr. Pitt when his health began to give way. The labour which he had to endure as a mere youth in sustaining the Government against overwhelming odds tended to undermine his constitution. One of his greatest speeches was delivered under much physical suffering. Now and then he took a holiday, and in imagination we may see him and Wilberforce at Holwood sallying forth with billhooks, cutting new walks from one large tree to another through the thickets of the Holwood copses. But continually it happened that he worked through nearly the whole of a recess, seldom allowing himself a single holiday. When the House of Commons met, his work was of course doubled, and he had to adapt himself to hours that ill-suited his feeble frame. Frequently the debates did not come to an end till six, seven, or even eight o'clock on the following morning. He wound up one of his most celebrated speeches—that on the Slave Trade, delivered in 1792, by welcoming as of good omen the morning beam that then shot across the House. As a usual thing, he had eight or ten hours of sleep, and he slept well. He had often to be woke up in the night to receive important news, and if his attendants went in upon him ten minutes afterwards they were sure to find him sleeping sound again. This was his salvation. When he received the news of Trafalgar he could not sleep after it, and rose to work at three in the morning. He mentioned this as something extraordinary, and as showing the tremendous importance of the tidings. But it showed also that his health was giving way, and that his nervous system was not so calm as it used to be. How could it be calm, considering the work which he had to go through? Even in his first Cabinet, when he had Dundas and Grenville at his side, he was overtoiled. He transacted the business of all departments except theirs, and when he transacted business we should understand what that means. He did nothing by deputy. He would not suffer any one to arrange his papers and extract the important points for him. Imagine this system of work carried on in a Government where he had no Grenville and no Dundas to assist him, where he stood almost alone, and when he had to bear up against health which was fast failing.—***Times review.***

Pitt could dilate or compress at pleasure: even in one member of a sentence, he could inflict a wound that was never healed. Mr. Fox having made an able speech, Mr. Erskine followed him with one of the very same import. Mr. Pitt rose to answer them: he announced his intention to reply to both; "but," said he, "I shall make no mention of the honourable gentleman who spoke last: he did no more than regularly repeat what was said by the member who preceded him, and regularly weaken all he repeated."

GEORGE III. AND HIS MINISTER, PITT.'

George III. had a sincere liking and regard for Pitt, though it is evident that much of that partiality was the merest selfishness. He was grateful to a Minister who saved him from the dictation of the great Whig families, and so long as it cost him nothing he was profuse in his expressions of attachment to Pitt. When Pitt proposed to resign in 1801 the King replied; "I hope Mr. Pitt's sense of duty will prevent his retiring from his present situation to the end of my life." So in the kindest way he forced Pitt to accept the Wardenship of the Cinque Ports, and afterwards, fearing for the safety of his Minister, he, without Pitt's knowledge, sent orders to Lord Amherst to stockade the ditch of Walmer Castle and station in it a picket of soldiers. When Pitt left office the King proposed to pay his debts, and for this purpose was anxious to put into the hands of Mr. Rose a sum of 30,000*l.* from the Privy Purse. When Pitt resumed office in 1804 he congratulated the King on looking much better than he did when Pitt last saw him in the spring of 1801. "That is not to be wondered at," said the King. "I was then on the point of parting with an old friend; I am now about to regain one." This was gracefully said; Pitt felt all the King's kindness, and it was not till afterwards that he learnt the full force of the King's selfish obstinacy. If the King could say that he owed his illness in 1801 to his Minister's persistence, that Minister could say that he owed his death to the King's unreasoning stubbornness. In forming his Cabinet Pitt was anxious to strengthen it with the names of Grenville and Fox, but the King would not hear of Fox, and without him Grenville would not join. Pitt, therefore, with enfeebled health was obliged to form a Cabinet so weak that on himself was imposed a load far beyond his strength. He knew this—he knew that he was risking his life, but it was against Lord Grenville that his resentment was directed. "I will teach that proud man that I can do without him, though it cost me my life," he said. But before long his weak Cabinet was rendered still weaker by the loss of his ablest lieutenant, Lord Melville. This was a terrible blow to Pitt, already overloaded with work. He again tried to induce the King to accept the services of Fox and Grenville. The King was inexorable. "I wish the King may not live to repent, and sooner than he thinks, the rejection of the advice which I pressed on him at Weymouth." In a few months Pitt sunk under his load of care, and the King had to be content with a Ministry of which Lord Grenville was the nominal head, and Fox was the presiding genius. He refused Fox, when by accepting him he might have saved Pitt's life, and in the end he only crushed Pitt and put Fox in his place.—***Times review.***

ELOQUENCE AND HUMOUR OF SHERIDAN.

One of the greatest tributes ever paid to eloquence, Mr. Sheridan received from Mr. Pitt, when, after Sheridan had, in opposition to him, advocated the prosecution of Warren Hastings, Pitt moved an adjournment, that "the House might have time to recover from the overpowering effect of Mr. Sheridan's oratory."

How little Sheridan's wit was the inspiration of the moment all men were aware who knew his habits; but a singular proof of this was presented by Mr. Moore, when he came to write his life; for we there find given to the world, with a frankness which must almost have made their author shake in his grave, the secret notebooks of this famous wit; and we are thus enabled to trace the jokes in embryo, with which he so often made the walls of St. Stephen's ring, in a merriment excited by the happy appearance of sudden unpremeditated effusion.

Take an instance from Moore, giving extracts from the commonplace-book of the wit: "He employs his fancy in his narrative, and keeps his recollections for his wit." Again, the same idea is expanded into—"When he makes his jokes you applaud the accuracy of his memory, and 'tis only when he states his facts that you admire the flights, of his imagination." But the thought was too good to be thus wasted on the desert air of a commonplace-book. So, forth it came at the expense of Michael Kelly, who, having been a composer of music, became a wine-merchant. "You will," said the **ready** wit, "import your music and compose your wine." Nor was this service exacted from the old idea thought sufficient—so in the House of Commons, an easy and apparently off-hand parenthesis was thus filled with it at Mr. Dundas's cost and charge, "(who generally resorts to his memory for his jokes, and to his imagination for his facts.)"

Pitt, in answer to an attack, in a debate on the Irish Union, said Sheridan seemed determined to have the last word; on which Sheridan replied that he was satisfied with having the last argument. When Dundas brought the sealed bag, containing the proofs which were to be examined, to show the necessity of a union, Sheridan, seeing there was not much in it, jocularly said to Dundas: "Confess the truth; is there anything in that bag, except the report the committee are to bring up."

During the debate on the India Bill, at which period John Robinson was secretary to the Treasury, Sheridan, one evening when Fox's majorities were decreasing, said, "Mr. Speaker, this is not at all to be wondered at, when a member is employed to corrupt every body in order to obtain votes." Upon this there was a great outcry made by almost every body in the House. "Who is it? Name him! name him!" "Sir," said Sheridan to the Speaker, "I shall not name the person. It is an unpleasant and invidious thing to do so, and therefore I shall not name him. But don't suppose, Sir, that I abstain because there is any difficult in naming him; I could do that, Sir, **as soon as you could say Jack Robinson."**

Again, during this memorable debate, the Apocalypse of St. John furnished images, which, by a slight effort of imagination, or by an immaterial deviation from the original text, were made to typify Fox, under the form of "the Beast that rose up out of the Sea, having *seven* heads." Their application to the Seven Commissioners appointed by the Bill, was at once so happy, and so natural, that it could not be mistaken: it was the suggestion of Mr. Scott, afterwards Lord Eldon. But Sheridan, though he could not possibly anticipate an attack of such a nature, yet having contrived in the course of the debate, to procure some leaves of the Book of Revelations, with admirable ability, found materials in it, equally suited for Fox's defence or justification; transforming him from "the Dragon and the Beast," under both which types he had been designated, to an angelic being, by producing other quotations from St. John, fully applicable to the Secretary of State.

Mr. Charles Butler once read to Sheridan the finest specimen of his poetry, his **Epistle to Semiramis.** "Oh! why did I not," he exclaimed, "uniformly addict myself to poetry; for *that* I was designed!" "But then," said Mr. Butler, "would you have been the admiration of the senate? Would London have emptied itself to hear your philippic on Mr. Hastings? Would you have been the intimate of Mr. Fox? Would you have been received, as doing honour to it, at Devonshire House?"— "What," he replied, "has all this done for me? What am I the better for the admiration of the senate, for Mr. Fox, for Devonshire House? I have thrown myself away. But you shall see to-morrow."

It was a general subject of wonder, that as Sheridan had shown how well he could write for the stage, he should write so little. "The reason is," said Michael Kelly, with exquisite felicity, "Mr. Sheridan is afraid of the author of the **School for Scandal."**

Occasionally Sheridan had brilliant sallies. On one occasion, he and Mr. Sheldon, of Weston, in Warwickshire, supped with Mr. Butler. Mr. Sheldon was born of Catholic parents, and brought up a Catholic; he embraced the Protestant religion, and sat in two Parliaments. The Catholic question being mentioned, Mr. Sheridan, supposing Mr. Sheldon to be a Catholic, told him he was quite disgusted at the pitiful, lowly manner in which the Catholics brought forward their case: Why should not you, Mr. Sheldon, walk into our House, and say,—"Here am I, Sheldon, of Weston, entitled by birth and fortune to be among you; but, because I am a Catholic, you shut the door against me." "I beg your pardon," said Mr. Sheldon, interrupting him, "I thought it the duty of a subject to be of the religion of his country; and therefore—" "You quitted," said Sheridan, interrupting him, "the errors of popery, and became a member of a church which you know to be free from error? I am glad of it You do us great honour." The subject then changed; but it was evident that Mr. Sheldon did not sit quite easy. At length, the third of the morning hour, arrived; Mr. Sheldon took his watch from his pocket, and holding it forth to Mr. Sheridan, "See," he said to him, "what the hour is; you know our host is a very early riser." "D—n your *apostate watch!*" exclaimed Sheridan, "put it into your Protestant fob."

Sheridan was very superstitious—a believer in dreams and omens. One sentiment of true religion Mr. Charles Butler often heard him express, with evident satisfaction; that, in all his writings, and even in his freest moments a single irreligious opinion or word had never escaped him.

Frequently, he disarmed those who approached him with savageness, and a determined resolution to insult him. He had purchased an estate [Polesden] in Surrey, of Sir William Geary, and neglected to pay for it. Sir William mentioned this circumstance to Mr. Butler; and the English language has not an expression of abuse or opprobrium, which Sir William did not apply to Sheridan. He then marched off in a passion; but had not walked ten paces before he met Mr. Sheridan. Mr. Butler expected a furious onset; but nothing like this took place. In ten minutes, Sir William returned, exclaiming, "Mr. Sheridan is the finest fellow I ever met with; I will teaze him no more for money."

Lord Derby once applied in the Green-room, to Mr. Sheridan, with much dignity, for the arrears of Lady Derby's [Miss Farren's] salary, and vowed he would not stir from the room till it was paid. "My dear Lord," said Sheridan, "this is too bad; you have taken from us the brightest jewel in the world, and you now quarrel with us for a little dust she has left behind her."

Politics was not a favourite subject with Sheridan: though he always voted for Catholic Emancipation, he did not speak for it; nor did he declare against it. "But," said he to an Irish Catholic of distinction, "though we don't show it, our hearts are with you." "And you, also," replied the gentleman of Ireland, "may be equally well assured, that if the French should land in Ireland, though we should not join you, our hearts will be with you."

POLITICAL LIFE.

Mr. Butler considers Sheridan's most splendid exhibition to have been his speech in the Court of Chancery, at the hearing of the cause upon the Bill filed against him by the trustees of Drury Lane Theatre. The court was crowded: Mr. Sheridan spoke for two hours, with amazing shrewdness of observation, force of argument, and splendour of eloquence. He was heard with great attention and interest: while his speech lasted, a pin might be heard to drop. But it did not prevent Mr. Mansfield from making a most powerful reply. He exposed, in the strongest terms, the irregularity of Mr. Sheridan's conduct as manager of the theatre; and the injuries done by it to the proprietor, creditors, and performers. Upon these, Mr. Mansfield commented in the bitterest terms; and every word he said sunk deep into Mr. Sheridan's heart. The Chancellor appeared to pity his calamities. He finished by conjuring Mr. Sheridan to think seriously of the words with which Dr. Johnson concluded his Life of Savage—that "those, who, in confidence of superior capacities or attainments, disregard the common maxims of life, will be reminded, that nothing will supply the want of prudence; and that negligence and irregularity long continued, will make knowledge useless, wit ridiculous, and genius contemptible."

Sheridan was very anxious to procure from Mr. Mansfield, something that had an appearance of retraction of the charges which he had brought against him. To obtain this he made many direct and indirect efforts. All he could obtain from Mr. Mansfield was a declaration, at a consultation with Mr. Charles Butler, at which Mr. Sheridan was present, that "he spoke from affidavits in the cause; so that his assertions and arguments depended, for their justice, on the truth of the facts mentioned in those." This was little, but it comforted Sheridan much.

The great blow to Sheridan was, however, the loss of his election at Stafford. It is worthy of remark, that his old friend, Mr. Richard Ironmonger, of Brighton, was some years after returned for Stafford, but did not live to take his seat.

Mr. Sheridan died at No. 17, Savile-row, in the front bedroom. In a short note to Mr. Rogers, dated Savile-row, May 15, 1816, six weeks before his death, he wrote—"They are going to put the carpets out of the window, and break into Mrs. S.'s room, and take me; for God's sake, let me see you." A present of 150*l.* from Mr. Rogers arrived in time.

ANECDOTES OF

Sheridan's remains were removed from Savile-row to Mr. Peter Moore's house, in Great George-street, Westminster, to be near Westminster Abbey for interment. This, probably, led to the story that the body had been removed to escape arrest—a popular error; for the body of a debtor could not be taken in execution after death, though such was the practice in Prussia, till its abolition by the Code Frédérique. The false notion in Sheridan's case may have been fostered through the misreading of the account of a sheriffs' officer threatening to arrest the dying man in his bed: "he would have carried him (Sheridan) off in his blankets, had not Dr. Bain assured him it was too probable his prisoner would expire on his way to the lock-up house."

At Holland House, where Sheridan often was, in his latter days, Lady Holland told Moore he used to take a bottle of wine and a book up to bed with him always;

the *former* alone intended for use. In the morning he breakfasted in bed, and had a little rum or brandy in his tea or coffee; made his appearance between one and two, and, pretending important business, used to set out for town, but regularly stopped at the Adam and Eve public-house, in the Kensington-road, for a dram, where he ran up a long score, which Lord Holland had to pay. This was the old roadside inn, nearly opposite the wall of the park: it has long since been taken down.

Sheridan one day said to Lord Holland: "They talk of avarice, lust, ambition, as great passions. Vanity is the great commanding passion of all. It is this that produces the most grand and heroic deeds, or impels to the most dreadful crimes. Save me from this passion, and I can defy the others. They are mere urchins, but this is a giant" Sheridan's strong wish to make his power felt in politics grew still stronger in his latter days from vanity and disappointment.

Francis Horner says, in a letter to Jeffrey, that Fox was ready to consent to Sheridan being a cabinet minister in 1806, but that the Duke of Bedford opposed him; and it is in the same place affirmed that Sheridan's "blabbing" propensities disqualified him. We have had some "blabbing" cabinet ministers since Sheridan's time.*

* See "Lives of Wits and Humourists," vol. ii. for several Anecdotes of Sheridan, hitherto unpublished.

HYDER ALLY'S PHYSIOGNOMY,

Governor Du Pré, in one of his interviews with Hyder Ally, was astonished to see that Hyder had no eyebrows; nor, indeed, a single hair left on any part of his face. A man constantly attended him, purposely to pull out, with a pair of nippers, any hair that made its appearance on the Sultan's face. Hyder, perceiving that Du Pré was surprised at this fact, said to him, "I observe that you wonder at my having no eyebrows, as well as my attention to cause every hair that appears on my face to be immediately eradicated. The reason I will explain to you. I am the Nabob of Mysore, and it is an object of policy with me that my subjects shall see no face in my dominions resembling the countenance of their sovereign." Du Pré, in relating this, added: "The impression which the Nabob's physiognomy made upon myself was not a little increased by this singularity." Hyder was generally of pleasing manners; but in his anger he was terrible, and often ferocious.

APOTHEOSIS OF WARREN HASTINGS.

At the time of the trial of Warren Hastings, it was said that at Benares, the very place in which the acts set forth in the first article of impeachment had been committed, the natives had erected a temple to Hastings; and this story excited a strong sensation in England. Burke's observations on the apotheosis were admirable. He saw no reason for astonishment, he said, in the incident which had been represented as so striking. He knew something of the mythology of the Brahmins. He knew that as they worshipped some gods from love, so they worshipped others from fear. He knew that they erected shrines, not only to the benignant deities of light and plenty, but also to the fiends who preside over small-pox and murder; nor did he at all dispute the claim of Mr. Hastings to be admitted into such a pantheon. "This reply," says Lord Macaulay, "has always struck us as one of the finest that ever was made in Parliament It is a grave and forcible argument, decorated by the most brilliant wit and fancy."

In the course of this protracted trial, Sheridan took occasion to refer to the "luminous page of Gibbon." Upon leaving Westminster Hall, at the close of the day's proceedings, the orator was joined by a friend, who asked him how he could pay such a compliment to a Tory, and an infidel? "My dear fellow," replied Sheridan, "I said *v*oluminous."

GROSVENOR-PLACE.

One of the pleasantest rows of houses in the metropolis is Grosvenor-place, Hyde Park Corner. It looks over the gardens of Buckingham Palace, which, if not the elysium intended by George IV., is a delightful specimen of landscape gardening. The tenants of Grosvenor-place owe this ***rus in urbe*** prospect to a strong-willed minister overruling his sovereign. When George III took up his residence at Buckingham House, and was adding a part of the Green Park to the new garden, the fields on the opposite side of the road were to be sold, and the King wished to purchase them, in order to prevent buildings being erected so as to look over his garden. The Lock Hospital then stood here alone; but it was apparent that the ground would soon be occupied, the King having fixed his abode so near. He, therefore, entered into a negotiation for its purchase: the price was 20,000*l.* This sum George. Grenville, then minister, refused to issue from the Treasury: the ground was, consequently, sold to builders, and Grosvenor-place was commenced building in 1767—the new row of houses looking over the King in his private walks, to his great annoyance.

A SMUGGLING AMBASSADRESS.

Not very many years since a package, directed to a French ambassadress in this country, was accidentally opened at the Custom-house, and found to contain French gloves, at that time liable to an exceedingly heavy duty. The authorities did not proceed against the ambassadress for smuggling, but sent the package through the Post-office. It was charged by weight, as a letter, and the postage, amounting to a formidable sum, was paid without observation.

Lady Holderness, in Mr. Grenville's administration, occasioned the putting of the laws against contraband goods into rigorous execution, having, at one journey from Paris, imported one hundred and fourteen gowns, which were seized. Her lord becoming afterwards Governor of the Cinque Ports, she carried on a smuggling intercourse at Walmer Castle, on the coast of Kent, for importing French clothes and furniture for herself—Dr. Doraris Notes to the Last Journals of Horace Walpole, italic vol i.

THE DUKE OF YORK AND MRS. CLARKE.

The story of Mary Ann Clarke, whose detection in trafficking with the Duke of York led to great improvement in our army administration, is a very extraordinary one, though told in various ways. Captain Gronow, in his **Reminiscences,** describes her first introduction to the Duke of York to have taken place when she was a sweet, pretty, lively girl of sixteen, residing at Blackheath; that she was first noticed by a cavalier as she was walking across the heath, that she returned his salute, and was by him introduced to a friend, and the acquaintance ripened into an amour. Captain Gronow tells us that not the slightest idea had the young lady of the position in society of her lover, until she accompanied him, on his invitation to the theatre, where she occupied a private box, and attracted much notice, which she accepted as a tribute to her beauty: on a second visit, she was addressed as Her Royal Highness; when she discovered that her lover was the son of the King, the Duke of York, who had not long before united himself to a lady, for whom she had been mistaken.

Another version of Mrs. Clarke's antecedents is that she was the daughter of a journeyman printer, named Farquhar, living in a court leading from Fetter-lane to Cursitor-street, where she was born about 1777. Ere she was thirteen, she engaged the love of James Day, a young compositor, one of the earliest literary acquaintances of Mr. John Britton, who relates this story. Day addressed sonnets to the charmer; but she soon eloped with Joseph Clarke, the son of a builder, on Snow-hill, and after living with him three years, they were married, and had children. Mr. Britton does not state *how* she became introduced to the Duke of York, but that the cohabitation began in 1802, and lasted for several years; while Captain Gronow dates its commencement shortly after the Duke's marriage—in 1791. Mr. Britton describes her as living openly with the Duke of York, at No. 31, Tavis-tock-place; thence she removed to Gloucester-place, Portman-square, where her establishment consisted of two carriages, eight horses, nine men-servants, &c., to support which the Duke allowed her 2,000*l.* a-year, which she considered barely sufficient to pay her servants' wages, and for their liveries. She soon found herself courted by persons of rank, and more especially by military men. The Duke was pleased with these attentions, and indulged her extravagance; she became embarrassed, and to raise money, persuaded the Duke to give her commissions in the army, which she could easily dispose of at a good price; and the traffic was extended from the army to the Church.

Among Mrs. Clarke's visitors was Colonel Wardle, the Radical M.P., who got intimately acquainted with her, and obtained from her the names of some of the parties who had purchased commissions of her. He was paying a clandestine visit to Mrs. Clarke, when a carriage with the royal livery drove up to the door, and the Colonel was compelled to take refuge under the sofa; but, instead of the royal duke, the caller was one of his aides-de-camp, who talked mysteriously to Mrs. Clarke, but led Wardle to believe that the sale of a commission was authorized by the Duke, though it afterwards appeared it was a private arrangement. At the Horse Guards, says Captain, Gronow, there was an unfathomable mystery connected with commissions, the list of promotions agreed on having new names added to it by Mrs. Clarke, whom the Duke had employed as his amanuensis; and he signed her autograph lists without examination. These scandalous transactions were inquired into in Parliament, in 1809, at the instigation of Colonel Wardle. Mrs. Clarke, whom the Duke had then abandoned, was called as a witness; and "the examination of this woman, and her various profligate intimates," occupied nearly three months, and that with an intenseness of anxiety seldom equalled. The Duke of York was acquitted from the motion made against him by a majority of 80; but so strong was the outcry against him out of doors, and so much was the nation convinced that all Mrs. Clarke said was true, and so little could they be brought to doubt that the Duke of York was a conscious and participant actor in all that person's schemes, that His Royal Highness resigned his office of Commander-in-Chief.

It appeared that Mrs. Clarke had strong inducements to furnish the information, Colonel Wardle having, in 1808, undertaken to furnish for her a house in Westbourne-place, Sloane-square, in part payment for her services in prosecution of the Duke of York at the bar of the House of Commons, This personal promise led to an action against Wardle for the recovery of 1,914 *l.,* the amount of the upholsterer's bill for articles of furniture supplied.

It is said that the whole exposure originated in the resentment of one M'Cullum against Picton (afterwards Sir Thomas Picton), for his oppressive conduct as Governor of Trinidad. M'Cullum, on reaching England, sought justice, but was baffled, as he suspected, by royal influence; he then exposed Picton in his Travels in Trinidad, and next ferreted out charges against the War Office, and through Colonel Wardle, exposed a suspicious contract for great-coats. This being negatived, M'Cullum then traced Mrs. Clarke, and arranged the whole of that exposure for Wardle and others. M'Cullum. worked night and day for months in getting up this case: he lodged in a garret in Hungerford Market, and often did not taste food for twenty-four hours; he lived to see the Duke dismissed from office, and to publish a Narrative of his exertions—and then died of exhaustion and want.

To return to Mrs. Clarke. In 1814, she was sentenced to nine months' imprisonment, for a libel on the Irish Chancellor of the Exchequer. She concocted a Memoir of her own Life and Adventures, upon the publication of which she consulted Mr. Gait "I told her," he says, "point-blank, she was in want of money, and that this was an expedient to raise the wind. She confessed the truth, and also that her debts had been paid to the amount of 7,000*l.,* and an annuity of 400*l.,*. granted to her on condition that she should not molest the Duke of York." The papers were unfit for publication, and by Mr. Galt's advice she suppressed the book.

The announcement of the Memoir had excited such expectation that the printer had worked off 10,000 copies, two volumes each, requiring 640 reams of paper, at 35*s.* per ream. The above settlement was made upon the condition that the whole should be **burnt,** and the manuscript delivered up to an agent under seven seals, being the number of the parties concerned. The work was accordingly **burnt** in the printing-office, in the presence of witnesses, and the conflagration was continued for three successive days, during which the smell of burnt paper excited repeated alarms near Salisbury-square, where this extraordinary transaction took place.

Meanwhile, incensed at the Duke's desertion of her, she threatened to publish his love-letters, which were likely to expose the whole of the Royal Family to ridicule, as they were often mentioned. Sir Herbert Taylor then bought the letters of Mrs. Clarke at an enormous price, on her signing an undertaking not to implicate the honour of any of the Royal Family. A pension was secured to her, on condition of her leaving England. She first went to Brussels; and then settled comfortably in Paris, where she died not long since.

Mrs. Clarke was of very agreeable manners, lively and rattling, and full of anecdotes, especially of the Royal Family; these she had received from the Duke of York, whom she used to prime with stories for the dinner-table: next morning, she used to say: "Well, Dukey, how did the story go off?" She was a pretty little fascinating woman: Galt, however, says, she had no pretensions to beauty; she dressed remarkably neat and plain; her hair was almost black, and her eyes sparkling. She possessed great powers of conversation, and was often witty, with flashes of shrewdness seldom seen in women: her mind was decidedly masculine. "The fact is," says Galt, "that she did not possess that extraordinary fascination which posterity may suppose from the incidents in which she was engaged; but she was undoubtedly clever, with a degree of tact, that, either in man or woman, would have been singularly "acute."

One of Mrs. Clarke's most noted rejoinders was, when under examination in the Court of King's Bench, and being asked under whose protection she then was—she replied, with a bow to Lord Ellenborough, who presided in the court—"Your Lordship's."

Mr. Cyrus Redding gives altogether a different version of Mrs. Clarke's antecedents to either yet related, which goes far to disprove the character fixed on her by Mr. Wilberforce as "a low, vulgar woman." Mr. Redding says:—

"The lady, while pronounced one of the ***canaille*** by the ministerial papers, was found at the bar of the House of Commons to be 'full of grace in her bearing,' and accomplished. Not free from feeling at the mode in which certain persons treated her, and replying to them in their own coin; this and perfect self-possession gave the contradiction at once to her mean origin and education. Not one paper stated the truth about her. I accidentally had twenty or thirty of her letters before me at one time. I read them, and they fully proved she was a woman who had been well educated. Time has removed the passions and prejudices of that period, neither reflecting honour on any of the actors in the scene, nor any advantage, except that the affair pushed up the fortunes of John Wilson Croker, whose acting in the comedy was not that of the worst performer. Again, let it not be supposed I knew the lady; I never coveted the honour or disgrace, whichever it might be. Mrs. Clarke was the daughter of Colonel Frederick, and grand-daughter of Theodore, King of Corsica, whose melancholy fate, as well as that of his son, need not be repeated here. She had a son, and, I believe, two daughters. Twice or thrice I well recollect seeing her, and one of her daughters. What business Mr. Clarke carried on when he married, I never heard, but that he had very scanty means of support was clear, for he accepted at one time a situation in the Excise at Dartmouth. As the daughter of Colonel Frederick, Mrs. Clark had been noticed by the Prince of Wales, Lady Jersey, and several persons of distinction before the Duke of York knew her, and she had received money from them in consideration of her misfortunes; perhaps his knowledge of her arose that way. One lady who died left her a hundred guineas in her will, in addition to former gifts."

WINDHAM'S ORATORY.

Of the mixed tenderness and figure in which Mr. Windham sometimes indulged, a specimen is afforded by his fine speech, in which, after comparing two plans of recruiting our army to a dead stick thrust into the ground, and a living sapling planted to take root in the soil, he spoke of carving his name upon the tree as lovers do when they would perpetuate the remembrance of their passions or their misfortunes. Of his happy allusions to the writings of kindred spirits an example is afforded in his speech about the peace of Amiens, when he answered the remarks upon the uselessness of the Royal title, then given up, of King of France, by citing the bill of costs brought in by Dean Swift against Marlborough, and the comparative amount of the charges of a Roman triumph, where the crown of laurel is set down at twopence. But sometimes he would convulse the House by a happy, startling, and most unexpected allusion, as when, on the Walcheren question, speaking of a *coup-de-main* on Antwerp, which had been its professed object, he suddenly said, "A *coup-de-main* in the Scheldt! You might as well talk of a *coup-de-main* in the Court of Chancery." Sir William Grant having just entered and taken his seat, probably suggested this excellent jest; and, assuredly, no man enjoyed it more. His habitual gravity was overpowered in an instant, and he was seen absolutely to roll about on the bench which he had just occupied. So a word or two artistically introduced would often serve him to cover the adverse argument with ridicule. When arguing that they who would protect animals from cruelty have more on their hands than they are aware of, and that they cannot stop at preventing cruelty, but must also prohibit killing, he was met by the old answer, that we kill them to prevent them overrunning the earth, and then he said in passing, and, as it were, parenthetically,—"An indifferent reason, by the way, for destroying fish." He happily caricatured Mr. Pitt's diction as a state-paper style, and that he believed he could speak a King's speech offhand.—***Lord Brougham's Historical Sketches.***

Of Mr. Windham's gaiety of spirits we have a trait in his halting to see "Punch and Judy:" he was then one of the Secretaries of State, and was on his way from Downing-street to the House of Commons, on a night of important debate; he paused before the street-show like a truant boy, until the whole performance was concluded, to enjoy a hearty laugh at the whimsicalities of the motley hero.

It was Mr. Windham who described the Parks as "the lungs of London;" for they were essential to the healthful respiration of its inhabitants.

He was an accomplished scholar and mathematician. Dr. Johnson, writing of a visit which Windham paid him, says: "Such conversation I shall not have again till I come back to the regions of literature, and there Windham is 'inter stellas luna minores.'" In a word, Mr. Windham has been described, and the description has been generally adopted as appropriate, as a model of the true English gentleman.

JOHN HORNE TOOKE.

This extraordinary man, the son of a poulterer named Horne, in Newport-street, a, "turkey merchant," as he told his schoolfellows, was educated for the Church, according to his father's wish, and took orders, but soon quitted the Church for the Bar. He had a quarrel with Frederick, Prince of Wales, his father's neighbour, at Leicester House, respecting a right of way, and defeated the Prince, which success seems to have had something to do with his turbulent after-life. Mr. Massey, M.P., in his recently published *History of England,* tells us:—

"For many years he had been the terror of judges, ministers of State, and all constituted authorities. He was that famous Parson Horne who attacked the terrible Junius, after statesmen, judges, and generals had fled before him, and drove him back defeated and howling with his wounds. He it was who silenced Wilkes. Some years afterwards he fastened a quarrel on the House of Commons, which he bullied and baffled with his usual coolness and address.

When put on trial for his life (for treason), "so far from being moved by his dangerous position, he was never in more buoyant spirits. His wit and humour had often before been exhibited in Courts of Justice; but never had they been so brilliant as on this occasion. Erskine had been at his request assigned to him as counsel; but he himself undertook some of the most important duties of his advocate, cross-examining the witnesses for the Crown, objecting to evidence, and even arguing points of law. If his life had really been in jeopardy, such a course would have been perilous and rash in the highest degree; but nobody in court, except, perhaps, the Attorney and Solicitor-General, thought there was the slightest chance of an adverse verdict. The prisoner led off the proceedings by a series of preliminary jokes, which were highly successful. When placed in the dock, he cast a glance up at the ventilators of the hall, shivered, and expressed a wish that their lordships would be so good as to get the business over quickly as he was afraid of catching cold. When arraigned, and asked by the officer of the court, in the usual form, how he would be tried? he answered, "I **would** be tried by God and my country—but—'and looked sarcastically round the court. Presently he made, an application to be allowed a seat by his counsel; and entered upon an amusing altercation with the Judge, as to whether his request should be granted as an indulgence or as a right. The result was that he consented to take his place by the side of Erskine as a matter of favour. In the midst of the merriment occasioned by these sallies, the Solicitor-General opened the case for the Crown."

Tooke took some delight in praising his daughters, which he sometimes did by those equivocatory falsehoods which were one of his principal pleasures. Of the eldest he said, "All the beer brewed in this house is that young lady's brewing." It would have been equally true to say, all the hogs killed in this house were of that young lady's killing, for they brewed no beer. When a member of the Constitutional Society, he would frequently utter sentences, the first part of which would have subjected him to death by the law, but for the salvo that followed; and the more violent they were, thus contrasted and equivocatory, the greater was his triumph.

When Tooke was justifying to the Commissioners his return of income under 60*l.* a-year, one of those gentlemen, dissatisfied with the explanation, hastily said, "Mr. Tooke, I do not understand you." "Very possibly," replied the sarcastic citizen, "but as you have not *half the understanding* of other men, you should have *double the patience.*"

Tooke told Mr. Rogers that in his early days a friend kindly gave him a letter of introduction to D'Alembert, at Paris. Dressed à-la-rnode, *he presented the letter, and was very courteously received by D'Alembert, who talked to him about operas, comedies, suppers, &c. Tooke had expected conversation on very different topics, and was greatly disappointed. When he took leave, he was followed by a gentleman in a plain suit, who had been in the room during his interview with D'Alembert, and who had perceived his chagrin. "D'Alembert," said the gentleman, "supposed from your gay apparel that you were merely a* petit maitre." The gentleman was David Hume. On his, next visit to D'Alembert, Tooke's dress was altogether different, and so was the conversation.

Tooke's *change of name* originated as follows. When he was rising into celebrity, the estate of Purley, near Croydon, belonged to Mr. William Tooke, one of four friends who joined in supplying him with an income, when, after quitting the Church, he studied for the Law. One of Tooke's richer neighbours, in wresting from him his manorial rights by a law-suit, had applied to Parliament, and nearly succeeded in effecting his purpose by means of an inclosure bill, which would have greatly depreciated the Purley estate. Tooke despondingly confided his apprehensions to Home, who resolved at once to avert the blow, which he did in a very bold and very singular manner. The third reading of the Bill was to take place the next day, and Horne immediately wrote a violent libel on the Speaker of the House of Commons, in reference to it, and obtained its insertion in the ***Public Advertiser.*** As might be expected, the first Parliamentary proceeding the next day was the appearance of the adventurous libeller in the custody of the Serjeant-at-Arms. When called upon for his defence, he delivered a most remarkable speech, in which he pointed out the injustice of the Bill in question with so much success, that it was reconsidered, and the clauses which affected his friend's property expunged. In gratitude for this important service, Mr. Tooke, who had no family, made Horne his heir; and on his death in 1803, the latter became proprietor of Purley: as one of the conditions of inheritance, he added the name of Tooke to his own, and from this time was known as John Horne Tooke.

His residence at Purley has been commemorated in the celebrated philological work which he wrote here, entitled the ***Diversions of Purley,*** which has exercised considerable influence upon almost all works in the English language published since its appearance. It is in two large volumes, and the title is said to have so misled an indulgent father as to induce him to order of a bookseller the "Diversions of Purley" as a toy-book for his son, then a boy. The great fault of Tooke's work is the love of hypothesis, and the absence, to a great extent, of that historical mode of investigation without which etymological studies are worse than useless: Its influence has considerably declined of late years: in ***Blackwood's Magazine,*** No. 514, will be found a searching paper upon the over-rated merits of Tooke's ***Diversions.***

FRENCH REVOLUTIONISTS.

It is remarkable, (says Bulwer,) that most of the principal actors of the French Revolution were singularly hideous in appearance—from the colossal ugliness of Mirabeau and Danton to the villainous ferocity in the countenances of David and Simon, to the filthy squalor of Marat, the sinister and bilious meanness of the Dictator's features. But Robespierre, who was said to resemble a cat, had also a cat's cleanliness: he was prim and dainty in dress, shaven smoothness, and the womanly whiteness of his lean hands. Rene Dumas, born of reputable parents, and well educated, despite his ferocity, was not without a certain refinement, which, perhaps, rendered him more acceptable to the precise Robespierre. Dumas was a beau in his way: his gala-dress was a ***blood-red coat,*** with the finest ruffles. But Henriot had been a lacquey, a thief, a spy of the police: he had drank the blood of Madame de Lamballe, and rose to his rank for no quality but his ruffianism; and Fouquier Tinville, the son of a provincial agriculturist, and afterwards a clerk at the Bureau of the Police, was little less base in his manners, yet more, from a certain loathsome buffoonery, revolting in his speech; bull-head, with black, sleek hair, with a narrow and livid forehead, and small eyes that twinkled with a sinister malice; strongly and coarsely built, he looked what he was, the audacious bully of a lawless and relentless Bar.

Robespierre was, perhaps, the coolest hand of the set: in making out the list of his victims for the guillotine, he wrote down the name of Jean Lambert Tallien, with a slow hand, that shaped each letter with a stern distinctness, saying—"That one head is ***my necessity!***"

One of the most extraordinary signs of these revolutionary times was the avidity with which the French people rushed to the theatres at night, as a relief to the bloody excesses of the day. "Night after night to the eighty theatres flocked the children of the Revolution, to laugh at the quips of comedy, and weep gentle tears over imaginary woes!"

However, the above strange taste is not exclusively characteristic of France. George Colman the elder relates that during the Riots in London, in 1780, on the 7th of June, when, day and night, desolation had attained its climax, and the metropolis was seen blazing in thirty-six different places, the receipts of the Haymarket Theatre exceeded twenty pounds! How, instead of twenty pounds' worth of spectators, twenty persons, or one person, could have calmly paid money to witness, in the midst of this general dismay, a theatrical entertainment, appears astonishing.

A TOUCH OF THE SUBLIME.

During the French Revolution, Jean Bon St. André, the Vendean leader, said to a peasant, "I will have all your steeples pulled down, that you may no longer have any objects by which you may be reminded of your old superstitions." "You cannot help leaving us the stars," replied the peasant, "and we can see them further off than our steeples."

LAST MOMENTS OF THE CONDEMNED.

Strange things have been said and done by the condemned, in their last moments. During the Reign of Terror, at Paris, in the same prison with Josephine Beauharnais was one of the daughters of Madame Coquet. When she too well surmised that her last hour was approaching, she borrowed a pair of scissors to cut off her hair, saying "the scoundrel executioner, at all events, shall not have that honour."

The executioner generally cut the hair of the condemned close off, it being his perquisite. Samson, one of this class possessed a cupboard at one time filled with the hair of the individuals, male and female, whom he had cropped before their execution—treasured, no doubt, for sale to hairdressers! The object of this operation was to prevent the edge of the axe, as it fell, from meeting with any resistance at the nape of the neck. The hair coming between the knife and the integument might deaden the edge. What an idea of ladies wearing false hair, supplied from the scissors of the executioner! Yet the fact cannot be doubted.

M. Brogle, only two hours before the fatal knife fell upon him, expecting the cart to take him to execution every moment, listened while M. Vigée, an author and fellow-prisoner, read to him one of his works, during which he took out his watch, and said: "My hour approaches; I do not know whether I shall have time enough left me to hear you out. No matter; go on till they send for me."

WAS BONAPARTE EVER IN LONDON?

This has been denied; but a letter appeared in the ***Birmingham Journal*** of April 21, 1855, affirming the fact, on the authority of one James Colman, then in his 106th year, and was living, in 1850, in the back parlour of No. 58, Castle-street, Leicester-square. Colman stated that he perfectly well knew N. Bonaparte, who resided in London for five weeks, in 1791 or 1792; he lodged at a house in George-street, Adelphi, and he passed much of his time in walking through the streets of the metropolis. Hence his marvellous knowledge of London, which used to astonish many Englishmen. The writer of the letter adds: "I have also heard, Mr. Mathews, the grandfather of the celebrated comedian, and a bookseller at No.,—,Strand; Mr. Graves, Mr. Drury, and my father, all of whom were tradesmen in the Strand, in the immediate vicinity of George-street, speak of Bonaparte's visit. He occasionally took his cup of chocolate at the Northumberland Coffee-house, (opposite Northumberland House,) occupying himself in reading, and preserving a provoking taciturnity to the gentlemen in the room; though his manner was stern, his deportment was that of a gentleman." [This is a very circumstantial story; but we must add, that, in two or three conversations we had with old Mr. Colman, in 1850, he did not mention his knowledge of Bonaparte, though he related several recollections of his long life: as, his birth in Church-court, Strand; his witnessing the funeral procession of George the Second; and his partaking of the Sacrament at the age of 100.]

BONAPARTE AN ANTI-REVOLUTIONIST.

It has repeatedly been observed from what little causes have sprung great tumults and revolutions which proper energy, at the right moment, might have nipped in the bud A remarkable instance was noted by Bonaparte, in 1792, when he was at Paris, and there met his old friend, Bourrienne, with whom he renewed his intimacy. He appears to have been then unemployed, probably unattached, while the army was undergoing a new organization. Napoleon and Bourrienne happened to be, on the 20th of June, 1792, at a café in the Rue St. Honoré, when the mob from the Faux-bourg, (a motley crowd, armed with pikes, sticks, axes, &c.) were proceeding to the Tuilleries. "Let us follow this *canaille"* whispered Napoleon to his friend. They went accordingly, and saw the mob break into the palace without any opposition, and the king afterwards appeared at one of the windows with the **red cap** on his head. "It is all over henceforth with that man;" exclaimed Napoleon: and returning with his friend to the café to dinner, he explained to Bourrienne all the consequences he foresaw from the degradation of the monarchy on that fatal day, now and then exclaiming indignantly: "How could they allow those despicable wretches to enter the palace? why a few discharges of grape-shot amongst them would have made them all take to their heels; they would be running yet at this moment!" He was collected and extremely grave all the remainder of that day: the sight had made a deep impression on him.

It will be remembered that a trifling disturbance by a few **gamins** of Paris, in February, 1848, was aggravated into a popular riot through the audacity of a few ultra-republicans.: Louis-Philippe felt that he stood alone and unsupported as a constitutional king, both at home and abroad, and that the soldiery were his only means of defence. He shrunk from employing their bayonets against his people: he fell in consequence, and his house fell with him.

TOM PAINE.

When Paine's **Rights of Man** reached Lewes, where he married a Miss Olive, the women, as with one voice, said: "Od rot im, let im come ear if he dast, an we'll tell im what the Rights of Women is; we'll toss im in a blanket, and ring im out of Lewes wi our frying pans."

THE BIRMINGHAM RIOTS, 1793.

Mr. Croker, in a MS. note to a Letter of Walpole, of the above date, states that he has read a communication from George III. to one of his ministers, on the subject of the Riots, in which Dr. Priestley's house was burned. His Majesty says, in his short emphatic way, that the Riots must be stopped *immediately;* that no man's house must be left in peril; and then he orders the march of certain troops, &c. to restore peace; and concludes with saying that as the mischief did occur, it was impossible not to be pleased at its having fallen on Priestley rather than another, that he might *feel* the wickedness of the doctrines of democracy which he was propagating.—Walpole's **Letters,** Cunningham's edit

THE MUTINY AT THE NORE.

In 1797, when Capt. William Under had the ***Thetis,*** and was returning to England, having on board the "Prussian subsidy," amounting to nearly half a million sterling, he was taken prisoner by the mutineer William Parker, and detained, with his vessel and valuable cargo, for a week at the Nore. The rebel, little suspecting the prize he had within his grasp, credited the assertion of Capt. Linder that the aid would shortly arrive, and that he was to be the medium of its transmission to this country. By this ***ruse,*** and a promise of assistance by which Parker decided that he would take the grand fleet into Brest, he obtained a pass (it is believed the only one given) from William Parker, and arrived safely with his immense treasure at the Tower, where he immediately landed his golden cargo, and forthwith proceeded to the Admiralty,—also giving information to the minister, Mr. Pitt, of his fortunate escape, which, had it been otherwise, would certainly have turned the tide of success of Old England at that time. Mr. Pitt generously offered him a commission; but Capt. Linder having a fine vessel of his own, and a noble and independent spirit, which he retained to the last, respectfully declined; nor could he be induced in after years to solicit for any recompense or popularity. He died in 1862, May 21, at the age of eighty-seven.—***Athenoeum.***

ASSASSINATION OF GUSTAVUS III. KING OF SWEDEN.

This accomplished but versatile prince fell a victim to a conspiracy of the nobility of Sweden, who, apprehending the loss of all their privileges through the arbitrary measures of Gustavus, resolved to murder him. A nobleman, named Ankastroem, whom he had personally offended, undertook the foul deed, at a masked ball, which was given on the 16th of March, 1792, at Stockholm. The King was warned by some anonymous friend, but he went to the ball, and was pointed out to the assassin by Count Horn, who tapped him on the shoulder and said, "Good evening, pretty mask." Upon this, Ankastroem shot the King through the body from behind, and mingled with the crowd of masks. The striking scene which ensued is thus given from a Swedish manuscript, which is considered authentic.

The King's surgeons having examined the wound, and the direction in which the pistol had been fired, saw at once how small was the chance of their royal patient's recovery. During this operation, which was excruciatingly painful, the King displayed that intense fortitude which few mortals ever possessed in a higher degree. As the surgeon applied his probe, the King thought his hand shook; suppressing the sense of pain, he said, with a firm voice, "Do not suffer your sorrow to affect your hand! Remember, sir, it is not possible that I can survive if the balls are not extracted." The surgeon paused a moment, as if to collect all his courage, and extracted. a ball and some slugs.

On his way from his palace to the opera-house, a few hours before, Gustavus stepped lightly down the broad flights of granite stairs to the vestibule below. He was now carried slowly back, stretched on a litter, borne on the shoulders of grenadiers, whose slightest motion gave him inexpressible pain. Although the doors were closed as soon as the King had entered, and none but courtiers and soldiers admitted, and even those not without selection, the whole of the colossal stairs were crowded to excess. Not a few of the ministers were clad in state dresses, and most of the courtiers and household officers still had on the fanciful robes worn at the fatal masquerade. The great diversity of splendid costume—the melancholy state of the King, stretched on the bier, lying on his side, his pale face resting on his right hand, his features expressive of pain subdued by fortitude, the various countenances of the surrounding throng, wherein grief, consternation, and dismay, were forcibly depicted; the blaze of the numerous torches and flambeaux borne aloft by the military; the glitter of burnished helmets, embroidered and spangled robes, mixed with the flashes of drawn sabres and fixed bayonets; the strong and condensed light thrown on the King's figure, countenance, litter, and surrounding group; the deep dark masses of shade that seemed to flitter high above, and far below the principal group, and the occasional illumination of the vast and magnificent outline of the structure, formed, on the whole, a spectacle more grand, impressive, and picturesque than any state or theatrical procession, in the arrangement of which the tasteful Gustavus had ever, been engaged.

In the midst of excruciating agonies his eyes lost not their brilliancy, and his finely expressive features displayed the triumph of fortitude over pain. Terrible and sudden as was this disaster, it did not deprive him of self-possession: he seemed more affected by the tears that trickled down the hard yet softened features of the veterans who had fought by his side, than by the wound which too probably would soon end his life. As the bearers of the royal litter ascended from flight to flight, he raised his head, evidently to obtain a better view of the grand spectacle of which he formed the principal and central object. When he arrived at the grand gallery, level with the state apartments, he made a sign with his hand that the bearers should halt, and looking wistfully around him, he said to Baron Armfelt, (who wept and sobbed aloud,) "How strange it is I should rush upon my fate after the recent warnings I had received; my mind foreboded evil; I went reluctantly, impelled, as it were, by some invisible hand. I am fully persuaded when a man's hour is come, it is in vain he strives to elude it!" After a short pause, he continued, "Perhaps my hour is not yet arrived- I would willingly live, but am not afraid to die. If I survive, I may yet trip down those flight of steps again, and if I die—why, then, enclosed in my coffin, my next descent will be on my road to the mausoleum in the Ridderholm church," The King died on the 29th of March.

The assassin, Ankastroem, was discovered, and executed; and many of the conspirators were banished out of the country. In the character of Ankastroem, and in his conduct during his last moments, a striking similarity may be traced to the wretched Bellingham, the assassin of Percival: the same fanatical satisfaction at the perpetration of the crime, the same presumptuous confidence of pardon from the Almighty.

It was the opinion of several officers of long standing and great experience in the Swedish service, that if the King had not been cut off by Ankastroem, the very army he was assembling with the view of invading France, in Normandy, and marching direct on Paris, would have hoisted the standard of revolt and destroyed the monarch whom once they adored.

Two chests containing papers were not to be opened, according to the injunction of Gustavus, until fifty years after his death. Accordingly, on April 29, 1842, these chests were opened: there was nothing found among the papers of any importance; but they proved that Gustavus enjoyed the reputation of being a great author without even knowing how to spell.

The fate of Gustavus has furnished the incidents of a very charming opera, composed by M. Auber: it is worthy of remark that this musical piece, terminating with the ***murder of a king,*** was produced ***for live French,*** who shudder at the death scenes of our tragic drama!

THE O'CONNORS OF CONNORVILLE.

Of the eccentricities of this Cork family, some amusing instances are related.

Roger Connor had high notions of his own dignity. At a Cork assize he walked across the table in the courthouse, in presence of the judge, conceiving that his personal importance gave him this privilege. The judge, who did not know him, gave him a sharp reprimand. Shortly after, the judge received, to his great surprise, a note from Mr. Connor, requiring either an apology, or "satisfaction at twelve paces." The judge was a man of peace, and as no hostile meeting occurred, it is not improbable that he apologised. A pun of this fiery gentleman's is recorded. Being asked by a guest at his table what description of wine they were drinking, Roger replied that it was Pontick ('pon ***tick***) wine—that is, it had not been paid for.

Robert O'Connor, although not in the army, had military tastes, and commanded a corps, or as he called it, a ***corpse*** of yeomanry cavalry, with which formidable body he sometimes frightened his wife by threatening to invade France at their head, seize Bonaparte, bring him to Ireland captive, and suspend him in an iron cage in his family hall! He was in constant communication with the Government at Dublin Castle, and with one of his political epistles he sent a map of the barony in which he resided, his own domain occupying so large a space as to leave but little room for the estates of all the other proprietors; on the map was written, in front of his mansion, "The finest station in the Barony for cannon." He once addressed to Sir Francis Burdett, then of radical politics, an epistle, concluding with, "Well, Sir Francis, what d'ye think of that?" "Excuse me, Connor," answered the Baronet, "I am not a judge of music," for the blotched and clumsy manuscript, with its underscored lines, bore a comical resemblance to an awkward attempt at musical notation.

Roger O'Connor, brother of Robert, when at Dublin College, "was allowed to be the best scholar in his division, and the most idle lad in his class." He grew up a strong insurgent, aiming to wield the Irish sceptre. He claimed to be descended from the royal O'Connors; and in the *"Chronicles of Eri,"* published by him, he is portrayed with his hand upon the Irish crown, and the legend, "Chief of a prostrate nation." His son Feargus records him to have exclaimed, in what we must suppose to have been a fit of patriotic frenzy, "My arm is yet young enough to wield the sword to recover my country's crown." His hatred to British domination naturally extended itself to taxes. During the continuance of the dog-tax, the collector called on him one day for payment Roger returned as meagre a list of taxable articles as possible. "Have you got no dogs?" inquired the collector. "Not one," answered the representative of Irish royalty. Just at this moment, a favourite dog came running into the courtyard, in which the collector and Roger were standing. The peril of detection was imminent, but Roger suddenly exclaimed, with well feigned alarm, "A mad dog! A mad dog!" and forthwith he took refuge in the house, as if to escape from the rabid animal—the collector followed in terror of a bite—the dog was properly disposed of, and Roger, no doubt, kept the tax in his pocket.—***Abridged from Sir Bernard Burke's Vicissitudes of Families.*** Second Series.

ADVENTUKES OF ARCHIBALD HAMILTON ROWAN.

Those who remember the streets of Dublin some forty years since, can scarcely have forgotten the above gigantic old man, in his old-fashioned dress; and following him two last of a race of dogs of a Danish breed, though called by him and supposed to be Irish wolf-dogs. Five-and-twenty years earlier, Rowan made a pedestrian tour of England with Lord Cloncurry; when Rowan's practice at starting from the inn, of a wet morning, was to roll himself in the first pool he met, in order that he might be beforehand with the rain. The laurels were then fresh which he had won by the performance of a grand feat, under the eyes of Marie Antoinette, and of which he was not a little proud. He had run a footrace in the presence of the whole French court, in jack-boots, against an officer of the Gardes de Corps, dressed in light shoes and silk stockings, and had won with ease, to the great admiration of the Queen, who honoured him with special marks of her regards.

Rowan was once master of a fortune of full 5,000*l.* a-year. He had always some adventure upon hand; and two or three of these, in which he rescued distressed damsels from the snares of rakes of rank, made a good deal of noise at the time; the particulars being made known by means of a private printing-press, which he kept in his house, ready for such occasions. When he was obliged to take refuge in America, he was frequently in pecuniary distress; and was, for a good part of the time, indebted for a livelihood to his mechanical knowledge, which enabled him to take charge of a cotton-factory in New York.—***Lord Cloncurry's Life and Times.***

THE HOUSE OF CROMWELL SNUBBED.

Lord Cloncurry, Archibald Hamilton Rowan, and Sir Thomas Frankland, once took a pedestrian tour together, and a pleasant party they made. Frankland was a man of considerable ability; but, what he chiefly valued himself upon, was his lineal descent from Oliver Cromwell, a fact with which he acquainted Sir Richard Arkwright, much to the astonishment of that ingenious knight. In passing through Derbyshire, the tourists were desirous of visiting Sir Richard's factory, and accordingly presented themselves at his door, and sent in their names. They were kept waiting in the hall a considerable time; and when, at length, Sir Richard made his appearance, in his morning gown and nightcap, he gave a very gruff and unwilling permission for the party to enter. They, nevertheless, made use of it; but not before

Frankland had read Sir Richard a lecture upon his discourtesy, and failure in the respect that was proper to be shown by a person in his position to a gentleman who, like himself was a descendant of the great Protector. The *ci-devant* barber treated the House of Cromwell with great contempt but did not withdraw the leave he had granted for the tourists to see his looms.

THE IRISH UNION.

At a dinner party, in the year 1795, at the house of John Macnamara, in Baker-street, at which Mr. Pitt was present, Lord Cloncurry, for the first time, heard of the contemplated project of a Union between Great Britain and Ireland. The news naturally acted as a ferment upon his Lordship's notions of patriotism and nationality; and he forthwith wrote a pamphlet of "Thoughts on the Projected Union." This brochure, published in Dublin, was the first blow at the ministerial scheme; it cost the author a heavy price, including his arrest as a "United Irishman," and subsequently to imprisonment for nearly two years in the Tower of London.

SUMMARY PUNISHMENT.

Some twenty years ago, one of the great organs of the Council of Edinburgh was James Laing; he was one of the clerks, and managed such police as Edinburgh then had; and though not an officer in the old Town Guard, could, as representative of the magistrates, employ it as he chose. It is incredible how much power this man had, and how much he was feared. He had more sense than to meddle with the rich, but over the people he tyrannized to his heart's content For example, about the year 1795, six or eight baker-lads of good character, being a little jolly one night, were making a noise in the street. This displeased Mr. Laing, who had a notion that nobody could be drunk with safety to the public except himself. So he had the lads apprehended; and as they did not appear in the morning, their friends became alarmed, and applied to Mr. (afterwards Sir Henry) Jardine, who next morning inquired about them, when Laing said that he need not give himself the trouble, because, **"they are all beyond Inchkeith by this time"** And so they were. He had them sent on board a tender lying in Leith Roads, which he knew was to sail that morning. This was done by his own authority, without a conviction, or a charge, or an offence. „They had been troublesome, and this was the very way to deal with such people. Such proceedings were far from uncommon; and legal redress was very seldom resorted to.

Laing had an incomprehensible reverence for Dugald Stewart. Stewart used to tell how he was walking in the meadows very early one morning, when he saw a number of people within the inclosure seemingly turning up the turf; and that, upon going up to them he found his friend, Jamie Laing, who explained that in these short light nights, there was nothing going on with the blackguards, "and so ye see, Mr. Professor, I've just brought oot the constables to try our hands at the mondieworts."—***Cockbun's Memorials.***

THE GREAT SEAL OF THE IRISH REPUBLIC.

At the time of Lord Edward Fitzgerald's arrest, his wife (the well-known Pamela), had taken refuge in the house of the father of Lord Cloncurry, in Merrion-street, Dublin, though without his knowledge. She was pursued there by the police in search of papers; and some which she had concealed in her bedroom were discovered and seized. Among other prizes taken, upon this occasion, was a seal, pronounced by the ***quidnuncs*** of the Castle to be the intended Great Seal of the Irish Republic. In Appendix, No. 23 of the Report of the Secret Committee of the Irish House of Commons, printed in 1799, there is an engraving of the impression of this seal "found in the custody of Lord Edward Fitzgerald, when he was apprehended," together with the following description:—"In a circle, Hibernia holding in her right hand an imperial crown over a shield. On her left hand is an Irish harp, over it a dagger, and at its foot lie two hogs."

Now, the Seal which the Committee of Secresy looked upon with so much horror, was a cast from an original cut for Lord Cloncurry, by Strongitharm, during one of his Lordship's earliest visits to London. The device is a harp, from which Britannia (not Hibernia,) has removed with the right hand, not an imperial but an Irish crown, and planted a dagger in its stead. Her left hand is represented breaking the strings of the harp; at the foot of which lie, not two hogs, but two Irish wolf-dogs sleeping at their post. All this is very plain to be seen. Britannia is arrayed in her ordinary helmet; and her child, bearing the cross of St George, lies beside her; the crown in her hand is as unlike the imperial crown as can well be imagined: it is manifestly the old Irish pointed-diadem. The seal itself was not designed for the broad seal of the Irish, or any other republic; but was simply a fancy emblem which Lord Cloncurry chose to illustrate his patriotic enthusiasm. There were subsequently a few casts from the original made in glass by Tassie, of Leicester-square: one of these casts given to Lord Edward Fitzgerald, became renowned in story under the *imprimatur* of the Committee of Secresy. In Lord Cloncurry's **Personal Recollections** are engraved the two seals.

REBELLION WINDFALLS.

When Lord Edward Fitzgerald became obnoxious to the law, Leinster House, the residence of his brother, the Duke of Leinster, was ransacked in the most insulting manner, in a search for criminatory documents; and when the Rebellion broke out, a number of the houses in the Duke's town of Kildare were wantonly burned, and several of his tenants hung upon the elm-trees in the avenue leading to his house at Carton. It is a curious fact, that both these brutal outrages involved incidents productive of very considerable advantages to the subject of them. By the burning of the houses in Kildare, a wholesale clearance of an idle and mischievous tenantry was effected, much to the benefit of the property, but which his Grace's kindness of heart prevented him from accomplishing. Among the tenants hanged, to annoy the landlord rather than to punish the immediate sufferers, was a man, upon the fall of whose life a number of leases expired, and a considerable addition to the Duke's income immediately accrued: so shortsighted do men often show themselves, in doing the bidding of their evil passions, no less than in their attempts to accomplish good.

LORD CLONMEL AND JOHN MAGEE.

Lord Clonmel one day said to Lord Cloncurry: "My dear Val, I have been a fortunate man in life. I am a chief justice and an earl; but, believe me, I would rather be beginning the world as a young sweep." A fortunate man, [observes Lord C] he certainly was, and in nothing more than in the period of his death, which took place the day before the outbreak of the Rebellion of 1798.

Lord Clonmel had a villa named Temple Hill, close to Sea-point, which was made the scene of an ingenious stroke of vengeance by John Magee, then printer of the **Dublin Evening Post** newspaper. Mr. Magee had been tried before his lordship for a seditious libel, and, as he thought, had been treated with undue severity by the Bench. He was subjected to very rigorous imprisonment, on the expiry of which he announced his intention of clearing off old scores. Accordingly, he had advertisements posted about the town, stating that he found himself the owner of a certain sum [14,000*l*.] 10,000*l*. of which he had settled upon his family, and the balance it was his intention, "with the blessing of God, to spend upon Lord Clonmel" Accordingly, he invited all his fellow-citizens to a *"bra pleasura"* to be held upon a certain day in the fields adjoining Temple Hill demesne. The fête was a strange one. Several thousand persons, including the entire disposable mob of Dublin, of both sexes, assembled early in the morning, and proceeded to enjoy themselves in tents and booths erected for the occasion. There were also various sports—such as climbing poles for prizes, running races in sacks, grinning through horse-collars, and so forth; and when the crowd had attained its maximum density, a number of active pigs, with their tails shaved and soaped, were let loose, and it was announced that each pig would become the property of any one who could catch and hold it by the tail. The pigs frightened and hemmed in by the crowd in all other directions, rushed through the hedges which then separated the grounds of Temple Hill from the open fields; forthwith all their pursuers followed in a body, and chasing over the shrubberies and parterres, soon revenged John Magee upon the noble owner.

FATE OF COLONEL DESPARD.

This gallant but unfortunate officer appears to have fallen into a sea of troubles through his devoted loyalty. In the course of his service he was the companion and friend of Lord Nelson, during his co-operation with whom, at the siege of Honduras, in his zeal for the public cause, he advanced large sums of money from his own resources, for the promotion of the operations of the war. For this, as well as for his gallantry and ability, he was thanked by Parliament, but *not repaid.* On his arrival in England, he pressed his claims for repayment upon the ministry; and irritated by the delays and difficulties thrown in his way by officials, he became passionate beyond control. He appealed to the House of Commons, but in vain. He then fell into pecuniary difficulties, became excited to desperation, wrote violent letters to Ministers, and having joined the London Corresponding Society, was taken up under the Act for suspending the writ of Habeas Corpus, and confined in Coldbath Fields prison. Here Lord Cloncurry found Despard, who had served many years in tropical climates, imprisoned in a stone cell, 6 feet by 8, furnished with a truckle-bed, and a small table; there was no chair, fireplace, or window, light being only admitted through a barred but un-glazed aperture over the door, opening into a paved yard, at the time covered with snow. Despard was confined, we believe, from the winter of 1797 until the spring of 1804, by which time he had grown worn and wan, and of unsound mind. In talking over the condition of Ireland with Lord Cloncurry, the Colonel said, that though "he had not seen his country for thirty years, he had never ceased thinking of it and of its misfortunes, and the main object of his visit [to Lord C] was to disclose his discovery of an infallible remedy for the latter—viz., a voluntary separation of the sexes, so as to leave no future generation obnoxious to oppression." This plan of cure would, he said, defy the machinations of the enemies of Ireland to interrupt its complete success.

A year after this conversation, this poor madman, at the Oakley Arms public-house, in Lambeth, was apprehended, with thirty-two other persons, on a charge of treasonable conspiracy, tending to destroy the King and subvert the Government—one feature of the plot being to take the Tower. In February following [1802] the Colonel, with nine associates, were tried by a Special Commission, and being all found guilty, seven of them, including Despard, were executed Feb. 21, on the top of Horsemonger-lane gaol.

BONAPARTE FIRST CONSUL.

Lord Cloncurry relates some interesting **Recollections** of the First Consul in 1802. His Lordship was, through Marshal Berthier, presented at the Tuileries, attended a grand review, and dined with the Emperor on the day of presentation. "The occasion," says Lord Cloncurry, "at which Lord Holland was also present, was a remarkable one. We were received in the magnificent rooms of the Tuileries, in great state; the stairs and ante-rooms being lined by men of the corps délite, *in their splendid uniforms, and baldricks of buff leather, edged with silver. Upon our introduction, refreshments were offered, and a circle was formed, as at a private* entrée. *Napoleon entered freely into conversation with Lord Holland and myself, inquiring, among other matters, respecting the meaning of an Irish peerage, the peculiar characters of which, and its difference from an English peerage, I had some difficulty in making him comprehend. While we were conversing, three knocks were heard at the door, and a deputation from the Conservative Senate presented itself, as if unexpectedly, and was admitted. The leader of the deputation addressed the First Consul in a set oration, tendering him the Consulate for life, to which he responded in an* extempore speech, which, nevertheless, he read from a paper concealed in the crown of his hat.

"Bonaparte was at that time very slight and thin in person, and, as far as I could judge, not possessed of much more information upon general subjects than of confidence in his own oratorical powers. Upon my expressing some surprise afterwards at the character of his remarks, I recollect General Lawless telling me that he and some other Irishmen, (I believe Wolfe Tone was among them) had a short time before been engaged in a discussion with him respecting a project for the invasion of Ireland, when, after making many inquiries, and hearing their answers, he remarked that it was a pity so fine a country should be so horribly infested with wolves! Lawless and his companions assured him that such was not the case, to which he deigned no reply, but a contemptuous *bah!*"

One of the Abbé Sièyes's constitutions proposed to have a grand functionary, with no power except to give away offices; upon which Napoleon, then First Consul, to whom the proposition was tendered, asked if it well became him to be made a "Cochon à l'engrais à la somme de trois milles par an? (a hog to be fatted at the rate of 120,000*l.* a-year.)

THE LAST OF THE STUARTS.

When Lord Cloncurry was at Rome, in 1803, he became somewhat of a favourite with the last of the Stuarts, Cardinal York, whom Lord C. always addressed as "Majesty," thus going a step further than the Duke of Sussex, who was on familiar terms with him, and always applied to him the style of Royal Highness.

The Cardinal was in the receipt of an income of eight or nine thousand pounds a-year, of which he received 4,000*l.* from his royal rival, George III., and the remainder from his ecclesiastical benefices. This revenue was then in Italy equivalent to at least 20,000*l.*; and it enabled his eminence to assume somewhat of royal state. He received visitors very hospitably at Frescati, where Lord Cloncurry was. a frequent visitor, and was often amused by a reproduction of the scenes between Sancho Panza and his physician, during the reign of the squire, in the island of Barataria. His Eminence was an invalid, and under a strict regimen; but as he still retained his taste for savoury meats, a contest usually took place between him and his servants for the possession of each rich dish which they formally set before him, and then endeavoured to snatch away, while he, with greater eagerness, strove to seize it in its transit. Among the Cardinal's most favourite attendants was a miserable cur dog, which one day attached itself to his Eminence at the gate of St. Peter's, an occurrence to which he constantly referred, as a proof of his true royal blood—the cur being, as he supposed, a King Charles spaniel, and, therefore, endowed with an instinctive, hereditary acquaintance with the House of Stuart.

Lord Cloncurry presented the Cardinal with a telescope, which he seemed to fancy, and received from him in return, the large medal struck in honour of his accession to his unsubstantial throne. Upon one side of this medal was the royal bust, with the Cardinal's hat, and the words, **Henries norms Dei gratia Rex,** and upon the other, the arms of England, with the motto:—**Hand desideriis Nominum, sed voluntate Dei.** The Cardinal was greatly delighted with the present, especially from its being of English manufacture.

INVASION PANIC OF 1803.

When the country was alarmed by the expected invasion of England by Bonaparte, George III. wrote, November 30, 1803, to Bishop Hurd, who was highly esteemed by the King:

"We are here in daily expectation that Bonaparte will attempt his threatened invasion. The chances against his success seem so many, that it is wonderful he persists in it. I own I place that thorough dependence on the protection of Divine Providence that I cannot help thinking the usurper is encouraged to make the trial that the ill-success may put an end to his wicked purposes. Should his troops effect a landing, I shall certainly put myself at the head of mine, and mine other armed subjects, to repel them. But as it is impossible to foresee the events of such a conflict, should the enemy approach too near to Windsor, I shall think it right the Queen and my daughters should cross the Severn, and shall send them to your episcopal palace at Worcester. By this hint I do not in the least mean that they shall be any inconvenience to you, and shall send a proper servant and furniture for their accommodation. Should this event arise, I certainly would rather have what I value most in life remain, during the conflict, in your diocese, and under your roof, than in any other place in the island."

FATE OF THE DUC D'ENGHIEN.

While the First Consul was meditating his descent upon England, in 1804, his life and government had been imperilled by the conspiracy of Georges, Moreau, and Pichegru. The Due d'Enghien, as is well known, was the innocent victim of this affair, having been arrested on neutral territory, and shot in a ditch, without a trial, in order to strike the Bourbons with terror. While the printed account shows that the plot was a formidable one, that the death of Napoleon and a counter-revolution were really not remote contingencies, and that there were some slight grounds to suspect an intrigue between Dumouriez and the Duke, it also impliedly acquits the Prince of any share in the main conspiracy, and throws the guilt of his cruel fate exclusively on the First Consul. From the list of charges against the Duke, entirely in Napoleon's writing, it is plain that he did not possess any proofs sufficient even for the tribunal of Vincennes to convict the prisoner of a design against his life

These monstrous charges speak for themselves, and accord well with the midnight dungeon, the irresponsible conclave, the undefended prisoner, and the grave dug before the trial for the victim! Moreover, the volume of Napoleon's **Correspondence,** in which these details are given, has not a trace of the alleged over-rapidity of Savory, of the suppression of the Prince's letter by Talleyrand, of the order said to have been given to Real to suspend the execution after the sentence, and to await the result of a regular examination—of the hundred and one excuses, in short, which have been urged for Napoleon by his apologists. On the contrary, from the following letter we infer that he wished to avoid discussion about a purpose already determined, and that he feared lest public opinion should condemn his design on the Due d'Enghien. It is addressed to the Commandant of Vincennes:—

"A person, whose name is to remain unknown, will be brought to the fortress confided to your care; you are to put him in a vacant cell, and to take every precaution for his safe keeping. The intention of the Government is to **keep all proceedings concerning him most secret.** No question is to be put to him as to who he is, or why he is detained. Even you are not to know who the prisoner is. No one is to communicate with him but yourself; no one else is to see him until fresh orders. He will probably arrive this night"

Napoleon's Government, though very despotic, was not, however, usually cruel; and this great crime which, perhaps, was caused by the haunting dread of an assassin's arm, was an exception to its general tenor.

NAPOLEON AND FOUCHÉ

Napoleon one day summoned Fouché, then Minister of Police, and told him, that he was astonished that a person of his noted dexterity did not do his business better; and that things were going on of which he knew nothing. "Yes," said the minister, "there are things which I was ignorant o£ but which I know now: for example, a little man, in a three-cornered hat, wearing a blue frock-coat, leaves the palace every second day; returns between eight and nine in the evening, by the small door of the pavilion Marsan, above the kitchens, and, accompanied by a single person, taller than himself, but habited in the same manner, gets into a hackney-coach, and goes straight to rue Chanteraine, No. 38, to the house of La Grazzini; the little man is yourself to whom this singular opera-singer is unfaithful in favour of Rode, the violin-player, who lodges in rue du Mont Blanc, **Hotel de l' Empire"** As soon as Fouché had done, Napoleon, turning his back upon the minister, began to walk up and down, with his hands behind him, whistling an Italian air; and Fouché retired without adding another word.

FRENCH DISTINCTION.

When, in 1805, Patrick Lattin, an officer of the Irish Brigade, was residing in Paris, a M. de Montmorency, whose Christian name was Anne, made his appearance, announcing that he was enabled to return to France, in consequence of the First Consul having scratched his name on the list of emigrés. "Apresent done" **observed Lattin,** "mon cher Anne, tues un zehre—un âne rayée."

AN IRISH ANTI-UNIONIST,

Wogan Browne, a virulent opponent of the Irish Union, was a magistrate of Kildare, Meath, and Dublin, and was highly popular and irreproachable as a magistrate of these three counties. Nevertheless, sometime in 1797, he was one Sunday riding past a field where the country-people were about to hold a football-match. The whole assembly paid their respects to him; and at their request, he got off his horse, and opened the sports by giving the ball the first kick—a sort of friendly sanctioning of the amusements of their neighbours, which was then not unusual among the gentry in Ireland. The custom, however, was not approved of by the Government; and Lord Chancellor Clare, upon being informed of what Wogan Browne had done, at once suspended him in the commission of the peace. He was soon afterwards restored by Chancellor Ponsonby, upon the accession of the ministry of All the Talents; but was again, without further cause, deprived of his commission for **two** of the counties, by Lord Chancellor Manners. This stupid insult, both to the individual and to the body of magistrates—for, if Mr. Browne was unfit to be a justice of the peace for two counties, it was an insult to associate him with the magistrates of a third—was warmly resented by the gentry of Kildare.

Another occurrence in Browne's history shows more forcibly how precarious was the hold which in those days, such a man enjoyed of his life. He was in the year 1798, seized as a rebel in the street of Naas, his county town, by some hostile soldiers, and a rope placed about his neck, for the purpose of hanging him, when the accidental arrival of a dragoon, with a letter addressed to him by the Lord Lieutenant, on public business, interrupted his captors in the work of murder.

Wogan Browne died at Castle Browne about five-and-thirty years ago; and the final scene was another illustration of a miserable phase of Irish society. He had been himself a Protestant; but his brother, and his sister, who, indeed, was a nun, were Roman Catholics. Upon these respective grounds, the two parties among his neighbours claimed the right of interring his body according to their particular customs; and they fought out the quarrel in the churchyard over his coffin: which party previled is not stated; but Lord Cloncurry, who relates the above, adds that "no man ever was buried, who, during life, exhibited or entertained less of sectarian rancour, or whose living feelings were less in unison with the passions which signalised his funeral"

NAPOLEON I. AND THE SENTINEL.

In the printshops may still be seen occasionally a representation of the Emperor Napoleon brought to a standstill by one of his own sentinels, in consequence of his inability to give the password. The veteran who, in obedience to his orders, was so near running his bayonet into His Majesty was Coluche, who gives the following account of the affair: "It was in 1809, after the victory of Ebersberg, that I was posted at the entrance of a half-destroyed building, in which the Emperor had taken up his quarters. My orders were not to allow anybody to pass unless accompanied by an officer of the staff. In the evening a person wearing a grey overcoat came towards my post and wanted to pass. I lowered my bayonet, and called out 'Nobody passes here.' Those were the words I used, and I never added 'even if you were the little corporal himself,' as has been wrongfully imputed to me since, because I did not know I had the Emperor before me. The person came on without seeming to notice what I said, and I then brought my bayonet to the charge, and called out, 'If thou takest another step I will run my bayonet into thy stomach.' The noise brought out the whole of the staff, the Emperor returned to his quarters, and I was carried off to the guardhouse. 'You are lost, my boy,' said my comrades; 'you have committed an assault on the Emperor!' 'Stop a bit,' I said, 'what of my orders? I shall explain all that to the court-martial.' The Emperor sent to fetch me, and when I came into his presence, he said, 'Grenadier, thou mayest put a red riband in thy buttonhole; I give thee the cross!' 'Thanks, my Emperor,' I answered, 'but there is no shop in this country where I can buy the riband.' 'Well,' replied the Emperor, with a smile, 'take a piece from a woman's red petticoat; that will answer the purpose just as well!'" Coluche continued to serve through all the campaigns, when he was not confined to the hospital by his wounds, till the concluding battle of Waterloo, after which he was discharged, returned to his village, and resumed his occupation as an agricultural labourer. The old soldier has been received at Fontainebleau by the present Emperor, who, according to the French journals, conversed with him a considerable time, and, among other questions, asked him, "Though you did not know it was the Emperor, would you really have shot him?" To which the veteran replied, "No, Sire, I would only have wounded him with my bayonet."

PREDICTIONS OF THE DOWNFAL OF NAPOLEON.

Brialmont and Gleig, in their *Memoirs of Wellington,* relate—Mr. Pitt received, during dinner, when Sir Arthur Wellesley and other eminent persons were present, intelligence of the capitulation of Mack, at Ulm, and the march of the Emperor upon Vienna. One of the friends of the Prime Minister, on hearing of the reverse, exclaimed, "All is lost! there are no other means of opposing Napoleon." "You are mistaken," said Pitt, "there is yet hope, if I can succeed in stirring up a national war in Europe—a war which ought to begin in Spain."—"Yes, gentlemen, Spain will be the first nation in which that war of patriotism shall be lighted up which can alone deliver Europe."

At a moment when the prestige of the Empire was accepted everywhere, Wellington not only expressed doubts as to the stability of that edifice, which seemed as if it must endure for ages, but pointed out distinctly the causes which must operate to throw it down, and the means by which its fall might be hastened.

In December, 1811, Wellington wrote to Lord William Bentinck, "I have long considered it probable that we shall see a general resistance throughout Europe to the horrible and base tyranny of Bonaparte, and that we shall be called upon to play a leading part in the drama, as counsellors as well as actors."

In a letter to Lord Liverpool, in 1811, Wellington wrote: "I am convinced, that if we can only hold out a little longer, we shall see the world emancipated." And to Dumouriez, July, 1811: "It is impossible that Europe can much longer submit to the debasing tyranny which oppresses it"

Brialmont and Gleig summarily observe: "It may truly be said that the Duke foretold in succession, the final success of the war in Spain—the influence which that war would exercise over public opinion in other nations—***the general rising of Europe against Bonaparte***—the fall of the Empire—the disastrous campaign in Russia—and the awakening of the public spirit in Germany."

ASSASSINATION OF MR. PERCEVAL.

On the evening of May 11, 1812, Mr. Spencer Perceval, then Chancellor of the

Exchequer, with his friend Mr. Stephen, was on his way to the House of Commons, sitting in Committee upon an important question. Mr. Perceval was later than the appointed time; and the first witness was being examined, when a messenger deputed to bring the minister, met him walking towards the House with Mr. Stephen, arm-in-arm. He instantly, with his accustomed activity, darted forward to obey the summons, but for which Mr. Stephen, who happened to be on his left side, would have been the victim of the assassin's pistol, which prostrated Mr. Perceval as he entered the lobby. He staggered forward with a slight exclamation, and fell expiring. The incident was so sudden, that the assassin was at first disregarded by the bystanders. He was at length seized, and examined, when another loaded pistol was found upon him. The wretched man, by name John Bellingham, had no kind of quarrel with Mr. Perceval, but complained of a suit at St. Petersburg having been neglected by our ambassador there, Lord Granville, whom he intended to have destroyed had not Mr. Perceval fallen first in his way. He never attempted to escape; but was taken, committed, tried, condemned, executed, dissected, all within one week that he fired the shot. Lord Brougham says of this indecent haste, "so great an outrage upon justice was never witnessed in modern times; for the application to delay the trial, until evidence of Bellingham's insanity could be brought from Liverpool, was refused; and the trial proceeded, while the courts the witnesses, the jury, and, the people, were under the influence of the feelings naturally excited by the deplorable slaughter of one of the most eminent and virtuous men,,in any rank of the community."

It appears that Mr. John Williams, of Scorrier House, near Redwith, in Cornwall, had a dream representing the assassination of Mr. Perceval on the night after its occurrence, when the fact could not be known to him by any ordinary means; and he mentioned the fact to many persons during the interval between the dream and his receiving notice of its fulfilment According to the account furnished to Dr. Abercrombie, Mr. Williams dreamt that he was in the lobby of the House of Commons, and saw a man enter, dressed in a blue coat and white waistcoat. Immediately after, he saw a man dressed in a brown coat with yellow basket-buttons, draw a pistol from under his coat, and discharge it at the former, who fell instantly, the blood issuing from a wound a little below the left breast. Mr. Williams saw the murderer seized by some gentlemen who were present, and observed his countenance; and on asking who the gentleman was who had been shot, he was told it was the Chancellor of the Exchequer. He then awoke, and mentioned the dream to his wife, who made light of it; but the dream was repeated a second and a third time. At breakfast, the dreams were the sole subject of conversation; and in the forenoon, Mr. Williams went to Falmouth, where he related the particulars of them to all the acquaintance that he met. Next day, Mr. Williams's daughter and son-in-law came to Scorrier House, when Mr. Williams described to the latter Mr. Perceval, although he, Mr. W., had never seen him, had any business with him, or been in the lobby of the House of Commons. Meanwhile, another of Mr. Williams's sons arrived from Truro, where he had seen a gentleman who had come by that evening's mail from London, and who, on the previous evening, had seen Bellingham shoot Mr. Perceval in the House of Commons lobby; and next Mr. Williams described particularly the appearance and dress of the assassin whom he had seen, in his dream, fire the pistol. About six weeks after, Mr. Williams, having business in town, went, accompanied by a friend, to the House of Commons, (where he had never been before,) and there, at the steps at the entrance, said, "This place is as distinctly within my recollection in my dream as any in my house," and he made the same observation when he entered the lobby. He then pointed out the exact spot where Bellingham stood, when he fired, and which Mr. Perceval had reached when he was struck by the ball, and when and how he fell The dress, both of Mr. Perceval and Bellingham also agreed with the description given by Mr. Williams, even to the most minute particulars. Mr. Williams died in April, 1841, after the publication of the account of his dream, the narrative of which, or any particulars of it, has never been contradicted; he is described as a man of strict integrity, proof against all temptation, and above all reproach.

Among the persons in the lobby of the House of Commons at the moment of the assassination, was Samuel Crompton, who was looking out for the reward promised him by the Chancellor of the Exchequer, for his invention of the spinning mule. Crompton was in conversation with Sir Robert Peel and Mr. Blackburn, upon the subject of his claim, which was about to be brought forward, when one of these gentlemen remarked, "Here comes Mr. Perceval." The group was immediately joined by the Chancellor of the Exchequer, who addressed them with the remark, "You will be glad to know that we mean to propose twenty thousand pounds for Crompton; do you think that will be satisfactory? "Mr. Crompton did not hear the reply, as he had left the party, and walked down a short stair leading out of the lobby; but before he left it, he heard a great rush of people, and exclamations that Mr. Perceval had been shot—which was indeed the fact The assassin, Bellingham, in an instant, had deprived the country of a valuable minister, and Crompton lost a friend and patron of the most critical importance to his fortune. Crompton did not, however, hear the shot, though so near the scene of the tragedy, nor did he see Mr. Perceval fall. The foundation on which his reasonable hopes were built was thus swept away.—French's *Life and Times of Crompton,* 2d. edit.

Mr. Perceval, when he was shot, had in his hand a memorandum, as follows: "Crompton

20,000 *l.*
10,000 *l*
5,000 *l*"

which was understood to signify not less than 5,000 *l.*, but 20,000 *l* if possible. After having haunted the lobby of the House of Commons for five wearisome months, the paltry sum of 5,000 *l.* was voted to Crompton for what he had done to extend the principal manufacture of the country!

GRAMMAR AND VIRTUE.

When Mr. Harris, of Salisbury, made his first speech in the House of Commons, Charles Townshend asked, with an affected surprise, who he was? He had never seen him before. "Ah! you must, at least, have heard of him. That's the celebrated Mr. Harris, of Salisbury, who has written a very ingenious book on *grammar,* and another on *virtue*"—"What the devil then brings him here? I am sure he will neither find the one nor the other in the House of Commons." Malone, however, states that Townshend knew Harris well; and the above was merely a trap for saying a good thing.

PAIRING OFF.

Soame Jenyns, seeing at the House of Commons some members pairing off in the Speaker's Chamber, said, "I think there are no happy pairs now in England, but those who pair here."

WATCHING AND SLEEPING.

When a Bill was introduced into the House of Commons, for better watching the metropolis; in order to contribute towards effecting which object, one of the clauses went to propose that watchmen should be **compelled** to sleep (luring the daytime; Lord Nugent, with admirable humour, got up, and desired that "he might be personally included in the provisions of the Bill, being frequently so tormented with gout, as to be unable to sleep either by day, or by night."

ELECTION REPARTEE.

When Mr. Wilberforce was a candidate for Hull, his sister, an amiable and witty young lady, offered the compliment of a new dress to each of the wives of those freemen who voted for her brother; on which she was saluted with the cry of "Miss Wilberforce *for ever!* when she pleasantly observed, "I thank you, gentlemen, but I cannot agree with you; for, really, I do not wish to be *Miss Wilberforce* for ever."

PARLIAMENTARY PERSONALITIES.

Lord Colchester relates that during his Speakership of the Commons, in the course of debate, Sir Joseph Yorke angrily called Whitbread "a brewer of bad porter." There was a violent uproar in the House. Whitbread instantly took the thing with good humour, and the Speaker refused to let anybody else speak till the uproar subsided. He then rose and said, "Mr. Speaker, I rise as a tradesman to complain of the gallant officer for abusing the commodity which I sell;" upon which the whole

House burst into laughter and approbation at the self-command and good humour with which Whitbread put an end to the fury of his friends.

Sir Joseph Yorke was addicted to personalities. One night, when speaking to a motion by Alderman Waithman, who was a linen-draper, Sir Joseph illustrated his argument, by assuming "a share or a *shawl,* it mattered not which."

RATIONALE OF RATTING—WRITTEN SPEECHES.

When the late Lord Dudley began life as Mr. Ward, he embraced, like most youthful politicians, the captivating theories of Whigism; but when he grew older, and came to his title, he became—like most men when they acquire "a stake in the country"—a Tory. Some time after the change, Lord Byron was asked what it would take to *rewhig* Dudley? The Poet replied, "he must first be re-Ward-ed."

Lord Dudley and Ward openly avowed and defended the practice of pre-writing speeches, learning them by heart, and reciting them in parliament. For this notion, and his severe treatment of Fox, in the *Quarterly Review* he was much assailed by the epigrammatists of the day, and among the results was Rogers's jeu-d' esprit:

"Ward has no heart, they say, but I deny it,
He has a heart, and gets his speeches by it."

A TUMBLE-DOWN.

It is curious to observe how, in some instances, great names and historical reputations are forfeited by some paltry means. Thus, Jorgen Jorgenson, the Dane, who deserves to be remembered for his singular career, and who, with an army of eight persons, established himself as Protector of Iceland, late in life was transported at the Old Bailey for pilfering from his lodgings in Warren-street, Fitzroy-square!

THE NATIONAL DEBT,

Charles Townshend and his brother George were at supper at the King's Arms, with some other young men. The conversation, somehow or other, rambled into politics, and it was started that the National Debt was a benefit. "I am sure it is not," said Mr. Townshend; "I can't tell why, but my brother Charles can, and I will send to him for arguments" Charles was at supper at another tavern, but so much the dupe of this message that he literally called for pen, ink, and paper, wrote four long sides of arguments, and sent word, that when his company broke up, he would come and give them more, which he did at one o'clock in the morning.

THE CIVIL LIST.

One of the candidates for the Dublin University, at an election, said of his opponent, that his speech proved but "the vulgarity of his own nature, which not eve? a University education could refine." To this the gentleman assailed replied that "it was a great pity when his opponent had secured a retiring pension of three thousand per annum on the consolidated fund, that he had not managed to put his tongue upon the civil list."

SIR FRANCIS BURDETT ARRESTED, AND COMMITTED TO THE TOWER.

The great event of the political career of Sir Francis Burdett was his committal by the House of Commons, in 1810, for a letter addressed to his constituents, denying the power of the House to imprison delinquents, which he published in Cobbett's ***Political Register,*** and which the House voted to be libellous and scandalous. Burdett was taken from the house, No. 80, Piccadilly, on the 6th of April The arrest had been made by forcing open the area windows and doors of the house, after a fruitless attempt to get by a ladder in at the drawing-room window. Sir Francis was then found in his drawing-room with his family, viz. his brother and son, with some ladies, and a tall, stout Irish gentleman (this was Roger O'Connor, the brother of Arthur O'Connor, the Irish traitor). About twenty or thirty persons, constables and magistrates, with the serjeant and deputy-serjeant at their head, went into the room. Sir Francis Burdett desired the serjeant to produce his authority and read his warrant, which he did. Sir Francis said it was illegal, and he should not go, unless forced. Then the serjeant touched him by the arm, and Sir Francis Burdett, with his brother and a servant, went downstairs to the coach, which was ready at the door. The deputy-serjeant and a messenger went with Sir Francis Burdett and Mr. Jones Burdett, his brother, in the coach; Sir Francis's servant behind it. The serjeant went on horseback before. The military force present at the arrest were the Guards and a large body of cavalry. The Life Guards attended the coach on each side, and before and behind. The 15th Light Dragoons led the way. They went round by Portland-street and the City-road, through Finsbury-square And the Minories to the Tower. Tower Hill was covered by the mob. Lord Moira received Sir Francis Burdett in the Governor's apartments in the Tower; and the Lieutenant gave Mr. Colman a receipt, and Sir Francis gave Mr. Col-man a letter to convey to Lady Burdett The carriage stopped at the palisade of the Tower, near the lions; and Sir Francis Burdett, with the serjeant, went on foot over the bridge, and under the gateway, to the Governor's apartments. Lord Moira gave him his hand upon his entrance, and offered him the whole range of the Tower if he would give his word and honour not to pass the gates; which Sir Francis undertook—and he kept his word.

While the news of the committal was the subject of conversation, a sentimental young lady inquired what Sir Francis had done? "Alas!" said her lover, "he is the victim of an unfortunate attachment." Tears of commiseration came into the lady's eyes; and when her informant left her, she indited some dozen stanzas on Constancy, and sent them to Sir Francis in prison. Having communicated this to her lover, he lost her favour for ever by explaining that Sir Francis, "so far *from* being a victim of the tender passion, had been only *attached* for high treason."

Sir Francis Burdett died January 23, 1844, in his 74th year. After reading the above account of his being besieged in his house in Piccadilly, his committal to the Tower, and his withstanding many subsequent years of strong political excitement, the story of his death reads strangely. He had been married to Lady Burdett fifty years; when, towards the close of 1843, her health gave way, and she died on Jan. 10 following. Her death sounded her husband's knell. Such was his grief that life became to him an insupportable burthen. Resolutely refusing food or nourishment of any kind, [as we learn from Sir Bernard Burke,] he died on the 23d of the same month; and husband and wife were buried side by side in the same vault, at the same hour, on the same day, in the church of Ramsbury, Wilts.

FIRE AND SMOKE.

When Curran visited France in 1814, he wrote in pencil on the column erected about a mile to the west of Boulogne, by Napoleon, to commemorate his attempt to invade England:

"When ambition achieves its desire,
How Fortune must laugh at the joke;
He rose in a pillar of fire,
To set in a pillar of smoke."

THE BATTLE OF WATERLOO.

Capt. Gronow, who, in his own words, "took but a humble part in this great contest, yet had opportunities of seeing and hearing much, both during and after the battle," has related these stirring episodes.

The whole of the British infantry not actually engaged, were, on the morning of the 18th, formed into squares; and, as you looked along our lines, it seemed as if we formed a continuous wall of human beings. "I recollect," says the Captain, "distinctly being able to see Bonaparte and his staff; and some of my brother officers, using the glass, exclaimed, 'There he is on his white horse.'"

"About 4 P.M. the enemy's artillery in front of us ceased firing all of a sudden, and we saw large masses of cavalry advance; not a man present who survived could have forgotten, in after life, the awful grandeur of that charge. You perceived at a distance what appeared to be an overwhelming, long moving line, which, ever advancing, glittered, like a stormy wave of the sea, when it catches the sunlight. On came the mounted host until they got-near enough, whilst the very earth seemed to vibrate beneath their thundering tramp. One might suppose that nothing could have resisted the shock of this terrible moving mass. They were the famous cuirassiers. In an almost incredibly short period, they were within twenty yards of us, shouting **'Vive l' Empereur!'** The word of command, 'Prepare to receive cavalry,' had been given, very man in the front ranks knelt, and a wall bristling with steel, held together by steady hands, presented itself to the infuriated cuirassiers.

"Just before this charge, the Duke entered by one of the angles of the square, accompanied only by one ***aide-de-camp;*** all the rest of the staff being either killed or wounded. Our Commander-in-Chief, as far as I could judge, appeared perfectly composed; but looked very thoughtful and pale. He was dressed in a grey great-coat with a cape, white cravat, leather pantaloons, Hessian boots, and a large cocked-hat á la Russe.

"The charge of the French cavalry was gallantly executed; but our long well-directed fire brought men and horses down, and ere long the utmost confusion arose in their ranks. The officers were exceedingly brave, and by their gestures and fearless bearing did all in their power to encourage their men to form again and renew the attack. The Duke sat unmoved, mounted on his favourite charger. I recollect his asking Colonel Stanhope what o'clock it was, upon which Stanhope took out his watch, and said it was twenty minutes past four, the Duke replied, 'The battle is mine; and if the Prussians arrive soon, there will be an end of the war.'

"During the terrible fire of artillery which preceded the repeated charges of the cuirassiers against our squares, many shells fell amongst us. We were lying down, when a shell fell between Captain (after Colonel) Colquitt and another officer. In an instant Colquitt jumped up, caught the shell as if it had been a cricket-ball, and flung it over the heads of both officers and men, thus saving the lives of many brave fellows.,,

Then comes the soldierly narrative of **the last Charge:**—"It was about five o'clock, that we suddenly received orders to retire behind an elevation in our rear. The enemy's artillery had come up **en masse** within a hundred yards of us. By the time they began to discharge their guns, however, we were lying down behind the rising ground, and protected by a ridge. The enemy's cavalry was in the rear of their artillery, in order to be ready to protect it if attacked; but no attempt was made on our part to do so. After they had pounded away at us for about half-an-hour, they deployed, and up came the whole mass of the Imperial infantry of the Guard, led on by the Emperor in person. We had now before us, probably, about 20,000 of the best soldiers in France, the heroes of many memorable victories; we saw the bear-skin rise higher and higher, as they ascended the ridge of ground which separated us and advanced nearer and nearer to our lines.

"It was at this moment that the Duke of Wellington gave his famous order for our bayonet charge, as he rode along the line; these are the precise words he made use of—'Guards, get up and charge.' We were instantly on our legs, and after ten weary hours of inaction and irritation at maintaining a purely defensive attitude—all the time suffering the loss of comrades and friends—the spirit which animated officers and men may easily be imagined. After firing a volley, as soon as the enemy were within shot, we rushed on with fixed bayonets, and that hearty hurrah peculiar to British soldiers.

"It appeared that our men, deliberately and with calculation, singled out their victims; for as they came upon the Imperial Guard, our line broke, and the fighting became irregular, the impetuosity of our men seemed almost to paralyze their enemy; I witnessed several of the Imperial Guard who were run through the body apparently without any resistance on their parts. I observed a big Welshman of the name of Hughes, who was 6 feet 7 inches in height, run through with his bayonet and knock down with the butt end of his firelock, I should think, a dozen, at least, of his opponents. This terrible contest did not last more than ten minutes, for the Imperial Guard was seen in full retreat, leaving all their guns and many prisoners in our hands."

WELLINGTON'S ACCOUNT OF THE BATTLE OF WATERLOO.

As might be expected, the Duke was applied to by several persons for details of this great battle. His replies are very characteristic; the first is dated from Cambrai, April 10th, 1816:—

"The Duke of Wellington presents his compliments to Sir John Sinclair, and is much obliged to him for the account of the defence of Hougoumont. The battle of Waterloo is, undoubtedly, one of the most interesting events of modern times; but the Duke entertains no hopes of ever seeing an account of all its details which shall be true. The detail, even, of the defence of Hougoumont is not exactly true; and the Duke begs leave to suggest to Sir John Sinclair, that the publication of details of this kind which are not exact cannot be attended with any utility."

But the persevering Scotchman was not to be so easily got rid of; he writes again, to which the Duke replies:—

"I have received your letter of the 20th. The people of England may be entitled to a detailed and accurate account of the battle of Waterloo, and I have no objection to their having it; but I do object to their being misinformed and misled by those novels called Relations,' 'Impartial Accounts,' &c. &c, of that transaction, containing the stories which curious travellers have picked up from peasants, private soldiers, individual officers, &c. &c, and have published to the world as the truth. Hougoumont was no more fortified than La Haye Sainte; and the latter was not lost for want of fortifications, but by one of those accidents from which human affairs are never entirely exempt. I am really disgusted with and ashamed of all that I have seen of the battle of Waterloo. The number of writings upon it would lead the world to suppose that the British army had never fought a battle before, and there is not one which contains a true representation, or even an idea, of the transaction; and this is because the writers have referred as above quoted, instead of to the official sources and reports. It is not true that the British army was unprepared. The story of the Greek is equally unfounded as that of Vandamme having 46,000 men;

upon which last point I refer you to Marshal Ney's report, who upon that point must be the best authority."

Mr. Mudford was then getting up a big hook about the battle: he pressed the Duke for information, and held out the inducement that the work should be dedicated to His Grace, who very rarely permitted this empty sort of compliment, and in this instance he felt the necessity of a refusal more than in any other. However, the Duke, after warning Mudford against the published accounts, gave him these details:—

"You now desire that I should point out to you where you could receive information on this event, on the truth of which you could rely. In answer to this desire, I can refer you only to my own despatches published in the **London Gazette.** General Alava's report is the nearest to the truth of the other *official* reports published; but even that report contains some statements not exactly correct The others that I have seen cannot be relied upon. To some of these may be attributed the source of the falsehoods since circulated through the medium of the unofficial publications with which the press has abounded. Of these a remarkable instance is to be found in the report of a meeting between Marshal Blucher and me at La Belle Alliance; and some have gone so far as to have seen the chair on which I sat down in that farmhouse. **It happens that the meeting took place, after ten at night, at the village of Genappe;** and anybody who attempts to describe with truth the operations of the different armies will see that it *could not be otherwise.* The other part is not so material; but, in truth, I was not off my horse till I returned to Waterloo, between eleven and twelve at night"

To Lady Frances Webster, the Duke wrote from Brussels, June 19, 1815, half-past eight, on the morning after the battle:—

"Lord Mountnorris may remain in Bruxelles in perfect security. I yesterday, after a most severe and bloody contest, gained a complete victory, and pursued the French till after dark. They are in complete confusion, and I have, I believe, 150 pieces of cannon; and Blucher, who continued the pursuit all night, my soldiers being tired to death, sent me word this morning that he had got 60 more. My loss is immense. Lord Uxbridge, Lord Fitzroy Somerset, General Cooke, General Barnes, and Colonel Berkeley are wounded. Colonel De Lancey, Canning, Gordon, General Picton, killed. *The finger of Providence was upon me, and I escaped unhurt?*

What the impulse was which dictated these extraordinary words, we leave to the opinion of those who read them..... When the dreadful fight was over, the Duke's feelings, so long kept at the highest tension, gave way, and as he rode amid the groans of the wounded and the reeking carnage, and heard the rout of the vanquished and the shouts of the victors, fainter and fainter through the gloom of night, he wept, and soon after wrote the words just quoted from his letter. Again, he feelingly wrote; "My heart is broken by the terrible loss I have sustained in my old friends and companions, and my poor soldiers. Believe me, nothing excepting a battle lost, can be half so melancholy as a battle won. The bravery of my troops has hitherto saved me from the greater evil; but to win such a battle as this of Waterloo, at the expense of so many gallant friends, could only be termed a heavy misfortune but for the result to the public."

Wellington would never have fought at Waterloo, unless certain of the aid of Blucher: it is idle, therefore, to speculate on the chance of what the event of the day might have been had this support been unexpectedly wanting. French writers assert that he must have been crushed; but from the following interesting passage we see that the Duke held a different opinion. The Rev. Mr. Gleig tells us that—

"After dinner, the conversation turned on the Waterloo campaign, when Croker alluded to the criticisms of the French military writers, some of whom contended that the Duke had fought the battle in a position full of difficulty, because he had no practicable retreat The Duke said, 'At all events, they failed in putting it to the test. The road to Brussels was practicable every yard for such a purpose. I knew every foot of the ground beyond the forest and through it. The forest on each side of the chaussée was open enough for infantry, cavalry, and even for artillery, and very defensible. Had I retreated through it, could they have followed me? The

Prussians were on their flank, and would have been on their rear. *The co-operation of the Prussians in the operations I undertook was part of my plan, and I was not deceived. But I never contemplated a retreat on Brussels. Had I been forced from my position, I should have retreated to my right towards the coast, the shipping, and my resources. I had placed Hill where he could have lent me important assistance in many contingencies, and that might have been one.* And, again, I ask, if I had retreated on my right, would Napoleon have ventured to have followed me? The Prussians, already on his flank, would have been on his rear. But my plan was to keep my ground till the Prussians appearedt and then to attack the French position, and I executed my plan.'"

It matters little whether it be a pleasing tradition or an historical fact, but it was commonly said that after the Peace, which crowned the immortal services of the Duke of Wellington, that great general, on seeing the playing-fields at Eton, said, there had been won the crowning victory of Waterloo.

THE SPA-FIELDS RIOTS.

When, in 1816, a monster meeting was held in Spa-fields, to petition the Prince Regent on the Corn Laws, Captain Gronow was sent, with a company of Guards, to occupy the adjoining prison. The leaders of the mob, including Major Cartwright, Henry Hunt, and Gale Jones, got information that the soldiers had orders, above all, to pick off the ringleaders, when the leaders left, and the meeting soon dispersed. Several years after this, at the time of the Reform Bill, Hunt was elected member of Parliament for Preston, and Captain Gronow was elected for Stafford. One evening, in the smoking-room of the House of Commons, the Captain told Hunt that if any attack had been made upon the prison at Spa-fields, he, (Gronow,) had given his men orders to pick off Major Cart-wright, himself (Hunt), and one or two more. Hunt was perfectly astonished; he became very red, and his eyes seemed to flash fire. "What, sir! do you mean to say that you would have been capable of such an act of barbarity?" "Yes, sir," said Captain Gronow, "and I almost regret you did not give us the opportunity, for your aim that day was to create a revolution, and you would have richly deserved the fate which you so marvellously escaped by the cowardice or lukewarmness of your followers."

In the riot which followed the Spa-fields Meeting, one Cashman, a sailor, who had joined the mob in plundering the shop of Beckwith, the gunsmith, in Skinner-street, was taken with a gun in his hand: he was tried, found guilty, and hung before Beckwith's shop-door, being the last instance of executing the criminal on the site of his guilt

POLITICAL PREDICTIONS.

Twenty weeks before the Chinese were compelled to take our opium, Mr. Weekes, of Tichborne-street, indulged in a curious prediction to Mr. Rush, the American resident in this country. "One of these days, (said Weekes,) England will oblige China to receive her wares by the strong arm of power." So it came to pass. "But," says Mr. Wade, "may not the hopes of the prophet have been father to his prediction, Mr. Weekes having accumulated an immense collection of ingenious mechanism, for which he only expected a remunerative opening in the Chinese market?"

When, in 1807, Hay don dined with Sir George and Lady Beaumont, he met there Humphry Davy, who was very entertaining, and make a remark which turned out a singularly successful prophecy; he said, "Napoleon will certainly come in contact with Russia, by pressing forward in Poland, and *there,* probably, will begin his destruction." This was said five years before it happened.

Lord Mulgrave, afterwards Marquis of Normanby, first raised Haydon's enthusiasm for the Duke of Wellington by saying, one day, at table, "If you live to see it, he will be a second Marlborough."

MRS. PARTINGTON AND HER MOP.

This "labour in vain" will be found in the Rev. Sydney Smith's speech at Taunton on the Lords' rejection of the Reform Bill, October 1831, in the following passage:

"The attempt of the Lords to stop the progress of reform reminds me very forcibly of the great storm off Sidmouth, and of the conduct of the excellent Mrs. Partington on that occasion. In the winter of 1824, there set in a great flood upon that town; the tide rose to an incredible height, the waves rushed in upon the houses, and everything was threatened with destruction. In the midst of this sublime and terrible storm, Dame Partington, who lived upon the beach, was seen at the door of her house with mop and pattens, trundling her mop, squeezing out the sea-water, and vigorously pushing away the Atlantic Ocean. The Atlantic was roused; Mrs. Partington's spirit was up; but I need not tell you that the contest was unequal. The Atlantic beat Mrs. Partington. She was excellent at a slop or a puddle; but she should not have meddled with a tempest,"

THE LAWS DELAY,

When the first cargo of Ice was imported into this country from Norway,—there not being such an article in the Custom House schedules, application was made to the Treasury and to the Board of Trade: after some delay, it was decided that the ice should be entered as *"dry goods;"* but the whole cargo had melted before the cargo was cleared up!

COOL SIR JAMES MACKINTOSH.

During Sir James Mackintosh's Recordership of Bombay, a singular incident occurred. Two Dutchmen having sued for debt two English officers, Lieutenants Macguire and Cauty, these officers resolved to waylay and assault them. This was rather a resolve made in a drunken excitement than a deliberate purpose. Fortunately, the Dutchmen pursued a different route from that which they had intended, and they prosecuted the two officers for the offence of lying in wait with intent to murder. They were found guilty, and brought up for judgment. Previous to his pronouncing judgment, however, Sir James received an intimation that the prisoners had conceived the project of shooting him as he sat on the bench, and that one of them had for that purpose a loaded pistol in his writing-desk. It is remarkable that the intimation did not induce him to take some precautions to prevent its execution—at any rate, not to expose himself needlessly to assassination. On the contrary, the circumstances only suggested the following remarks: "I have been credibly informed that you entertained the desperate project" of destroying your own lives at that bar, after having previously destroyed the judge who now addresses you. If that murderous project had been executed, I should have been the first British judge who ever stained with his blood the seat of justice. But I can never die better than in the discharge of my duty." All this eloquence might have been spared. Macguire submitted to the judge's inspection of his writing-desk, and showed him that, though it contained two pistols, neither of them was charged. It is supposed to have been a hoax—a highly mischievous one, indeed—but the statement was primâ facie so improbable, that it was absurd to give it the slightest credit.

Sir James Mackintosh had a very Parson-Adams-like for-getfulness of common things and lesser proprieties, which was very amusing. On his arrival at Bombay, there being no house ready for his reception, the Governor offered his garden-house for the temporary accommodation of Sir James and his family, who were so comfortable in their quarters, that they forgot to quit, month after month, till a year had elapsed, when the Governor took forcible possession of his own property. Again, Sir James and his lady, on requesting to inspect the seat of Lord Melville, in Perthshire, were invited to stay two or three days, which were protracted to as many months, till every species of hint was thrown away upon them.

Mackintosh, at his first arrival in London, in the year 1783, lodged with Fraser, a wine-merchant, in Clipstone-street, Fitzroy-square. Sir James died in No. 15, Langham-place, Regent-street, May 30, 1832, through a small portion of the breast-bone of a chicken lodging in his throat—his health having been long debilitated from the effects of his residence in India. His learning was abundant; but he wanted method and elegance, which led an ill-natured political opponent to liken him to "a half-polished Scotch pebble."

THE SIDMOTTTH PEERAGE.

The foundation of the Sidmouth Peerage is traceable to one of those fortunate turns which have much to do with worldly success. It is related that while Lord Chatham was residing at Hayes, in Kent, his first coachman being taken ill, the postillion was sent for the family doctor; but not finding him, the messenger returned, bringing with him Mr. Addington, then a practitioner in the place, who, by permission of Lord Chatham, saw the coachman, and reported his ailment. His lordship was so pleased with Mr. Addington, that he employed him as apothecary for the servants, and then for himself; and, Lady Hester Stanhope tells us, "finding he spoke good sense on medicine, and then on politics, he at last made him his physician." Dr. Addington subsequently practised in the metropolis, then retired to Reading, and there married; and in 1757 was born his eldest son, Henry Addington, who was educated at Winchester and Oxford, and called to the bar in 1784 Through his father's connexion with the family of Lord Chatham, an intimacy had grown up between young Addington and William Pitt when they were boys. Pitt was now First Minister of the Crown, and through his influence Addington entered upon his long political career, and became in very few years Prime Minister of England: his administration was brief; but he was raised to the peerage in 1805, and held various offices until 1824, when he retired. Lord Sidmouth was an unpopular minister, and not a man of striking talent; but his aptitude for official business was great He came in for much of the satire of the day upon the Tory Administration, to which, in evil days, he was attached. He was familiarly called "the Doctor," partly from his father's profession, and partly from his having himself prescribed for George III., in his illness of 1801, a pillow of hops as a soporific. This gave Canning the opportunity of calling him the Doctor, and George Cruikshank, ***pari passu,*** the caricaturing of him in the prints of Hone's clever political squibs, with a clyster-pipe hanging out of his pocket.

Family reputation generally proves an insecure stock to begin the world with: the Chatham' and Sidmouth families exemplify the reverse of this observation. Nevertheless, there is much truth in the experience of Lord Mahon (now Earl Stanhope), who says: "In public life I have seen full as many men promoted for their father's talents as for their own."

MR. ROGERS'S REMINISCENCES OF LORD ERSKINE.

When Lord Erskine heard that somebody had died worth 200,000 *l*., he observed, "Well, that's a very pretty sum to begin the next world with."

"A friend of mine," said Erskine, "was suffering from a continual wakefulness, and various methods were tried to send him to sleep, but in vain. At last his physicians resorted to an experiment which succeeded perfectly: they dressed him in a watchman's coat, put a lantern into his hand, placed him in a sentry-box, and—he was asleep in ten minutes."

To all letters soliciting his "subscription" to anything, Erskine had a regular form of reply; viz.: "Sir, I feel much honoured by your application to me, and I beg to subscribe"—here the reader had to turn over the leaf—"myself your very obt servant," &c.

Erskine used to relate to Mr. Rogers many anecdotes of his early life with much spirit and dramatic effect. He had been in the navy, and he said that he once managed to run a vessel between two rocks, where it seemed almost impossible that she could have been driven. He had also been in the army; and on one occasion saved the life of a soldier who was condemned to death, by making an earnest appeal in his behalf to the general in command and his wife. Erskine, having got the pardon, rode off with it at full speed to the place of execution, where he arrived just as the soldier was kneeling, and the muskets were levelled for the fatal shot.

When he had a house at Hampstead he entertained the best company. Mr. Rogers says: "I have dined there with the Prince of Wales—the only time I ever had any conversation with his Royal Highness. On that occasion the Prince was very agreeable and familiar. Among other anecdotes which he told us of Lord Thurlow, I remember these two:—The first was, Thurlow once said to the Prince, "Sir, your father will continue to be a popular King as long as he continues to go to church every Sunday, and to be faithful to that ugly woman your mother; but you, Sir, will never be popular." The other was this:—"While his servants were carrying Thurlow up-stairs to his bedroom, just before his death, they happened to let his legs strike against the banisters, upon which he uttered—*the last words he ever spoke*—a frightful imprecation on "all their souls."

CHANCELLOR'S CHURCH PATRONAGE.

"When Erskine was made Lord Chancellor, Lady Holland never rested till she prevailed on him to give Sydney Smith, her father, a living (Foston-le-Clay, in Yorkshire). Smith went to thank him for the appointment. "Oh!" said Erskine, "don't thank me, Mr. Smith, I gave you the living because Lady Holland insisted on my doing so; and if she had desired me to give it to the devil, *he* must have had it."

Lord Chancellor Thurlow, on reading Horsley's Letters to Dr. Priestley, at once obtained for the author a Stall at Gloucester, saying that "those who supported the Church should be supported by it."

OPPOSITION TO GAS LIGHTING.

Miss Martineau in her *History of England during the Thirty Years' Peace*, thus vividly paints the difficulties which beset the introduction of this great social invention.

"The brilliantly-lighted, carefully-watched, safe, orderly, and tranquil London of the present day, presents as great a contrast to the London of 1816, as that again, contrasted with the London of 1762—the year in which the Westminster Paving and Lighting Act was passed. Street-robberies, before that period, were the ordinary events of the night. For half a century after this the metropolis had its comparative safety of feeble oil-lamps and decrepid watchmen. The streets were filled with tumultuous vagabonds; and the drowsy guardians of the night suffered every abomination to go on in lawless vigour, happy if their sleep were undisturbed by the midnight row of the drunken rake. In 1807 Pail-Mall was lighted by gas. The persevering German (Winsor,) who spent his own money and that of the subscribers to his scheme, had no reward. The original gas company, whose example was to be followed not only by all England, but the whole civilized world, were first derided, and then treated in Parliament as rapacious monopolists. We turn to the Debates, and we see how they were encouraged in 1816—nine years after it had been found that the invention was of unappreciable public benefit:—'The company,' said the Earl of Lauderdale, 'aimed at a monopoly, which would ultimately prove injurious to the public, and ruin that most important branch of trade, our whale fisheries' Alderman Atkins, 'contended that the measure was calculated to ruin that hardy race of men, the persons employed in the Southern and Greenland whale-fisheries, in each of which a million of money and above a hundred ships were engaged. If the Bill were to pass, it would throw out of employ ten thousand seamen, and above ten thousand ropemakers, sailmakers, mastmakers, &c, connected with that trade.' At every step of scientific discovery which promises to impart new benefits to mankind, however certain and unquestionable be the benefit, we are called upon to maintain the' ancient state of things, amidst the terrible denunciations of ruin to some great interest or other. There never was a nation doomed to such perils by the restless character of its people. They will not let well enough alone, as the only wise men say. In 1816 they risked the existence of the British navy, which depended upon the whale-fisheries, for the trifling advantage of making London as light by night as by day, and bestowing safety and peace-fulness upon its million of inhabitants. And yet, at the very moment that this ruin was predicted to oil, it was admitted that we could not obtain a sufficiency of oil"

To these facts may be added another anecdotic testimony. When Winsor first applied to Parliament to charter a company, to light the streets, the testimony of Accum, the chemist, in favour of the practicability of gas-lighting was bitterly ridiculed by Mr. William Brougham; and Sir Humphry Davy, then President of the Royal Society, asked the inventors, "if it were intended to take the dome of St Paul's for a gasometer"

Soon after the establishment of the first gas-works at Westminster, 1810-12, an extensive explosion took place on the premises, when a Committee of the Royal Society, was, by request of the Government, appointed to investigate the cause of the catastrophe. They met several times at the gas-works to examine the apparatus, and made a very elaborate Report, in which they stated as their opinion, that if gas-lighting was to become prevalent, the gas-works ought to be at a considerable distance from all buildings; and that the reservoirs should be small and numerous, and always separated from each other by mounds of earth, or strong party-walls!

THE BOMBARDMENT OF ALGIERS..

There is, perhaps, nothing in the history of warfare more terrific in its consequences than the first broadside that the British fired at Algiers, in 1816. On the morning of August 27, as Lord Exmouth, with the British fleet, was nearing Algiers, his Lordship despatched his interpreter, Mr. Salamé with two letters, one for the Dey, the other for the British Consul The letter to the Dey demanded the entire abolition of Christian slavery; the delivery of all Christian slaves in the kingdom of Algiers; the restoration of all the money that had been paid for the redemption of slaves by the King of the Two Sicilies and the King of Sardinia; peace between Algiers and the Netherlands; and the immediate liberation of the British Consul who had been put in chains, and two boats' crews who had been detained with him. The commander's letter to the Consul of course contained an assurance that every effort should be made for his safety; but who, under such circumstances, could forget that when the French Admiral Duquesne, in 1682, bombarded Algiers, the Dey fastened the unhappy French Consul to the mouth of a cannon, and blew him to atoms, in savage defiance of the hostile armament? At eleven o'clock the interpreter reached the mole, in a boat bearing a flag of truce, and delivering his letters to the captain of the port, demanded an answer to the letter addressed to the Dey in one hour. The Algerine engaged that an answer, if answer were returned at all, should be given in two hours; and in the mean time the interpreter remained in a sufficiently uncomfortable situation, within pistol-shot of thousands of the people on the walls and batteries. The interpreter, with his flag of truce, waited for his answer from eleven o'clock till half-past two, but in vain.

During this time a breeze sprung up, the fleet advanced into the Bay, and lay-to within half a mile of the city of Algiers. The interpreter then hoisted the signal that no answer had been given, and the fleet immediately began to bear up, and every ship to take her position. Salamé reached the Queen Charlotte, Lord Exmouth's ship, in safety. Then he saw the change which comes over a brave and decided man at the moment when resolve passes into action. "I was quite surprised to see his Lordship was altered from what I left him in the morning, for I knew his manner was in general very mild; and now he seemed to be all fightful, as fierce as a lion which had been chained in its cage and was set at liberty. With all that, his Lordship's answer to me was, 'Never mind, we shall see now;' and at the same time he turned towards the officers, saying, 'Be ready.' The Queen Charlotte passed through all the batteries without firing a gun, and took up a position within a hundred yards of the mole-head batteries. At the first shot, which was fired by the Algerines at the Impregnable, Lord Exmouth cried out, "That will do; fire, my fine fellows!" The miserable Algerines who were looking on, as at a show, with apparent indifference to the consequences, were swept away by hundreds by this first fire from the Queen Charlotte. "There was a great crowd of people in every part, many of whom, after the first discharge, I saw running away under the walls like dogs, walking upon their feet and hands." From a quarter before three o'clock till nine, the most tremendous firing on both sides continued without intermission, and the firing did not cease altogether until half-past eleven. During this engagement of nine hours, the allied fleet fired a hundred and eighteen tons of gunpowder, and five hundred tons of shot and shells. The Algerines exclaimed that hell had opened its mouth upon them through the English ships. That the Algerines had plied their instruments of destruction with no common alacrity is sufficiently shown by the fact, that eight hundred and fifty-two officers and men were killed in the British squadron, and sixty-five in the Dutch.

Lord Exmouth says in his despatch: "There were awful movements during the conflict which I cannot now attempt to describe, occasioned by firing the ships so near us." Salamé adds one of the Algerine frigates, which was in flames, drifted towards the Queen Charlotte within about fifty feet of her; but a breeze springing up carried the burning frigate towards the town. The Algerine batteries around Lord

Exmouth's division were silenced about ten o'clock, and were in a complete state of ruin and dilapidation; but a fort at the upper angle of the city continued to annoy our ships, whose firing had almost ceased. This was the moment of the most serious danger to our fleet Our means of attack were well-nigh expended; the upper batteries of the city could not be reached by our guns; the ships was becalmed. "Providence at this interval," says Lord Exmouth, "gave to my anxious wishes the usual land-wind, common in this bay, and my expectations were completed. We were all hands employed warping and towing off, and by the help of the light, air the whole were under sail, and came to anchor out of reach of shells about two in the morning, after twelve hours' incessant labour." There, when the ships had hauled out beyond the reach of danger, a sublime spectacle was presented to the wondering eyes of the interpreter, who had ventured out of the safety of the cockpit to the poop of the Queen Charlotte Nine Algerine frigates and a number of gun-boats were burning within the bay; the storehouses within the mole were on fire; the blaze illumined all the bay, and showed the town and its environs almost as clear as in the day-time; instead of walls the batteries presented nothing to the sight but heaps of rubbish; and out of these ruins the Moors and Turks were busily employed in dragging their dead. When the fleet had anchored there arose a storm of thunder and lightning which filled up the measure of sublimity, at the close of the twelve awful hours of battle and slaughter.

Next morning, Lord Exmouth offered by letter terms of peace to the Dey, saying: "if your receive this offer as you ought, you will fire three guns." The three guns were fired, the Dey made apologies, and treaties of peace and amity were fully signed, to be very soon broken again. The enduring triumph of this expedition was the release, within three days of the battle, of one thousand and eighty-three Christian slaves, who came from the interior, and were immediately conveyed to their respective countries. "When I arrived on shore," says Salamé, "it was the most pitiful sight to see all these poor creatures, in what a horrible state they were; but it is impossible to describe the joy and cheerfulness of them. It was, indeed, a most glorious and an ever-memorably merciful act for England, all over Europe, to see these poor slaves, when our boats were shoving with them off the shore, all at once take off their hats and exclaim in Italian, 'Viva il Ré d' Ingliterra, il padre eterno!

e'l Ammiraglio Inglese che ci ha liberate da questo secondo inferno!' ('Long live the King of England, the eternal father! and the English Admiral who delivered us from, this second hell!')"

It is worthy of remark that, in the debate in Parliament, in the spring of the year, after Lord Exmouth had acceded to a suspension of hostilities with the Dey, and returned to England with his fleet, Lord Cochrane maintained "that two sail of the line would have been sufficient to compel the Dey of Algiers to accede to any terms. The city of Algiers was on the sea-shore, the water was deep enough for first-rates to come up to the very walls, and those were mounted only with a few pieces of cannon, with the use of which the barbarians were scarcely acquainted." Lord Cochrane qualified this assertion in the subsequent session. It was fortunate that such an assertion was not the cause of an inadequate preparation and a fatal repulse. Lord Exmouth had his own observation for his guide.—*Abridged from Miss Marti-neau's History of England during Thirty Years' Peace.*

SHERIDAN AND PEEL.

During the debate in Parliament, in the session of 1819, on the Royal Household or Windsor Establishment Bill, the task of answering Tierney's (Opposition) speech was undertaken by Mr. Peel, at that time Secretary for Ireland. He relied principally upon the determination expressed by the Duke of York to accept of no salary which should come from the privy purse, and upon the sacredness and inviolability which had hitherto been held to attach to that fund. When he mentioned Mr. Sheridan and Mr. Adam (now become Lord Chief Commissioner of the Scotch Jury Court) as two eminent Whig authorities who had been accustomed to preach this doctrine about the privy purse in its highest strain, the House, or at least the Opposition, testified by loud derisive cheers how it was disposed to account for the high monarchic principles on this point entertained or professed by these personal friends of the Prince of Wales. Mr. Peel, however, dexterously chose to understand the manifestation in a somewhat different sense. "If" he exclaimed, "what I have heard from the other side be meant as a cheer of derision at the name of Mr. Sheridan, I must say that I could not expect such an expression towards an individual who was one of the most able supporters the party from which it proceeded ever had the honour to possess, while he was, by universal confession, one of the greatest ornaments of whom that House and the British empire ever had reason to be proud."

PEEL'S LOVE OF TRUTH.

When, upon the death of Sir Robert Peel, the Duke of Wellington sought to express what seemed to him most admirable in the character of his friend, he said that he was **the truest man he had ever known;** adding: "I was long connected with him in public life. We were both in the councils of our sovereign together, and I had long the honour to enjoy his private friendship. In all the course of my acquaintance with Sir Robert Peel, I never knew a man in whose truth and justice I had a more lively confidence, or in whom I saw a more invariable desire to promote the public service. In the whole course of my communication with him I never knew an instance in which he did not show the strongest attachment to truth; and I never saw, in the whole course of my life, the smallest reason for suspecting that he stated any thing which he did not firmly believe to be the fact."

THISTLEWOOD, THE TRAITOR.

Southey relates this touching anecdote of the last hours of Thistle wood, the chief of the Cato-street conspirators of 1820:

"When the desperate and atrocious traitor Thistlewood was on the scaffold, his demeanour was that of a man who was resolved boldly to meet the fate he had deserved: in the few words which were exchanged between him and his fellow-criminals, he observed, that the grand question whether or not the soul was immortal would soon be solved for them. No expression of hope escaped him; no breathing of repentance, no spark of grace, appeared. Yet (it is a fact which, whether it be more consolatory or awful, ought to be known), on the night after the sentence, and preceding his execution, while he supposed that the person who was appointed to watch him in his cell was asleep, this miserable man was seen by that person repeatedly to rise upon his knees, and heard repeatedly calling upon Christ his Saviour to have mercy upon him, and to forgive him his sins."—The Doctor, chap. lxxi.

HOOD AND GRATTAN.

The celebrated altercation between these two patriots has rarely been equalled in virulence. Hood called Grattan "a mendicant patriot, who had sold his country for prompt payment;" and Grattan retorted on Hood as an ill-omened bird of prey, with broken beak and cadaverous aspect, &c. Hood's nose was disfigured, which occasioned the allusion to the broken beak.—***Croker.***

LAST MOMENTS OF GRATTAN.

At the end of May, 1820, Mr. Grattan came, for the last time, to London—in Baker-street. On the first day of the following June, Mr. Charles Butler called; and being informed that he was extremely ill, was retiring, without having seen him; but Mr. Grattan, having heard that he was in the house, sent for him. It was evident that he neared the moment of his dissolution;—but the ethereal vigour of his mind was unsubdued, and his zeal for the Catholic cause unabated. He pressed Mr. Butler by the hand: "It is," he said, "all over!—yes—all over!—but I will die in the cause,—I mean to be carried to the House of Commons tomorrow,—to beg leave of the Speaker to take the oaths sitting,—and then to move two resolutions." These he mentioned to Mr. Butler; but spoke so indistinctly that Mr. B. could only perceive generally that they were substantially the same as the clauses which he had prefixed to the Bill, which, in 1812, he brought into Parliament for the relief of the Catholics. He again pressed Mr. Butler by the hand, repeated the intention of being carried to the House, and desired Mr. B. to attend him to sit,—but Grattan died in the ensuing night.

Lord Brougham, in characterizing the oratorical genius of Grattan, says that "Dante himself never conjured up a striking, a pathetic, and an appropriate image in fewer words than Mr. Grattan employed to describe his relation towards Irish independence, when, alluding to its rise in 1782, and its fall twenty years later, he said: 'I sat by its cradle—I followed its hearse.' "

THE DEVELOPMENT THEORY.

During the debate on Sir Robert Peel's tariff the admission of asses duty free caused much merriment. Lord T,——who had just read ***Vestiges of the Natural History of Creation,*** remarked that the House had, he supposed, passed the donkey clause out of respect to its ancestors. "It is a wise measure," said a popular novelist, "especially as it affects the importation of food; for, should a scarcity come, we should otherwise have to fall back on the food of our forefathers." "And pray what is that," asked an archaeologist. "Thistles," replied Lord T——***Family Jo. Miller***

"PROSPERITY ROBINSON" AND THE PANIC OF 1825.

Cobbett gave this memorable ***sobriquet*** to the Right Hon. F. J. Robinson, as Chancellor of the Exchequer, who, in 1825, boasted in Parliament of an expanded circulation exceeding by nearly 50 per cent, the amount in 1823. This was the era of "Prosperity Robinson" (afterwards first Earl of Ripon), who boasted of "dispensing the blessings of civilization from the portals of ancient monarchy." In the King's speech of 1825, his Majesty said: "There never was a period in the history of the country when all the great interests of society were at the same time in so thriving a condition." But the sunshine was succeeded by the murkiest of gloom—"the Panic of 1825," when one-eighth of the country banks were ruined, and six of the London banks stopped payment; and the two years' increase in the circulating medium was annihilated in a few weeks.

The panacea was the issue of one-pound Bank of England notes, which is stated to have originated as follows:

The incidental mention to one of the Directors that there was a box of one-pound notes ready for issue, turned the attention of the authorities to the propriety of attempting to circulate them; and the declaration of Mr. Henry Thornton, in 1797, probably occurred, that it was the want of small change, not a necessity for gold, that was felt; and as the pressure on the country banks arose from the holders of the small notes, it was suggested to the Government that the public might, perhaps, receive one-pound notes in place of sovereigns. The Government approved of the idea, and the panic was at its height, when, on Saturday, the 17th of December, the Bank closed its doors with only 1,027,000 *l.* in its cellars. (In the pamphlet published by Lord Ashburton is the following remarkable paragraph. After saying "I was called into counsel with the late Lord Liverpool, Mr. Huskis-son, and the Governor of the Bank," his Lordship proceeds: "The gold of the Bank was drained to within a very few thousand pounds; for although the published returns showed a result rather less scandalous, a certain Saturday night closed with nothing worth mentioning remaining.") It has been frequently stated, that by a mere accident the box of one-pound notes was discovered. But such was not the case. A witness stated that "he did not recollect that there were any one-pound notes; they were put by; it was the casual observation that there were such things in the house, which suggested to the directors that it would be possible to use them." Application was made to the Government for permission to issue them; and this was granted, subject to certain stipulations.

MONEY PANIC OF 1832.

Panics have been produced sometimes by extraordinary means. Thus, in May, 1832, a "run upon the Bank of England" was produced by the walls of London being placarded with the emphatic words, "To stop the duke, go for gold;" advice which was followed, as soon as given, to a prodigious extent. The Duke of Wellington was then very unpopular; and on Monday, the 14th of May, it being currently believed that the duke had formed a cabinet, the panic became universal, and the run upon the Bank of England for coin was so incessant, that in a few hours upwards of half a million was carried off. Mr. Doubleday, in his ***Life of Sir Robert Peel,*** states it to be well known that the above placards were "the device of four gentlemen, two of whom were elected members of the reformed Parliament. Each put down 20 *l.;* and the sum thus clubbed was expended in printing thousands of these terrible missives, which were eagerly circulated, and were speedily seen upon every wall in London. The effect is hardly to be described. It was electric."

MINISTERS RESIGNING.

When, in May, 1833, the Lord-Advocate (Jeffrey) called upon Lord Althorp to ask what he should do about his resignation, his reception was as follows. Lord Althorp's secretary could not give him any information, and Lord A—desired he would walk upstairs. Up Jeffrey walked. Lord A—had just done washing, and one arm was bare above the elbow, and rather hairy. His razor was in the other, and he was about to shave. "Well, Mr. Advocate," said his Lordship, "I have the pleasure to inform you that we are no longer His Majesty's Ministers. We sent in our resignations, and they are accepted." When they returned, Jeffrey called again. Lord A—was looking over his fowling-piece, and said to Jeffrey, "Confound these political affairs; all my locks are got out of order," in his usual grumbling, lazy way. This graphic account is told by Haydon, who received it from Lord Jeffrey.

PROFOUND INVESTIGATION.

In 1833, M. Thiers made a ten-days' journey in England, and pledged himself to Louis Philippe to learn in that time all that was worth knowing of the politics, commerce, revenues, religion, arts, sciences, and social economy of this nation. While here he wrote to a gentleman connected with the Treasury the following note: "My dear Sir,—Would you give me a short quarter of an hour, to explain to me the financial system of your country? Always yours, T."

THE MINISTERIAL FISH DINNER.

Every year, the approach of the close of the Parliamentary Session is indicated by what is termed "the Ministerial Fish Dinner," in which Whitebait forms a prominent dish; and Cabinet Ministers are the company. The Dinner takes place at a principal tavern, usually at Greenwich, but sometimes at Blackwall: the dining-room is decorated for the occasion, which partakes of a state entertainment. Formerly, however, the Ministers went down the river from Whitehall in an Ordnance gilt barge: now, a Government steamer is employed. The origin of this annual festivity is told as follows. On the banks of Dagenham Lake or Reach, in Essex, many years since, there stood a cottage, occupied by a princely merchant named Preston, a baronet of Scotland and Nova Scotia, and sometime M.P. for Dover. He called it his "fishing cottage," and often in the spring he went thither, with a friend or two, as a relief to the toils of parliamentary and mercantile duties. His most frequent guest was the Rt Hon. George Rose, Secretary of the Treasury, and an Elder Brother of the Trinity House. Many a day did these two worthies enjoy at Dagenham Reach; and Mr. Rose once intimated to Sir Robert, that Mr. Pitt, of whose friendship they were both justly proud, would, no doubt, delight in the comfort of such a retreat. A day was named, and the Premier was invited; and he was so well pleased with his reception at the "fishing cottage"—they were all two if not three bottle men—that, on taking leave, Mr. Pitt readily accepted an invitation for the following year. For a few years, the Premier continued a visitor, always accompanied by Mr. George Rose. But the distance was considerable; the going and coming were somewhat inconvenient for the First Minister of the Crown. Sir Robert Preston, however, had his remedy, and he proposed that they should in future dine nearer London. Greenwich was suggested: we do not hear of Whitebait in the Dagenham dinners, and its introduction, probably, dates from the removal to Greenwich. The party of three was now increased to four; Mr. Pitt being permitted to bring Lord Camden. Soon after, a fifth guest was invited—Mr. Charles Long, afterwards Lord Farnborough. All were still the guests of Sir Robert Preston; but, one by one, other notables were invited,—all Tories—and, at last, Lord Camden considerately remarked, that, as they were all dining at a tavern, it was but fair that Sir Robert Preston should be relieved from the expense. It was then arranged that the dinner should be given, as usual, by Sir Robert Preston, that is to say, at his invitation; and he insisted on still contributing a buck and champagne: the rest of the charges were thenceforth defrayed by the several guests; and, on this plan, the meeting continued to take place annually till the death of Mr. Pitt.

Sir Robert was requested, next year, to summon the several guests, the list of whom, by this time, included most of the Cabinet Ministers. The time for meeting was usually after Trinity Monday, a short period before the end of the Session. By degrees, the meeting, which was originally purely gastronomic, appears to have assumed, in consequence of the long reign of the Tories, a political, or semi-political character. Sir Robert Preston died; but Mr. Long, now Lord Farnborough, undertook to summon the several guests, the list of whom was furnished by Sir Robert Preston's private secretary. Hitherto, the invitations had been sent privately: now they were despatched in Cabinet boxes, and the party was, certainly, for some time, limited to the members of the Cabinet. A dinner lubricates ministerial as well as other business; so that the "Ministerial Fish Dinner" may "contribute to the grandeur and prosperity of our beloved country."

LORDS STOWELL AND ELDON.

William, Lord Stowell, the eldest son of Mr. John Scott, coal-fitter, of Newcastle-upon-Tyne, was born under circumstances which had a remarkable effect on his early prospects, and his fortune in after life. In 1745, the city of Edinburgh having surrendered to the army of the Pretender, his road to London lay through Newcastle, the town-walls of which bristled with cannon, and the place was otherwise prepared for a siege. Mrs. Scott was at this time in such a condition as made her anxious to be removed to a more quiet place. This, however, was a matter of some difficulty; for Mr. Scott's house was situated in one of the narrow lanes of Newcastle, between which and the river Tyne ran the town-wall, the gates of which were closed and fortified. In this dilemma, Mrs. Scott was placed in a basket, and, by aid of a rope, hoisted over the wall to the water-side, whence a boat conveyed her to Heworth, a village about four miles from Newcastle, but on the southern bank of the town, within the county palatine of Durham, where, within two hours after the above removal, Mrs. Scott gave birth to the twins, William and Barbara. Lord Stowell having been thus born in the county of Durham, was eligible for a scholarship, which fell vacant for that diocese, in Corpus Christi College, Oxford: this he succeeded in obtaining; and thereby laid the foundation, not only of his own, but of his still more successful brother (Lord Eldon's) prosperity.

Lord Eldon's birth-place no longer exists; but the ancient and picturesque house on Sandhill (No. 41, now inhabited by a grocer), from which the future Chancellor stole his young bride, yet remains. "The lattice by which Miss Surtees escaped has a blue pane of glass in the centre, to distinguish it from the rest of the window. The biographer of Lord Eldon, in describing the attractions of the lady, says 'her form was slender.' It must have been so, or she could not have got through so narrow an aperture."

Tyne-side has long been celebrated for the excellence of its port wine: from the date of the Methuen Treaty to the present time its coal-trade has brought to its wharves the best of Portugal's vintage. When Lord Eldon had mounted to the woolsack, he showed little anxiety to strengthen his connexion with his birth-place; but he knew well what it was good for, and to the last he had the choicest of his beloved port, as well as his coals, from the black city. Good wine needs no bush: when the Chancellor's butler put Newcastle port on the table, the host had no need to recommend it to his guests by declaring its vintage, or mentioning the name of his wine-merchant.

Much has been said of the brothers, Lords Stowell and Eldon, their chances and successes, and plodding industry. But the supposed marvel is at an end when we learn that the property left by his father to Lord Stowell amounted to 25,000 *l.;* and Lord Eldon had as fair a start in point of birth and connexion as nineteen out of twenty of his contemporaries. We do not say this to detract from their merits, but to fix the precise value of the examples they hold up.

Lord Eldon had no particular liking for work. "I have now (he said late in life) a letter in which Lord Thurlow promised me a commissionership of bankruptcy, when it would have been most valuable to me in point of income; he never gave it to me, and he always said it was a favour to me to withhold it What he meant was, that he had learnt (a clear truth) that I was by nature very indolent, and it was only want that could make me industrious." On another occasion, he wrote as follows to a ward of his court:—"You will shortly become entitled to a small property, which will prove to you either a blessing or a curse, according as you use it. It was, perhaps, fortunate for me that I was not situated in my early life as you are now. I had not, like you, a small fortune to look to. I had nothing to depend upon but my own exertions, and, so far from considering this a misfortune, I now esteem it a blessing;

for if I had possessed the same means which you now enjoy, I should, in all probability, not be where I now am. I would, therefore, caution you not to let this little property turn your mind from more important objects, but rather let it stimulate you to cultivate your abilities, and to advance yourself in society."

As for the self-accusation of indolence, it is not at all unusual to find an extraordinary capacity for mental labour combined with an extreme reluctance to undertake it. Dr. Johnson, for example, seldom put pen to paper except to get money when he wanted it. He complained that the setting his mind in motion was always attended with pain, though, when it was thoroughly warmed and in full play, the excitement was pleasurable. In the same spirit, Sir Walter Scott declared he could never work so well as when the printing-machine was "banging at his heels." Perhaps John Scott felt the same; or, to take a more obvious solution, perhaps Lord Thurlow got up the charge as the best excuse for his own breach of promise, and Lord Eldon assented to it, without reflecting that all of us are by nature indolent, if this means that we are frequently disinclined to work.

LORD ELDON'S EDUCATION.

The brothers, William and John Scott, received their early education at the Grammar-school of Newcastle. Lord Collingwood was John Scott's classical fellow. "We were placed at that school," said Lord Eldon, "because neither his father nor mine could afford to place us elsewhere." They lay under no disadvantage on that account, and Lord Eldon felt that they did not. He was always eager to do justice to the merits of his old master, the Rev. Mr. Moises, and told, with evident satisfaction, the anecdote of the King (George III.), expressing his surprise how a naval officer could write so excellent a despatch as that which contained Collingwood's account of the battle of Trafalgar, and suddenly adding, "but I find he was educated by Moises."

The foundation of the two brothers' fortune was laid by William (Lord Stowell), who, in his sixteenth year, obtained a scholarship at Corpus Christi College, Oxford: he soon wrote home for his brother, advising that he should be sent up to him. This was done, and he was entered a commoner of University College. He took his bachelor's degree in February, 1770. "An examination for a degree at Oxford," he used to say, "was a farce in my time. I was examined in Hebrew and in History. 'What is the Hebrew for the place of a skull?' I replied, 'Golgotha.' 'Who founded University College?' I stated (though, by the way, the point is sometimes doubted) 'that King wAlfred founded it' 'Very well, sir,' said the examiner, 'you are competent for your degree.' "

In the year following he won the Chancellor's prize for the best composition in English prose—the subject being the "Advantages and Disadvantages of Foreign Travel." It would be unreasonable to expect any depth of thought on such a subject from an untravelled lad, and the essay is never wanting in good sense; but the style is turgid, and the clumsy construction of the sentences would lead us to infer that Mr. Moises had taken less pains with John Scott than with Collingwood, did we not bear in mind how intimately style is connected with character. He who thinks decidedly, will write clearly, if not forcibly; he who has made up his mind what he is going to say, can say it; and the difference between Lord Eldon's and Lord Collingwood's mode of writing is neither more nor less than that which existed to the last between the energetic seaman and the hesitating judge. Lord Eldon's style did not improve materially in after-life. It ceased to be turgid, but it never ceased to be confused and ungrammatical. He might have said of grammar what the roué Due de Richelieu said of spelling,—"We quarrelled at the outset of life, and never made up our differences."—*Edinburgh Review,* No. 163.

LORD ELDON'S MARRIAGE.

The young John Scott eloped to Scotland with Miss Betty Surtees, a beautiful girl of Newcastle, and married her. Neither of them had sixpence, independent of their parents: the Newcastle gossip was that the poor lad was undone; and his own brother condemned it as a very foolish act, adding I that John was completely ruined, nor can anything now save him from beggary. He was obliged to relinquish his fellowship; but, in the year of grace allowed him, he began the study of the law, with the view (to use his own words,) of having two strings to his bow: while keeping his terms at the Temple, he continued his residence at Oxford, employed partly as utor at University College, and partly as Deputy-Professor of Law, for which service he received 60 *l* a-year. Soon after the marriage, the law professor sent Mr. Scott the first lecture, which he had to read *immediately* to the students, and which he began without knowing a single word that was ????　It was upon the statute of ***young men running away wits mardens.*** In after-life, Lord Eldon, in relating the above, used to say, "Fancy me reading with about one hundred and forty boys and young men all giggling at the Professor. Such a tittering audience no one ever had." He used also to say the church was "his first mistress;" and it was not until all chance of a college living was at an end that he decided "to pursue a profession which had much less of his affection and respect."

When he had become Chancellor, Lord Eldon's care and vigilance in preventing elopements among the young ladies who were wards in Chancery, did not protect him against a domestic visitation of a similar description. His eldest daughter, Elizabeth, after some unsuccessful attempts, to obtain his consent to her marriage with Mr. George Stanley Repton, made her escape from Lord Eldon's house in Bedford Square, on the morning of the 27th of November, 1817; and, the bridegroom having made all requisite preparation, they were married by licence at St. George's, Hanover Square. Although in this instance the lady had only followed the example of her father and mother, yet the head of the law would not allow the validity of his own precedent; and it was not until the year 1820 that a reconciliation took place.

LORD ELDON'S MAXIMS.

"I have seen it remarked," says Lord Eldon in his ***Anecdote-Book,*** "that something which in early youth captivates attention, influences future life in all stages. When I left school in 1766 to go to Oxford, I came up from Newcastle to London in a coach, then denominated, on account of its quick travelling as travelling was then estimated, a fly; being, as well as I remember, nevertheless, three or four days and nights on the road: there was no such velocity as to endanger overturning or other mischief. On the panels of the carriage were painted the words ***'Sat cito, si sat bene:'*** words which made a most lasting impression on my mind, and have had their influence upon my conduct in all subsequent life. Their effect was heightened by circumstances during and immediately after the journey. Upon the journey a Quaker, who was a fellow-traveller, stopped the coach at the inn at Tuxford, desired the chamber-maid to come to the coach-door, and gave her a sixpence, telling her that he forgot to give it her when he slept there two years before. I was a very saucy boy, and said to him, 'Friend, have you seen the motto on this coach?'—'No.'—'Then look at it: for I think giving her only sixpence *now* is neither **sat cito** nor **sat bene.**' After I got to town, my brother, now Lord Stowell, met me at the White Horse in Fetter-lane, Holborn, then the great Oxford house, as I was told. He took me to see the play at Drurylane. Love played Jobson in the farce, and Miss Pope played Nell. When we came out of the house, it rained hard. There were then few hackney-coaches, and we got both in one sedan-chair. Turning out of Fleet-street into Fetter-lane, there was a sort of contest, between our chairmen and some persons who were coming up Fleet-street, whether they should first pass Fleet-street, or we in our chair first get out of Fleet-street into Fetter-lane. In the struggle, the sedan-chair was overset with us in it. This, thought I, is more than **sat cito,** and it certainly is not **sat bene.** In short, in all that I have had to do in future life, professional and judicial, I have always felt the effect of this early admonition, on the panels of the vehicle which conveyed me from school, **'Sat cito, si sat bene.'** It was the impression of this which made me that deliberative judge—as some have said, too deliberative;—and reflection upon all that is past will not authorize me to deny that, whilst I have been thinking **'sat cito, si sat bene'**, I may not have sufficiently recollected whether **'sat bene, si sat cito'** has had its due influence."

A clergyman had two churches, Newbury and Bibury; and instead of dividing the duties equally between them, chose always to perform the morning service at the former, and the evening service at the latter. Being asked his reason, he made answer: "I go to **nubere** in the morning, because that is the time **to marry;** and I go to **bibere** in the evening, because that is the time to **drink.**"

When Lord Eldon was at an inn at Rusheyford, the landlord of which was more than an octogenarian, his Lordship gave him the following sound advice: "I hear, Mr. Hoult, you are talking of retiring from business, but let me advise you not to do so. Busy people are very apt to think a life of leisure is a life of happiness; but believe me, for I speak from experience, when a man who has been much occupied through life arrives at having nothing to do, ***he is very apt not to know what to do with himself.***"

LORD ELDON'S ESCAPE.

When John Scott was an undergraduate at Oxford, he had a narrow escape of his life. He was skating on Christchurch meadow, and venturing on too weak ice, fell into a ditch deep enough to allow him to sink to the neck. When he had scrambled out, and was dripping from the collar, and oozing from the stockings, a brandy vendor shuffled towards him, and recommended a glass of something warm; upon which, Edward Norton, of University College, a son of Lord Grantley, sweeping past, cried out to the retailer: "None of your brandy for that wet young man; he never drinks but when he is dry."

SIR WILLIAM SCOTT'S HUMOUR.

When some sudden and somewhat violent changes of opinion were imputed to a learned Judge, who was always jocosely termed Mrs.——,"Varium et mutabile semper femina," was Sir William Scott's remark. A celebrated physician having said, somewhat more flippantly than beseemed the gravity of his cloth, "Oh, you know, Sir William, after forty, a man is either a fool or a physician!" "Mayn't he be both, doctor?" was the arch rejoinder—with a most arch leer and an insinuating voice half drawled out. "A vicar was once," said his Lordship, "presiding at the dinner of the Admiralty Sessions, so wearied out with his parish-clerk confining himself to the 100th Psalm, that he remonstrated, and insisted upon a variety, which the man promised; but, old habit proving too strong for him, the old words were as usual given out next Sunday, 'All people. that on earth do dwell.' Upon this the vicar's temper could hold out no longer, and, jutting his head over the desk, he cried, 'D—n all people that on earth do dwell!'—a very compendious form of anathema!" added the learned chief of the Spiritual Court. As Sir William Scott could imagine nothing better than the existing state of any given thing, he could see only peril and hazard in the search for anything new; and with him it was quite enough to characterise a measure as "a mere novelty," to deter him at once from entertaining it—a phrase of which Mr. Speaker Abbot, with some humour, once took advantage to say, when asked by his friend what that mass of papers might be, pointing to the huge bundle of the Acts of a single session, "Mere novelties, Sir William—mere novelties."

When Sir William Scott, in his 68th year, married the Dowager Marchioness of Sligo, his acquaintance sometimes made merry on the match; the more because it was suspected that the lady was inclined to preserve, in her wedlock, a good deal of the independence of her widowhood. On the door of their house in Grafton-street, which had been her abode before the marriage, was a brass plate, displaying her name, and beneath it, Sir William placed another, bearing his own. "Why, Sir William," said Mr. Jekyll, who had left his card of congratulation upon the wedding, "I am sorry to see you knock under." Sir William made no answer at the time, but transposed the plates. "Now, Jekyll," said he, when next they met, "you see I no longer knock under." "No, Sir William," said the unrelenting wit, "I see you knock up now."

LORD STOWELL'S LOVE OF SIGHT-SEEING.

Lord Stowell loved manly sports, and was not above being. pleased with the most rude and simple diversions. He gloried in Punch and Judy—their fun stirred his mirth without, as in Goldsmith's case, provoking spleen. He made a boast on one occasion that there was not a puppet-show in London he had not visited, and when turned fourscore, was caught watching one at a distance with children of less growth in high glee. tie has been known to make a party with Windham to visit Cribb's, and to have attended the Fives Court as a favourite resort. "There were curious characters," he observed, "to be seen at these places." He was the most indefatigable sightseer in London. Whatever show could be visited for a shilling, or less, was visited by Lord Stowell In the western end of London there was a room generally let for exhibitions. At the entrance, as it is said, Lord Stowell presented himself eager to see "the green monster serpent," which had lately issued cards of invitation to the public. As he was pulling out his purse to pay for his admission, a sharp but honest north-country lad, whose business it was to take the money, recognised him as an old customer, and knowing his name, thus addressed him: "We can't take your shilling, my lord; 'tis the old serpent which you have seen twice before in other colours; but ye shall go in and see her." He entered, saved his money, and enjoyed his third visit to the painted beauty. This love of seeing sights was, on another occasion, productive of the following whimsical incident. Some thirty years ago, an animal, called a "Bonassus," was exhibited in the Strand. On Lord Stowell's paying it a second visit, the keeper very courteously told his lordship that he was welcome to come, gratuitously, as often as he pleased. Within a day or two after this, however, there appeared, under the bills of the exhibition, in conspicuous characters, "Under the patronage of the Right Hon. Lord Stowell;" an announcement of which the noble and learned lord's Mends availed themselves, by passing many a joke upon him; all of which he took with the greatest good humour.—***Townsend's Lives of the Twelve Judges.***

LORD ELDON'S CHANCELLORSHIP.

The brightest period of Lord Eldon's judicial career was his Chief-Justiceship of the Common Pleas. "How I did love that court!" is his parenthetical exclamation in the ***Anecdote-Book;*** and once, during a walk with Mr. Farrer, after comparing the harassing duties of the Chancellorship with the quiet of the Common Pleas, he suddenly turned round, and emphatically adjured his companion never to aspire to the Great Seal—a curious piece of advice to a young barrister.

Early in 1801, when Mr. Pitt's resignation was anticipated, it was understood that Lord Eldon was to succeed Lord Loughborough as Chancellor; but Lord Eldon maintained a cautious reserve on the subject, which he justified by an anecdote. "Lord Walsingham, the son of Lord Chief-Justice de Grey, told me that his fattier, the Chief-Justice, gave a dinner to his family and friends, on account of his going to have the Great Seal as Chancellor next morning, but that in the interim, between the dinner and the next morning, Mr. Justice Bathurst, it was determined, should be Chancellor, and received the seal."

The Great Seal was delivered to Eldon on the 14th of April, 1801. He used to say he was the King's Chancellor, not the Minister's. "I do not know what made George III so fond of me, but he *was* fond of me. Did I ever tell you the manner in which he gave me the seals? When I went to him he had his coat buttoned thus, (one or two buttons fastened at the lower part,) and putting his right hand within, he drew them from out the left side, saying, 'I give them to you from my heart.'"

In compliance with Lady Eldon's feeling, Lord Eldon often applied to King George III. to allow him to dispense with his wig, at times when he was not engaged in performing official functions. He pressed on the King the fact, that in former days, under the reigns of some of His Majesty's predecessors, (as James I. and Charles I.) wigs were not worn by the Judges. "True," replied the King good humouredly, "I admit the correctness of your statement, and am willing, if you like it, that you should do as they did; for though they certainly had no wigs, yet they wore their beards."

When Lord Eldon received the Great Seal from George IV., and kissed hands on his appointment, the King conversed with him, and said, when his Lordship was about to retire, "Give my remembrance to Lady Eldon:" Lord E. acknowledged this condescension, and intimated that he was ignorant of Lady Eldon's claim to such a notice. "Yes, yes," answered the King, "I know how much I owe to Lady Eldon. I know that you would have made yourself a country curate, and that she has made you my Lord Chancellor."

It is remarkable that George IV., who, as he confessed, began by hating Lord Eldon, ended by becoming as much attached to him as George III. "On Monday," says Lord Eldon, in a letter to his grandson describing his final resignation, "your grandfather attended with the rest of the ministers to give up the seals of office, and was, of course, called in first The King was so much affected that very little passed; but he threw his arms round your grandfather's neck and shed tears."

That resignation took place in April 30, 1827, on the formation of Mr. Canning's government. After allowing for the secession during the Whig government in 1806-7, it appears that Lord Eldon held the Great Seal twenty-four years, ten months, and twenty-three days—a longer period than any other Chancellor held it.—*Edinburgh Review,* No. 163.

LORD ELDON AND JOSEPH HUME.

Lord Campbell relates the following, of the Chancellor and Joseph Hume. On the presentation of the Report of the Commission of Inquiry into the Court of Chancery, on a petition being presented to the House of Commons from a person very properly committed for a contempt of the Court of Chancery, Mr. Hume, sometimes more zealous than discreet, created a strong feeling in favour of the Chancellor, by declaring that "the greatest curse which ever fell on any nation was to have such a Chancellor and such a Court of Chancery." Lord Eldon, rather pleased with this attack, treated it thus merrily, in a letter to Lord Encombe:—"You see Mr. Hume called your grandfather a *curse to the country.* He dignified also the quietest, meekest man in the country, with the title of a *firebrand, i. e.* the Bishop of London. I met the Bishop at the Exhibition, and as it happened to be an uncommonly cold day, in this most unusually cold weather, I told him that *the curse of the country* was so very cold that I hoped he would allow him to keep himself warm by sitting next to the *firebrand;* and so we laughed, and amused ourselves at this fellow's impertinence."

A GRATEFUL LADY.

At the time of passing the Catholic Relief Bill, Lady Clerk wrote to Lord Eldon congratulating him upon the energetic stand he had made to prevent the Bill becoming law. His answer was laconic and neatly thus:—"Dear Molly Dacre, I am happy to find you approve of my endeavours to oppose the Catholic Relief Bill. I have done what I thought my duty. May God forgive me if I have done wrong, and may God forgive my opponents (*if he can*). Yours affectionately, Eldon."

DILATORY INCLINATIONS.

Sir Robert Peel, speaking of Lord Eldon, remarked, that "even his failings leaned to virtue's side;" upon which a bystander observed, that his lordship's failings resembled the leaning tower of Pisa, which, in spite of its long inclination, had never yet *gone over!*

THE RT. HON. GEORGE CANNING.

George Canning, who was educated at Hyde Abbey School, near Winchester, whence he was sent to Eton, at an early age obtained great distinction in Latin versification; and in his sixteenth year started a periodical called the ***Microcosm,*** which was published at Windsor weekly, for nine months. From Eton he went to Christchurch, Oxford, on leaving which he went to study at Lincoln's Inn, but soon gave up the law for the political career that was opening to him. He had, however, nigh adopted the stage. Mrs. Canning, through the influence of Queen Charlotte, was introduced by Garrick to the stage as her profession, and she subsequently married Reddish, the actor. [Note 1: Mr. Canning resided in the parish of Marylebone, London, where his son was born, 1770: the father died in the following year, and was buried in the recently-consecrated cemetery on the south side of Paddington-street, where is a monument to his memory, though the inscription is scarcely visible.]. Meanwhile, her son George had become the associate of actors of a low class, from which influence he was rescued by Moody, the comedian, who stated the boy's case to Mr. Stratford Canning, and thus opened the road by which he advanced to power and fame.

His college vacations were usually passed in the house of Mr. Sheridan, who introduced him to Burke, Fox, Lord John Townsend, the Duchess of Devonshire, and other leading Whig partisans. He is thought to have given up the law by the advice of Sheridan, whose political opinions it was expected he would have adopted, and have joined the opposition; but Canning accepted the proposals of the Tory party, and was brought into Parliament by Mr. Pitt in 1793. This preference is thought to have arisen from Canning's having seen "the difficulties which even genius like his would experience in rising to the full growth of its ambition under the shadowy branches of the Whig aristocracy, and that superseding influence of birth and connexions which had contributed to keep such ones as Burke and Sheridan out of the cabinet." (Moore's Life of Sheridan.) *Mr. Pitt found Canning a powerful ally; and during his absence from power was much indebted to Canning's friendship for writing the song of "The Pilot that weathers the Storm," which became exceedingly popular. He had already distinguished himself in this way by contributing poetry, burlesques, and* jeux d' esprit *to the* Anti-jacobin.

Canning shone in early life at the Clifford-street Society, which met at the Clifford-street Coffee-house, at the corner of Bond-street. He was then the most handsome man about town; and his fine countenance glowed, as he spoke, with every sentiment which he uttered. It was customary, during the debates, for pots of porter to be introduced by way of refreshment. One night, when the topic was the leaders of the French Revolution, Canning, in an eloquent tirade against Mirabeau, handled the peculiar style of the Count's oratory with great severity. The president had, during this part of Canning's speech, given a signal for a pot of porter, which had been brought in and placed before him. It served Canning for an illustration. "Sir," said he, "much has been said about the gigantic powers of Mirabeau. Let us not be carried away by the fake jargon of his philosophy, or imagine that deep political wisdom resides in trained and decorated diction. To the steady eye of a sagacious criticism, the eloquence of Mirabeau will appear to be as empty and as vapid as his patriotism. It is like the beverage that stands so invitingly before you—foam and froth at the top, heavy and muddy within!"

In 1809, Mr. Canning fought a duel with his colleague, Lord Castlereagh, by whom he was wounded. At this time he resided at Gloucester Lodge, Old Brompton, where he received a visit from the Princess of Wales; and in 1820, when Queen Caroline's conduct was brought before Parliament, Mr. Canning, rather than bear any part in the proceedings, resigned his office; then he made the somewhat fine nourish styling the Queen "the grace, the life, and ornament of society."

Sydney Smith, ludicrously compared Canning in office to a fly in amber: "Nobody cares about the fly; the only question is—How the devil did it get there? Nor do I attack him, (continues Sydney,) from the love of glory, but from the love of utility, as a burgomaster hunts a rat in a Dutch dyke, for fear it should flood a province. When he is jocular, he is strong, when he is serious, he is like Samson in a wig. Call him a legislator, a reasoner, and the conductor of the affairs of a great nation, and it seems to me as absurd as if a butterfly were to teach bees to make honey. That he is an extraordinary writer of small poetry, and a diner-out of the highest metre, I do most readily admit After George Selwyn, and perhaps Tickell, there has been no such man for the last half century."

Mr. Canning's fund of animal spirits, and the extreme excitability of his temperament, (it is stated in the **Quarterly Review,**) were such as invariably to hurry him, ***nolentem volentem,*** into the full rush and flush of conviviality. At the latter period of his life, when his health began to break, he would sit down with an evident determination to be abstinent, partake sparingly of the simplest soup, take no sauce with his fish, and mix water in his wine; but as the repartee began to sparkle, and the anecdote to circulate, his assumed caution was insensibly relaxed, he gradually gave way to temptation, and commonly ended by eating of everything, and taking wine with everybody—the very beau-idèal of an amphitryon. Yet this is emphatically disputed by Lord Brougham.

When Mr. Canning retired from the office of Under-Secretary, in 1801, he settled upon his mother, of whom he was exceedingly fond, the pension of 500*l* a year, to which he was entitled. He paid her an annual visit at Bath, and made it a rule, with which no engagements were allowed to interfere, to write to her every Sunday. Even during his embassy to Lisbon, when there was usually an interval of several weeks between the mails, the Sunday letter was never omitted, and the packet frequently brought four or five together.

When Mr. Moore was collecting materials for his **Life of Sheridan,** he was told that one night Sheridan sent to the House of Commons a draft upon Mr. Canning to be accepted, which, upon hearing the state Sheridan was in, Mr. readily Canning did.

The opposition in the House of Commons to Mr. Canning, after he became Premier, was of the most formidable and irritating character; though labouring under anxiety and sickness, his rhetorical power and sparkling wit never failed him. Soon after the close of the Session, he retired, for change of air, to Chiswick, where he died on the 8th of August, 1827.

Shortly before Mr. Canning's death, appeared Mr. Plumer Ward's ***De Vere, or the Man of Independence,*** in which the public dwelt with keen interest on a portraiture of this able minister, whose career was then about to close in his premature death. The contention in the mind of this illustrious statesman between literary tastes and the pursuits of ambition is beautifully delineated in one passage of ***De Vere,*** which has been often quoted.

Among the coincidences in Canning's political career, it may be mentioned that he was the same age as his fellow collegian, the Earl of Liverpool, and each became Premier. The last of Mr. Canning's public acts was his signing a treaty for the settlement of the affairs of Greece; and one of the first poems he wrote, when a youth, was a lament on "the Slavery of Greece."

It is related that, one day, on the breaking up of a meeting of the Council, Mr. Canning undertook to guess the thoughts of any of those present in less than twenty questions. Eighteen or nineteen had been asked, when Canning guessed rightly, "The Wand of the Lord High Steward." "The success of the question," says ***Notes and Queries,*** No. 274, "depended upon his power of logical division, and with this aid it rarely requires even twenty questions to arrive at the object thought of."

The late Lady Holland, though possessing greatness and strength of mind, well-informed, without pretension, and decidedly incredulous—for she shared with her husband the philosophical ideas of the eighteenth French century—was accessible to ***presentiments.*** M. Guizot relates that "she had been slightly ill, was better, and admitted it. 'Do not speak of this' she said to me, 'it is unlucky.' She told me that, in 1827, Mr. Canning, then ill, mentioned to her that he was going for change and repose to Chiswick House, a country seat of the Duke of Devonshire. She said to him, 'Do not go there; if I were your wife, I would not allow you to do so.'—'Why not?' asked Mr. Canning,—'Mr. Fox died there' Mr. Canning smiled; and an hour after, on leaving Holland House, he returned to Lady Holland, and said to her, in a low tone, 'Do not speak of this to any one, it might disturb them.'—'And he died at Chiswick,' concluded Lady Holland, with emotion."—***An Embassy to the Court of St James's.***

The room in which Fox died is a small but cheerful apartment, hung with tapestry; the bed and bedstead, with chintz curtains, are preserved.

The chamber in which Canning died is a small low room which he chose himself: it has not even a cheerful view from the window, but overlooks a wing of the house: nothing can be more cheerless. At Chiswick House, Mr. Canning passed the last three weeks of his life: in a room downstairs, he read prayers to the family each Sunday. His pious feeling is evinced in the pathetic lines which he wrote on the death of his eldest son.

BROUGHAM AND HIS MASTER.

Henry Brougham, when at the High School, Edinburgh, made "his first public explosion," as Lord Cockburn calls it "He dared to differ from Luke Fraser, a hot but good-natured old fellow, on some small bit of latinity. The master, like other men in power, maintained his own infallibility, punished the rebel, and flattered himself that the affair was over. But Brougham reappeared next day, loaded with books, returned to the charge before the whole class, and compelled honest Luke to acknowledge that he had been wrong. This made Brougham famous throughout the whole school." "I remember," adds Cockburn, "as well as if it had been yesterday, having had him pointed out to me as 'the fellow who had beat the master.' It was there that I first saw him."

LORD BROUGHAM'S CHANCELLORSHIP PREDICTED.

It may take the reader by surprise to be told that, astounding as the career of Lord Brougham has been, the rise of this distinguished man to the highest honour of the realm appears to have been predicted thirty years before its attainment At the Social Science dinner at the Crystal Palace, Sydenham, on June 14th, 1862, at which Lord Brougham presided, Mr. J. W. Napier, ex-Chancellor of Ireland, related that he remembered, some years previously, meeting an old and respected lady in the north of England, who was present at a party when the first writers in the *Edinburgh Review,* including Henry Brougham, dined together at Edinburgh, after the publication of the Second Number of the Review (in 1802.) On that occasion, the lady's husband, Mr. Fletcher, remarked that the writer of a certain paper in the Review, of which he knew not the author, was fit to be anything. Mr. Brougham hearing this, observed, "What! do you think he is fit to be Lord Chancellor?" The reply was, "Yes; and I tell you more: he will be Lord Chancellor;" and the old lady had the happiness to live thirty years after this, and to see her friend Lord Chancellor of England. Lord Brougham well remembered old Mrs. Fletcher, and corroborated the accuracy of Mr. Napier's anecdote. Mr. Napier then proposed, in an affectionate manner, the health of Lord Brougham, whose answer was, as he said, but a repetition of words he had spoken thirty years ago elsewhere: "When I cease from my labours, the cause of freedom, peace, and progress, will lose a friend, and no man living will lose an enemy."

A LECTURE ON BREWING.

Shortly after Lord Brougham's appointment to the office of Lord High Chancellor, he visited, along with some other Ministers of the Cabinet of Earl Grey, one of the most extensive breweries in the metropolis, and had there what is colloquially called a "beef-steak dinner." After it was finished, a proposition was made that they should inspect the works; and, in order that the party might understand the use of each and all of them, the foreman, a cautious, but intelligent Scotchman, was desired to attend and explain them. They had scarcely got into the first room, before Lord

Brougham, with a slight motion of the hand, put aside his Scotch *cicerone,* who was volunteering an explanation, and said, with his usual cool, good-natured *nonchalance:* "Young man, I will save you the trouble you are about to undertake; I understand all this perfectly well, and will explain it myself to my noble and distinguished friends." His Lordship then proceeded, without farther preface, to explain to Earl Grey and other members of this convivial party, every stage in the process of brewing; but unfortunately, did not explain one of them right, even by accident The Scotchman, who perceived, but was too prudent to expose, the ignorance of his countryman, was astounded by his unceasing volubility: and, in speaking of it in a mixed company, where the informant was present, observed: "Gude faith, sirs, but it made my hair staun on en to hear the Lord High Chancellor o' Great Britain tellin the Lord High Treasurer a lang tale aboot maut and the brewing o't, and nae word o' truth fra beginnin to en. It made a thinking mon reflect what a terrible pass things must ha come till, when ae Minister could jist tell, and anither Minister jist believe, sic awful cantrips. Eh, sirs! nae barrel can be gude that that blatherin' chiel has got the brewin o'."

This anecdote is related in the Life of Sir Thomas Fowell Buxton.

HOW LORD BROUGHAM MISSED THE GREAT SEAL.

Upon the restoration of the restoration of the Melbourne Cabinet, in 1835, a luminary of the first magnitude failed to re-appear in the ministerial constellation. Dislike on the part of William IV. with a similar feeling on the part of some of the ministers, seems to have been the chief reason why the Great Seal was placed in commission. But neither the King nor his ministers committed themselves to any open avowal of aversion; and the dazzling prize of the Chancellorship was long suspended, holding out a delusive hope, and so averting the dread ire of its former possessor, Lord Brougham. His Lordship wrote a letter to the King to mollify his resentment (***Life of Lord Langdale,*** p. 413.) It is stated on the same authority that Lord Melbourne sounded his Majesty on the re-appointment of the ex-chancellor; but the latter evaded by stating that it was his (the minister's) duty to name the person he thought most fit Where the chief blame rested does not clearly appear;

but "never more shalt thou be servant of mine," seems to have been the common understanding.—Wade's ***England's Greatness,*** p. 686.

It was suspected at the time, that the indiscreet use of the Queen's name, as having been the means of breaking up the first Melbourne cabinet, led the King to a stern resolve to exclude the author of it from his future councils: "the Queen has done it all" were the obnoxious words communicated to the press, the next day acknowledged to be a piece of misinformation, which the misled journalist did not soon forget.

FATHER MATHEW AND LORD BROUGHAM.

During his stay in London, Father Mathew was invited to meet many distinguished men of the day. He created no small amusement to a large party at the hospitable mansion of an Irish nobleman by his attempts, partly playful, but also partly serious, to make a convert of Lord Brougham, who resisted, good-humouredly but resolutely, the efforts of his dangerous neighbour. "I drink very little wine," said Lord Brougham: "only half a glass at luncheon, and two half glasses at dinner; and though my medical advisers told me I should increase the quantity, I refused to do so"—"They are wrong, my lord, for advising you to increase the quantity, and you are wrong in taking the small quantity you do; but I have my hopes of you." And so, after a pleasant resistance on the part of the learned lord, Father Mathew invested his lordship with the silver medal and ribbon, the insignia and collar of the Order of the Bath. "Then I will keep it said Lord Brougham, "and take it to the House, where I shall be sure to meet the old Lord the worse of liquor, and I will put it on him." The announcement of his intention was received with much laughter, for the noble lord referred to was a persistent worshipper of Bacchus. Lord Brougham was as good as his word; for, on meeting the veteran peer, who was so celebrated for his potations, he said: "Lord—, I have a present from Father Mathew for you," and passed the ribbon rapidly over his neck. "Then I'll tell you what it is, Brougham: by—! I will keep sober for this day," said his lordship, who kept his word to the great amusement of his friends.—***Life, by Maguire.***

A SECRET AGENT.

One of the "strange bedfellows" with which the misery of Haydon, the painter, [Note 1: Memoirs, vol. ii.] made him acquainted, was a Dr. Mackay, who was employed by Canning to arrange and negotiate the treaty of commerce and independence with South America. Dr. Mackay, [Haydon tells us,] had resided many years in Mexico, and knew all the parties thoroughly. He made a fortune, and returned to England. He was sent for by Canning, and after all due preliminary caution sent out to Mexico. Mr. Haydon met him in 1827: like a true politician, or employé politique, he began to suspect the painter. "Remember," said the Doctor, "before I proceed, you make no use of this." I gave him my word, and he proceeded. Vittoria was his old friend. On his way to Mexico, under pretence of pressing business, he called on Vittoria, and found him in actual negotiation with Spanish commissioners. That evening a treaty was to be signed and settled. Vittoria begged him to dine. He refused a long time, but Mackay making him promise to put off the commissioners till next day, he agreed. Vittoria sent word he was ill, and Mackay was received as an English physician and friend. That night the ground was broken. Vittoria complained they were forsaken by England. Mackay opened his powers, and it was agreed that Vittoria should continue ill, Mackay visiting and prescribing every day. He did so, and at last Vittoria got better, and received full authority from Mexico, and Mackay and he used to walk out to take a little air and retire unobserved into a by-street, to a room hired for the purpose. In this way the treaty of independence and commerce was finally settled. One party proposed an article; after discussion it was written in a book, each party being at liberty to reflect till next day. When they met again, the article proposed and agreed to was restated and discussed again, and if nothing had occurred to alter and amend, it was finally entered into a separate book, whence there was no appeal. In this way, Dr. Mackay said the whole treaty was settled. As he knew the Spaniards well, and that pride was their failing, he got nothing by downright opposition, but carried everything by yielding and persuading them that even he would not have so favoured England by such a proposition, &c. Mr. Canning was highly delighted and gave him great praise.

Dr. Mackay had lost 40,000*l.* (which he had amassed in Mexico by a long life of labour) in speculations on the Stock Exchange. Haydon found him in the Queen's Bench planning steam coaches, and talking of setting off for Mexico as soon as he was free and undisturbed. He seemed to have a very great idea of Canning's genius, and spoke of him with the greatest respect.

OBSTACLES TO IMPROVEMENT.

In illustration of the difficulties which beset the introduction of inventions or improvements, it is related that when Mr. Joseph Whitworth introduced a Street Sweeping Machine, by which one man and a horse would do the work of twenty sweepers, he offered its use to ensure twice the amount of cleanliness for the same expenditure of rates. Of the feet of the return of service on his condition, there could be no doubt; but the increase of service was no stimulus to the adoption of the machine, and did not prevail against the patronage and influence of dust-contractors and scavengers, and the mere trouble of making a change of practice in the larger districts. He proposed his machine to the local authorities at New York. His agent was at once frankly told that there was a fatal objection to the working of the machine in that city—viz. it had no votes, and it interfered with the patronage, not of the master scavengers as in England, but of the journeymen scavengers who had votes. With an excessive expenditure of rates, New York is described as being often ankle deep in mud, and as filthy as the worst parts of London—all the filth being traceable to patronage. A former political member of the American Government told the writer that he found the votes and the patronage of the great numbers serving as the scavengers of New York the most difficult to deal with of any matter he had met with in the agitation in which he had been engaged for the election of a president.

THE BIRMINGHAM TRADES UNIONISTS.

When the great Reform Meeting of the Trades Union took place at Newhall Hill, near Birmingham, it occurred to Haydon that the moment the vast concourse joined in the sudden prayer offered up by Hugh Hutton would make a fine subject for a picture. The Birmingham leaders were pleased with the idea. Haydon wrote to Lord Grey to ask his patronage for the picture. This, of course, was at once refused, but the refusal (which approved itself on reflection, to the painter's better judgment,) was softened by a profession of Earl Grey's readiness to give any assistance in his power to a painting of any subject connected with the Reform Bill to which the same objection would not apply. Haydon's visit to Birmingham brought him in contact with the leaders of the movement there, and his account of it contains some curious disclosures, showing how near, in the opinion of those leaders, matters then were to revolution.

Haydon now saw Mr. Parkes, who consented to be one of the trustees to take charge of subscriptions for the picture. The painter notes: "He (Mr. Parkes) was not up, and sent for me, and begged me to come in. I went in, and there was this Birmingham man, half dozing, and telling me all about the energy of the Union, and what they meant to do.

"He said warrants were made out against the whole of them, and that if Wellington had succeeded, they would all have been taken up, and then the people would have fought it out I went on talking to him of the sublimity of the scene at Newhall Hill He said, 'You are the same man in prison as out I'll be your trustee.' So having a pivot to go on, I advertised directly."

Attwood, while Haydon was sketching him, told the whole history of the Union. "In one of his speeches, he said to the people: 'Suppose, my friends, we had two millions of threads; suppose we wound these two millions of threads into a good strong cord; suppose we twisted that cord into a good strong rope; suppose we twisted that rope into a mighty cable, with a hook at the end of it, and put it into the nose of the boroughmongers, d'ye think we would not drag the Leviathan to shore?' (Immense shouts.)"

"Attwood said some other strong things. 'After poverty, sir, there is nothing so much hated as independence. We are become a nation of petty, paltry corporations, and love of wealth. The five-pounder adores the ten; and the ten the twenty.' He told Lord Melbourne, 'If the people do not get their belly full after this, I shall be torn to pieces.' 'And so much the better. You deserve it,' said Lord Melbourne. 'Yes, my Lord,' said Attwood, 'but they will begin, with you. I do not despond of seeing you all tried for your conduct, Commons and all.'

"At one time," said Attwood, "I used to question whether it was best for us or the United States to sink. I thought it would be better for us. But now I do not think so. We have redeemed ourselves."

He said Lord Grey asked him what he thought would be the end of the Unions. He replied, as people get prosperous and satisfied, they would die away. "I am much inclined to be of your opinion," said Lord Grey.

He said one of the Ministers, (Lord Durham,) told him they owed their places to the Birmingham Union.

"Attwood," (says Haydon,) "is an extraordinary man, and really a leader. The other members seem to have an awe of him. In conversation I found the influence of the leaders of this Union was not from temporary causes, but connected with their predictions on finance—that they had predicted all the ruin which had taken place to Ministers, and thus gained the confidence of the people, and led the way to the establishment of a body which should take the lead."

Hatton is described as a highly powerful and intellectual young man. "The more I see of these Birmingham gentlemen, (says Haydon,) the less am I astonished at their late energy. Hutton had in his study portraits of the great Reformers. Hutton is a high-principled person, ripe to do all he has done. He told me he paved his garden, and made up his mind to fight His dinner was simple, and showed narrow circumstances.

"They had been so excited lately they are absolutely languid in conversation. But they are high in feeling—Roman quite—and will be immortal in their great struggle. I shall be proud to commemorate it"

Jones, a leader, told Haydon that when the tax-gatherer called during the three days, he said to him, "If you dare, sir, to call again, I will have you nailed by the ear to my door, with a placard on your breast, saying who you are."

The cause of the strong republican feeling at Birmingham is their connexion with America.

The Newhall Hill picture was begun, and several subscriptions to it obtained, both in London and Birmingham. "But," added Haydon, "the hardy hammer-men had no real heart in the matter, and without minutely recording the ups and downs of the work, I may dismiss the subject by saying that it came to nothing."

HONEST LORD ALTHORP.

Haydon relates some characteristic traits of Lord Althorp—"not so conversational as Lord Melbourne, but the essence of good nature." The painter continues: "I said, 'My Lord, for the first time in my life I scarcely slept, when Lord Grey was out during the Bill—were you not deeply, anxious?' 'I don't know,' said Lord Althorp, 'I am never very anxious.' Lord Althorp seems heavy. I tried to excite him into conversation. He said Sir Joshua painted him when a boy. He said nothing remarkable."

Haydon tells this droll incident, upon another sitting. "Lord Althorp had made an appointment with an engraver at the same hour, and had not had time to tell me: so, in walked his Lordship, half laughing, saying he had done so, and begging to know if it would interrupt me. I said 'No.' by his side stood his secretary with papers. The door opened, and in toddled——, with his clump foot, and a large portfolio. Lord Althorp roared with laughter, and so did I. The whole thing was dramatic All this so disturbed me—so perplexed my thoughts—was so unlike the solitude of my own study, where I can indulge in visions, that I only thought how to get out of it in peace. Lord Althorp, who is a heavy man, stood up for the head, that the engraver might touch it. The graceless way in which he stood was irresistible. I could paint a picture of such humour as would ruin me.

"The fact is [continues Haydon], one should never forget what is due to one's self. The moment I found Lord Althorp made no gentlemanly appeal to me, as the whole rencontre was his fault, I should very quietly have daubed out the whole head, and merely made generalities. The truth was, he seemed to think it a devilish good joke—not knowing I have no intercourse with artists; and that though I could not help laughing, it was little better than an insult. What had I in common with an engraver, let him be ever so eminent? I was there by Lord Grey's desire, and as his representative, and I ought to have been treated with marked distinction."

When Haydon was painting the great picture of the Reform Banquet, the Whigs had been cursing Attwood for a radical and a fool, and begging the painter not to put him in. Lord Althorp said: "Oh yes, he was prominent in the cause. He ought to be in." "This," says the painter, "was noble; all party feelings vanished in Lord Althorp's honest heart."

MR. COKE'S REMINISCENCES.

When Mr. Coke was sitting to Haydon for his portrait, he told some amusing anecdotes of Fox. He said, the first time he came into power he dined with him. He went on talking before the servants. After they were gone some one said; "Fox, how can you go on so before the servants?" "Why the devil," said Fox, "should they not know as much as myself?"

One night, at Brookes's, Fox made some remark on Government powder, in allusion to something that had happened. Adams considered it a reflection, and sent Fox a challenge. Fox went out, and took his station, giving a full front. Fitzgerald said, "You must stand sideways." Fox said, "Why I am as thick one way as the other." "Fire" was given—Adams fired, Fox did not, and when they said he must, he said, "I'll be d—d if I do, I have no quarrel." They then advanced to shake hands. Fox said, "Adams, you'd have killed me if it had not been Government powder." The ball hit him in the groin.

Lord Mulgrave once said at table it was a fact that Charles Fox would have agreed to come in under Mr. Pitt latterly, as Secretary for Foreign Affairs. Mr. Coke said there was such a report, and he wrote Fox, saying if it were so, they must separate. Fox assured him on his honour it was not so, and he kept the letter till his death.

Fox is described to have been as fond of shooting as a schoolboy. He went out one morning. It came on to rain. Fox stood under some firs with a gamekeeper, who was a great talker. All the day it rained incessantly. As the ladies were all waiting dinner, in came Fox: "Where have you been, Charles," said Mr. Coke. "Why, talking to that fellow all day. There is hardly a man I can't get something from if he talks" said Mr. Fox.

When Burke was dying, Fox went to see him; but Burke would not see Fox. When he came back, Mr. Coke was lamenting Burke's obstinacy. "Ah," said Fox, "never mind, Tom, I always find every Irishman has got a piece of potato in his head."

George IV. is said to have sworn he would knight Coke once, when a very violent petition was being brought up by him. Mr. Coke said he had made up his mind that if the King attempted it he would have knocked off the sword

Mr. Coke said he remembered a fox killed in Cavendish-square, and that where Berkeley-square now stands was an excellent place for snipes.

A LESSON FOR A GOVERNOR.

Sir Francis Head, in 1835, was appointed governor of Upper Canada; and one of his first experiences in his new post he thus felicitously relates:

"Within a week after my arrival at Toronto," says the Governor, "I had to receive an address from the Speaker and Commons' House of Assembly; and on inquiring in what manner I was to perform my part in the ceremony allotted to me, I was informed that I was to sit very still on a large scarlet chair with my hat on. The first half was evidently an easy job; but the latter part was really revolting to my habits and feelings, and as I thought I ought to try and govern by my head and not by my hat, I felt convinced that the former would risk nothing by being for a few minutes divorced from the latter, and accordingly I determined with white gloves to hold the thing in my hands; and several of my English party quite agreed with me in thinking my project not only an innocent but a virtuous act of common courtesy: however, I happened to mention my intention to an Upper Canadian, and never shall I forget the look of silent scorn with which he listened to me. I really quite quailed beneath the reproof which, without the utterance of a word, and after scanning me from head to foot, his mild, intelligent, faithful countenance read to me, and which but too clearly expressed—'What! to purchase five minutes' loathsome popularity, will you barter one of the few remaining prerogatives of the British Crown? Will you, for the vain hope of conciliating insatiable Democracy, meanly sell to it one of the distinctions of your station? Miserable man! beware, before it be too late, of surrendering piecemeal that which it is your duty to maintain, and for which, after all, you will only receive in exchange contumely and contempt!' I remained for a few seconds as mute as my Canadian Mentor, and then, without taking any notice of the look with which he had been chastising me, I spoke to him on some other subjects; but I did not forget the picture I had seen, and accordingly my hat was tight enough on my head when the Speaker bowed to it, and I shall ever feel indebted to that man for the sound political lesson which he taught me,"

"PATRIOTIC GREEKS."

"Laman Blanchard and Douglas Jerrold met by accident before either friend had reached his majority. The latter was pushing his way, by slow degrees, into the tramway of the current journalism; the former was writing graceful poesy, to be presently gathered into a volume of "Lyric Offerings," and published by Harrison Ainsworth. Yet their common subject just now, as they stood under the gateway protected from the rain, was of Byron and liberty. The noble was their idol of the' hour. He was a bard, and he was the champion of liberty. Why should they not follow him—join him in Greece? The two friends were roused to frenzy with the idea, and the fair, blue-eyed one, suddenly seeing the ludicrous position of two Greek crusaders sneaking out of a shower of rain, dashed into the wet, saying, "Come, Sam, if we're going to Greece we mustn't be afraid of a shower of rain."—*Blanchard Jerrold's Life of his Father.*

TALLEYRAND'S DIPLOMACY AND WIT.

Only three months before his death, Talleyrand said: "A minister of foreign affairs must possess the faculty of appearing open, at the same time that he remains impenetrable; of being in reality reserved, although perfectly frank in his manner." The precept was his own portrait. His power of **concealing his opinions,** and his steady adherence to the principle of allowing attacks upon his character to dissipate by time for want of opposition, have had the effect of keeping his contemporaries ignorant of his real character. This taciturnity has frequently occasioned his being subject to imputations which he did not deserve; at times it has, beyond a doubt, acquired for him a reputation for ability greater than he deserved.

On the murder of the Duke d'Enghien by the order of Bonaparte being mentioned, Talleyrand is reported to have said—"It was worse than a crime—it was a blunder." "We believe," says Charles Butler, "that such an expression was never uttered by an Englishman, and that it would be heard by no Englishman without disgust."

Talleyrand was one of the few men who had the art of ***doing*** witty things. On the death of Charles X. he drove through Paris for a couple of days, wearing a white hat. He carried a crape in his pocket. When he passed through the Fauxbourg of the Carlists, the crape was instantly twisted round his hat; when he came into the quarter of the Tuileries, the crape was instantly stripped off and put into his pocket again.

At a public dinner Talleyrand's health was drank. Before the noise was over, he got up, made a mumbling, as if speaking—spoke nothing—made a bow, and sat down; at which the applause redoubled, though all those immediately about him knew he never said a word.

The only *mot* recorded of Charles X., as uttered on his return to France in 1814, on seeing that the adversaries of his family had disappeared, was—"There is only one Frenchman the more." This was the suggestion of M. Talleyrand. He afterwards proposed, in like manner, to Charles's successor, that the foolish freaks of the Duchess de Berri should be visited with this rescript to her and her faction: "Madame, no hope remains for you. You will be tried, condemned, and pardoned."

The Prince was enjoying his rubber, when the conversation turned on the recent union of an elderly lady of respect able rank. "How ever could Madame de S——make such a match?—a person of her birth to marry a valet-de-chambre!" "Ah," replied Talleyrand, "it was late in the game; at nine we don't reckon honours."

Talleyrand being asked, if a certain authoress, whom he had long since known, but who belonged rather to the last age, was not "a little tiresome?" "Not at all," said he; "she was perfectly tiresome."

A gentleman was one day making a somewhat zealous eulogy on his mother's beauty, dwelling upon the topic at uncalled-for length—he himself having certainly inherited no portion of that kind under the marriage of his parents. "It was your father, then, apparently, who may not have been very well favoured," was Talleyrand's remark, which at once released the circle from the subject.

When Madame de Staël published her celebrated novel of **Delphine,** she was supposed to have painted herself in the person of the heroine, and M Talleyrand in that of an elderly lady, who is one of the principal characters. "They tell me," said he, the first time he met her, "that we are both of us in your novel, in the disguise of women."

Rulhières, the celebrated author of the work on the Polish Revolution, having said, "I never did but one mischievous work in my life."—"And when will it be ended!" was Talleyrand's reply.

"Is not Geneva dull?" asked a friend of Talleyrand, "Especially when they amuse themselves," was the reply.

"She is insupportable," said Talleyrand, with marked emphasis, of one well known: but, as if he had gone too far, to take something off what he had said, he added, "It is her only defect."

A friend was conversing with Talleyrand on the subject of Mademoiselle Duchesnois, the French actress, and another lady, neither of them remarkable for beauty; and the first happening to have peculiarly bad teeth, the latter none at all. "If Madame S." said Talleyrand, "only had teeth, she would be as ugly as Mademoiselle Duchesnois."

"Ah; I feel the torments of hell," said a person, whose life had been supposed to be somewhat of the loosest. "Already?" was the inquiry suggested to M. Talleyrand. The Cardinal de Retz's physician is said to have made a similar expression on a like occasion.

Talleyrand had a confidential servant, excessively devoted to his interests, but withal superlatively inquisitive. Having one day entrusted him with a letter, the Prince watched his faithful valet from the window of his apartment, and, with some surprise, observed him coolly reading the letter *en route.* On the next day a similar commission was confided to the servant; and to the second letter was added a postscript couched in the following terms:—"You may send a verbal answer by the bearer; he is perfectly acquainted with the whole affair, having taken the precaution to read this previous to its delivery."

A creditor to whom the Prince was indebted in a heavy sum, waited on him as he was setting off on his last departure for this country; not to take so great a liberty as to ask for his money, but merely to ascertain any time, however remote, when he might presume to ask for a part of it. The diplomatist's only reply to the inquisitive intruder was, "Monsieur, vous êtes bien curieux;" and no one but the diplomatist could have made *such* a reply.

Talleyrand's cook, Marie-Antoine Carême, contrasting the good and evil features of his vocation, exclaimed enthusiastically, "The charcoal kills us; but *n'importe,*—our years are few in number, but full of glory."

PRESENTIMENT TO TALLEYRAND.

Dr. Sigmond received from the widow of M. Colmache, the private secretary and friend of M. de Talleyrand, the following remarkable anecdote.

One day, in the presence of the minister, the conversation had turned upon the subject of those sudden warnings which have been looked upon as communications from the world of spirits to man: some one observed, that it would be difficult to find a man of any note, who had not, in the course of his life, experienced something of the kind.

"I remember," said Talleyrand, "upon one occasion, having been gifted, for one single moment, with an unknown and nameless power. I know not to this moment whence it came; it has never once returned, and yet upon that one occasion it saved my life. Without that sudden and mysterious inspiration I should not have been here to tell my tale. I had freighted a ship in concert with my friend Beaumetz. He was a good fellow, Beaumetz, with whom I had ever lived on the most intimate terms. I had not a single reason to doubt his friendship. On the contrary, he had given me, on several occasions, most positive proof of his devotion to my interest and well-being. We had fled from France; we had arrived at New York together, and we had lived in perfect harmony during our stay there. So, after having resolved upon improving the little money that was left by speculation, it was, still in partnership and together, that we freighted a small vessel for India, trusting to all the goodly chances which had befriended us in our escape from danger and from death, to venture once more conjointly to brave the storms and perils of a longer and yet more adventurous voyage. Everything was embarked for our departure; bills were all paid, and farewells all taken, and we were waiting for a fair wind with most eager expectation, being prepared to embark at any hour of the day or night, in obedience to the warning of the captain. This state of uncertainty seemed to irritate the temper of poor Beaumetz: he grew remarkably restless: one day, he entered our lodging, evidently labouring under great excitement, although commanding himself to appear calm. I was engaged at that moment in writing letters to Europe; and looking over my shoulder, he said, with forced gaiety, 'What need to waste time in penning those letters! they will never reach their destination. Come with me, and let us take a turn on the Battery; perhaps the wind may be chopping round; we may be nearer our departure than we imagine.' The day was very fine, and though the wind was blowing hard, I suffered myself to be persuaded. Beaumetz, I remembered afterwards, displayed an unusual offciousness in aiding me to close my desk, and put away my papers, handing me with hurried eagerness, my hat and cane, and doing other services to quicken my departure, which, at the time, I attributed to his restless desire for change. We walked, through the crowded streets, to the Battery. He had seized my arm, and hurried me along. When we had arrived at the broad esplanade—the glory of New York—Beaumetz quickened his step still more, until we reached close to the water's edge. He talked loud and quickly, admiring in energetic terms the beauty of the scenery, the Brooklyn heights, the shady groves of the island, the ships riding at anchor, and the busy scene on the peopled wharf, when suddenly he paused in his mad, incoherent discourse—for I had freed my arm from his grasp, and stood immovable before him. Staying his wild and rapid steps, I fixed my eye upon his face. He turned aside, cowed and dismayed. 'Beaumetz,' I shouted, you mean to murder me: you intend to throw me from the height into the sea below. Deny it, monster, if you can.' The maniac stared at me for a moment; but I took especial care not to avert my gaze from his countenance, and he quailed beneath it. He stammered a few incoherent words, and strove to pass me, but I barred his passage with extended arms. He looked vacantly right and left, and then flung himself upon my neck, and burst into tears. "Tis true—'tis true, my friend! The thought has haunted me day and night, like a flash from the lurid fire of hell It was for this I brought your here. Look! you stand within a foot of the edge of the parapet: in another instant the work would have been done.' The demon had left him; his eye was unsettled, and the white foam stood in bubbles on his parched lips; but lie was no longer tossed by the same mad excitement under which he had been labouring, for he suffered me to lead him home without a single word. A few days' repose, bleeding, abstinence, completely restored him to his former self, and what is most extraordinary, the circumstance was never mentioned between us. MY FATE was at work."

It was whilst watching by the bedside of his friend that Talleyrand received letters which enabled him to return to France; he did so, and left Beaumetz to prosecute the speculation alone. The Prince Talleyrand could never speak of the preceding event without shuddering, and to the latest hour of his existence believed that "he was for an instant gifted with an extraordinary light, and during a quick and vivid flash the possible and the true was revealed to a strong and powerful mind," and that upon this the whole of his destiny hinged. "This species of momentary exaltation," says Dr. Sigmond, "which is not again repeated, but is remembered with the most vivid impression, is what is more immediately known by the name of fantasia:" in France and England it is named presentiment—Dr. Forbes Window's Psychological Journal.

THE PRINCESS TALLEYRAND.

In the Memoirs of Prince Talleyrand we find the following portrait of his strange relative:—'She was the most eccentric person I ever met with—the last of a race of which it will be impossible, from the change in human ideas, ever to behold another specimen. In her youth she had been most beautiful, and still retained, saving the loss of an eye, traces of loveliness even in advanced age. She could not be called either clever or witty, but was the cause of such interminable wit on the part of others, of such endless good sayings on the part of the Prince, that Valancay, to those who were accustomed to her society, seemed dull à perir *when she was not there. She had the greatest fund of originality and natural vivacity that could be possessed by any human being. Her ideas could not be made, by any force of reasoning or persuasion, to follow the tide of improvement of the times; and she could never be taught to believe that the Revolution had wrought any change in the relative positions of the aristocracy and the people, but continued, to the latest period of her life, to treat all plebeians and* roturiers *as though they had still been serfs and vassals, subject at her will and pleasure to* détresse *and* corvée. *She was an invaluable specimen of the old insolent* noblesse; *and after a day spent in her company you might retire to rest, no longer wondering at the horrors of the great Revolution, nor yet at the hatred by which they had been instigated. On one occasion she had nearly set the whole province in uproar by an unseasonable display of what the Prince was wont to call her* impertinence régents. *A large party had been invited to dinner at the* château, a party in honour of the arrival of some high and illustrious visitor at Valançay. I think there were even scions of Royalty among the guests. In short, it was one of the gaudy days of the castle, when the flaming yellow liveries, and the antique silver, and the Royal gifts, were all displayed. Of course, the préfet *of the department, the* maire of Valançay, the curé and, in short, all the authorities of the place, had been invited, and with true provincial punctuality had arrived at the exact hour named in the invitation, which, as usual in modern times, was long before the princely host expected to receive his guests, and, when they were ushered into the drawing-room, they found that none of the family had as yet appeared, and that they would be consequently compelled to amuse themselves as they best could until the ringing of the bell, which would gather together the stray members of the household. In a short time, however, the great doors of the drawing room were thrown back with a loud *fracas,* and in sailed, in all the majesty of stiffened silks and fluttering Plumes, her Highness the Princess T——. The troubled provincials immediately with one accord turned from the chimney, where they had been talking in mysterious murmurs concerning the mighty individuals whom they were to meet at dinner, and moved in a body, with sundry low bows, and a great display of gymnastic prostrations, towards the fair Princess. The latter stood for a moment, and gazed as they advanced, then turning suddenly round to the grinning domestic, who had remained standing at the door, "Fool!" exclaimed she indignantly, "did I not bid you ascertain if anybody had arrived, before I troubled myself to come down to the *salon?*" "Yes, Princess, and I came myself to see," answered the servant, looking rather puzzled and embarrassed, first at his mistress, then at the guests, who stood wondering where the questioning would lead to, "and when I found these gentlemen here, I"——"Idiot!" interrupted the Princess, "not to know your business better; remember that such as these are not anybody, but ***nobody.***" With these words she tossed out of the room, pointing with her fan over her shoulder at the poor stupified provincials, whose rage and mortification defy description.'

TALLEYRAND AND BONAPARTE.

Bourrienne is not the best of authorities, but the earlier volumes of the memoirs which pass under his name are less falsified than the later; and an anecdote which he relates of Talleyrand's interview with the First Consul, after being reappointed minister of foreign affairs, is so characteristic, that its truth is highly probable:—"M. de Talleyrand, appointed successor to M. de Reinhart at the same time that Cambacères and Lebrun succeeded Sièyes and Roger Ducas as consuls, was admitted to a private audience by the First Consul. The speech which he addressed to Bonaparte was so gratifying to the person to whom it was addressed, and appeared so striking to myself, that the words have remained in my memory:—'Citizen Consul, you have confided to me the department of foreign affairs, and I will justify your confidence; but I must work under no one but yourself. This is not mere arrogance on my part: in order that France be well governed, unity of action is required: you must be first consul, and the first consul must hold in his hand all the mainsprings of the political machine—the ministries of the interior, of internal police, of foreign affairs, of war, and the marine. The ministers of these departments must transact business with you alone. The ministries of justice and finance have, without doubt, a powerful influence upon politics; but it is more indirect. The second consul is an able jurist, and the third a master of finance: leave these departments to them; it will amuse them; and you, general, having the entire management of the essential parts of government, may pursue without interruption your noble object, the regeneration of France.' These words accorded too closely with the sentiments of Bonaparte to be heard by him otherwise than with pleasure. He said to me, after M. de Talleyrand had taken his leave, 'Do you know, Bourrienne, Talleyrand's advice is sound. He is a man of sense' He then added smilingly:—Talleyrand is a dexterous fellow: he has seen through me. You know I wish to do what he advises; and he is in the right.

Lebrun is an honest man, but a mere book-maker; Cambacéres is too much identified with the Revolution: my government must be something entirely new."

Napoleon and Talleyrand may be said to have understood each other, and that in a sense not discreditable to either. The good sense of both was revolted by the bloodshed and theatrical sentiment, the blended ferocity and coxcombry of the Revolution; both were practical statesmen, men with a taste and talent for administration, not mere constitution-makers. They resembled each other—neither was remarkably scrupulous as to the means by which he attained his ends; though this laxity of sentiment was kept in check by the natural humanity of both. Their very points of difference were calculated to cement their union. Each of these men felt that the other was a supplement to himself. Talleyrand readily admired and appreciated Napoleon. If he flattered him, it was by the delicate method of confirming him in the opinions and intentions which met his approbation.

The imperturbability of Talleyrand may have been coarsely exaggerated; but it was, doubtless, very great His reserve, probably constitutional, but heightened by the circumstances of his early life, and cultivated upon principle, was impenetrable. In advanced life it seemed even to have affected his physical appearance. When at rest, but for his glittering eye it would have been difficult to feel certain that it was not a statue that was placed before you. When his sonorous voice broke upon the ear it was like a possessing spirit speaking from a graven image. Even in comparatively early life, his power of banishing all expression from his countenance, and the soft and heavy appearance of his features, were remarked as contrasting startlingly with the manly energy indicated by his deep powerful voice. Mirabeau in the beginning, Napoleon at the close of the Revolution, threw him into the shade; but he outlasted both. The secret of his power was patience and pertinacity; and his life has the appearance of being preternaturally lengthened out, when we recollect the immense number of widely-removed characters and events of which he was the contemporary. It may be said on the one hand that he accomplished nothing which time did not in a manner bring about; but on the other it may be said, with equal plausibility, that scarcely any of the leading events which have occurred in France in his day would have taken the exact shape they assumed had not his hand interfered to give them somewhat of a bias or direction. Next to Napoleon I., he certainly was the most extraordinary man the revolutionary period of France gave birth to.

CELEBRITIES OF HOLLAND HOUSE.

Of this once great meeting-place for Whig politicians, for poets, painters, critics, and scholars, placed in a domain of deep seclusion, at "courtly Kensington," a scholarly hand wrote thus eloquently, and we fear prophetically, in 1842, two years after the death of the lamented statesman who contributed so greatly to the fame of the mansion.

"Yet a few years, and the shades and the structures may follow their illustrious masters. The wonderful city, which, ancient and gigantic as it is, still continues to grow, as a young town of logwood by a water-privilege in Michigan, may soon displace those turrets and gardens which are associated with so much that is interesting and noble; with the courtly magnificence of Rich, with the loves of Ormond, with the councils of Cromwell, with the death of Addison. The time is coming, when perhaps a few old men, the last survivors of oar generation, will seek in vain, amidst new streets and squares, and railway stations, for the site of that dwelling, which in their youth was the favourite resort of wits and beauties, of painters and poets, of scholars, philosophers, and statesmen; they will remember with strange tenderness, many objects familiar to them—the avenue and terrace, the busts and the paintings, the carving, the grotesque gilding, and the enigmatical mottoes. With peculiar tenderness, they will recal that venerable chamber, in which all the antique gravity of a college library was so singularly blended with all that female grace and wit could divine to embellish a drawing-room. They will recollect, not unmoved, those shelves loaded with the varied learning of many lands and many ages; those portraits in which were preserved the features of the best and wisest Englishmen of two generations; they will recollect how many men who have guided the politics of Europe, who have moved great assemblies by reason and eloquence, who have put life into bronze or canvas, or who have left to posterity things so written that it will not willingly let them die, were there mixed with all that was lovely and gayest in the society of the most splendid of capitals.

"They will remember the singular character which belonged to that circle, in which every talent and accomplishment, every art and science, had its place. They will remember how the last debate was discussed in one corner, and the last comedy of Scribe in another; while Wilkie gazed with modest admiration on Reynolds's Baretti; while Mackintosh turned over Thomas Aquinas to verify a quotation; while Talleyrand related his conversation with Barras, at the Luxembourg, or his ride with Lannes, over the field of Austerlitz. They will remember above all, the grace, and the kindness, far more admirable than grace, with which the princely hospitality of that ancient mansion was dispensed; they will remember the venerable and benignant countenance and the cordial voice of him who bade them welcome; they will remember that temper which years of sickness, of lameness, of confinement, seemed only to make sweeter and sweeter; and that frank politeness, which at once relieved all the embarrassment of the youngest and most timid writer or artist, who found himself for the first time among ambassadors and earls. They will remember, that, in the last times, which he traced, he expressed his joy that he had done nothing unworthy of the friend of Fox and Grey; and they will have reason to feel similar joy, if in looking back on many troubled years, they cannot accuse themselves of having done anything unworthy of men who were distinguished by the friendship of Lord Holland."—*John Fisher Murray's Environs of London.*

"It is remarkable," says Lord Brougham, "that, like his uncle, Lord Holland, though fond of poetry [and himself a poet], had no relish for the kindred art; the other branch of harmony, Music, was positively disagreeable to them both—a remarkable instance of Shakspeare's extravagant error in a well-known passage of his plays." [Note *: "The man that hath no musick in himself,
Nor is not mov'd with concord of sweet sounds,
Is fit for treasons, stratagems, and spoils;
The emotions of his spirit are dull as night,
And his affections dark as Erebus:
Let no such man be trusted."
Merchant of Venice, Act v. Sc. 1.]

[His Lordship called on Lord Lansdowne a little before his death, and showed him his epitaph of his own composing, "Here lies Henry Vassall Fox, Lord Holland, &c, who was drowned while sitting in his elbow-chair;" he died, in this house, in his elbow-chair, of water on the chest.—*Gun ningham.*]

POLITICAL RISE OF LORD LYNDHURST.

This very able judge did not succeed in attracting public attention until the year 1817, when Serjeant Copley was counsel, in conjunction with Sir Charles Wetherell, for James Watson the elder, who was indicted for high treason. Lord Campbell, in his Life of Lord Ellenborough, says that Lord Castlereagh was sitting on the bench during the trial, and he adds the statement, which Lord Lyndhurst resented—viz. that Lord Castlereagh, expressing great admiration of Mr. Serjeant Copley's Republican eloquence, is said to have added, "I will set my **rat-trap** for him, baited with **Cheshire cheese.**" This anecdote was probably a joke of circuit invention; but it had just this basis of actual fact, that Mr. Serjeant Copley in the year following (1818) was made by the Government Chief Justice of Chester.

This story is usually termed "the Cheshire-cheese joke;" but it has been stated, upon indisputable authority, in the ***Edinburgh Review,*** No. 216, that "it was during the trial of a prosecution against the publisher of the ***Quarterly Review*** for an alleged libel on Colonel Maceroni that Lord Lyndhurst (then Serjeant Copley) first fixed the attention of the Tory leaders as a desirable auxiliary. He conducted the defence, and the Duke of Wellington, Lord Liverpool, with other members of the Government, having been subpœnaed as witnesses, were seated on the bench. Shortly afterwards, the successful advocate was requested to call on the Prime Minister, who told him that if he wished to come into Parliament a seat was at his disposal, and requested him to take time to consider. The reply was an immediate acceptance, and Mr. Serjeant Copley was forthwith elected member for Yarmouth, Isle of Wight, on the nomination of Mr. Holmes. No pledge, promise, or condition of any sort was required, offered, suggested, or imposed." This paragraph was based on information supplied to the writer of the article in the ***Edinburgh Review*** by Lord Lyndhurst himself, and it was read over to him, and declared correct, prior to publication.

On the 6th of March, 1827, Copley delivered his able and memorable speech against Catholic Emancipation, to which Canning retorted so effectually by citing his opinion as law officer of the Crown. Canning remarked, with some appearance of justice, that "had he been required to predict the quarter from which the attack would proceed, the quarter from which it had proceeded would have been the last he should have conjectured." He also charged Sir John Copley with not being original in his remarks. "I have met them," said he, "in print," alluding to the pamphlet of Dr. Philpotts, afterwards Bishop of Exeter, and which, having then just appeared, it is said Sir John actually held in his hand, when Mr. Lushington, or some one looking over his shoulder, communicated the circumstance to Canning, who thereupon made the observation reported in his speech; and further, it is said, exclaimed in the words of the song;

"Dear Tom, this brown jug which now foams with mild ale
Was once *Toby Philpotts.*"

This brush between Mr. Canning and the Master of the Bolls did not cause the slightest diminution of the regard which subsisted between them.

A most significant proof of this was in fact afforded a few weeks afterwards. Dissensions on the Catholic claims, together with the death of Lord Liverpool, having broken up the Cabinet, and Lord Eldon having resigned for the very last time, after twenty-five years' occupancy of the woolsack, and an extended series of threatened leave-takings, Canning made an offer of the Chancellorship to Sir John Copley, with the definite intimation "*non obstante Philpotto.*" It is stated that when Lords Liverpool and Eldon were discussing his succession to the Mastership of the Rolls, while Lord Liver pool considered that his claims to that office were paramount, Lord Eldon even went so far as to add that "he goes to school in the lower form (the Rolls) to qualify him to remove into the higher, if he takes the Chancellorship." His Lordship probably found that this contingency occurred sooner than he anticipated, and certainly he had some difficulty in reconciling himself to his own surrender of that dignified office. Yet it was quite in due-course that it should fall to the lot of Sir John Copley to succeed him as Chancellor, and Sir John therefore, on the 20th of April, 1827, was created Baron Lyndhurst, of Lyndhurst, and very properly, "**non obstante Philpotto.**"

A pleasant story is related of the damasking of the Great Seal (the perquisite of the Lord Chancellor) at the demise of George IV. Lord Lyndhurst then held the Seal, but Lord Brougham was its Keeper when the Seal of William IV. was completed; hence there were two claimants for the damasked Seal, one arguing that it was really a Seal of the preceding reign, and as such vested in him at the death of the Sovereign; the other that it was in full force till it was actually defaced. King William was appealed to to settle the dispute, and decided that each of the two Lords should have half the old Seal: his Majesty ordered his goldsmith to insert the two halves in two superb silver salvers, which he presented to Lord Lyndhurst and Lord Brougham, recommending them to "toss up" which should have the obverse and which the reverse of the Seal Another story of Lord Lyndhurst resigning the Great Seal, and, on his descending the palace staircase, being addressed with "Lord Lyndhurst, can I do anything for you!" was told with much humour by the ex-Chancellor himself.

Lord Lyndhurst, undoubtedly, did not like to be reminded of his ever having been a Whig and something more. When he was canvassing Cambridge University, and asked Musgrave, afterwards Archbishop of York, for his vote, the reply was, "I am a Whig, still, Sir!" Musgrave's dog was couchant under the chair on which the candidate was sitting, and ha was advised to "take care of that dog; he's a terrible fellow for vermin!"

"The courtesy of Lord Lyndhurst was as marked a feature in him as his learning as a lawyer and his ability as a statesman. It probably pained him, when he was Chancellor, to be uncivil even to a Lord Mayor, as he was obliged to be, according to ancient custom. When a new Lord Mayor invites the other Judges to dine with him they bow, by way of assent, but when the same invitation is made to the Lord Chancellor, he listens, gives no sign, and the Mayor departs without an answer."—Memoir in Athenœum.

Many are the instances related of the generosity of Lord Lyndhurst Mr. Gale Jones, the violent Radical, addressed a long letter to his lordship, detailing the distressing circumstances in which he was placed through ill-health, and the infirmities of old age, and soliciting charity. Lord Lyndhurst read the letter attentively, and handed it to his secretary, saying, "Make out a cheque on my bank for five pounds for this poor man." The secretary, on looking at the signature, said, "My lord, are you aware who this man is?" "No," said his lordship, "I do not recollect having before seen the name" "Why, this is the notorious Gale Jones, who has been for so many years so grossly and virulently abusing your lordship" Lord Lyndhurst looked again at the letter; and then said, "Oh, never mind what he has been in the habit of saying, about me; the poor man seems to be in a very distressed condition; get the cheque ready, and send him the money."

Here is a more playful instance of Lord Lyndhurst's good nature. When Cleave, the newsvendor, was tried in the Court of Exchequer, on a Government information, he conducted his own case, and was treated with much indulgence by Lord Lyndhurst, the judge. Cleave began his defence by observing that he was afraid he should, before he sat down, give some rather awkward illustrations of the truth of the adage, that "he who acts as his own counsel has a fool for his client." "Ah! Mr. Cleave," said his lordship, with great pleasantry, "ah, Mr. Cleave! don't you mind that adage; it was framed by the **lawyers.**"

It is gratifying to add that of this illustrious man "the end was peace;" and that nothing so called forth Lord Lyndhurst's perpetual gratitude to God as that he had enabled him, by extending his life far beyond the allotted time, to "redeem the time." And nobly did he redeem the time. His mind was fully occupied with the importance of religion. He was incessant in the earnest preparations which he made for death. He applied all the power of his marvellous intellect and all his apprehensive quickness to the study of religion. Great as he was, he bowed down before the greatness of the Supreme Being. Through religion his natural kindliness and loving disposition were refined into the highest Christian graces, which were profusely shown in his relations with all who came in contact with him—wife, daughter, servants, everybody. His last articulate words were "Happy, happy, happy," and happy he was indeed. Those who ministered to him knew his true humility, his hearty repentance, his serene and earnest hope. He died in peace and charity with all mankind. [Note *: Sermon, preached at St. George's Church, Hanover-square.]

MACAULAY IN PARLIAMENT.

M. Megnet, the French historian, in a brief sketch of the debates on the Reform Bill, thus vividly describes Macaulay.

"During that long and solemn discussion Mr. Macaulay spoke often and eloquently. He delivered five speeches successively, all worthy to be preserved. In merely considering his magnificent talent, which suggested comparisons with Burke, it may be said with truth that he placed himself by his copious diction, his elevation of thought, and his energy, in the rank of the great political orators. He enters vigorously on his subject, and masters it. His reasoning is solid rather than pompous, firm as well as rhetorical. In his short or in his swelling periods, incisive or harmonious, he indulges in no details which would weaken the interest of his subject He no more abuses history, from which he draws his telling evidence, than he does the eloquence with which he inflicts such unerring blows. His speeches, carefully studied as they were, seem as if they were conceived the moment they were delivered. They show consummate labour, and yet the movement of improvisation; and they combine studied eloquence with freedom. The moment he stood up to speak, Whigs and Tories crowded the benches of the House. Without the external qualities of the orator, he produced great oratorical effect. On a massive bust (it is thus he is represented) rose a strong and expressive head. His feet remained as if fixed to the ground. His left arm flung behind him, while with his right, and by some abrupt movements, he seemed to push, as it were, his words before him. It was in this rigid attitude, and in a tone of voice at first grave, that he opened those florid but ardent discourses, copious but impetuous, which gradually acquired an irresistible force. Then it grew to be a torrent of strong ideas, of convincing facts, of able considerations, of noble sentiments, of close reasonings, of splendid images, all of which rolled on without confusion, and carried everything before it His hearers, among whom were as many adversaries as partisans, followed him, astonished or delighted, and he obtained, from the approval of his ideas by some, applauses which admiration of his talents drew from others."

SIR JAMES GRAHAM IN PARLIAMENT.

When, in a time of great political agitation, a Bill was introduced prohibiting any person from taking part in the proceedings of a town meeting who was not an inhabitant or freeman of the place, Mr. (afterwards Sir James) Graham wished to know if a member who sat for a borough of which he was neither inhabitant nor freeman would come within the mischief of the Act? He paused to listen for the report of his shot; but few were attending, and nobody cried "Hear." He looked to see if it had hit; but the Under-Secretaries were talking to one another on the Treasury Bench, and Lord Castlereagh was occupied in smelling the hothouse flower in his button-hole. Mr. Graham repeated his question in other words, but with no better effect. He felt half vexed with himself at having got up, but he was up and must go on; so he thought he would argue the point. The case was not an imaginary one, he said, for it was his own, as he happened to sit for a borough, of which he was neither a freeman nor an inhabitant, and of which he was not likely to become either, having no connexion with the place. At this unlucky proffer of irrelevant information, he heard, or thought he heard, something like a suppressed laugh. He felt himself getting confused, a little at first, and then very much so. For a few minutes he rambled on through commonplace and reiteration, but no timely cheer came to his rescue, and he sat down without any distinct recollection of what he had said or what he had intended to say. Mr. Henry Lascelles, who sat opposite, whispered to a mutual friend, "Well, there is an end of Graham; we shall hear no more of him."—*Life by Torrens.*

When, in 1834, Sir Robert Peel was about to form his ministry, a King's messenger was despatched to Sir James Graham, who was found about to dine at the rectory at Artharet, and with certain politicians of a strong blue tint. One of these, bursting with impatience, suddenly asked him, "Well, Sir James, what are you thinking of doing?" "The only thing I am thinking of doing just now," he answered, "is of eating a good dinner."

It was during the debate on the Address, at the opening of the next Session of Parliament, that (O'Connell quoted the lines of Canning as descriptive of Sir James Graham and those who, with him, were then led by Lord Stanley,—neither a party nor a faction. What is it, he asked, that—

Down thy hill, romantic Ashburne, glides!
The Derby Dilly carrying six insides.

"No political *sobriquet*," remarks Mr. M'Cullagh Torrens, "ever stuck more closely, and few ever more effectually served their purpose."

Personally, Sir James Graham was, in 1844, the most unpopular statesman of the day. "How do you account for it," said a mutual friend standing one day below the bar to a noble lord whom Sir James had lately complimented highly in debate, and towards whom he had certainly never shown anything like disrespect "How? Why just look at him, as he sits there, with his head thrown back, and his eyes fixed on the windows over the gallery, as if there was nothing going on in the House worth his listening to." Another distinguished supporter, when asked why so many people hated him, replied, "He has cocked his hat on the wrong side of his head; and depend upon it, that's a mistake not easily got over."

In 1847, when addressing the House one evening, on the oft-debated subject of the connexion between the rate of wages and the price of food, Sir James reiterated his declaration that experience had convinced him that the former had a constant tendency to rise in proportion as the latter fell Lord George Bentinck, who was sitting on the front Opposition bench below him, threw back his head, and, looking at him, exclaimed, "Ah I yes, but you know you said the other thing before." A shout of laughter, in which Sir James joined, was followed by cheers and counter-cheers; and curiosity was on tip-toe for the retort From his perch, as he used to call it, the ex-minister looked down at his noble antagonist, and said in a tone of ineffable humour,—"The noble Lord's taunts mil harmless upon me; I'm not in office now."

In 1852 he again stood for Carlisle, abolishing all necessity for apologies and explanations by the simple words, "Well, gentlemen, the wanderer has returned." He was elected, and. returned thanks. "Somebody had said that if he were returned, Carlisle would be called a refuge for the destitute. Well, that was a better name for it to bear than an hospital for the incurable."

No one knew better than Sir James Graham how to ward off an attack on the hustings. In 1859, when a squib was published styling him a **weather-cock,** he retorted, "Well, I think it very likely that on the day of election I shall show which way the wind blows."

In power of work Sir James Graham and Sir Robert Peel were the admiration of each other, and of all who knew them. When Sir Philip Crampton, on one occasion, found Sir Robert Peel not looking over well, he ventured to suggest that the Premier did not allow himself sufficient time for rest and relaxation. "Do you think so?" was Peel's reply. "Why, what I do in the way of work is nothing to what Graham does."

Mr. Torrens relates the following instance of want of graciousness in this unpopular statesman:—"In 1837, on the death of King William, Lord John Russell came to the bar of the House of Commons charged with a Message from the Queen. Hats were immediately ordered off, and even the Speaker announced from the chair that members must be uncovered. Every one complied with the injunction except Sir James Graham, who continued to wear his hat until the first words of the Message were pronounced. His doing so Was the subject of some unpleasant remarks in the newspapers; and at the meeting of the House next day he rose to explain that in not taking off his hat until the word *Regina* was uttered he but followed the old and established custom—a custom which he deemed better than that observed by everybody else in the House. The Speaker then said that Sir James Graham was quite right, that he was strictly within rule in not uncovering until the initiatory word of the Message was delivered. If Sir James Graham had the letter of the law on his side, still there was a stiffness in his conduct which, considering that the message came from a young Queen, and was her first message to her faithful Commons, was not over attractive.

WELLINGTONIANA.

Sir Walter Scott once described the Duke of Wellington's style of debating as "slicing an argument into two or three parts, and helping himself to the best."

Colonel Gurwood relates, the Duke complained that liberties were taken with him. He said, when he went to Court, after William the Fourth's death, the Duke of Cambridge said, "Why, Duke, why d'ye have your hair so short?" Directly after, the Duke of Sussex said, "Why are you not in mourning, Duke?" The Duke said, "I ordered black, your Royal Highness." "Ah," said he; "it is not black. It is what the French call tête-de-negre." ***"The Duke of Marlborough," said the Duke to Gurwood, "because he was an old man, was treated like an old woman. I won't be. And the reason why I have a right never to have a liberty taken with me, is because I never take a liberty with any man." Colonel Gurwood said that the Duke, although he had known Lord Fitzroy Somerset from a boy, always called him*** Lord Fitzroy.

"The rat has got into the bottle" was the Duke's favourite saying, when people tried to persuade him to do what he had made up his mind not to do. "This not very intelligible expression," says Mr. Tom Taylor, "may refer to an anecdote I have heard of the Duke's once telling, in his later days, how the musk-rats in India got into bottles, which ever after retained the odour of musk." "Either the rats must be very small," said a lady who heard him, "or the bottles very large." "On the contrary, madam," was the Duke's reply, "very small bottles, and very large rats." "That is the style of logic we have to deal with at the Horse Guards" whispered Lord—.[Note *: Note to Lord Haydon's Autobiography and Journals; one o the best Anecdote-books of our time.]

The saying of the Duke ought never to be forgotten, that "success can only be obtained by tracing every part of every operation from its origin to its concluding point."

It was àpropos **to the county of Dublin meeting, in January, 1821, that the celebrated** môt of the Duke of Wellington was uttered in the House of Lords. "County meetings" said his Grace, "are farces." "On this occasion," retorted the Duke of Leinster, "it was not the fault of the authorities that the farce did not turn out a tragedy."

Lord Strangford was staying with the Duke of Wellington at Walmer Castle, when, one morning at breakfast, the Duke informed him that he was obliged to go up to London immediately, as all his razors required setting, but he would be back to dinner. Lord Strangford very naturally offered to lend the Duke his razors, which his Grace did not accept Lord S. then offered to take the razors to Dover; but the Duke replied: "The man who always sharpens my razors has sharpened them for many years; I would not trust them with any one else. He lives in Jermyn-street, and there they must go. So you see, Strangford, every man has a weak point, and my weak point is about the sharpening of my razors. Perhaps you are not aware that I shave myself and brush my own clothes. I regret that I cannot clean my own boots; for servants bore me, and the presence of a crowd of idle fellows annoys me more than I can tell you."

Occasionally, besieging correspondents got the better of the gallant Duke. A Mrs. Dowell, who kept a tobacconist's shop, at the entrance to Wilton-place, Knightsbridge, was so partial to the Duke, that she was continually inventing some new plan whereby to express her regard. She sent him patties, cakes, and other delicacies; and, as it was useless to attempt to defeat the old woman's pertinacity, everything sent was taken in. To such a pitch did she carry this mania, that she regularly laid for his Grace at her table, constantly expecting he would call in.

The Duke was once asked by a friend, with ill-timed familiarity, if he was ever surprised? "No," replied his Grace; "but I am now."

The Duke had, however, some escapes at home. One day, in May, 1845, as he was walking up the roadway of Park-lane, when opposite Gloucester House, a carter came along with a country wagon and team of horses: he called aloud to the Duke, who, being very deaf, did not hear the man, who had very nearly, with his wain, thrown down and driven over the hero of a hundred fights! We happen to know a gentleman who took his Grace almost from under the horses of an omnibus, opposite the Earl of Cadogan's house, in Piccadilly.

The Duke, when assailed by the mob, on his return from the Tower, during the Reform Bill excitement, had an escape of another sort. A young man, in a gig, or taxed-cart, kept close to the Duke's horse the whole way through the City, in such a manner as completely to guard one side. He never once looked up, nor had the air or manner of one who was doing anything out of the way; and we believe he remains to this day unknown, though the greatest disgrace that could have fallen on the nation was, in all human probability, averted by him.

It was during the unhealthy excitement, when the Reform Bill mob clung to the wheels of the Lord Mayor's state-coach, as it rolled into the court-yard of St James's, that Apsley House was attacked by the lawless brawlers, who threw stones at the very gallery in which was celebrated every year the victory which saved England and Europe! It was to protect his mansion, after the windows had been broken by the mob, that the Duke had affixed to the windows bulletproof iron Venetian blinds. Nor were these blinds removed during the Duke's lifetime. "They shall remain where they are," was his remark, "as a monument of the gullibility of a mob, and the worthlessness of that sort of popularity for which they who give it can assign no good reason. I don't blame the men that broke my windows. They only did what they were instigated to do by others who ought to have known better. But if any one be disposed to grow giddy with popular applause, I think a glance towards these iron shutters will soon sober him." In the general repair of Apsley House, some time after the Duke's death, these iron blinds were removed by order of the present Duke: to our thinking, it was most discreet to leave the farther lesson to be recorded in history.

On going over Apsley House, soon after the death of the Duke of Wellington, we were shown, on the lawn in the rear of the mansion, next Hyde Park, the garden-engine with which the Duke was wont to enjoy exercise, just *as did his great antagonist, Napoleon, at Longwood.* For, in Captain Nicholls's journal, in Sir Hudson Lowe's Letters and Journals, we find: "Jan. 2, 1820. General Bonaparte was amusing himself with the pipe of the fire-engine, spouting water on the trees and flowers of his favourite garden."

In 1839, Haydon went to Walmer Castle, to paint the Duke for a Liverpool Committee; the artist has given a minute account of the visit in his journal

"In the evening, the Duke talked of the sea encroaching at Dover, and of the various plans to stop it 'What, there are plans?' said Sir Astley Cooper, who was one of the party. 'Yes, yes, there are as many Dover doctors as other doctors,' said he, and we all laughed.

"The Duke said, when he came to Paris, in 1814, Madame de Staël had a grand party to meet him. The Abbé du Pradt was there. In conversation he said, 'Europe owes her salvation to one man. But before he gave me time to look foolish,' added the Duke, 'Du Pradt put his hand on his own breast, and said, "*C'est moi.*"'

"He then talked of Bonaparte's system. Sir Astley used the old cant—'it was selfish.' 'It was,' said the Duke, 'bullying and driving.' Of France he said, 'they robbed each other, and then poured out on Europe to fill their stomachs and pockets by robbing others.'

"He spoke of Don Carlos—said he was a poor creature. He saw him at Dorchester House two days before he escaped. He advised him not to think of it. He told him 'all we are now saying will be in Downing-street in two hours.' 'You have no posts Carlos said, 'Zumalacaragui will take me on.' 'Before you move,' replied his grace, 'be sure *he* has got one.' (Here was the *man.*) The Duke said Don Carlos affected sickness—somebody got into his bed, and kept the farce up—that medicine came—that the French ambassador behaved like a noodle. Instead of telegraphing up to

Bayonne, which would have carried the news there in two hours, he set off in his post-carriage and four after Don Carlos, when he must have got to Bayonne or near it.

"The Duke talked of the want of fuel in Spain—of what the troops suffered, and how whole houses, so many to a division, were pulled down, and regularly paid for, to serve as fuel He said every Englishman who has a home goes to bed at night. He found bivouacking was not suitable to the character of the English soldier. He got drunk, and lay down under any hedge. Discipline was destroyed. But when he introduced tents, every soldier belonged to his tent, and, drunk or sober, he got to it before he went to sleep. I said, 'Your Grace, the French always bivouac.' 'Yes,' he replied, 'because French, Spanish, and all other nations, lie anywhere. It is their habit. They have no homes.'

"The Duke said the natural state of man was plunder. Society was based upon the security of property alone. It was for that object men associated; and he thought we were coming to the natural state of society very fast."

A delightful scene with children, of whom the Duke was very fond, is described next morning, at breakfast. "In the midst, six dear noisy children were brought to the windows. 'Let them in,' said the Duke, and in they came and rushed over to him, saying, 'How d'ye do, Duke? how do d'ye do, Duke?' One boy, young Grey, roared, 'I want some tea, Duke.' 'You shall have it, if you promise not to slop it over me, as you did yesterday.' Toast and tea were then in demand. Three got on one side, and three on the other, and be hugged them all. Tea was poured out, and I saw little Grey try to slop it over the Duke's frock-coat. Sir Astley said, 'You did not effect this.' They then rushed out on the leads, and after breakfast I saw the Duke romping with the whole of them, and one of them gave his Grace a devil of a thump. I went round to my bedroom. The children came to the window, and a dear little black-eyed girl began romping. I put my head out, and said, 'I'll catch you!' Just as I did this, the Duke, who did not see me, put his head out at the door, close to my room, No. 10, which leads to the leads, and said 'I'll catch ye!—ha, ha, I've got ye!' at which they all ran away. He looked at them, and laughed, and went in."

In the evening, the Duke seated himself in the drawing-room, put a candle on each side of him, and read the **Standard** through. Sir Astley had left in the morning, and in talking of the Duke's power of conversation, related that when some one said, "Habit is second nature," the Duke remarked, "It is ten times nature."

Garwood said, the Duke told him he gave 1,000$l.$ a-year away, because the Government would not put the demands relating to his Wardenship of the Cinque Ports on the Estimates.

Gurwood also said that the year when Alexander's bank failed, the Duke gave away at least 6,000$l.$ One day, he found the Duke sealing up bank-notes, and sending off envelope after envelope, and his Grace said he ought to be as rich as Crœsus, and have mines without end.

Alava, who acted as the Duke's aide-de-camp at Waterloo, used to relate that as he was joining the Duke early on the field, he thought to himself 'I wonder how he feels and looks with Napoleon opposite.' The Duke shortly joined, and called out in his bluff manner, 'Well, how did you like the ball last night?' Putting up his glass, and sweeping the enemy's ground, he then said to Alava, 'That fellow little thinks what a confounded licking he'll get before the day is over.' "

An interesting little girl was present during a sitting of the Duke to Mr. Weigall, for his portrait; when she amused herself with some childish attempt at drawing "the window of the opposite house," to which she desired to draw the Duke's attention. Patting her on the head, he observed, "Very meritorious! very ingenious! I'm considered a great favourite with children. I was at the house of Lord S——the other day, and a fine little fellow was there who had evidently been told that I was coming, and was on the look out for me. He called soldiers ***Rub-a-dubs.*** As soon as I went in, he came up to me, and said, "You are not a Rub-a-dub at all, for you don't wear a red coat" His Grace, however, remarked that he was not always fortunate with children. "I was lately," said the Duke, "in the house of a French marquis: they brought in a little child to see me; I wanted to take it in my arms, but the child seemed to have a great aversion to me, and shrunk from me; so, I said to the little thing, 'Pourquoi,' and clinging to the nurse, it said, 'Il bat tout le monde!' I suppose she had heard her nurse say so, and thought I should beat her."

Mr. Weigall remarked to the Duke, at the above sitting; that he did not wear his orders, when he took them out of his pocket in a crumpled piece of paper, and placed them on his breast, observing—"I did not put them on before coming out, for the worst of it is, I find the people think I am after something. Now, on Saturday, when I was coming here, I saw a fellow running by my side. I turned round my horse, and asked him where he was running to? He said, *'To see where you are going to!'* 'Well, then' I remarked, 'I am going through Stanhope Gate,'—and darted off."

One evening, the ladies pressed the Duke for some of his stories. For some time he declared all his stories were in print. At last, he said, Well, I'll tell you one that has not been printed In the middle of the battle of Waterloo, he saw a man in plain clothes, riding about on a cob in the thickest fire. During a temporary lull, the Duke beckoned him, and he rode over. He asked him who he was, and what business he had there. He replied, he was an Englishman accidentally at Brussels, that he had never seen a fight, and wanted to see one. The Duke told him he was in instant danger of his life; he said, "not more than your Grace" and they parted. But, every now and then the Duke saw the cob-man riding about in the smoke, and at last having nobody to send to a regiment, he again beckoned to this little fellow, and told him to go up to that regiment, and order them to charge—giving him some mark of authority the colonel would recognise. Away he galloped, and in a few minutes the Duke saw his order obeyed. The Duke asked him for his card, and found in the evening, when the card fell out of his sash, that he lived at Birmingham, and was a button manufacturer! When at Birmingham, the Duke inquired of the firm, and found he was their traveller, and then in Ireland. When he returned, at the Duke's request he called on him in London. His Grace was happy to see him, and said he had a vacancy in the Mint of 800*l.* a-year, where accounts were wanted. The little cob-man said it would be exactly the thing, and the Duke installed him—much to his Grace's honour.

Of the Duke's perfect coolness on the most trying occasions, Colonel Gurwood related this instance. He was once in great danger of being drowned at sea. It was bed-time, when the captain of the vessel came to him, and said, "It will soon be all over with us." "Very well," answered the Duke, "then I shall not take off my boots."

To the oft-repeated question, "Was the Duke ever wounded, we may quote the following, from the *Life of General Sir William Napier,* published in 1864:

"After dusk, at the battle of Salamanca, the Duke rode up *alone* behind my regiment, and I joined him; he was giving me some orders, when a ball passed through his left holster, and struck his thigh; he put his hand to the place, and his countenance changed for an instant, but only for an instant; and to my eager inquiry if he was hurt, he replied, sharply, 'No!' and went on with his orders. Whether his flesh was torn or only bruised I know not."

The Duke is known to have been an early riser; the advantages of which were illustrated throughout his long life. His service of the Sovereigns and the public of this country for more than half a century,—in diplomatic situations and in councils, as well as in the army,—has scarcely a parallel in British history. His Despatches are the best evidence of his well-regulated mind in education. No letters could ever be more temperately or more perspicuously expressed than those famous documents. They show what immense results in the aggregate were obtained by the Duke, solely in virtue of habits which he had sedulously cultivated from his boyhood—early rising, strict attention to details, taking nothing ascertainable for granted, unflagging industry, and silence, except when speech was necessary, or certainly harmless. His early habit of punctuality is pleasingly illustrated in the following anecdote: "I will take care to be punctual at five to-morrow morning" said the engineer of New London Bridge, in acceptance of the Duke's request that he would meet him at that hour the following morning. "Say a quarter before five," replied the Duke, with a quiet smile; "I owe all I have achieved to being ready a quarter of an hour before it was deemed necessary to be so; and I learned that lesson when a boy."

Whoever has seen "the Duke's bedroom" at Apsley-house, and its plain appointments, will not regard it as a chamber of indolence. It was, a few years since, narrow, shapeless, and ill-lighted; the bedstead small, provided only with a mattress and bolster, and scantily curtained with green silk; the only ornaments of the walls were an unfinished sketch, two cheap prints of military men, and a small portrait in oil: yet here slept the Great Duke, whose "eightieth year was by."

"THE TENTH OF APRIL."

The great Chartist Demonstration of 1848 was brought to a ridiculous issue, by the unity and resolution of the Metropolis, backed by the judicious measures of the Government, and the masterly military precautions of the Duke of Wellington. "On our famous 10th of April, his peculiar genius was exerted to the unspeakable advantage of peace and order. So effective were his preparations that the most serious insurrection could have been successfully encountered, and yet every source of provocation and alarm was removed by the dispositions adopted. No military display was anywhere to be seen. The troops and the cannon were all at their posts, but neither shako nor bayonet was visible; and for all that met the eye, it might have been concluded that the peace of the metropolis was still entrusted to the keeping of its own citizens. As an instance, however, of his forecast against the worst, on this memorable occasion, it may be observed that orders were given to the commissioned officers of artillery, to take the discharge of their pieces on themselves. The Duke knew that a cannon-shot too much or too little might change the aspect of the day; and he provided by these remarkable instructions, both for imperturbable forbearance as long as forbearance was best, and for unshrinking action when the moment for action came."—*Memoir; Times.*

WATERLOO QUERIES.

Haydon asked the Duke of Richmond if there ever was a moment when he desponded at Waterloo. He said: "Never. For an instant some young officers might fear, when the cavalry were on the hill, that they had got possession of the artillery;

but all old ones knew that cavalry getting possession of artillery was nonsense."

When Haydon dined at Lord Palmerston's, he sat next to Lord Hill, and this conversation ensued: "I said, 'My Lord, I feel great interest in seeing your Lordship after reading so much about you.' 'Ah!' said Lord Hill, 'those days are past' 'But,' said I, 'not forgotten.' He seemed pleased at my attention, and came home with me to see the picture.

"While in the carriage I said, 'My Lord, was there ever any time of the day at Waterloo when you desponded?' 'Certainly not,' he replied 'There never was any panic?' 'No. There was no time of the day.' I said, 'I apologise; but Sir Walter Scott asked the Duke the same thing, and he made the same reply.' Lord Hill said, in the simplest manner, 'I dare- say.' "

A coincidence rarely remembered, may be mentioned here. During the visit of the Allied Sovereigns to this country, George IV. (then Prince Regent) was entertained at a costly, banquet at Guildhall, London, with Alexander, Emperor of Russia, and Frederick William III., King of Prussia, June 18, 1814; and on the first anniversary of this Festival, June 18, 1815, was fought the battle of Waterloo.

THE WELLINGTON FAMILY AND TALLEYRAND.

Talleyrand, it is told, suggested to Bonaparte, after the battle of Leipsig, 1813, the idea of raising the Duke of Wellington to the throne of England! The details are thus related in Rovigo's *Memoirs:*—"The Emperor asked him to explain himself, and M. de Talleyrand continued: 'There is in England a family which has acquired a distinction favourable to the encouragement of every kind of ambition. It is natural to suppose that it possesses ambition, or at least; that, by showing a disposition to second its ambition, we may excite in it the desire of elevation; and also, that there are in England a sufficient number of adventurous men to turn the chances of its fortune. At all events, such a proposition could do us no harm. On the contrary, if it were listened to, it might bring about changes which would soon place us in a state in which we would have little to repair. Another consideration is, that your allies have failed you, you can do nothing solid except with new men connected from the beginning with the conservation of your system.' The Emperor listened to M. de Talleyrand, but desired him to speak out more plainly, remarking that he was always the same, and that there was no knowing what he would be at. Thus pressed, Talleyrand mentioned the Wellesley family, and said, 'Look at Wellington, who may be supposed to have something in view. If he submit to live on his reputation, he will soon be forgotten. He has several examples before his eyes; and a talent such as his will not be stopped, so long as there is something to be desired.' The Emperor did not adopt these suggestions. He observed, that before helping the ambition of others, it was fit that he should be in a condition to make himself respected in his government, and added, that at the present moment he could give his attention to nothing else. M. de Talleyrand, however, told me, that the Emperor appeared much impressed with what he had stated. He indeed expected that the Emperor would have again spoken to him on the subject."

THE MARQUES WELLESLEY.

Lord Wellesley's prosperous career of civil service was more flattering to his ambition than productive of emolument. His father's debts were paid by him voluntarily, but he was unable to preserve the family estates. On the fall of Seringapatam, the sum of 10,000*l.* was set apart for the Marquess—a grant which, on his suggestion, was abandoned to the army.

The Marquess, unlike his illustrious brother, the Duke of Wellington, was a lover of dress, and carried the spirit of foppery so far, that he would often play the coxcomb for his own amusement. He would sit in his own room for hours with no other spectator than what he saw reflected in the mirror, dressed in full costume, and decorated with the blue riband and the Garter, as if meant to appear at a chapter, or a royal levee.

O'CONNELL AND HAYDON.

The painter, during O'Connell's sittings to him, contrived to draw from him some interesting talk about the politics of the time, of which Haydon, with his accustomed tact, made the following entries in his Diary:—

"At twelve I went to O'Connell's, and certainly his appearance was very different from what it is in the House of Commons. It was, on the whole, hilarious and good-natured. But there was a cunning look. He has an eye like a weasel. Light seemed hanging at the bottom, and he looked out with a searching ken, like Brougham, something, but not with his depth of insight.

"I was first shown into his private room. A shirt hanging by the fire, a hand-glass tied to the window-bolt, papers, hats, brushes, wet towels, and dirty shoes, gave intimation of 'Dear Ireland.' After a few moments O'Connell rolled in in a morning-gown, a loose black handkerchief tied round his Heck, God knows how; a wig, and a foraging-cap bordered with gold lace. As a specimen of character, he began, 'Mr. Haydon, you and I must understand each other about this picture. They say I must pay for this likeness.' 'Not at all, sir' This is the only tiling of the sort that has happened to me.

"He sat down, and I sketched him. He talked of Repeal. 'What did ye think of me when I first started the question?' 'That you were mad,' said I. 'Do you not think, sir,' I said, 'that Ireland being the smaller, must always be subject to England, the larger island?' 'No,' said O'Connell. 'Is not Portugal a smaller country than Spain?' 'Yes, but she is a separate country'.

" 'One great mistake of the Liberals,' said he, 'is their in fidelity. Now, there are no infidels in Ireland.' 'No,' said I, 'they are too poetical' O'Connell looked at me as if he thought that was new and true. I succeeded in his head. It is a head of hilarity and good humour, while his nose and eyes denote keen cunning. His voice is melodious and persuasive, and there is a natural poetry about his mind that renders him interesting. There were no less than five papers in the room, in which O'Connell read alternately. He said, 'I got a scolding from Peel last night I told him I spared him this once—but the next time——.' "

Of another sitting: "O'Connell came in his best wig, and looking in great health and vigour. O'Connell has a head of great sentiment and power, but yet cunning. The instant he came in he looked at the picture, and said, 'Ah, there's Stanley, with a smile I never yet saw on his countenance—Melbourne, Graham, Russell,—Grey, but too handsome;—Althorp, the bitterest enemy of Ireland, but he shall never legislate for her.'

"O'Connell was in great good humour, and I begged him to give me a history of his early life. He did so immediately, explained their first meeting to consider the grievances of the Catholics—their being interrupted by a company of soldiers, &c. The poetical way in which he described the crashing of the muskets on the stones at 'Order arms,' was characteristic. I said, 'It is somewhat ungrateful, after getting emancipation, to turn round, and demand repeal.' 'Not in me,' said O'Connell, 'I always said repeal would be the consequence of emancipation, and I always avowed such to be my object. 'Do you think you will carry it?' 'Not a doubt of it,' said O'Connell 'If you get repeal, what will you do?' 'Have an Irish Parliament directly.' 'But an Irish Parliament,' said I, 'was always corrupt.' 'Yes,' said he, 'in borough-mongering times; but now there is a constituency. Besides, corrupt as it was, it carried important measures.'

" 'Upon my word," I said, 'you take up more time in the House than you ought.' 'We can't help it,' said O'Connell 'Don't you think the Irish people barbarous? said I. O'Connell was shaken, and he tried to explain why they were not, but did not succeed. O'Connell spoke of himself with great candour. He said, 'How could the Government expect after the character and publicity I gained by emancipation, I could relapse into a poor barrister? Human vanity would not permit it.'

" 'How they bore you,' said I, 'in the House about Barrett.' 'Ah,' said O'Connell, with one of his wicked arch smiles, 'Barrett and I understand each other. He makes 1,500*l.* or 2,000*l.* a-year by my organs.'

THE DUKE OF WELLINGTON AND LORD ELDON.

A strange scene took place between these two statesmen, on the forming of the Duke's Administration, early in 1828. The day after his Grace received the King's commands, he wrote to Lord Eldon, declaring his intention of calling on him the next day. By Lord Eldon's account, the meeting was an awkward one; the ex-chancellor evidently expecting the offer of some post in the Administration, though too old to resume his seat on the woolsack. "From the moment of his quitting me," writes Lord Eldon, "to the appearance in the papers of all the appointments, I never saw his Grace. I had no communication with him, either personally, by note, letter, by message through any other person, or in any manner whatever, and for the whole fortnight I heard no more of the matter than you did,—some of my colleagues in office—(and much obliged to me too)—passing my door constantly, on their way to Apsley House, without calling upon me. In the meantime rumour was abroad that I had refused all office." However, it being somehow communicated that Lord Eldon was much hurt at this sort of treatment, brought the Duke to him again, and the object of his visit seemed to be to account for all this. "He stated in substance," says Lord Eldon, "that he had found it impracticable to make any such administration as he was sure I should be satisfied with, and therefore, he thought he should only be giving me unnecessary trouble in coining near me—or to that effect." Then came out the old politician's soreness about not having been offered the office of President of the Council, and about being considered impracticable, which he was sure nobody had any reason to suppose; and about being neglected for a whole fortnight! The Duke gave as a justification for having concluded that Lord Eldon would not have approved the composition of the Ministry, that he seemed as if he did not like it, now the whole ministry was complete, to which Lord Eldon emphatically replied, that he thought it a d——d bad one. "We conversed together," he continued, "however, till it seemed to me we both became a good deal affected."

"NO MISTAKE."

In 1827, the death of Mr. Canning having led to the formation of the Goderich

Administration, the Duke of Wellington resumed, on the 27th of August, the command of the army. In January following, the ***pro tempore*** Administration of Lord Goderich having broken down, the Duke was called upon by the King to form a ministry. His first impulse was to decline the mission; but, finding a great difficulty in getting another individual to fill the place, and it being the unanimous wish of those with whom he usually acted, that he should take office, he determined to accept it. When installed, the Duke went to work in true military style: he exacted the most prompt and entire obedience from his subordinate colleagues. Mr. Huskisson, who had been retained, soon felt this. The Duke, like all military men, hated ideologists; and he looked on Mr. Huskisson, with his liberal Toryism, and Free-Trade tendencies, as one of this class. It was not long before he found an excuse for getting rid of him. On the last Retford Bill, Mr. Huskisson gave a vote different from that which the ***mot d'ordre*** had prescribed The same night, feeling the importance of the step, he sat down, in excitement, and wrote a letter, in which he conditionally placed his office at the Duke's disposal Had the Duke desired to retain him, he would have given him time to reflect; but the opportunity was tempting, and the Duke chose to regard the letter as an unconditional resignation. He even proceeded to clench the matter by filling up Mr. Huskisson's place. In vain did Lord Palmerston endeavour to patch up a reconciliation. The Duke was immovable; and, in answer to a suggestion that there had been a mistake, wrote his celebrated words: "It is no mistake; it can be no mistake; it shall be no mistake." This positiveness settled the affair. The people thought it a capital joke to see these theoretical men thus sent to the right about by the practical soldier; and it is on record that when the news of Huskisson's dismissal was known, numerous vessels in the Thames hoisted their flags in token of satisfaction—because Mr. Huskisson was known to be a Free-Trader.

THE DUKE AND THE LORD HIGH ADMIRAL.

In 1829, the Lord High Admiral, the Duke of Clarence, was thought by the straightforward and simple-mannered Premier (Wellington) to have mixed up too much of the popularity-seeking heir-presumptive with the business of his office. There had been a vast deal of jaunting and cruising about, presenting of colours, preparations of shows on sea and land, which appeared to the Duke of Wellington to be more expensive and foolish than in any way serviceable; and it was believed that the retirement of the Lord High Admiral was caused by a plain expression of the Premier's opinion on the matter. On a long account for travelling expenses being sent in to the Treasury by the Duke of Clarence, the Premier endorsed the paper: "No travelling expenses allowed to the Lord High Admiral;" and dismissed it Yet, this was not a whit more curt than the "No mistake" endorsement of the Huskisson letter.

Equally characteristic of the Duke's brevity was his answer to an officer of the 46th, for the renewal of a six months' leave of absence: the officer was stationed at Cape Coast Castle: the Duke's emphatic reply consisted of three short words: "Sell or sail."

PRINCE WILLIAM HENRY A MIDSHIPMAN

It was, probably, in resentment for the behaviour of his brother, the Duke of Cumberland, at the trial of Admiral Keppel, that George III determined to send his third son, a boy nine or ten years of age, to sea in one of the fleets that were to sail, as a hint to the Duke of Cumberland that he was never to be Lord High Admiral, which he would have been otherwise.

When Prince William Henry **was** sent to sea, he had, at least, to make and fight his way among his young shipmates. "I am told," says Dr. Doran, "on reliable authority, that in the first week of his cruise, for some impertinence at mess, he received a drubbing from one of his mates. The Prince threatened to tell his father. 'Ah,' replied the mate, 'I would serve your father in the same way if he were in your place, and behaved as unlike a gentleman.' The mate was living at Deal when the Duke of Clarence became Lord High Admiral, and summoned his old shipmate up to town. At the interview, the Duke began by asking, 'Are you the man who gave me my first **hiding** at sea?' 'Oh! your Royal Highness,' said the veteran, 'I—I am sorry for it.' 'Well, I am not,' replied the Duke, 'for it helped to make a man of me; and now I want to do something for you.' The mate returned to Deal a step or two in rank. In these later days, the Navy has seen, with surprise, a young prince sent to sea with a protector; and it has created something more than surprise that this guardian, or 'governor,' is not an officer in the navy, but a lieutenant of engineers I"—**Notes to Walpole's Last Journals,** vol. ii. p. 332.

VISCOUNT MELBOURNE.

Of this amiable man and popular Minister, Haydon records some very interesting traits, in his **Memoirs.**

Lord Melbourne said: "I remember Reynolds. [Sir Joshua.] He was a hard-working old dog. When I sat to him, he worked too hard to be happy."

Haydon attended an Irish Church debate in the House of Lords in 1833. "The Duke spoke well, and without hesitation. There was a manly honour about his air, and when he read a quotation, to see him deliberately take out his glasses and put them on was extremely interesting. He enforces what he says with a bend of his head, striking his hand forcibly, as if convinced, on the papers. He finished, and to my utter astonishment, up started Lord Melbourne like an artillery rocket. He began in a fury. His language flowed out like fire. He made such palpable hits that he floored the Duke of Wellington as if he had shot him. But the moment the stimulus was over, his habitual apathy got ahead. He stammered, hemmed, and hawed. But it was the most pictorial exhibition of the night He waved his white hand with the natural grace of Talma; expanded his broad chest, looked right at his adversary, like a handsome lion, and rappled him with the grace of Paris."

Hay don notes: "November 11th—The scene at the Lord Mayor's dinner at Guildhall last night was exquisite—the mischievous air of over-politeness with which Lord B——handed in the Lady Mayoress,—the arch looks of Lord Mel bourne,—the supercilious sneer of Lord S——at 'a city affair,' as he called it.

"In the ball-room I said to Lord S——Lord Melbourne enjoyed it. 'There is nothing, Lord Melbourne does not enjoy,' said he. Can there be a finer epitaph upon a man? It is true of Lord Melbourne, who was all amiability, good humour, and simplicity of mind.

"Lord Melbourne, (says Mr. Tom Taylor,) being now at the head of the administration, Haydon availed himself of his easy good humour and accessible habits, to urge on him, as he had done on his predecessor for twenty years, the duty of providing public employment for artists. But the charming insouciance of Lord Melbourne was worse than the most frigid formality of any of his predecessors. He was always ready to listen when Haydon talked, but as to impressing him with any sense of the importance of the subject! In one of these conversations—a "set-to"—in reply to Lord Melbourne's declining a grant, here is Haydon's remonstrance with the minister. 'You say the Government is poor: you voted 10,000$l.$ for the Poles, and 20,000$l.$ for the Euphrates.' 'I was against 10,000l-. for the Poles. These things only bring over more refugees,' said Lord Melbourne. 'What about the Euphrates? Why, my Lord, to try if it be navigable, when all the world know it is not?" Then Lord Melbourne turned round, full of fun, and said, 'Drawing is no use, it is an obstruction to genius. Corregio could not draw, Reynolds could not draw.' 'Ah, my Lord, I see where you have been lately.' Then he rubbed his hands, and laughed again, &c.

"I said, 'Do you occupy Downing-street? He said, 'No,' with hesitation. I fancy he fears his lease; but he is a man fond of leisure, and by keeping his house, he is out of the way of bore till business hours. Lord Grey was always in it Of another of these interviews, Hay don, being admitted, says, Lord Melbourne, looked round with his arch face, and said, 'What now?' as much as to say, 'What the devil are you come about?—art, I suppose.' Then began the set-to, in the course of which the painter urges: 'You say you can't afford it In Lord Bexley's time, the same thing was said, and yet 30,000$l.$ was spent to build an ophthalmic hospital—it failed—5,000$l.$ was fetched by the sale of the materials, and 4,000$l.$ voted to Adams, for putting out the remaining eyes of the veterans.' 'No doubt,' said Lord Melbourne, 'a great deal of money has been uselessly spent.' 'I take the excuse of poverty as a nonentity,' I said. He did not reply.

"Now, my Lord, Lord Grey said there was no intention of taking down the tapestry. **It's down.** [This was said three days after the burning of the House of Parliament, in 1834.] A new House must be built Painting, sculpture, and architecture must be combined. Here's an opportunity that never can occur again. Burke said it would ultimately rest on a minister; have you no ambition to be that man?' He moved, but did not reply. 'For God's sake, Lord Melbourne, do not let this slip,—for the sake of art—for your own sake—only say, you won't forget art.' [Haydon offers to undertake it.] No reply. 'Depend on my discretion. Not a word shall pass from me; only assure me it is not hopeless.' Lord Melbourne glanced up with his fine eye, and looked into me, and said, 'It is not.' 'There will be only a temporary building till Parliament meets. There's time enough."

At another interview, the following dialogue ensued: 'Well, my Lord, have you seen my petition to you?' 'I have.' 'Have you read it?' 'Yes.' 'Well, what do you say to it?' He affected to be occupied, and to read a letter. I said, 'What answer does your Lordship give? What argument or refutation have you?' 'Why, we do not mean to have pictures. We mean to have a building with all the simplicity of the ancients' 'Well, my Lord, what public building will you point out without pictures?'

When Lord Melbourne followed Lord Grey, with him went Haydon's hopes of State encouragement for high art. In a few days, however, the painter had another set-to with the ex-minister. "He advised me to try Peel, which I shall do. He would not open his lips about politics, and was impressionless on art." "The fact is," said Haydon, "you are corrupted, you know you are, since I first talked to you. Calcott, after dinner at Lord Holland's, has corrupted you, sneered you out of your right feelings over your wine." He acknowledged there was a good deal of truth in this, and laughed heartily.

"He advised me," adds Haydon, "to attack Peel, and told me how to proceed to get a sum in the Estimates. This is exactly Lord Melbourne. He has no nerve himself; he seemed ashamed, and now, willing not to lose some of the credit, pushes me off on Peel. We shall see."

Here is an entry early in the following year, in a more lively vein of banter:

"February 1st Sunday. Called on Lord Melbourne. He was lounging over the *Edinburgh Review.* He began instantly, 'Why here are a set of fellows who want public money for scientific purposes, as well as you for painting; they are a set of ragamuffins.' That's the way' said I, 'nobody has any right to public money but those who are brought up to politics. Are not painting and science as much matter of public benefit as political jobbing? You never look upon us as equals; but any scamp who trades in politics is looked upon as a companion for my Lord.' 'That is not true,' said he. 'I say it is,' said I; and he then roared with laughter, and rubbed his hands. 'I could not get him to touch on politics. 'Lord Melbourne, will you make me a promise?' 'What is that?' 'Pass your word to get a vote of money for art, if you are premier again.' Not a word. No old politician ever speaks on politics so as to give you a notion of what is going on."

Early in 1836, "in walks an execution." "I wrote to Lord Melbourne, Peel, and the Duke of Bedford. Lord Melbourne sent me directly a cheque for 70*l.* This was kind-hearted. He told me I must not think him hard, but decidedly he could not repeat it I concluded my grateful reply by telling him that I should think nothing hard but his building the House of Lords without pictures—at which he laughed heartily, I will be bound."

Sir Bulwer Lytton characterises Lord Melbourne as one who, if not among the greatest Ministers who has swayed this country, was one of the most accomplished and honourable men who ever attained to the summit of constitutional ambition. Lord Melbourne was once heard to say that he rejoiced to have been Prime Minister, for he had thus learnt that men were much better, much more swayed by conscience and honour, than he had before supposed; a saying, honourable to the Minister, and honourable still more to the public virtue of Englishmen.

Lord Melbourne was proverbially a good-natured man; but in preferences he acted with a sense of duty more stringent than might have been expected. It appears that Lord John Russell had applied to Lord Melbourne for some provision for one of the sons of the poet Moore; and here is the Premier's reply:

"My dear John,—I return you Moore's letter. I shall be ready to do what you like about it when we have the means. I think whatever is done should be done for Moore himself. This is more distinct, direct, and intelligible. Making a small provision for young men is hardly justifiable; and it is of all things the most prejudicial to themselves. They think what they have much larger than it really is; and they make no exertion. The young should never hear any language but this: 'You have your own way to make, and it depends upon your own exertions whether you starve or not'—Believe me, &c. MELBOURNE."

When Alfred Bunn, accompanied by his brother of the rod, Duruset, was fishing at Brocket, Lord Melbourne's seat in Hertfordshire, from cockcrow until sundown, Bunn reflected: "Is it not passing strange, that a man possessing so delightful a domain as Brocket, to sustain which he hath ample means, should consent to take upon himself the government of a country for which he hath NO means? But Brocket is a fine place, and Byron, my Lord, hath been here, and poor Lady Caroline! And then, its waters have noble fish in them; and, it is too bad to abuse the man who allows you to pull them up; but alas!" &c.

A ROYAL SPEECH BY CANDLELIGHT.

The opening day of the Session of Parliament in 1836, (February 4,) was unusually gloomy; which, added to an imperfection in the sight of King William IV., and the darkness of the House, rendered it impossible for his Majesty to read the Royal Speech with facility. Most patiently and good-naturedly did he struggle with the task, often hesitating, sometimes mistaking, and at others correcting himself. On one occasion, he stuck altogether, and after two or three ineffectual efforts to make out the word, he was obliged to give it up; when, turning to Lord Melbourne, who stood on his right hand, and looking him most significantly in the face, he said in a tone sufficiently loud to be audible in all parts of the House, "Eh! what is it?" Lord Melbourne having whispered the obstructing word, the King proceeded to toil through the speech; but by the time he got to about the' middle, the librarian brought him two wax-lights, on which he suddenly paused; then raising his head, and looking at the Lords and Commons, he addressed them, on the spur of the moment, in a perfectly distinct voice, and without the least embarrassment or the mistake of a single word, in these terms:

"My Lords and Gentlemen,—

"I have hitherto not been able, from want of light, to read this speech in the way its importance deserves; but as lights are now brought me, I will read it again from the commencement, and in a way which, I trust, will command your attention."

The King then again, though evidently fatigued by the difficulty of reading in the first instance, began at the beginning, and read through the speech in a manner which would have done credit to any professor of elocution.

"THE OLD WHIG POET TO HIS OLD BUFF WAISTCOAT."

In the middle of 1838, died, in his 93rd year, at his delightful retreat in Surrey, Captain Morris, the political and anacreontic song-writer. His remains rest in the churchyard of Betchworth, where his grave is simply marked by a head and foot stone.

Attaching himself politically, as well as convivially, to his table companions, Morris composed the ballads of "Billy's too young to drive us," and "Billy Pitt and the Farmer." His humorous ridicule of the Tories, however, was but ill repaid by the Whigs, on their accession to office; at least, if we may trust the following Ode, which was found in MS. left among the papers of Alexander Stephens, in 1823.

"Farewell, thou poor rag of the muse,
In the bag of the clothesman go lie:
A sixpence thou'lt fetch from the Jews,
Which the hard-hearted Christians deny.

Twenty years in adversity's spite,

I bore thee most proudly along!
Stood jovially **buff** to the fight,
And won the world's ear with my song.

But, prosperity's humbled thy case,
Thy friends in full banquet I see,
And the door kindly shut in my face,
Thou'st become a **fools garment** to me!

Poor rag! thou art welcome no more,
The days of thy **service** are past,
Thy toils and thy glories are o'er,
And thou and thy master art **cast.**

But though thou art forgot and betray'd,
Twill ne'er be forgotten by me,
How my old lungs within me have play'd,
And my spirits have swell'd thee with glee.

Perhaps they could swell thee no more,
For Time's icy hand's on my head;
My spirits are weary and sore,
And the impulse of Friendship is dead.

Then adieu! tho' I cannot but fret
That my constancy with thee must part,
For thou hast not a hole in thee yet,
Though through **thee** they have wounded my heart.

I change thee for sable, more sage,
To mourn the hard lot I abide;
And mark upon **gratitude's** page
A blot that had buried my **pride.**

Ah! who would believe in these lands,
From the **Whigs** I should suffer a wrong,
Had they seen how with hearts and with hands
They followed in frenzy my song?

Who'd have thought, though so eager their claws,
They'd condemn me thus hardly to plead?
Through my **prime** I have toil'd for your cause,
And you have left me, when aged, in need.

Could ye not midst the favours of fate
Drop a mite where all own it is due?
Could ye not from the feast of the **state**
Throw a **crumb** to a servant so true?

In your **scramble** I stirr'd not a jot,
Too proud for rapacity's strife;
And sure that all hearts would allot
A scrap to the **claims of ray life.**

But go, faded rag, and while gone,
I'll turn thy hard fate to my ease;
For the hand of kind Heaven hath shewn
All crosses have colours that please.

Thus a **bliss** from thy shame I receive,
Though my body's had treatment so foul,
I can suffer, forget, and forgive,
And get comfort more worth for my **soul.**

And when seen on the rag-seller's rope,
They who know thee'll say ready enough,

'There service hangs jilted by hope,
This once was poor M—rr—s's buff.'

If they let them give virtue her name,
And yield an example to teach,
Poor rag, thou hast served in thy *shame,*
Better ends than thy *honours* could reach.

But though the soul gains by the loss,
The stomach and pocket still say,
Pray what shall we do in this cross?'
I answer, 'be *poor* and be gay.'

Let the muse gather mirth from her wrong,
Smooth her wing in *adversitys shower;*
To new ears and new hearts time her song,
And still look for a *sunshining hour.*

"While I, a disbanded old Whig,
Put up my discharge with a smile;
Face about—prime and load—take a swig,
And march off to the opposite file.

G. R. *August* 1, 1815

ADMINISTRATIVE EXPERIENCE.

M. Thiers, in a conversation with Mr. Senior, gave the following account of his experience as a minister, in respect to the Civil Service in France, which is corroborative of the general account of it given by M. Balzac. "When," said he, "I was minister, I used constantly to find my orders forgotten, or neglected, or misinterpreted. As I have often said to you, men are naturally idle, false, and timid (*menteurs, laches, paresseux*). Whenever I found an employé supposed that because

THE INDIAN MUTINY.

The following extract from an interesting letter, addressed to the Rev. Secretary of the London Missionary Society, from the Rev. A. F. Lacroix, one of the Society's missionaries in India, is striking: the letter is dated Calcutta, June 3, 1857:

"We are passing through a most critical period, such as I have never seen during my thirty-six years' residence in India, and which, I believe, has not been witnessed before. It is strange that it should happen just a century after the taking of Bengal by the British, under Lord Clive; the battle of Plassy, which decided the fate of the country, having been fought on the 23rd of June, 1757. There has been for many years a Brahminical prediction, current among the natives, and which I have often heard referred to, viz. that the British rule in India would last just one hundred years; and I should not be surprised that this pseudo-prophecy may have had some influence in inducing the Sepoys to revolt at the present time."

In the *Record,* of Wednesday, Sept. 23, 1857, is a letter bearing the signature of "E. A. W., of Haselbury, Bryan, Dorset," in which the writer states that, "for upwards of fifty years, the Mohammedans have been looking forward to the year 1857 as the year in which they were to regain their dominion in the ancient Mogul empire," and cites a passage from the ***Journals and Letters of the Rev. Henry Martyn*** (2 vols.), edited by S. Wilberforce, to prove this assertion. It occurs vol. ii. p. 2, Jan. 8, 1807:—

"Pundit was telling me to-day that there was a prophecy in their books that the English should remain one hundred years in India, and that forty years were now elapsed of that period. (This is a mistake; it should have been said *fifty years,* since 1757, the year of the battle of Plassy.) That there should be a great change, and they should be driven out by a king's son who should be born. Telling this to Moonshee, he said that about the same time the Mussulmans expected some great events, and the spread of Islamism over the earth."

Mrs. Torrens, the widow of General Torrens, residing at Southsea, near Portsmouth, about a year previous to the Indian mutiny, dreamed that she saw her daughter, Mrs. Hayes, and that daughter's husband, Captain Hayes, attacked by Sepoys; and a frightful murderous struggle ensued, in which Captain Hayes was killed. She wrote instantly to entreat that her daughter and the children would presently come home; and in consequence of her extreme importunity, her grandchildren arrived by the following ship. This was before an idea was entertained of the mutiny. Mrs. Hayes remained with her husband, and suffered the whole horrors of the siege of Lucknow, where Captain Hayes fell by the hands of the Sepoys—who first put out his eyes, and then killed him. (See **Predictions Realized in Modern Times**.)

THE NATIONAL ANTHEM.

Mr. T. Raikes, in his Journals, published in 1856, notes: "Our National Anthem of God save the King' composed in the time of George I., has always been considered of English origin; but, on reading the amusing Memoirs of Madame de Créquy it appears to have been almost a literal translation of the cantique which was always sung by the Demoiselles de St. Cyr when Louis XIV. entered the chapel of that establishment to hear the morning prayer. The words were by M. de Brinon, and the music by the famous Sully. It appears to have been translated and adapted to the, House of Hanover by Handel, the German composer:

" 'Grand Dieu, sauve le Roi!
Grand Dieu, venge le Roi!
Vive le Roi!
Que toujours glorieux,
Louis victorieux,
Voye ses ennemis
Toujours soumis?
Grand Dieu, sauve le Roi!
Grand Dieu, venge le Roi!
Vive le Roi!' "

In the **Familie Magazijn** for 1859, (quoted in **Notes and Queries**), we find the following strange story:—

"As King William III. of England, the Stadtholder of the Netherlands, was besieging Namur, in 1695, sundry soldiers from his army, through the want which reigned in the camp, went marauding, though such a transgression of the martial law had been forbidden on pain of death. Most of these marauders were caught by the country people, and killed; only two of them reached the camp unscathed; but they were sentenced to death. They were both brave soldiers, and the general-in-chief wanted to save one of them, and thus commuted the judgment in so far, that they should have to throw at dice for their life, as was the custom in former times in such cases.

"On the morning appointed for the execution, both the marauders were led to a drum, in order thereupon to cast the decisive throw; while, at a few paces further, the fatal pole already stood erect Full of painful expectation, a group of officers, the regimental chaplain, and the executioner, surrounded the poor fellows. With a trembling hand, one of the condemned took up the dice: he threw—two sixes! In the next moment, he saw that his fellow had also thrown—two sixes!

"The commanding officers were not a little stricken at this strange occurrence: but their orders were precise, and so they commanded both the men to throw again. This was done: the dice were cast, and in the throw of both there turned up—two fives! The spectators now loudly called out that both should be pardoned; and the officers, to ask for new directions, momentarily put off the execution. They applied to the court martial, which they found assembled; and, after a long discussion, the disheartening reply was that the delinquents should decide their lot with new dice. Once more both of them cast, and, lo—each threw two fours!

" 'This is the finger of God!' said all present.

"The officers again submitted the strange case to the court martial This time, even the members of the court shuddered; and they resolved to leave the decision to the general-in-chief, who was momentarily expected.

"The Prince of Vaudemont came. He caused the two Englishmen to appear before him: they related to him the trying circumstances of their desertion. The Prince listened attentively, and relieved the poor culprits with the welcome 'Pardon,' adding, 'it is impossible in such an uncommon case not to obey the voice of Divine Providence.'"

THE SUPERIOR MAN.

Sir E. Bulwer Lytton, in his **Caxtonia** gives this clever portrait of the safe or superior man, winning success by his silence:—

"A certain nobleman, some years ago, was conspicuous for his success in the world. He had been employed in the highest situations at home and abroad, without one discoverable reason for his selection, and without justifying the selection by one proof of administrative ability. Yet at each appointment the public said, 'A great gain to the government! Superior man!' And when from each office he passed away, or rather passed imperceptibly onward towards office still more exalted, the public said, 'A great loss to the government! Superior man!' He was the most silent person I ever met. But when the first reasoners of the age would argue some knotty point in his presence, he would, from time to time, slightly elevate his eyebrows, gently shake his head, or, by a dexterous smile of significant complacency, impress on you the notion how easily he could set those babblers right, if he would but condescend to give voice to the wisdom within him.

"I was very young when I first met this superior man; and chancing the next day to call on the late Lord Durham, I said, in the presumption of early years, 'I passed six mortal hours last evening in company with Lord——. I don't think there is much in him.'

" 'Good heavens!' cried Lord Durham, 'how did you find that out? Is it possible that he could have—talked?' "

THE SEA-SICK MINISTER.

The Earl of Aberdeen, as Minister, had to attend Queen Victoria in her cruisings, very much against his will, or at least against his stomach. He was one of the gravest and most laconic men in the world. The Queen, one day, undertook to reconcile him to his fate. "I believe, my lord," said she, graciously, "you are not often sea-sick." "***Always,*** madam," was the grave reply. "But," still more graciously, "not *very* sea-sick." With profounder gravity, "VERY, madam!" Lord Aberdeen, more than once, declared that if Her Majesty persisted in her cruisings, he should have to resign.

THE MASONIC GRIP.

Sir A. Alison, at a Masonic festival at Glasgow, related the following anecdote of what is familiarly termed as above:—

"In the Crimean war, during the assault on the Redan, an Eglish officer led a small party of soldiers up to one of the guns place in a recess of the Redan, and most of the men fell before the tremendous fire with which they were received. The others were attacked by a body of Russians, and the English officer was about to be bayoneted, when he chanced to catch the hand of a Russian officer, and had presence of mind enough to give him a masonic grip. The Russian in a moment struck up the bayonet of the soldier, led his newly-found brother to the rear, and treated him with all the kindness of a Mason."

THE ART OF PUBLIC SPEAKING.

The late Marquess of Lansdowne one day remarked to Thomas Moore, that he hardly ever spoke in the House of Lords without feeling the approaches of some loss of self-possession, and found that the only way to surmount it was to talk on at all hazards. He added, what appears highly probable, that those ***commonplaces*** which most men accustomed to public speaking have ready cut and dry, to bring in on all occasions, were, he thought, in general used by them as a mode of getting out of those blank intervals, when they do not know ***what*** to say next, but, in the meantime, must say ***something.***

Scarcely any person has ever become a great debater without long practice and many failures. It was by slow degrees, as Burke said, that Fox became the most brilliant and powerful debater that ever lived. Fox himself attributed his own success to the resolution which he formed when very young, of speaking, well or ill, at least once every night. "During five whole sessions," he used to say, "I spoke every night but one; and I regret only that I did not speak that night too."

A MINISTER OF FOREIGN AFFAIRS FOR FIVE MINUTES.

During the great French revolution, a person named Alexandre, who had been originally an Exchange porter, was the Foreign Minister of France for the space of five minutes! It happened thus: Citizen Alexandre was the friend and understrapper of the influential terrorist, Santerre, and had shown himself a ready and sanguinary Jacobin agent on many infamous occasions. He was therefore known to Robespierre; and on the 22nd of June, 1793, just after the Girondins were destroyed, the Committee of Public Safety wanted, on a sudden vacancy, a Minister of Foreign Affairs. Robespierre, in the hurry, named Alexandre, and the name was instantly transmitted to the Convention. The obsequious president of that assembly at once ratified the nomination and sent the appointment to the ***Moniteur,*** where it appeared. Scarcely however had he done so, when such a man as Alexandre appeared so utterly ridiculous for such a place that some members of the Convention present, despite even their fear of Robespierre, carried an amendment, that the appointment should be suspended, and a list to choose from should be made out of persons suited for the office. This effectively cut short Alexandre's official career, and he relapsed into such obscurity that his name never appeared publicly again in the annals of the Revolution.

PREVISION OF WILLIAM IV.

When, in 1789, the Duke of Clarence went to live at Richmond, he became so popular that had the place been a borough, and he not reached his title, but still retained his idea of standing candidate, he would certainly have been elected there. He paid his bills regularly himself locked up his doors at night that his servants might not stay out late, and never drank but a few glasses of wine. "Though the value of crowns," writes Walpole, "is mightily fallen of late in the market, it looks as if his Royal Highness thought they were still worth waiting for; nay, it is said that he tells his brothers that he shall be King before either. This is fair at least." [Slender as his chance was in 1789, Clarence came to the Crown in 1830, on the death of his elder brother, at this time (1789) the Prince of Wales.—***Cunningham.***]

GEORGE THE FOURTH.

The Eight Horn George Rose, in his ***Diary,*** published in 1860, tells us that George the Third could not bear that any of his family should want courage. To which Mr. Rose replied, he hoped his Majesty would excuse him if he said he thought a proper attention to prevent the ill effects of an accident, that **had** happened, was no symptom of a want of courage. The King then said, with some warmth, "Perhaps it may be so; but I thank God there is but one of my children who wants courage, and I will not name HIM, ***because he is to succeed me.***"

There is a curious feet in the history of Newspapers worth remembering, viz., that the celebrated Cardinal Richelieu was a frequent Correspondent of the Mercurie Français; and that the King himself, Louis XIII., often contributed to its columns. D'Israeli the elder, who gives us this information, adds, "Many articles in the Royal handwriting, and corrected by the Royal hand, are still in preservation."—***Dr. Rimbault.***

THE FRENCH REVOLUTION OF 1848.

On the evening of the 24th of February, 1848, whilst the House of Commons was in session, a murmur of conversation suddenly arose at the door, and spread throughout the house, when was witnessed—what never occurred before or since, in the writer's experience—a suspension for a few minutes of all attention to the business of the house, whilst every member was engaged in close and earnest conversation with his neighbour. This intelligence had arrived of the abdication and flight of Louis Philippe, and of the proclamation of the Republic. The monarch and his ministers, whose ambitious projects had furnished the pretexts for our warlike armaments, and the gallant prince, whose pamphlet had sounded like a tocsin in our ears, were now on their way to claim the hospitality of England.

Mr. Cobden, who thus relates the eventful news, adds that he was sitting by the side of Mr. Joseph Hume when the tidings reached their bench. Sir Robert Peel was on the opposite front seat, alone, his powerful party having been broken and scattered by his great measure of Corn Law Repeal. "I'll go and tell Sir Robert the news," exclaimed Mr. Hume; and stepping across the floor, he seated himself by his side, and communicated the startling intelligence. On returning to his place, he repeated, in the following words, the commentary of the ex-minister:—"This comes of trying to carry on a government by means of a mere majority of a chamber, without regard to the opinion out of doors. It is what these people (pointing with his thumb over his shoulder to the protectionists behind him) wished me to do, but I refused."

During the Peninsular Campaign there appeared in the **Morning Chronicle** certain letters, which criticised severely, and often unjustly, the military movements of Lord Wellington. His lordship's attention being drawn to these comments, he at once perceived, from the information which they contained, that they must have been written by an officer holding a high command under him. Lord Wellington soon discovered the author of the letters to be no other than Sir Charles Stewart, the late Marquis of Londonderry. As soon as Lord Wellington had made himself master of this fact, he summoned Sir Charles Stewart to head-quarters at Torres Vedras, and without the least preface, thus addressed him:—

"Charles Stewart, I have ascertained with deep regret that you are the author of the letters which appeared in the ***Morning Chronicle,*** abusing me, and finding fault with my military plans."

Lord Wellington here paused for a moment, and then continued:—

"Now, Stewart, you know your brother Castlereagh is my best friend, to whom I owe everything; nevertheless, if you continue to write letters to the ***Chronicle,*** or any other newspaper, by God, I will send you home."

Sir Charles Stewart was so affected at this rebuke, that he shed tears, and expressed himself deeply penitent for the breach of confidence, and want of respect for the Articles of War. They immediately shook hands, and parted friends.—***Captain Gronow's Reminiscences.***

THE WILBERFORCE OAK.

The spot whereon Wilberforce resolved to set about his great work, the Abolition of the Slave Trade, may almost be regarded as "holy ground." This truly Christian resolution was made beneath a venerable oak in the grounds of Mr. Pitt's retreat at Holwood, in the parish of Keston, five miles south from Bromley. In Wilberforce's own words—"I got together, at my house, from time to time, persons who knew anything about the matter....When I had acquired so much information I began to talk the matter over with Pitt and Grenville.

Pitt recommended me to undertake its conduct, as a subject suited to my character and talents." Earl Stanhope has recently commemorated this meeting, with excellent taste, by causing to be erected upon the spot a seat, the oval portion of the back of which bears the following inscription:—

FROM MR. WILBERFORCE'S DIARY, 1788.

"At length, I well remember, after a conversation with Mr. Pitt, in the open air, at the root of an old tree at Holwood, just above the steep descent into the vale of Keston, I resolved to give notice on a fit occasion, in the House of Commons, of my intention to bring forward the Abolition of the Slave Trade."

ERECTED BY EARL STANHOPE, 1862.

After quoting the above passage in his *Life of Pitt,* Lord Stanhope notes: "I may add that this very tree, conspicuous for its gnarled and projecting root, on which the two friends had sat, is still pointed out at Holwood, and is known by the name of 'Wilberforce's Oak.' "—Vol. i. p. 318. The carrying out of this wisdom-tempered resolve was, through illness, postponed by Mr. Wilberforce till the following year (1789), when, on May 12, he brought the question before the House of Commons, as Burke said, "in a manner the most masterly, impressive, and eloquent....The principles were so well laid down, and supported with so much force and order, that it equalled anything he had heard in modern times, and was not, perhaps, to be surpassed in the remains of Grecian eloquence." The Wilberforce Oak is almost the only memorial of interest now remaining at Holwood. The estate was disposed of by Pitt in 1802. To part with his favourite retreat must have been to him a bitter pang; yet Lord Stanhope has not found a word of complaint upon the subject in any of his letters or conversations that is recorded. But he once said to his friend Lord Bathurst. "When I was a boy, I used to go bird's-nesting in the woods of Holwood, and it was always my wish to call it my own."

www.bookjungle.com email: sales@bookjungle.com fax: 630-214-0564 mail: Book Jungle PO Box 2226 Champaign, IL 61825

The Codes Of Hammurabi And Moses
W. W. Davies

QTY

The discovery of the Hammurabi Code is one of the greatest achievements of archaeology, and is of paramount interest, not only to the student of the Bible, but also to all those interested in ancient history...

Religion ISBN: *1-59462-338-4* Pages:132 *MSRP $12.95*

The Theory of Moral Sentiments
Adam Smith

QTY

This work from 1749. contains original theories of conscience amd moral judgment and it is the foundation for systemof morals.

Philosophy ISBN: *1-59462-777-0* Pages:536 *MSRP $19.95*

Jessica's First Prayer
Hesba Stretton

QTY

In a screened and secluded corner of one of the many railway-bridges which span the streets of London there could be seen a few years ago, from five o'clock every morning until half past eight, a tidily set-out coffee-stall, consisting of a trestle and board, upon which stood two large tin cans, with a small fire of charcoal burning under each so as to keep the coffee boiling during the early hours of the morning when the work-people were thronging into the city on their way to their daily toil...

Childrens ISBN: *1-59462-373-2* Pages:84 *MSRP $9.95*

My Life and Work
Henry Ford

QTY

Henry Ford revolutionized the world with his implementation of mass production for the Model T automobile. Gain valuable business insight into his life and work with his own auto-biography... "We have only started on our development of our country we have not as yet, with all our talk of wonderful progress, done more than scratch the surface. The progress has been wonderful enough but..."

Biographies/ ISBN: *1-59462-198-5* **Pages:300** *MSRP $21.95*

www.bookjungle.com email: sales@bookjungle.com fax: 630-214-0564 mail: Book Jungle PO Box 2226 Champaign, IL 61825

The Art of Cross-Examination
Francis Wellman

QTY

I presume it is the experience of every author, after his first book is published upon an important subject, to be almost overwhelmed with a wealth of ideas and illustrations which could readily have been included in his book, and which to his own mind, at least, seem to make a second edition inevitable. Such certainly was the case with me; and when the first edition had reached its sixth impression in five months, I rejoiced to learn that it seemed to my publishers that the book had met with a sufficiently favorable reception to justify a second and considerably enlarged edition. ...

Reference   ISBN: *1-59462-647-2*   Pages: 412   MSRP *$19.95*

On the Duty of Civil Disobedience
Henry David Thoreau

QTY

Thoreau wrote his famous essay, On the Duty of Civil Disobedience, as a protest against an unjust but popular war and the immoral but popular institution of slave-owning. He did more than write—he declined to pay his taxes, and was hauled off to gaol in consequence. Who can say how much this refusal of his hastened the end of the war and of slavery?

Law   ISBN: *1-59462-747-9*   Pages: 48   MSRP *$7.45*

Dream Psychology Psychoanalysis for Beginners
Sigmund Freud

QTY

Sigmund Freud, born Sigismund Schlomo Freud (May 6, 1856 - September 23, 1939), was a Jewish-Austrian neurologist and psychiatrist who co-founded the psychoanalytic school of psychology. Freud is best known for his theories of the unconscious mind, especially involving the mechanism of repression; his redefinition of sexual desire as mobile and directed towards a wide variety of objects; and his therapeutic techniques, especially his understanding of transference in the therapeutic relationship and the presumed value of dreams as sources of insight into unconscious desires.

Psychology   ISBN: *1-59462-905-6*   Pages: 196   MSRP *$15.45*

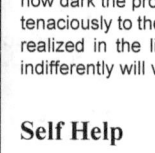

The Miracle of Right Thought
Orison Swett Marden

QTY

Believe with all of your heart that you will do what you were made to do. When the mind has once formed the habit of holding cheerful, happy, prosperous pictures, it will not be easy to form the opposite habit. It does not matter how improbable or how far away this realization may see, or how dark the prospects may be, if we visualize them as best we can, as vividly as possible, hold tenaciously to them and vigorously struggle to attain them, they will gradually become actualized, realized in the life. But a desire, a longing without endeavor, a yearning abandoned or held indifferently will vanish without realization.

Self Help   ISBN: *1-59462-644-8*   Pages: 360   MSRP *$25.45*

www.bookjungle.com *email: sales@bookjungle.com fax: 630-214-0564 mail: Book Jungle PO Box 2226 Champaign, IL 61825*
QTY

- [ ] **The Rosicrucian Cosmo-Conception Mystic Christianity** by *Max Heindel* ISBN: *1-59462-188-8* **$38.95**
  The Rosicrucian Cosmo-conception is not dogmatic, neither does it appeal to any other authority than the reason of the student. It is: not controversial, but is: sent forth in the, hope that it may help to clear... New Age/Religion Pages 646

- [ ] **Abandonment To Divine Providence** by *Jean-Pierre de Caussade* ISBN: *1-59462-228-0* **$25.95**
  "The Rev. Jean Pierre de Caussade was one of the most remarkable spiritual writers of the Society of Jesus in France in the 18th Century. His death took place at Toulouse in 1751. His works have gone through many editions and have been republished... Inspirational/Religion Pages 400

- [ ] **Mental Chemistry** by *Charles Haanel* ISBN: *1-59462-192-6* **$23.95**
  Mental Chemistry allows the change of material conditions by combining and appropriately utilizing the power of the mind. Much like applied chemistry creates something new and unique out of careful combinations of chemicals the mastery of mental chemistry... New Age Pages 354

- [ ] **The Letters of Robert Browning and Elizabeth Barret Barrett 1845-1846 vol II** ISBN: *1-59462-193-4* **$35.95**
  by *Robert Browning* and *Elizabeth Barrett* Biographies Pages 596

- [ ] **Gleanings In Genesis (volume I)** by *Arthur W. Pink* ISBN: *1-59462-130-6* **$27.45**
  Appropriately has Genesis been termed "the seed plot of the Bible" for in it we have, in germ form, almost all of the great doctrines which are afterwards fully developed in the books of Scripture which follow... Religion/Inspirational Pages 420

- [ ] **The Master Key** by *L. W. de Laurence* ISBN: *1-59462-001-6* **$30.95**
  In no branch of human knowledge has there been a more lively increase of the spirit of research during the past few years than in the study of Psychology, Concentration and Mental Discipline. The requests for authentic lessons in Thought Control, Mental Discipline and... New Age/Business Pages 422

- [ ] **The Lesser Key Of Solomon Goetia** by *L. W. de Laurence* ISBN: *1-59462-092-X* **$9.95**
  This translation of the first book of the "Lernegton" which is now for the first time made accessible to students of Talismanic Magic was done, after careful collation and edition, from numerous Ancient Manuscripts in Hebrew, Latin, and French... New Age/Occult Pages 92

- [ ] **Rubaiyat Of Omar Khayyam** by *Edward Fitzgerald* ISBN:*1-59462-332-5* **$13.95**
  Edward Fitzgerald, whom the world has already learned, in spite of his own efforts to remain within the shadow of anonymity, to look upon as one of the rarest poets of the century, was born at Bredfield, in Suffolk, on the 31st of March, 1809. He was the third son of John Purcell... Music Pages 172

- [ ] **Ancient Law** by *Henry Maine* ISBN: *1-59462-128-4* **$29.95**
  The chief object of the following pages is to indicate some of the earliest ideas of mankind, as they are reflected in Ancient Law, and to point out the relation of those ideas to modern thought. Religion/History Pages 452

- [ ] **Far-Away Stories** by *William J. Locke* ISBN: *1-59462-129-2* **$19.45**
  "Good wine needs no bush, but a collection of mixed vintages does. And this book is just such a collection. Some of the stories I do not want to remain buried for ever in the museum files of dead magazine-numbers an author's not unpardonable vanity..." Fiction Pages 272

- [ ] **Life of David Crockett** by *David Crockett* ISBN: *1-59462-250-7* **$27.45**
  "Colonel David Crockett was one of the most remarkable men of the times in which he lived. Born in humble life, but gifted with a strong will, an indomitable courage, and unremitting perseverance... Biographies/New Age Pages 424

- [ ] **Lip-Reading** by *Edward Nitchie* ISBN: *1-59462-206-X* **$25.95**
  Edward B. Nitchie, founder of the New York School for the Hard of Hearing, now the Nitchie School of Lip-Reading, Inc, wrote "LIP-READING Principles and Practice". The development and perfecting of this meritorious work on lip-reading was an undertaking... How-to Pages 400

- [ ] **A Handbook of Suggestive Therapeutics, Applied Hypnotism, Psychic Science** ISBN: *1-59462-214-0* **$24.95**
  by *Henry Munro* Health/New Age/Health/Self-help Pages 376

- [ ] **A Doll's House: and Two Other Plays** by *Henrik Ibsen* ISBN: *1-59462-112-8* **$19.95**
  Henrik Ibsen created this classic when in revolutionary 1848 Rome. Introducing some striking concepts in playwriting for the realist genre, this play has been studied the world over. Fiction/Classics/Plays 308

- [ ] **The Light of Asia** by *sir Edwin Arnold* ISBN: *1-59462-204-3* **$13.95**
  In this poetic masterpiece, Edwin Arnold describes the life and teachings of Buddha. The man who was to become known as Buddha to the world was born as Prince Gautama of India but he rejected the worldly riches and abandoned the reigns of power when... Religion/History/Biographies Pages 170

- [ ] **The Complete Works of Guy de Maupassant** by *Guy de Maupassant* ISBN: *1-59462-157-8* **$16.95**
  "For days and days, nights and nights, I had dreamed of that first kiss which was to consecrate our engagement, and I knew not on what spot I should put my lips..." Fiction/Classics Pages 240

- [ ] **The Art of Cross-Examination** by *Francis L. Wellman* ISBN: *1-59462-309-0* **$26.95**
  Written by a renowned trial lawyer, Wellman imparts his experience and uses case studies to explain how to use psychology to extract desired information through questioning. How-to/Science/Reference Pages 408

- [ ] **Answered or Unanswered?** by *Louisa Vaughan* ISBN: *1-59462-248-5* **$10.95**
  Miracles of Faith in China Religion Pages 112

- [ ] **The Edinburgh Lectures on Mental Science (1909)** by *Thomas* ISBN: *1-59462-008-3* **$11.95**
  This book contains the substance of a course of lectures recently given by the writer in the Queen Street Hall, Edinburgh. Its purpose is to indicate the Natural Principles governing the relation between Mental Action and Material Conditions... New Age/Psychology Pages 148

- [ ] **Ayesha** by *H. Rider Haggard* ISBN: *1-59462-301-5* **$24.95**
  Verily and indeed it is the unexpected that happens! Probably if there was one person upon the earth from whom the Editor of this, and of a certain previous history, did not expect to hear again... Classics Pages 380

- [ ] **Ayala's Angel** by *Anthony Trollope* ISBN: *1-59462-352-X* **$29.95**
  The two girls were both pretty, but Lucy who was twenty-one who supposed to be simple and comparatively unattractive, whereas Ayala was credited, as her Bombwhat romantic name might show, with poetic charm and a taste for romance. Ayala when her father died was nineteen... Fiction Pages 484

- [ ] **The American Commonwealth** by *James Bryce* ISBN: *1-59462-286-8* **$34.45**
  An interpretation of American democratic political theory. It examines political mechanics and society from the perspective of Scotsman James Bryce Politics Pages 572

- [ ] **Stories of the Pilgrims** by *Margaret P. Pumphrey* ISBN: *1-59462-116-0* **$17.95**
  This book explores pilgrims religious oppression in England as well as their escape to Holland and eventual crossing to America on the Mayflower, and their early days in New England... History Pages 268

www.bookjungle.com *email:* sales@bookjungle.com *fax:* 630-214-0564 *mail:* Book Jungle PO Box 2226 Champaign, IL 61825

QTY

The Fasting Cure *by Sinclair Upton*   **ISBN:** *1-59462-222-1*   **$13.95**
In the Cosmopolitan Magazine for May, 1910, and in the Contemporary Review (London) for April, 1910, I published an article dealing with my experiences in fasting. I have written a great many magazine articles, but never one which attracted so much attention... New Age/Self Help/Health Pages 164

Hebrew Astrology *by Sepharial*   **ISBN:** *1-59462-308-2*   **$13.45**
In these days of advanced thinking it is a matter of common observation that we have left many of the old landmarks behind and that we are now pressing forward to greater heights and to a wider horizon than that which represented the mind-content of our progenitors... Astrology Pages 144

Thought Vibration or The Law of Attraction in the Thought World   **ISBN:** *1-59462-127-6*   **$12.95**
by William Walker Atkinson   *Psychology/Religion Pages 144*

Optimism *by Helen Keller*   **ISBN:** *1-59462-108-X*   **$15.95**
Helen Keller was blind, deaf, and mute since 19 months old, yet famously learned how to overcome these handicaps, communicate with the world, and spread her lectures promoting optimism. An inspiring read for everyone... Biographies/Inspirational Pages 84

Sara Crewe *by Frances Burnett*   **ISBN:** *1-59462-360-0*   **$9.45**
In the first place, Miss Minchin lived in London. Her home was a large, dull, tall one, in a large, dull square, where all the houses were alike, and all the sparrows were alike, and where all the door-knockers made the same heavy sound... Childrens/Classic Pages 88

The Autobiography of Benjamin Franklin *by Benjamin Franklin*   **ISBN:** *1-59462-135-7*   **$24.95**
The Autobiography of Benjamin Franklin has probably been more extensively read than any other American historical work, and no other book of its kind has had such ups and downs of fortune. Franklin lived for many years in England, where he was agent... Biographies/History Pages 332

Name	
Email	
Telephone	
Address	
City, State ZIP	

☐ Credit Card   ☐ Check / Money Order

Credit Card Number	
Expiration Date	
Signature	

Please Mail to: Book Jungle
                    PO Box 2226
                    Champaign, IL 61825
or Fax to: 630-214-0564

ORDERING INFORMATION

web: *www.bookjungle.com*
email: *sales@bookjungle.com*
fax: *630-214-0564*
mail: *Book Jungle PO Box 2226 Champaign, IL 61825*
or PayPal *to sales@bookjungle.com*

Please contact us for bulk discounts

DIRECT-ORDER TERMS

**20% Discount if You Order
Two or More Books**
Free Domestic Shipping!
Accepted: Master Card, Visa,
Discover, American Express

www.ingramcontent.com/pod-product-compliance
Lightning Source LLC
Chambersburg PA
CBHW081838230426
43669CB00018B/2747